THE EDUCATION OF A CITIZEN SOLDIER

DASH

GARY ELLER
LIEUTENANT COLONEL (RET)

DASH
by Gary Eller

Published by Red Roof Books
redroofbooks.us

Printing History
Red Roof Books Books Edition
November, 2004

Cover and book design
by Mark Kashino
kashino.com

Publisher
Red Roof Books
Address 3139 N 2900 E
Twin Falls, Idaho 83301

ISBN: 0-9761516-0-X

Printed in the United State America

CONTENTS

DEDICATION

—

*This book is dedicated to all the great
soldiers, sailors, airmen, and marines
who chose to serve our great nation.
Among these, my special thanks to that
elite brotherhood of warriors — our
nation's Special Operations forces, past
and present, and to the families
of those who never returned.*

—

Lieutenant Colonel
Gary Eller (Ret)

INTRODUCTION

During one of those moments in life when, for whatever reason, you found yourself having to walk through a cemetery, did you ever pause and note the inscription on a stranger's tombstone? For instance:

JOHN DOE
HUSBAND & FATHER
1920-1997

The inscription tells no tales, provides no anecdotal evidence of who John was or what he accomplished during his lifetime. Simply that he was born, lived for a period of time, married with children, and now is dead. It is abrupt, without context or meaning, as cold as the rock it is written upon. Just the acknowledgement that beneath this stone is someone, who once was, but is no more.

Like most, you probably read the inscription, mentally calculated how old the person was when he or she died, then moved quickly on before thoughts of your own mortality crept in.

There are, however, tombstones and grave markers that are little harder to walk away from.

JOHN DOE
SERGEANT MAJOR, US MARINE CORPS
WORLD WAR II-KOREA-VIETNAM
1920-1997

Tombstones such as these conjure up images of a life different from most of the others buried beside him. Without further written explanation, for those with an eye for such things, it can be imagined that his life was one of travel and adventure, of death and danger. For a fact, he was a participant in many events that have since become recorded history. The records of war on his tombstone a clear indication that he was not one of those who simply watched history happen. Rather, he was one of those individuals who made history.

For the curious among us, especially with America's current war against terrorism raging around us, such a person might be considered to have an opinion worth listening to. I know from my own personal experiences that if given the choice between sharing a moment with a group of soldiers just having returned from Iraq or Afghanistan, or attending a university seminar to discuss either with a visiting professor, I will choose the company of soldiers every time. As individuals who have lived it, their stories are usually far more illuminating than the theoretical opinions discussed at the university. Be those stories pro or con. This is one of those stories.

I have never been a politician or a general. Therefore, I am not presumptuous enough to consider myself qualified to question the decisions made by either. The complexity of their jobs far exceeds any that I have ever had. I also know, with rare exception, that both politicians and generals are decent human beings who make the best decisions possible with the information they have been given. Neither would deliberately harm our nation or its children in the absence of what they consider to be sufficient justification. However, like the Sergeant Major listed above, I have seen war from a soldier's perspective and I know that the view one gets of it through a rifle sight differs greatly from that painted with words and pictures on the nightly news or discussed during senate hearings. As a soldier I have both buried friends and torn the fingernails off my hands digging in the rubble caused by a terrorist bomb trying to find others. I have also drunk gallons of tea with people on a first-name basis with those who built the bombs that buried them. Few, though not many, generals or politicians have done either. For me, war was a personal journey of brotherhood and brutal reality, not a theoretical exercise of infallible military strategies and good political manners. Past the half-century mark, I have now lived long enough to see the reemergence of a war in Iraq that resembles the one of my youth when politicians were required to justify the why of it. And, like Vietnam, Iraq may be the beginning of a mistake for it has been my life experience that whenever an explanation is required, i.e. it is not an obvious act of self-defense instinctively understood by all, it will be a nagging problem for all of us. Today's warriors are not the first generation of soldiers who will ask, "Why am I here?"

Although my life has had its share of memorable moments, I cannot be so audacious as to describe it in autobiographical form. A reader would quickly become as bored with reading about my life as I would become in writing about it. Therefore literary license has been invoked to maintain interest. The events described occurred on my watch, the locations and settings are real; some I had personal experience with, and some I did not. Likewise, the main characters in this novel are composites of the many hundreds of fine young men I had the pleasure of serving with. Any similarities to any one person living or dead are purely coincidental. The political views expressed are my own; they are not the products of a "vast military conspiracy" attempting to wrest control from civilian masters.

I hope for this story to be entertaining as well as provocative. As anyone who has had the pleasure of drinking beer with a group of World War II paratroopers from the famed 82nd, 11th or 101st Airborne Divisions can attest, the stories rival the best that Hollywood has ever produced. And unlike Hollywood, the paratroopers' stories are mostly true. Well, kind of. As their memories of events and places long ago and far away become less accurate perhaps there are some embellishments. But as long as the beer continues to flow these men will hold spellbound their most strident critic with tales of bravery and friendships that are riveting to listen to. Often delivered by the storyteller with such a stoic nonchalance that the listener is left with the impression that bravery and self-sacrifice were as routine a part of their young lives as a morning cup of coffee was to those who missed the experience.

My own military experience began as an enlisted Marine during the turbulent 1960's and ended with retirement as an Army Special Operations Lieutenant Colonel at the cusp of the new millennium. It was a career encompassing two declared wars and several undeclared ones, literally sending me around the world, living, working and playing in some exotic, or some not so exotic parts of the globe.

This is a familiar story to some as it has been and is still being lived by thousands of Americans. Yet those same thousands stand in stark contrast to the vast majority of post-draft Americans whose idea of personal sacrifice is to sell a stock short, not to be placed in physical danger for a belief in something larger than themselves.

This is also the story of a life that will one day be abbreviated with a dash on my own gravestone. For that reason I want to tell it as one who has experienced modern war; a war of liberation where the enemy is more of an idea than an army. The objective of which is not territory but dominion over the very soul of mankind. To be free to live as we choose to live will be the definition of victory for all sides. But there are two other, less obscure reasons that I want to tell this story.

First, even though my time has passed many other young men and women now find themselves in harm's way and are being asked to do the seemingly impossible. I can only counsel those soldiers, sailors, airmen, coastguardsmen and marines fighting today's battles to keep the faith and recognize that your stories are being told. Perhaps with the growing crescendo of our collective voices someday the world's multitudes will finally heed our words and say to the politicians, "You are not Caesar! These soldiers are not your personal legions! Enough is enough! If old, fat, bald-headed men want to fight one another then they can carry their own muskets."

Then again, today's soldiers are probably discovering the same lessons those who served before them discovered. Evil does exist. It is often built on stupidity or wanton desire for power and privilege. It must be confronted when and where it is found and soldiers, better than anyone else can, recognize that evil exists on both sides of the firing line.

On one side of this line exists evil that must be confronted by violence and death. That is a soldier's job. No one does it better. On the other side of this line evil exists in those who would knowingly place soldier's lives in danger simply for selfish self-interests. These people must be confronted by the wisdom of 20/20 hindsight that comes with the passage of time. This is my job. I hope that I am up to it.

Which leads to my second reason for wanting to tell this story. Mysterious forces appearing from the primordial ooze like evil apparitions did not perpetrate the September 11, 2001 attack on America. Any elected official pretending to have been unaware of the growing threat posed by Muslim extremists is either newly elected and doesn't know any better, or they are a liar. The now publicly familiar names of Osama bin-Laden and Al-Qaida, Mullah Omar and the Taliban, Saddam Hussein and the Ba'ath party have been known to Washington political insiders for decades. Also known to these same insiders were the evil personalities and intentions of each group. All, at one time or another, in varying degrees of "friendship," have been allies of the United States.

The people who hate America more than they love their own lives are the by-product of a flawed American foreign policy that consistently suffers from amnesia and disinterest once American political party objectives have been achieved. As a nation, America has been a fickle ally in large part because of special interests and domestic politics often at odds with the goals and objectives of the people we profess to be helping. And at the epicenter of our fickleness is our schizophrenic concept of democracy. Schizophrenic because America demands that other countries be free and open markets for the exchange of ideas and goods while refusing to acknowledge that many of those same countries are not represented by governments chosen by the people living there; a fundamental concept of democracy. In fact, in many of these countries the people are often at war with their own government. Consequently, when American business interests work with that same government it is seen by the people living there as an attack on them, which makes America a lightning rod for all the internal problems. Then, for some illogical, inexplicable reason, (Profits?) the American public is told that *we* are now responsible for fixing those internal problems because a "friendly" government is under attack. Later, when American business interests are attacked directly — and they always are — a hue and cry is emitted by the electorate, closely joined at the hip with those business interests under attack to "send in the Marines!" And they go! This, in a nutshell, is American foreign policy: supporting governments that do not have the support of their own people but are willing to do business with us. This is what we have been trying to sell to the world as democracy, and it is not working, despite our many promises that it will.

If reneging on the promise to help create a real democracy in these countries is a viable option without immediate consequences, then a quick review of recent history will clearly show that American politicians will trip over each other in the rush to be popular with the voting public. Meeting the expectations of foreigners who do not vote has never been a high priority for the electorate. Internationally, this rush to ignore, modify, or simply forget past promises in order to get elected or reelected has metastasized into a suicidal policy of hatred for those who have been on the receiving end of our schizophrenia. The hope that America can now simply kill her way to peace without giving due consideration to the origins of some of this hatred is a false illusion. So too, following the 9-11 attack and the subsequent invasion of Iraq by American forces is failing to respond to those same forces of hate. During my years of living and working with foreign troops I discovered a great void separating the promises of democracy and freedom for developing nations and the expectations non-Americans hold for both. For most Americans democratic freedom means opportunity, for many people caught up in an evolving political system, it means wealth. And, unfortunately, all too often it means wealth without effort or a willingness to change.

For those who wish to find hidden in the pages of this book vivid tales of conspiracies or glossy death and destruction, you will be sadly disappointed. This is not a Sergeant Rock Comic Book. This story does not describe how soldiers deal with life threatening situations; it describes why they find themselves in such situations. It is a story emphasizing why we fight rather than how we fight and a great deal of time will be spent describing the emotions and opinions of the adversary, the coalition partners, and the typical American soldier. Though there will be the telling of both death and killing, these will be described realistically, with no artificial vestiges of romance or glory. For real, violent death rarely has either. I certainly have never heard the angels sing or trumpets blare while viewing the recent dead, and I don't think anyone else has either. Unfortunately, real deaths are never choreographed to end as they do in the movies.

But there is an even more humanistic reason for not glorifying the killing in any war – respect for human life. As a young man, I was as gung-ho about finding and killing America's enemies as the next man; and my country presented me with several opportunities to do it. But as I age this attitude of "kill them all" has mellowed considerably. I now realize that it takes guts to go onto a battlefield and anyone who does so is worthy of respect. Making a soldiers death a necessity of war, not a celebration. Soldiers who have endured the untold horrors of life on a battlefield places all who have done so in a common brotherhood. For a writer to seemingly brag about how the sons and daughters of one side are able to kill some other mother's son or daughter on the other side, somehow making their position superior, is not an emotion many veterans share. They know all to well that it is more often luck, not right and wrong, that determines who lives and who dies. To wish this truth away takes the simple mind of a child to assume that being lucky or unlucky is synonymous with righteousness or God's will. The death of any brave young man or woman, regardless of whose flag they profess allegiance to, should never become the stuff of entertainment for those who have failed themselves to live a life dedicated to duty, honor, and country.

However, this mutual respect is granted only if these opponents were soldiers fighting for a belief in something larger than themselves. If they were simply bandits or thugs bent only on personal enrichment at the expense of others, and not truly soldiers, then to hell with them. During my time in service I had the opportunity to share the field with both soldiers and thieves. Consequently, it should not be difficult to distinguish between the two when reading this story.

The Author
November 2004

CHAPTER 1

The big cat moved from his tangled lair the way all cats move, with grace and in complete silence. As fascinating as it is to watch any cat move with such stealth, it was particularly astonishing to watch this cat creep silently forward. He was no ordinary cat. At a mature weight of six hundred pounds, he was large even by the standards of his breed, the Bengal Tiger.

As the cat slowly emerged from the dense underbrush he paused, stretched his sinewy muscles and sniffed the wind. More than anything he was hungry and in need of a fresh meal, his last being a paltry human leg dragged from the top of a nearby bush following a B-52 arc-light strike in the Que Son Mountains of Vietnam, a place called Charlie Ridge by the American Marines.

Adjacent to the city of Da Nang, the Que Son mountain range separates South Vietnam from neighboring Laos like a serpent's spine with some of the most inhospitable, inaccessible, mountainous terrain to be found on the Asian continent. Those soldiers and marines that operated in this part of Vietnam often equated a mission in the Que Son Mountains with a step backward in time. Even as late as 1969, it was still undeveloped and beautiful. Ancient tribes such as the Kinh, Co Tu, and Xe Dang still inhabited the area, much as they had since before the time of Christ and the flora and fauna were reminiscent of the Jurassic era. It was in fact, if not in imagination, a land that time had truly forgotten. It was a place where tigers were free to be tigers.

That portion of the Que Son mountain range hunted by the big cat ran west from the coastal low lands of Quang Nam province to the Laotian border. The marines had aptly named the area because of the numerous North Vietnamese Army (NVA) and Viet Cong (VC) forces operating there. Phonetically, the VC were known as Victor Charlie, hence the name Charlie Ridge.

Charlie Ridge as well as the surrounding terrain had been further subdivided into several areas with their own unique *nom de jure*; one of which was the aptly named Rocket Belt Region. During the war both the NVA and the VC operated with relative impunity in the thickly canopied mountainous jungle of Charlie Ridge, taking advantage of the relative safety enjoyed by transporting huge amounts of supplies and ammunition over the vast maze of mountain paths comprising the Ho Chi Minh Trail. As a result of the heavy losses suffered during the 1968 Tet Offensive, the enemy forces had now adopted a less aggressive strategy of long-range attacks against the Americans.

As the war stalemated, increasingly large portions of supplies being transported over the jungle trails along Charlie Ridge consisted of long-range rockets capable of hitting the air base at Da Nang and the large American supply base just outside the city at Marble Mountain. With the introduction of these rockets, the VC began launching lethal, harassing attacks on the American occupied sites with increasing regularity.

As a result of these attacks a nearby marine unit, the 3rd Battalion, 1st Marine Regiment (3/1) had been given the mission of conducting a sweep of the Rocket Belt region. The stated purpose of the sweep was to kill, capture, or generally disrupt the NVA and VC forces from their favorite pastime, rocketing the air base. After a month of chasing the elusive foe up and down the steep mountainsides, the marines were now exhausted, depleted and of a general agreement that it was time to call the whole thing off before someone really got hurt.

***

The marines of 3/1 were similar to personnel of other military units operating in Vietnam during the latter stages of the war. Ideologically the battalion consisted of two polar opposites connected by an ill-defined middle. On the right were men who wanted to serve in Vietnam, or at least felt that it was necessary for them to be there to protect America from encroaching Communism. On the left were those who had no desire to be in Vietnam under any circumstances short of going to prison for not being there. Between these two extremes were those marines making up the majority of the unit; men who had nothing better to do with their time, or had few alternatives from which to choose, or had simply been drafted into a war they knew very little about. Like mercenaries of old, many of them were in Vietnam seeking adventure or increased opportunity once they returned home, if they returned home.

It was this largest group of marines that entered Vietnam without preconceived notions regarding the politics of the war. Like the stereotypical "show me" Missourian, these men made up their minds based upon personal experience. They were neither naive nor blindly patriotic. This group of men would learn through first hand experience, doing something first and withholding judgment regarding the merits of the event until they could describe it for themselves. These men didn't need some intellectual describing their opinions for them or telling them how they were supposed to feel about something. They could make up their own minds, being perfectly capable of separating fact from fiction.

Like their respective peer groups in the United States, the marines could generally be divided along the political spectrum as being pro-war or anti-war based upon age or education. Many of the older marines seemed to be pro-war while the younger but often more educated seemed to be anti-war. Those marines caught between these two political extremes represented the majority of the men serving in Vietnam who had not yet had the opportunity or the desire to analyze the merits of the war. Now that they were seeing Vietnam for themselves, they had the intellectual capacity to compare what they were seeing and doing with what the Marine Corps leadership and American politicians were telling citizens regarding who was winning the war. The most obvious result of this analysis was disillusion and disgust as these men quickly saw enough to recognize that the war was circular; it had no real beginning and no foreseeable end. If America was winning the war as they were being told, then it was not apparent from their unique perspective as frontline soldiers. All they ever saw was just more of the same inconsequential bullshit of watching people die every day for no apparent gain and for no apparent reason. To them, the prevailing opinion was that Vietnam remained as much a lost cause after a friend's death as before, and it always would be.

Those marines on the right of the political spectrum had either participated in or grown up in the shadow of World War II glory. Seeing Vietnam as their opportunity to protect America from encroaching communism and to build a career as a professional marine. These men continued to prosecute the war regardless of how they might have personally felt about the politics because they firmly believed it to be their duty to do so. This group of men, the leaders, wanted to win the war and they were perfectly content to allow the politicians to define the conditions for victory. Their opinion of the war was based on their perceived reality of what war was supposed to be, winning at any cost, with the underlying assumption that this was also what the politicians wanted as well. To these men, the enemy was seen with crystal clarity as being the evil communist forces and anyone agreeing with them.

The group of men on the left of the political continuum, the less pro-war group, seemed to want to quit the war and have America apologize to the world for its intransigence. These men felt that it was impossible to win a war for the hearts and minds of the people when America seemed to be hated more by the South Vietnamese civilians than the supposed enemy. Their opinion of the war was based on a perceived reality of what war should not be, standing between an oppressed people and their repressive government, regardless of any possible economic, social, or political benefits derived from doing so. Many of these men saw the enemy with crystal clarity as being the United States government and anyone not opposed to American involvement in Vietnam.

The largest group of men, the one in the middle, simply wanted to survive by any means necessary and go home. Who was winning or who was losing the war was of very little consequence to them. They didn't give a damn why America thought she had to be there. Each of them simply felt that they would achieve a personal victory if they survived until their date of expected return from overseas (DEROS) and they could wave goodbye to Vietnam through the bottom of a beer bottle while aboard the Freedom Bird. It was the best that they could hope for. These men felt themselves to be powerless to either win the war or to put a stop to it. This group's opinion of the war was based on their belief that all wars suck and that theirs simply sucked a little more than most. The men in this group did not see the enemy with the same crystal clarity as the other two groups. They instinctively knew that the pro-war and anti-war groups were both right and wrong and that the stubborn arrogance with which each group disregarded the opinions of the other was probably the real enemy. But they were certain of one thing, however. They clearly saw who their only friends were, the marine holding a rifle and sharing a foxhole with them. This group was by far the most realistic of the three groups. These men pragmatically believed that both politics and war have always been a dirty, nasty business with few, if any, redeeming qualities to recommend either as a remedy for centuries of human failure. If they had to risk their lives fighting for something larger than themselves, they needed to look no further than the man standing next to them. Everything and everyone else was simply superfluous bullshit.

**

The marines both suffered and inflicted casualties over the course of the operation in the Que Son Mountains and as they neared the Laotian border the veterans among them cautioned of the threats still remaining. During similar campaigns involving company-size or larger unit operations near the Laotian border, it had been the veterans' experience that the heavy fighting began only when the marine unit posed a real threat to the enemy supply lines. To their great dismay the combat veterans' realized that they were starting to do exactly that as a full battalion of marines wormed their way through the thick undergrowth surrounding Charlie Ridge. True to form, the firefights were becoming more intense and of longer duration. The enlisted marines were becoming anxious, not only because of the Vietnamese enemy soldiers confronting them.

Those marine riflemen fortunate enough to have survived their first three or four months of combat had done so by learning to run patrols and ambushes where they suspected the enemy *would not* be, not where the enemy *would* be. The implied logic being that if they didn't aggressively seek the enemy then the enemy would not aggressively seek them. The technique for accomplishing this was known as "sandbagging," running ghost patrols where a squad would call in checkpoints as if they were moving while they were in fact still in the safety of a bunker or nearby village. Sandbagging patrols and ambushes quickly became a common method of survival for experienced marines and few, if any, infantry troops that survived Vietnam are unfamiliar with the term. By all recollections sandbagging was a method of survival reciprocated by their Vietnamese opponents as both sides consciously sought to avoid making contact with one another whenever given the opportunity. If you didn't bother them then they wouldn't bother you seemed to be the unspoken rule at the squad level.

Only when leaders, Officers and Noncommissioned Officers (NCO's) became involved in operations did this unspoken gentlemen's agreement stop working. When "lifers," as the junior enlisted derisively called any marine above the pay grade of E-4 Corporal, accompanied them on operations, people always ended up dead, which was not a problem for the professionals. To this group of marines both killing and dying are supposed to take place during a war. They would have found it incomprehensible to believe that a war could be won in any other way.

Although it was not the leaders' desire that a fellow marine should be maimed or killed, the seasoned professionals considered it an anathema to actually seek to avoid gaining and maintaining contact with the enemy. It was something that marines simply did not do, or so they mistakenly believed.

At the junior-enlisted level, realities were often much different. As a result of these differences, in the macro sense, after several years of seeing the same tired bullshit and resultant body bags, these lifers were experiencing increasing difficulties convincing the troops that it was necessary to aggressively seek out the enemy. They weren't having any luck at all convincing the young marines that it was always going to be the other guy who ended up dead. The troops were much smarter than the lifers believed; they knew better.

As a result of the draft, many of these enlisted troops were better educated than their superiors. Several had college degrees and were older than some of the sergeants put in charge of them. By the late 1960's a growing number of these troops were arriving in the Marine Corps after having first been exposed to the anti-war protests raging across America's college campuses. Consequently, they were beginning to question the logic and rationale of what they were being asked to participate in. The company grade officers, the lieutenants and captains, were experiencing great difficulty in explaining it to them. Just as the field grade officers, the majors, colonels, and generals were having difficulty in explaining it to the company grades and, completing this circle, the politicians were having difficulty explaining it to the field grade officers.

"What the hell is America trying to accomplish by being in Vietnam?" Seemed to be the million-dollar question that always resulted in a ten-cent answer. The only answer given was that the spread of communism had to be stopped and that Vietnam was similar to Korea, where maintaining the status quo would be considered a victory.

"It is the purpose of modern war," skeptics would be told. "To achieve complete victory would require a real war and in the nuclear age America doesn't want to risk destroying the world in order to win." A truism, to be sure, but this explanation never adequately addressed the concerns of the men fighting and dying in Vietnam. The combat troops in Vietnam were intimately aware that a marine killed at the Chosen Reservoir in Korea or Khe Sahn in Vietnam was just as dead as a World War II marine killed on the road to Tokyo. Unfortunately, by comparison, the marine killed while conducting "wars of containment" sacrificed his life for far less gain than did his WW II predecessor.

Most of the young men serving in Vietnam had relatives who had served during the Korean Conflict. (It was not politically correct to call Korea a war.) Technically it hadn't been war. It had been a United Nations police action, a conflict rather than a war, and therein lay the problem for the young men fighting in Vietnam.

American culture demands winners. Despite the foreign policy expert's weak attempt to explain it, a tie is not the same thing as a win when fighting a war. These young men had both read and heard about Korea and, except for the bravery of the thousands of young men and women who had fought there, there was nothing good that could be said about it. Which is the principle reason Korea has been recorded in the annals of American history as "The Forgotten War." Americans simply don't want to talk about it.

The young men fighting and dying in Vietnam were growing more aware with each passing day that Vietnam was going to end the same way, or in a worse way, than the Korean Conflict had ended. There would never be an official flag of surrender, nor would there ever be victory parades celebrating the wars end. In their opinion the Vietnam War was something that would simply continue on for, well, forever.

Also, quietly lurking in the back of everyone's mind was the unsettling knowledge that neither Korea nor Vietnam had attacked America so troops had not been sent to either as a matter of self-defense. Instead, America had voluntarily offered the blood of its young men and women for a cause fighting wars of containment that even the "best and brightest" could not succinctly articulate to an increasingly distrusting American public.

Yet these political thoughts were mere background noise for most marine riflemen as they had a more immediate concern to deal with. They were growing openly disdainful of the belief held by the lifers that killing Vietnamese, as was being tracked by an official "body count," would actually make a difference in who was ultimately going to win this war. Philosophically, this disagreement was becoming a growing problem for those doing the actual fighting. For when fighting troops don't clearly understand the reason they are being asked to kill, then they sure as hell will never understand why they are being asked to die.

Lack of clarity, purpose and justification were disconcerting issues in the minds of the marines sweeping Charlie Ridge in December 1969. They all knew that as they closed on the Laotian border that, any day now, these goddamn lifers were going to ask them to start dying for some ambiguous reason that no one could adequately explain to them. Yet the fear of death was the only thing they all clearly understood.

These marines were not cowards. They fought bravely for what they believed in – one another. However, unlike World War II, which was the formative grounds for both the upper echelons of the chain of command and the politicians who ruled them, this was a war that few of the enlisted marines were trying to win; it was one they were only trying to survive.

In the minds of the men being asked to die, if avoiding fighting was an option that worked, then it was certainly all right with them. After all, it was rationalized, they were involved in a war that had been going on since many of them were in grade school. By all appearances it was one that would still be going on when their own children were in grade school. What difference would their efforts make? For these troops the unspoken mantra was, "Stay alive any way you can and wait for your DEROS."

All of these disparate emotions, combined with the psychosis of what would later imprint the meaning of the Vietnam War on the American psyche were at work that night on Charlie Ridge as the Marine Rifle Company dug into the hillside. In the humid jungle heat sweaty, filthy, disillusioned young men took brief moments to share their hopes and dreams of returning home to a better life with those around them.

Nearby, also seeking to survive, hidden among the cluster of NVA, VC, and marine forces was at least one very large, very hungry, Bengal Tiger.

***

Over the course of the past several days there had been a significant increase in the small arms fire being exchanged between the trapped NVA forces and elements of 3/1. As a result of the escalating gunfire, the big cat had gone into hiding three days prior with nothing more to eat than a small Vietnamese leg and very little to drink. Only the rainwater that slowly puddled around his lair, a well-camouflaged crevasse ensconced between two huge boulders provided him with needed moisture. It had been much too dangerous for him to venture forth on a hunting foray and the big cat was still frightened by the sounds of the bombs and mortar fire that had driven him into hiding. After three days of hiding, his fear of gunfire was rapidly being overcome by his hunger pangs. He needed fresh meat; he needed it tonight, and the scent of nearby prey wafted on the dank jungle breeze.

The big cat had acquired a taste for human flesh primarily because of the abundance of dead and wounded Viet Cong and North Vietnamese Army soldiers that he had recently fed upon. He had not yet taken to actually stalking and preying upon healthy human beings, being satisfied instead with the carrion that is the aftermath of all battlefields. During the American Civil War, Southern farmers often used hogs to clean up the battlefields. In this remote part of Vietnam nature was still being left to its own traditional methods for doing away with the dead, and the tiger was very much in keeping with the traditions of nature.

But tonight there were no dead nearby and the familiar smell of the Vietnamese had been replaced by a different human smell. Less like the fishy smell of Nuc Bam, a fermented fish staple favored by the Vietnamese and more like the smell of a dairy because of the high fat diet enjoyed by the Americans.

In fact, to the tiger, the smell of the Americans reminded him of the lactating buffalo cows he had frequently killed before the fighting had driven them from the area. His primitive brain recalled those pleasurable times of abundance and his mouth salivated in anticipation of a fresh kill. But the lactating buffalo cows were gone. Now, all that he had to feed upon were the humans who had replaced them, and his belly ached because of the delicious aroma emanating from the nearby fighting position.

Tonight the tiger would have to make do with what he could catch.

***

That he smelled delicious would have come as a great surprise to LCPL Bob Lipre, a rifleman with 2nd Platoon, India Company, 3/1. Like all the marines participating in the operation, Lipre had seen neither soap nor water nor a toothbrush for thirty days now. The jungle crust had caked to him like ripening garbage and his sweat stained fatigues could have stood at "parade rest."

All of this mattered little to Lipre as he busily settled into digging a two man fighting position with his buddy, PVT Mike Scanlon, who smelled just as delicious as Lipre.

In the rapidly darkening sky, the two marines were given the responsibility of digging in for the night as part of a platoon perimeter that would tie their squad in with an adjacent squad on their left flank. While tactically sound, the perimeter was more of a straight line than the classic horseshoe shaped perimeter favored by marines and Lipre and Scanlon were the last position on the right flank, tied into nothing but the rugged terrain by two large boulders and a seemingly inaccessible, dense undergrowth.

"Finally get to take a break from humping these goddamn hills," said Lipre to no one in particular.

"Yeah," came Scanlon's reply as he scooped yet another shovel full of red clay mud with his entrenching tool. "If we could just get someone to dig this damn hole for us, we could almost pretend to be humans again and get some real sleep."

Exhausted from the continual march against a rapidly withdrawing NVA force, the marines had had little time for sleep and for the first time since the operation kicked off it appeared that there was going to be a brief pause. But first came over an hours worth of digging.

With sweat dripping from his nose, Lipre finally settled back into his finished fighting position and drew a large drink of warm water from his canteen. Letting the water dribble down his chin and onto his chest, he wiped his face with a dirty arm and turned to Scanlon asking, "Mike, you want first watch or do you want me to wake you up?"

"No man. I'm beat. You take first and wake me up in a couple hours," replied Scanlon. "But first, what do you say we burn one?"

Lipre glanced over his shoulder to make sure that there weren't any lifers nearby and, satisfied that the coast was clear, responded, "Sure, why not? Zips wouldn't dare attack us up here anyway."

With that Scanlon produced a finger-sized joint of marijuana from the cargo pocket of his tattered jungle fatigues, lit it, inhaled deeply, and passed it to Lipre. The joint had been safely stored in his pocket along with nine others in a baggie known to the marines as a "party pack." These party packs could be obtained from any Vietnamese child willing to take the time to roll the abundant marijuana plants growing wild throughout Vietnam into a cigarette. And many did. A party pack containing ten finger-sized joints could be purchased from them at a cost of one U.S. dollar. Conversely, one warm Budweiser beer could be purchased at any of the base camps for fifty cents. For troops seeking a mental escape from the horrors of Vietnam it wasn't even a contest when asked to choose between the two. A hot beer for half a dollar or a joint guaranteed to blow your boots off for ten cents. If for no other reason, basic economics would lead Americans to choose drugs over alcohol in Vietnam, though both would be consumed in abundance.

Lipre took the marijuana "super cigmo" from his friend and took a long deep hit, exhaling only when he had run out of breath. Getting stoned and trying to stay that way had become a routine habit for them, as it had for many of the line marines digging in that night on Charlie Ridge.

"You know, Mike," Lipre finally said, exhaling what little smoke remained in his lungs into the damp jungle air, "when I finally get out of this hellhole, I'm going to go back to Seattle and finish my degree at UW. It seems as if I've been here forever, and if it hadn't been for that damn blonde, I wouldn't have ever been here at all."

Mike Scanlon nodded his head in acknowledgement to Lipre's words and thought to himself, "Jesus Christ, not again!"

Scanlon had politely listened before to Lipre's brokenhearted remembrances. Patiently enduring Lipre's tales of how falling head over heels in love with a blonde University of Washington sorority girl had caused him to change his political science major to that of beer drinking and wild sex, neglecting his studies and consuming his finances. With the loss of both his student status and, after dad saw his sons grades, his father's money, it wasn't long before Lipre lost the blonde sorority girl as well. Scanlon knew that, among other reasons, Lipre had ultimately joined the Marine Corps so he could return to school with GI Bill benefits in the hopes of rekindling the romance. In Scanlon's estimation, Lipre seemed overly concerned with impressing others. His insecurity often showed in the things that he did while trying to fit in. He knew that Lipre had joined a fraternity while going to college because he enjoyed the elitist atmosphere of belonging to a select group. It had probably been this same compulsion of achieving excellence by identifying with a select group that had caused him to enlist in the Marine Corps as well. Lipre's compulsion to surround himself with people he might have felt inferior too baffled Scanlon. All he wanted out of life was for educated idiots and elitists to simply leave him alone. After all, it was because of the decisions made by those who thought they were "smarter and prettier" than everyone else that five hundred thousand unhappy young Americans were still in Vietnam. The fact that he was one of them did not endear Scanlon to those who professed to possess a special insight that allowed them, and only them, to know what was best for all of mankind.

It was Lipre's all too obvious ambition to get through life by riding the coattails of people imagined to be superior to himself that made Scanlon doubt his commitment as a team player. He was a nice enough guy, but in the world of "I'll watch your back and you watch mine" combat, Scanlon always felt a little uneasy about Lipre's willingness to risk life and limb for anyone other than himself – or perhaps someone he was desperately trying to impress. Which was in large part why the two of them were sharing a foxhole tonight, and had been for the past thirty days. Although Lipre carried the MOS 0311, basic rifleman, because of his expensive private school education and organizational skills he had become the First Sergeant's "office pog," or admin clerk, and had spent no time in the bush. Consequently, Lipre had not qualified for the Combat Action Ribbon, the only award signifying that he had exchanged hostile fire with the enemy. With his time in Vietnam coming to an end, Lipre was growing desperate to punch this last ticket before leaving and had convinced his First Sergeant to allow him to participate in the current mission.

Lipre believed that if he was to fulfill his ambition of building a political career after completing college that combat awards and medals would distinguish him from the crowd of other budding politicians who had avoided military service altogether. He was intelligent enough to understand that form, rather than substance, was often all that it took to launch a political career. He hoped to capitalize on this knowledge by wearing some "form" on his uniform when he returned from Vietnam.

Scanlon wasn't bothered by the fact that Lipre was a badge collector – a lot of military people are badge collectors. He was quite content to simply take advantage of Lipre's inexperience by allowing him to do all the heavy lifting that went with life in the bush. Scanlon had casually smoked a cigarette while Lipre did most of the digging of their new fighting position.

Nor was Scanlon bothered by his awareness that Lipre had befriended him because he had had the dubious distinction of having been awarded the Silver Star as well as the Bronze Star with V-device during his combat tour. Awards that Lipre himself had helped prepare by typing the citations. Two combat awards for valor are difficult for a person of any rank to receive, and Lipre was practically salivating at the thought of getting one himself. Enhancing his chance was the fact that Scanlon was still a private, having been reduced twice in rank from PFC, and his low rank had made it doubly difficult for him to receive a medal. What the awards meant to the junior enlisted like Lipre was that Scanlon, or any other private awarded a medal for valor, had actually performed the feats of bravery that the citations said he had performed. Something that those with combat experience knew to often be untrue when officers and senior enlisted received these same awards. In fact, experienced marines often felt that when an officer or senior NCO wore an award for valor and did not have an accompanying purple heart, it was a phony award, pencil whipped by a compliant headquarters admin geek for a fifth of Jack Daniel's whiskey.

Scanlon suspected, but wasn't interested enough to question him about it, that Lipre had ended up in Vietnam in order to spite his father for cutting off his college funds. In fact, that is precisely what Lipre had tried to accomplish, first by joining the Marines, again by volunteering for Vietnam. But his efforts had backfired on him. Lipre's father, a World War II draftee who had been in the first wave at Omaha Beach, responded to his son's threats to join the military by telling him, "Any twenty year old young man with a backbone shouldn't want to keep his hand in his dad's pocket." Mister Lipre felt that all children should make their own way in life and if going into the military was what it took to wean any kid off their parents, then so be it. A self-made millionaire, Mister Lipre had never felt obligated to pay for his son's education. Nobody had paid for his education when he returned from Europe; instead he had astutely taken advantage of the GI Bill and gone to law school. If earned government benefits had worked to launch his career then he reasoned that his son could damn well do the same thing. A staunch advocate for tough love, Mister Lipre had reluctantly paid his son's college tuition simply because it had been easier for him to part with the money than to put up with his wife's nagging for, "not caring enough about our son's future." But he'd be damned if he was going to pay college tuition just so his son could party and get laid. Telling his wife as much following receipt of a copy of Lipre's grades sent to him by a confidant who worked at the University of Washington. "Maureen," he told her as they reviewed the long list of

F's on the grade report, "its time to break his plate. He will either sink or swim, but it is going to be his effort rather than our money that makes the difference." Against her best wishes, mom finally agreed. On the day he left for Vietnam, Mister Lipre's parting words to his son had succinctly been, "good luck and write to your mother whenever you get the chance."

In keeping with Lipre's fetish for surrounding himself with superior people he had actively sought Scanlon to be his "bush buddy," hoping to capitalize on his fondest dream that Scanlon would receive another award for valor and that he would receive one as well just for being there.

"Hell," Scanlon silently thought as Lipre droned on, "they had all heard the story of Lipre's love life before, several times." But, since he didn't have anything that he wanted to talk about himself, Scanlon allowed Lipre to continue with his broken hearted reminiscing and pretended to care.

"Yep, two more months and I'm finally out of here. Gonna show up on campus driving a new set of wheels and with money in my pocket. See what that bitch and all her sorority sisters think about me now." Lipre confidently said it more to impress himself than to impress anyone else.

"What the hell do you care what a woman thinks about you, man?" Responded a genuinely perplexed Mike Scanlon. "More pussy on that campus than one man could wear out in an entire lifetime. Go find another one to bang."

Oblivious to the fact that Lipre or any other man could fall blindly in love with something as fickle as a woman made Scanlon a poor matrimonial counselor. For him all any girl had ever represented was a neighborhood semen receptacle with legs. Just like his own mother had been while parading a constant stream of lovers through his young life, trying to pass each one off as a surrogate father for him and his seven siblings.

The concept that a man could actually love a woman as much as Lipre obviously did was not an emotion he had grown up with. "Hell," he thought, "in my world even the girls don't think love is like that." Most of them had either had a child or an abortion by the time they were thirteen. Few knew or even cared who the father was.

To a street-wise young man like Scanlon, a man who wore his vulnerabilities like a neon sign as plainly as Lipre did would have been considered prey in the world of his youth. In the slums of Atlanta, it didn't pay for a young black man to show any sign of weakness, and Mike Scanlon firmly believed that valuing a woman's opinion more than his own was about as weak as any man could get.

"Hell, man," Lipre replied with just a hint of anger in his voice. "I'm not just talking about the women. It's the whole college scene. If you want to be somebody in America you've got to get that sheepskin. You know what I mean? You won't go anywhere without it. And the contacts I've already made with my fraternity brothers will reap big dividends down the road. It just pisses me off that since I'm no longer a college student, those who are seem to think that they're better than me, you know?"

"Yeah, life's a bitch, man," responded an adamant and unconcerned Scanlon as he took the joint back from Lipre. Except for his own, Scanlon could have cared less about opinions regarding what it took to be successful in life. He stifled the impulse to tell Lipre, "All you tight-ass white boys are too damned concerned with where you fit into the pecking order. Quit worrying about being the top dog all the time!" Instead he replied, "Almost everyone I've ever met has thought that they were better than me. It don't mean jack shit, man!" Adding defensively, "you and I are better than any of those college motherfuckers already!"

In their many conversations, Lipre received brief glimpses into what Mike Scanlon's childhood life must have been like. By all accounts, it hadn't been pretty. Lipre had heard stories of the abuse that Scanlon had suffered at the hands of a violent stepfather while growing up in Atlanta. Although Scanlon was black and Lipre was white, their life together over the past month had given them the opportunity to share many intimate details of their pre-Vietnam lives. Many of the stories consisted of the usual braggadocio of sexual conquests, hell raising, and one-upmanship of young males trying to out-lie one another. Other stories, those usually told at more vulnerable moments, were much more revealing to a man with Lipre's education.

Scanlon, while in a drunken stupor bought and paid for by Lipre before commencement of the current operation, had told Lipre about the time that his stepfather, while in a drunken rage, had once beaten him so badly that he had fractured his skull. Shattered it, actually. His mother had refused to call for help because she hadn't wanted to see her new husband go back to prison. Mercifully, neighbors hearing his screams had called the police before he had been killed. Later that night Child Protective Services had taken him to a hospital for emergency brain surgery to relieve the swelling. The scar where the team of doctors had opened his skull was clearly visible when his head was uncovered.

Unlike Lipre, Scanlon did not have the excuse of having failed out of college as his reason for joining the Corps. He had enlisted because a judge offered him the choice between military service or prison. Even at the tender age of seventeen, Scanlon knew he didn't want to do time in prison. Besides, he had an uncle who was a former marine and on those rare occasions he had spoken with him, he sensed a pride in his uncle that he did not sense in those who had never served.

So, with his mother's signature of permission on the enlistment documents, Mike Scanlon joined the Marines for a two-year hitch. At the time it seemed such an easy decision to make. Now, after ten months in Vietnam he almost wished that he had gone to prison instead.

Lipre, who had grown up in an upper class family on Mercer Island, an upscale community east of Seattle, often marveled at how a human being like Scanlon could recover from such a tragic childhood and appear to be so strong and self-assured. He himself had grown up surrounded by the yuppie life style of Seattle and had never really known a hard day in his life until he had joined the Marines. Since that time it seemed to him that every day was now hard and he couldn't wait to get out of the Corps. The hardships didn't really seem to bother his buddy Scanlon, however.

But Lipre also knew that deep down Scanlon was constantly fighting off the distant demons from his past. He was a heavy drinker and had shot heroin at least twice while Lipre was present. One time, with Credence Clearwater Revival's *"Bad Moon On The Rise"* playing in the background, Lipre had found him sprawled, spread eagle and unconscious, on the floor of the tent they shared back on Hill 55 before the start of Operation Oklahoma Hills. He was genuinely concerned about where Scanlon was going to go with his life when they returned to the world, if they returned to the world. Then again, he had thought at the time, *"drugs and alcohol are such a part of life in Vietnam that I'll be surprised if we aren't all in a detox program before our tour is over."*

"I've got to get some sleep, man. I'm outta here," a sleepy voice said.

Taking a final hit from the joint, Scanlon removed his flak vest and rolled it into a pillow, placing the rolled up vest on the lip of the fighting position. He then laid his head upon it and was asleep before the sound of his own voice carried away. His upper torso was pointing invitingly at two large boulders approximately fifty feet away.

***

Naturally blessed with superb night vision, the big cat patiently watched from the shadows, observing all that was going on between Lipre and Scanlon. He watched Scanlon drop his head and drift off in a deep sleep. He watched Lipre's eyes scan the bushes in which he now hid. He watched the two marines smoke the joint, fascinated by the sounds these strange animals made. Had he been human and understood their words, he might have felt sorry for them. But he was not human. He was the embodiment of all of nature's violent fury, an emotionally detached predator stalking its prey.

The tiger only reacted to the basic law of the jungle, that in nature the strong survived by preying on the weak, and the weak simply died as a result. How the weak felt about that was not really a matter of concern. As he coiled his legs tightly underneath his body he could feel the adrenaline course through his tightly bunched, quivering muscles. Now, after remaining undetected and completely motionless for more than one hour, he was watching Lipre's head drop as he too succumbed to the need for sleep.

The speed of the attack was incredible. Lipre thought he saw movement on the right, but in the twilight zone between being almost asleep and almost awake, he couldn't really be sure. He thought for a brief instant that the marijuana had him hallucinating. What he was sure of, however, staring at the now empty space beside him was that Private Mike Scanlon was gone, quickly whisked away by something very large and incomprehensible to a drugged mind rapidly awakening, yet shocked by the information it was being asked to process.

Unlike Lipre, it took Scanlon but an instant to realize that something was terribly wrong. Although he had felt no pain when the six-inch fangs penetrated his left shoulder just below the collarbone, crushing both the clavicle and the scapula, Scanlon dangled like a large black and green rat from the Tiger's massive jaws. He felt the sensation of being carried through the air as if his one hundred and eighty pound frame was but a mere feather. And with the instant realization that he was about to be killed and eaten, Scanlon emitted a scream unheard by man since the Neanderthal was the favored prey of the Saber Toothed Tiger.

The marines of 2nd Platoon, India Company, 3rd Marine Battalion, 1st Marine Regiment, 1st Marine Division, responded to his screams.

CHAPTER 2

A t the time of the "Night of the Tiger," as the marines came to call it, Corporal Tom Dash had been in Vietnam for nine months of what was to be a thir- teen-month tour of duty. A member of a Force Reconnaissance Unit, Dash had already seen his share of killing, usually up close and very personal. By now, after nine months of ambushes, snipers, booby traps, prisoner interrogations and dead bodies, extreme violence should have become as familiar to him as forced breathing is to a snorkeling swimmer. Like a State Trooper arriving at the scene of a fatal car wreck, he should have been comfortable with compartmentalizing the human tragedy of war and perform his job as routinely as if he were walking the family dog. But he wasn't. Instead just the opposite had occurred.

For Dash and a growing number of marines, rationalizing the killing was becoming more difficult with each day they remained in Vietnam. This sweep was the third time that his team had run long-range reconnaissance patrols (LRRP's) over this same terrain. The first had been before Operation Oklahoma Hills, the second during, and now this sweep. Despite their efforts the environment was as dangerous now as it had been the previous two times, maybe even more dangerous. Yet despite their awareness of the growing threat, the leadership always insisted that if they stayed the course America would win the war.

It wasn't that the team members objected to the killing that takes place during a war. After all, the Marine Corps had trained them to kill with great efficiency and, enhancing the effects of this training, each individual possessed an unusually ag- gressive, martial spirit. None of them would have been in the Corps, much less an elite Special Operations unit like Force Reconnaissance if they objected to the idea of killing another human being. What they were beginning to object to, however, was that they had to kill people in the same location each time they returned to the area. Which, at least in Dash's mind, defeated the purpose for having killed in the first place. If killing and the fear of death didn't modify or change people's behavior, what exactly was the purpose for it? Worse yet, since killing the Vietnamese was not having the desired effect on them, when would it no longer be necessary to kill them? Or, were they simply supposed to kill all of them?

His doubts were not exclusively concerned with all of the unnecessary killing; they also centered on unnecessary dying as well. This sweep had already resulted in two Americans being killed in a violent encounter along the Laotian border when they had detonated an unexploded American 155mm-artillery shell rigged as a booby trap by NVA forces. The booby trap had been placed on a trail that the marines had walked many times before; undoubtedly placed there with the complicit knowledge of people they had helped before as well, if not actually having been placed there by one of these same people.

Compounding these growing doubts, the South Vietnamese LRRP team operating jointly with them had developed the nasty habit of torturing villagers by smashing the fingers of old women with their rifle butts to obtain information from them that none of the marines found useable or even particularly relevant. After thirty days of this nonsense, it had seemed to them that the allied LRRP team had become a little too exuberant with their interrogation techniques and the torture was beginning to wear on the marines.

The only reason they had not put a stop to the abuse was because it was Vietnamese on Vietnamese violence that they had learned to ignore as best they could. Both the NVA and the VC did similar horrendous things to the villagers if they suspected them of aiding the Americans or the Thieu Government in Saigon. Although they didn't like it, the Americans knew that the villagers were caught between a rock and a hard place that neither they nor the Marines Corps could do a damn thing about.

Unlike their civilian counterparts, these marines had experienced the reality of war often enough to know that there are no good sides to a war; just those who can only loosely be described as winners because they ultimately write the peace agreement, and losers, those who are subjected to it. That noncombatants are always swept up in the violence is not a surprise to those fighting in a war, especially civil wars where compliance, if not the actual loyalty of the civilian population is the main objective. That civilians would not be used and abused by both sides during modern warfare are the thoughts of a dreamer, small children, politicians, theologians or people who actually believe that an all-powerful God has a personal stake in the outcome.

Their awareness of the harsh realities of warfare, coupled with the fragile belief that they were fighting a war ostensibly for the very survival of western civilization, each other, and America were the only things that kept the marines going back out to fight. But since they were still going out to fight a war, by God, they were intent on winning it. The Marine Corps had made it a point of emphasis during boot camp to teach new recruits that both God and history were on their side. The Corps failed to mention that victory, as defined by one winner and one loser, was not what Vietnam was about. However, by 1969 the young marines called upon to do the fighting were beginning to figure that part out for themselves.

Following nine months of working and living with the South Vietnamese as part of the "Vietnamization" program encouraging them to do more of the fighting, Dash was no longer under any illusions that Vietnam was a war that America should feel confident in winning. Beginning with his first day in Vietnam when he had been told the self-defeating and widely held American belief to "never trust the Vietnamese civilians; they are all either VC or VC sympathizers." To his growing awareness that the political rhetoric from Washington and the facts on the ground were totally out of sync with one another.

The statement regarding all Vietnamese as communists was a logic that completely escaped Dash's analytical mind. *"If the country has already gone communist, then what the hell are we trying to prevent from happening?"* he remembered thinking when he first heard it. Such a statement validated the convoluted and tragic logic of a story he had read while a college freshman at Utah State University. It was an interview a high-ranking American officer had given to a New York Times reporter questioning him about the military strategy in Vietnam. The reporter had asked why a particular airbase had been placed where it was. The officer had responded that it was there to protect the troops. The reporter then asked why the troops were there. The officer had replied that they were there to protect the airbase. Particularly frightening was that the officer had not seen anything wrong with what he was trying to explain to the reporter. To him it made good tactical sense, completely missing the point that neither the troops nor the airbase had to be there in the absence of the other.

Dash had also watched an equally illogical yet politically correct statement given to the press by a colonel from the U.S. Army 1st Cavalry Division when he gave a television interview to a reporter during the chaos of the 1968 TET offensive near Saigon. While Dash casually sipped a hot coffee in the student union cafeteria, the TV reporter questioned the colonel by asking why America was involved in a war in Asia that, obvious to all, was a Vietnamese civil war. The good colonel had responded with the unforgettable line, said with total conviction and a deep southern drawl, "There is an American spirit inside every South Vietnamese. We are here to help set free that American spirit."

"Wow," Dash thought when he had first heard it. *"How can anyone not know that you cannot take freedom away from the unwilling without killing them and you cannot give freedom to the unwilling unless they are willing to fight and die for it themselves."* To not understand this basic principle is pure idiocy. Now, after 273 days in Vietnam he was clearly seeing the results of such idiocy firsthand.

There was an even more troubling doubt creeping into the minds of the marines during the latter stages of the war. They were begrudgingly developing a growing admiration of both the VC and the NVA soldier's willingness to endure incredible danger and deprivation to win the war. It was not an admiration built upon them as human beings, after all the marines were still in the business of killing them, but rather an admiration of respect born of the shared misery that is the life of an infantry soldier.

As miserable as Dash had been in Vietnam, and misery was the life of any combat soldier in Vietnam, he always felt that, as bad as it was, the enemy was enduring even greater hardships. Yet the enemy continued to achieve successes.

In essence, the admiration was based upon the mutual respect that only grunts can have for one another while simultaneously killing each other. Like prizefighters entering the ring, you can't help but admire the courage and skills of a worthy opponent, even while he is trying to knock you out.

It was obvious that the team was not alone in feeling this way as Dash sensed a growing desperation within the military and political leadership to "sell" the legitimacy of the war to all the men and women serving in Vietnam. These leaders would greatly exaggerate the significance of American accomplishments, of which there were many, but conveniently ignored the obvious; the harder those fighting the war worked at reducing the volume, the deeper the shit was getting.

As a result, Dash's disillusionment with what was being said and what was being seen and experienced grew more pronounced every day. The politically correct rhetoric was that America was winning, yet actions on the ground clearly told him that everyday was simply a repeat of the day before it, leaving those fighting to stay alive feeling like Bill Murray's character in the film, *"Groundhog Day."* No matter what a marine did today, tomorrow would simply be a repeat of yesterday, unless he died, in which case, there would be no more tomorrows.

After nine months it was becoming obvious to Dash that the enemy soldiers had a far greater resolve to win than did their South Vietnamese counterparts, the Army of the Republic of Vietnam (ARVN) troops that Dash had worked with. By comparison, at least in Dash's estimation, ARVN troops were, with rare exception, a motley collection of homosexual delinquents who would rather play hide the weenie under a poncho than endure anything approaching the hardships enemy soldiers were being exposed to on a daily basis.

Yet, despite their growing doubts, the Americans were still very intent on finding, killing, or capturing enemy soldiers. After all, it was what Marines get paid to do.

Playing a pivotal role in the sweep operations, Dash's Force Reconnaissance Team had been given the responsibility of screening the forward movement of the battalion by conducting long range patrols well in advance of the lead element, I/3/1. Initially they had performed an admirable job collecting intelligence on enemy movements, finding NVA troop concentrations, directing helicopter fire, artillery, and coordinating air strikes with the omnipresent F4 Phantoms orbiting the area.

Unfortunately, that had all come to an end two days earlier when they had been forced to ambush a ten-man squad of North Vietnamese regulars who had been, ostensibly, sent across the Laotian border to ambush them. This ambush effectively ended the teams' ability to operate under the enemy's radar screen and continue to collect valuable information. But it was something they all felt had to be done.

The team had been alerted of the presence of the enemy squad by a villager they had previously befriended when they provided medical assistance for a child that had a foot blown off when she stepped on a booby trap that was meant for the Americans.

Team member Sergeant Danny Overton, from Orlando, Florida, had personally bound the wound of the child and Team Leader Staff Sergeant Glenn Meadows, from Raleigh, North Carolina, had called in a MEDEVAC helicopter to send her to a triage facility near Da Nang. Meadows had subsequently arranged to have her flown back to her village once she was fit to travel. The father had never forgotten the kindness of the marines and he felt that he owed them something for their efforts.

There was a lesson to be learned from this experience that Tom Dash would remember for the remainder of his military career. He learned the importance of showing hopeless and desperate people how much better life could be if they kept the Americans alive. He also learned the importance of doing deeds for people that they could not do for themselves; deeds that would one day be repaid in spades.

Dash learned that the more often he did these things the more indispensable he became to the people he was helping. Even if it was mistakenly believed by some of those same people that they had found a naive fool to take advantage of. It is always better to be seen as a fool than to be seen as the enemy, especially when living among people who may in fact be the enemy.

Dash learned to never do what he had seen the ARVN soldiers do to gain compliance; threaten to kill people who are hanging on to hope by a thin thread. Such a technique never gives people a reason to keep soldiers alive, it only gives them a good reason for wanting to see them dead. After all, civilian noncombatants live with the threat of death everyday, from both sides, and threatening to harm them only makes them angrier, putting marines and soldiers in the same long line with others wishing them ill. As Dash watched the ARVN troops intimidate, torture and even kill villagers in failed attempts to obtain information from them, he knew that America was fighting a losing battle for winning their hearts and minds.

Finally, Dash learned that when one had gained the trust of the people and they pointed out the actual enemy, that enemy was killed just as dead as yesterday's alarm clock. Violently, with no remorse or compassion. One killed them until they were all dead, maimed, or prisoners. Hopefully, such action would demonstrate to the villagers that America, this time, was there to finish the job.

The information the girl's father had provided them alerted the marines to the fact that they had been observed by a soldier from the enemy squad in one of the villages recently visited. The marines decided to use this knowledge to their own advantage.

Just before darkness, but with enough light remaining that they could be seen from a distance, both the Recon team and their Vietnamese LRRP shadows occupied a night position at the base of the mountains about a quarter mile from the nearest tree line. Their intent was to be clearly visible to anyone watching from the mountains; and the enemy was watching.

When darkness fell the team of marines, leaving the LRRP unit as bait to be watched by the hidden NVA soldiers, silently slipped into the current of the Song River and floated downstream to establish an ambush site at a right angle to their former position.

The ambush site was approximately fifty yards outside the once distant tree line where they had been observed occupying the night position by anxious eyes belonging to this group of NVA soldiers, who began salivating at the prospects of killing them tonight.

The marines knew that if they had been observed occupying the initial site, the NVA soldiers would react once they felt the time was right. So they quickly established their linear ambush position ninety feet from a well-traveled paddy dike leading into and out of the tree line. Confident that this would be the path their prospective killers would follow to get to where they last seen the marines. It was a classic bait and switch operation the marines had successfully performed many times before.

Once they occupied the ambush site both Overton and Dash each placed a Claymore mine out. One at the beginning and one at the end of what they hoped would soon become a kill zone. The experienced marines submerged the mines in the shallow paddy water and radically angled the deadly devices skyward towards the ridge of the paddy dike.

This was done so the water in the rice paddy would help absorb the backblast from the mines, allowing the marines the advantage of being as close to the kill zone as possible when they were detonated. The two mines were wired together and connected to one clacker, or detonator, that Dash would control from the far end of the kill zone.

Finally, with their deadly preparations finished, the six man Recon team slipped silently into the murky waters of the rice paddy and settled in to wait for their wishful killers to emerge from the security of the tree line.

Initially Dash thought they had misjudged the accuracy of the information. The wait was interminable. After lying motionless for three hours in the leech-infested water, there was nothing that he would have liked more than to be able to remove a particularly aggressive leech busily trying to slip inside his nostrils. He wanted with every fiber of his body to take the little bastard in his hand, hurl it to the ground, and then stomp the life out of it. But he couldn't; he was already set in position for the ambush. Dash continued to just lie there instead, forced to tolerate the presence of the persistent leech, seeking the source of the carbon dioxide that had attracted him.

All in all Dash found the leech to be rather annoying. *"At least I don't have to worry about falling asleep,"* he was thinking when suddenly, out of the corner of his eye, he saw movement. Silhouetted against the moonlit tree line, Dash could clearly see that it was not an animal, but rather a small man wearing a pith helmet and carrying an AK-47. There was another similarly armed man right behind him.

***

No matter how many times Dash experienced intense feelings before in his life, nothing would ever compare with the adrenaline rush he always experienced when he was about to kill another human being. Particularly when he could almost reach out and touch them, yet they had no idea that the next few seconds would be their last on earth.

Dash had grown up hunting deer and small game in Idaho and he had heard of hunters experiencing a case of "buck fever," or case of shaky nerves, when an elk or deer or some other type of animal came into view. He had always enjoyed the excitement of hunting and had felt both a sense of satisfaction and an adrenaline rush any time he had been fortunate enough to bring meat home for the table. But he had never experienced anything close to buck fever, a case of nerves that left hands shaking and mouth so dry that he couldn't have produced saliva to win a hundred dollar bet. Not until Vietnam where he experienced the effects of buck fever many times, always after having made the kill, never before or during.

As a result of these experiences he now understood how predatory animals contained these feelings when they were about to make a kill, being excited yet remaining in control of themselves until the job was finished. Controlling their emotions is something all predators have to do if they want to survive. For man, whether he likes to admit it or not, the excitement of killing comes as naturally to him as it does to a tiger.

As a result of his wartime experiences, Dash grew to pity the frailty of humans who found the killing of an unarmed animal by shooting them from a safe distance with a high powered rifle to be so exciting that it produced similar feelings of buck fever. He found it especially annoying that these hunters lacked the self-discipline to control their emotions.

Though as a poor newly wed college student Dash would continue to employ both his rifle and shotgun to put meat on the table, the excitement of hunting animals for sport would never be the same after Vietnam. While in college, with little money to buy food, killing animals became an occurrence born more of necessity than pleasure. After Vietnam Dash found that killing animals now lacked excitement because in hunting them there was no danger of being killed himself.

Despite the protestations of the "Great White Hunters," such a feeling of vulnerability when confronting another armed human is one that hunting even the most dangerous big game animals cannot replicate. Unless, of course, those same "dangerous animals" are themselves given high power rifles in order to return fire, leveling the playing field and greatly reducing the number of Great White Hunters purchasing hunting licenses each year.

"Put a person susceptible to bouts of buck fever in an environment where the animals shoot back and he will pee down both legs," Dash often thought. *"He certainly won't go hunting more than once."*

In addition to learning to control emotions during combat, Dash also marveled at how easy it had been to make the transition from a civil society to one of death and destruction. Perhaps mankind has not evolved as far from his predatory roots as some would like to believe Dash would later argue with his college sociology professors.

"We're just animals ourselves," he would tell them. "We are only fooling one another by failing to acknowledge that the dark side of man's nature hasn't changed for thousands of years. Only his methods of killing have changed, not his desire to want to kill."

Tonight, as he watched the enemy soldiers move into the kill zone he felt no guilt, no shame in knowing that he was about to kill a fellow human being. The feelings he had at such moments were similar to those he had experienced when shooting ground squirrels on the family farm in Idaho. He didn't care one way or the other about killing the squirrels, but they were pests that made life difficult for him when he irrigated the fields and the corrugate of water kept disappearing down a burrow. Their burrows posed a hazard to the horses that he often rode through those same fields. Besides, he often rationalized, it is the fickle hand of fate at work. If the squirrels didn't want to be shot, then they simply could have hauled their bushy little butts out of his fields. It's not as if he was going to follow them. But they didn't leave his fields, making their death as much a fault of their own choosing than of his.

He was now experiencing those same detached feelings as he watched the enemy soldiers emerge from the tree line. If they had not come here tonight, they wouldn't be dead by his hand. But they were here, and they were dangerous. They had to be dealt with and, like the ground squirrels back in Idaho, he didn't care one way or the other how it had to be done. As ten NVA soldiers cleared the tree line he smiled within and thought, *"Come on you little bastards, just a bit further."*

***

As the NVA troops emerged from the cover of the tree line, it was obvious they were unaware that the marines had moved from where they had last seen them, repositioning to a location where they could now almost reach out and touch one another. Which, in a macabre sense, they were about to do.

The NVA troops hurried down the paddy dike in a clustered mass of excitement, behaving as if they were on their way to their own kill, throwing caution to the wind. Only the first and last two soldiers maintained any dispersion, minimal at best, making themselves a target for the taking. When the clump of six soldiers centered themselves in the kill zone, Dash closed his eyes and squeezed hard on the clacker.

Lying directly behind and only fifty feet from the simultaneous explosion of two claymore mines, even when fired from under water, is an ear shattering experience. Being twenty feet in front of those same two exploding mines would have to be a near death experience even if they missed. But they didn't miss. Six of the ten NVA troops immediately disappeared in a tremendous blast of muddy water, blood, guts, bone, teeth and hair. Body parts were blown one hundred feet across the rice paddy, splashing into the muddy water like raindrops from a summer storm.

The remaining four soldiers who escaped the shotgun blast of shrapnel fired from the claymores were either knocked from their feet and flattened to the paddy dike by the concussion, or they simply collapsed in shock. Either way they died where they fell when the marines sprang from the water and rushed toward them while firing quick bursts from their weapons. Closing on the comatose men they ended their assault with a bullet through each mans brain.

At the front of the kill zone, Sergeant Corky Reeves from Des Moines, Iowa, fired one-pause, two-pause, three-pause, four rounds back into the tree line where the Vietnamese had first emerged. No return fire followed, indicating that all present were dead; their bodies sprawled haphazardly along the paddy dike and scattered around the surrounding paddy waters like so much debris.

Satisfied that these were the only soldiers sent to kill them, the marines quickly searched the four intact corpses and body parts of the others for information, then raced to a nearby rally point to begin their exfiltration, their LRRP shadows bringing up the rear. With their cover blown, the marines now sought the safety of the large force approaching from the east, being led by the second platoon, India Company, Third Battalion, First Marine Regiment.

CHAPTER 3

The reconnaissance team had learned through trial and error that the best way to coordinate anything as complicated as conducting a linkup, or establishing restricted firing areas, was to do so face to face, especially at night, when everyone is a little trigger happy. After entering the battalion radio net and affecting the necessary control measures, the team approached the marine lines, fired a green star cluster signifying friendly forces, and entered their perimeter. Dressed in their black pajamas, sandals, and carrying AK-47's, the team looked more like Ninja warriors than combat marines and their arrival at the Battalion TOC, Tactical Operations Center, caused quite a stir.

While his team members began to renew old acquaintances, and the LRRP squad returned to their own Vietnamese parent unit, SSGT Meadows sought out the battalion operations officer. The S-3 had not expected them and had no pre-planned missions, providing them instead with cursory guidance to move into a hide position behind 2nd Platoon, I/3/1, and await further instructions. They were in the process of occupying this position when Scanlon began screaming.

***

Although Lipre wasn't quite sure what was happening his marine instincts told him to start firing his M-16 and sort out the facts later. In the dim light his first shot hit nothing but air, but it did cause the tiger to change direction and start running towards the recon team, Scanlon still hanging from his jaws, screaming like a banshee. Lipre was now pumping out rounds at a feverish pace as his brain came to grips with what was happening.

Both the sights of the cat and the gunfire directed towards them were events completely unexpected by the Recon team. They were anticipating getting a good night's sleep behind the protective barricade of marine riflemen manning the line. For men well trained to always expect the unexpected, even the hard core Recon marines had difficulty comprehending what they had unwittingly become a party to.

As the outline of the tiger and screaming marine vaguely appeared before the team other marines along the perimeter began firing into the jungle at targets that existed only in their imaginations. So exuberant was this volley of fire that at least two Claymore mines were detonated, and shouts of "There they are! Over there! Fire! Fire!" could be heard up and down the line as the contagious excitement of combat swept the entire marine perimeter.

As this "mad minute" rose to a deafening crescendo someone, to the good fortune of all, popped a parachute flare and in the ghostly light Lipre could vaguely make out the cat's silhouette. More importantly, he could also see his front sight blade. With calm deliberation he began placing effective fire on the cat, hitting him at least twice but neither of the little armor piercing bullets broke a bone nor hit a vital organ or, most distressing of all, caused it to relinquish its grip on Mike Scanlon.

As Lipre's firing became more accurate, Scanlon's screams could distinctly be heard over the roar of gunfire. With each passing second his screams became less like the primal sounds of being prey to the high-pitched squeal of being a target as bullets whizzed past the cat's head.

In typical firefight chaos, even though only one side is doing all of the shooting, instinct rather than forethought becomes modus operandi. It was instinct that caused Recon team member SGT Corky Reeves to fire a burst of rifle fire at the cat, one a tracer round, hitting and killing it. Thus it was the sharply honed instinct of Corky Reeves that saved the life of Mike Scanlon. It was this same instinct, honed to a razors edge in Bob Lipre as well, a split second later, that took the life of Corky Reeves.

The first and most basic survival skill learned in Vietnam was the ability to recognize the distinctive firing sound made by an AK-47 and an M-16. The AK makes a "cacking" sound when fired while the M-16 makes a "popping" sound. In addition to the differing sounds made by the two weapons, the AK-47 ammunition used in Vietnam consisted of green tracer rounds while the M-16 fired orange tracers. The AK-47 was the chosen weapon of the NVA and the M-16 that of the Marines. This was a lesson that Bob Lipre, inexperienced though he was, had already learned. When Reeves fired his three round burst at the cat with his AK-47 Bob Lipre had no idea that the Recon team had sequestered itself to his immediate rear. No one had bothered to tell him. Since the cat was running directly at the team's location, Lipre already had his weapon aimed in their general direction.

The muzzle flash of the AK coupled with the tell-tale streak of the tracer round prompted Lipre to make a minor adjustment before sending a bullet through the chest of Corky Reeves and another through the leg of Tom Dash.

The first 5.56mm, .223 caliber, 55 grain armor piercing bullet broke through Reeve's chest at a speed of 3600 feet per second, bursting his heart as if it were an over inflated party balloon, severing his spine between the fourth and fifth vertebra. Death was instantaneous.

Lipre's next bullet entered the front quadriceps of Tom Dash's left leg and exited through his hamstring, narrowly missing both the femur and the femoral artery before burying itself in the mud between his feet. Gratefully, Lipre's following shots went over the heads of the other startled team members.

If it was a soldier's instinct that killed both the cat and Reeves, it was calculated thought that caused the marines to run from the kill zone rather than return Lipre's fire. Though no one spoke a word, they all knew that returning fire would be a huge mistake as the other marines, already firing wildly into the jungle at imaginary targets, would return the AK fire with a vengeance. Besides, they instinctively knew that Lipre had done exactly what they themselves would have done under the same circumstances.

In the dim glow of the dying parachute flare, the remaining four members of the Recon team hurriedly scooped Dash up by the arms, leaving Reeves where he had fallen, and sprinted towards two large boulders into what had once been the lair of the now dead Bengal Tiger. Fortunately for them, Lipre stopped shooting in order to reload, allowing the team to reach the entrance to the lair unscathed. It was here that they first heard Lipre screaming the dreaded refrain that caused the neck hairs of many a marine rifleman to stand on end, "GOOKS IN THE WIRE!"

Everything had happened so fast up to this point that all the team members were in a virtual state of shock. But when Lipre began screaming for help, they quickly realized that they had little time to react before he and the now gathering storm of excited marine riflemen saturated the lair with small arms fire, hand grenades, and 40mm rounds from their M-79 grenade launchers. Anticipating this reaction, Meadows feverishly removed a green star cluster flare from the back of the PRC-77 radio and fired it into the air. Simultaneously all of the team members began screaming, AMERICANS! AMERICANS! STOP SHOOTING, STOP SHOOTING!

The sight of the green flare, signifying friendly forces, and the sound of the marines' voices seemed to dissuade the other marines from firing, but Lipre couldn't resist. He had seen many strange and unbelievable things within the last several seconds but he was absolutely certain that the people he had been shooting at were not marines. They were not dressed like marines and they were not carrying M-16's. In his mind both the flare and the spoken English had to be some sort of VC trick. For these reasons Lipre ignored both the flare and the screams.

Rushing forward he fired another 20 round magazine into the brush masking the team. Fortunately, because of all that Lipre had witnessed within the past few seconds, he was in acute sensory overload. His hands were shaking like a stop sign in a hurricane. Except for the noise of the gunfire, which caused the team members to flatten out as best they could on the dirt and bone covered floor, nothing of consequence penetrated the sanctity of the lair. But the rapid fire did attract the attention of Lipre's Platoon Sergeant, who had been told about the recon team. Fearing the worst, he shouted orders for Lipre and the other marines to hold their fire, going so far as to personally tear the weapon from Lipre's trembling hands.

The nightmare for that night was finally over, a nightmare that would live with those who experienced it for the rest of their lives. None more so than Bob Lipre, who had done nothing wrong, but would carry the burden of undeserved guilt for having killed one of his own.

"Recon! Is that you?" Shouted the platoon sergeant.

"Yes, goddamn it! Stop your shooting!" Came the chorus of replies as everyone answered at once.

"All right, but come out one at a time and with your weapons above your heads," replied the platoon sergeant, a crusty gunnery sergeant on his third tour of duty in Vietnam. Gunny had not survived as long as he had by being careless and he wasn't about to start now.

As the team members emerged from the lair, an 81mm mortar fired a continuous illumination mission and in the eerie light all could see the "What the hell just happened?" expression on everyone's face as they silently looked into one another's eyes.

Good order and discipline quickly replaced a numbed silence as the marines began to react as the hardened veterans they had become. In the aftermath of the chaos, orders were shouted out, the wounded administered to, accusatory looks exchanged, and Marine Corps NCO professionalism emerged. The perimeter was quickly reestablished, the wounded and dead gathered for evacuation.

As Meadows helped a Naval Corpsman tighten a battle dressing around Dash's leg, the platoon sergeant approached and stated matter-of-factly, "You have one dead and my man Scanlon is in a deep state of shock. Lipre isn't a hell of a lot better off but I think he will be all right."

The gunny briefly glanced at Dash's leg while continuing to speak to Meadows in a hushed tone, offering professional guidance. "Doc tells me that this wound is a through and through so he will be choppered out in the morning along with the other casualties. I told the squad leaders you were moving around to our rear, but they obviously didn't put the word out. I'm sorry about that, but shit happens. Learn from it and move on, but don't dwell on it." With that said he spun on his heels and brusquely walked away. There was nothing more that anyone could have said that would have made a whit of difference.

***

At first light, Tom Dash was unceremoniously loaded into the back of a CH-47 helicopter along with the body of Corky Reeves and the ambulatory but still in shock Mike Scanlon. Both Dash and Scanlon would be separated from the body upon their arrival at the Naval Aid Station Hospital in Da Nang. Reeves' body would be placed in the morgue, joining dozens of other bodies collected from all over I Corps to await further processing and eventual return to the States for burial.

Dash and Scanlon would be admitted to wards full of other wounded marines to await further evacuation to hospitals outside of Vietnam. Both would eventually be sent to the Naval Hospital at Agana, Guam and subsequently to the Naval Hospital at Bremerton, Washington, where they would recover from their wounds and ultimately receive their honorable discharges from the United States Marine Corps.

Tom Dash would briefly return to his life in Idaho and earn a college degree. Mike Scanlon would disappear into the bowels of Atlanta, never to be seen or heard from again. Following two years of unsuccessful psychiatric treatment at Bethesda Naval Hospital and numerous syringes of black tar heroin, with visions of a political career long dissolved by feelings of guilt, Bob Lipre would put a bullet through his own brain, finally bringing to an end the predators, human and animal, that had haunted him his entire life.

In the interim, across America Marine Corps recruiters and Navy chaplains were mobilized to conduct next of kin notification. Dreaded knocks on doors in Twin Falls, Idaho and Atlanta, Georgia were answered with silent prayers and anxious anticipation as the detailed recruiters read:

"The Commandant of the Marine Corps regrets to inform you that your son (FILL IN NAME) has been WOUNDED IN ACTION..."

Followed by immediate sighs of relief and questions concerning the extent of injuries, none of which could be satisfactorily answered and the uncomfortable recruiter would silently stare at his shoes as he wished he were anywhere but here.

In Des Moines, Iowa a somber recruiter read to a young wife and mother:

"The Commandant of the Marine Corps regrets to inform you that your husband (FILL IN NAME) has been KILLED IN ACTION..."

Followed by a burst of tears and a nodding condolence from the Chaplain as he holds the newborn son who will never know his brave father, Sergeant Corky Reeves. The body of Corky Reeves arrived in Des Moines three days after his wife received notification of his death. He was buried December 24, the day before Christmas, 1969, on a clear, crisp Iowa winter day.

The warrior Marine was buried with full military honors in a non-descript cemetery, next to a creek bed on the outskirts of the city. During the ceremony the cheerful appearance of a bright blue sky compensated for the vision of the dreary, snow covered burial ground. In the biting winter chill, the tears of those in attendance froze to exposed cheeks, giving the mourners' the appearance of zombies, causing many of them to look exactly as they felt. Corky Reeves was only nineteen.

As a young wife and mother wept over the flag draped casket of her fallen Marine, other nineteen-year-old college fraternity brothers, home for Christmas break, celebrated the holidays with their families and worried about how they were going to pay their Christmas bills. They dreamed of touring Europe in the summer and casually contemplated what life would be like when they were finally forced to leave the childish world of a college fraternity and grow up to become real men.

In accordance with his last request, and much to the chagrin of the mortician observing the proceedings, the Marine Honor Guard, following the viewing, reached inside the casket and turned the body face down. Corky Reeves, Sergeant, United States Marine Corps, as a last request, had asked that he be buried in this manner so, in his own words, *"all those college fraternity pussies can kiss my Marine Corps ass!"*

CHAPTER 4

onvalescing in hospitals for three months gave Dash plenty of time to ponder his future. Like most young people faced with a major transition in their life, he was not certain what he wanted to do now that his enlistment in the Marine Corps was coming to an end. Realistically, he hadn't given the future much thought since arriving in Vietnam nine months earlier. He never expected to live long enough to have a future, choosing instead to live day to day. Now that he had survived Vietnam, he had to pull the cobwebs from his mind, contemplate tomorrow, and then do his best to prepare for it.

But for all his uncertainties about what he would do with the rest of his life, there was one thing he was absolutely certain of; sending young men to die in Vietnam had been a mistake. Not a mistake because he and others had answered the call, but a mistake by the government to which he had sworn his allegiance.

Yet as he lay in his hospital bed contemplating the myriad forces that had put him there, he realized that American involvement in Vietnam had not been the mistake many of the peace protestors he was watching on television were proclaiming it to be. A mistake willfully created by the military and industrial complex to further enrich overly greedy American businessmen. With twenty-twenty hindsight, intelligent people believing in such a conspiratorial reason for going to war was almost as bad as intelligent people believing that America needed to send its sons and daughters to Vietnam because God personally called her to shine the light of freedom on all of mankind.

The real mistake made in Vietnam, besides America's overreaction to the fear of communism, was that well-intentioned people had foolishly believed that wars could be successfully waged as a zero sum game ending with no clear winner and no real loser. These same people mistakenly believed that when given the opportunity to address internal grievances, rational people would always choose economic prosperity over nationalism and political power, foolishly believing that reason and logic would trump mankind's irrational passion for violence. Unfortunately these well-intentioned people forgot that history has many more examples of where such beliefs were proven to be wrong than it has of when they were proven to be right.

As he lay in his hospital bed, Dash swore to himself that he would make every effort to ensure that a debacle like Vietnam never victimized America again. He didn't yet know how he was going to affect such a thing, he just knew that he wanted to try. In the meantime, he anxiously waited for the day he would return to the world of hamburgers and beer, of music and laughter, of busty, long legged women, and fast cars; a world that he had left far behind 58,229 lifetime's ago.

***

Becoming a "lifer" himself, a career military man, was not something that Tom Dash had often considered while serving in the Marine Corps. He had done his time and with his experiences behind him it was time to get on with his life. He accomplished that by marrying his former high school sweetheart and going back to college, earning a bachelor's degree with a dual major of sociology and political science. A degree that even then had the same job prospect associated with it that a degree in Art History has when the holder lives in a small town — none at all.

The only reason he had chosen his field of study was that he had become fascinated by the decision making process of a group of intelligent and well-meaning people who chose to intervene in a civil war in Southeast Asia as a way to protect America. Studying the interactions of the many and varied special interest groups, comprised of veterans, academics, and politicians who should have clearly known better than to become embroiled in a land war on the Asian continent, was a thought that intrigued him. How so many learned people could arrive at such an erroneous conclusion was a thought that would haunt him for the remainder of his life.

But as life in small town America, with all of its ups and downs and limited options began to catch up to him, career decisions had to be made at some point and the military was certainly one option among the many available to him. His inquisitiveness into all things political and social was rapidly being replaced by both his and his new wife Janet's desire to eat. In addition, like many returning veterans confronted by daily death, once he had the opportunity, Dash quite willingly surrendered to the impulse of procreation – he and Janet quickly had two children. As a consequence, he had to get serious about starting a career with a paycheck attached to it; contemplating theoretical concepts would have to wait until later.

Dash initially thought about following the same career path his wife had chosen and become a schoolteacher. But as he weighed the possibilities of a teaching profession he came to the stark realization that despite the rhetoric of the profession, he could not recall one single instance where he had been personally inspired to excel by a teacher. Not in elementary school, not in high school, and certainly not in college. To him, high school hadn't been so much a place of inspiration and challenge as it had been a place to compete in sports. College was just something to be tolerated while he prepared to look for a job. As he looked back over his student career, he realized that the only real learning that had taken place had been in grade school when he had first learned to read and write. The rest of his formal education had been more akin to being in an adult day care than in a creative, challenging, learning environment. Looking back on his civilian educational experiences, he realized that it had been the most boring time of his life. Being a teacher probably wouldn't be any more exciting.

It wasn't until he enlisted in the Marines that all of that had changed. Dash found the military experience to be new and exciting, challenging beyond anything he had ever experienced before. And he would have had to remove his shoes in order to account for the number of officers and NCO's that had inspired him to excellence while he was a marine. Dash possessed a natural flair for leadership, having graduated at the top of every military school he had ever attended. He had also done well as a civilian student, remaining on the Dean's list throughout his college career, a significant accomplishment since he found campus life and the classroom exceedingly boring when compared to his experiences as a combat marine. As a veteran, Dash had not had a high opinion of his post-Vietnam college experience. It had been mind numbingly routine. Once a person has experienced the life and death reality of a battlefield it is slightly absurd to believe that he will feel the "pressure" of a semester final is something to fret over. Trying to convince combat veterans that all that "personal responsibility" experienced in college will lead to maturity is even more absurd. In fact, many veterans feel that going straight to college after high school delays growing up and offers a sanctuary for those desperate to extend juvenile adolescence for as long as possible. Something very easy to do if daddy pays for college and the student joins a sorority or fraternity, trading one mother for another to continue shielding them from life's harsh realities.

As a civilian working mundane jobs to put food on the table and bored with college, Dash began to yearn for those days when he and others had accomplished feats the difficulty of which most civilians could not even begin to comprehend. As a decorated and wounded veteran, he was certainly no stranger to danger and hardships.

Dash weighed his many career possibilities realizing that despite the political negatives of Vietnam, such as the wrong war in the wrong place at the wrong time for all the wrong reasons, his actual military experiences had been pretty good. To him the profession of arms was an honorable trade and one that would not lock him into an "office box" for the remainder of his life. With his brief taste of military adventure fresh in his mind, Dash scorned the possibilities of living the remainder of his life as just another eight to five stuffed shirt as being akin to going to prison without the possibility of parole. A form of vertical death. These thoughts in mind, he enrolled in the Reserve Officer Training program, ROTC, at Idaho State University. His recent experiences and upbringing seemed a perfect fit.

***

Dash had grown up during the 50's and 60's, a typical baby boomer enjoying a small town *"Leave-It-To-Beaver"* childhood, regaled with the American glory that had been World War II. His Father, several uncles, and virtually every other adult male that Tom had met while growing up in Idaho had participated in what Studs Turkle so aptly called the *"Good War."*

Described as a classic confrontation between good and evil, World War II had left little room for misinterpreting which side had been good and which side had been evil. Unless of course, one happened to be German or Japanese, then a difference of opinion can be found. But inside America it was virtually unanimous that it had been a just war fought with American reluctance but a vengeance reminiscent of the Christian crusades.

Americans like moral clarity and World War II patriotism was worn like a badge of honor by those who had participated in it. It also ended with clear winners and clear losers; or so it was believed by the young men listening to the veterans recount their wartime experiences.

Only later, much later, as veterans themselves, would the young men understand the untold stories that were carefully kept hidden just beneath the surface as American culture painted a picture of war that was too rosy to be realistic. And the retiring crop of politicians refused to admit that much had been left undone following the war. Much of this unfinished business, more political than military, would lead directly to future wars. Also missing from the stories told by the veterans themselves were those of mistakes and doubts, of despair and fear. Of being deceived if not openly lied to by the very government that had sent them to war. Stories of lives delayed, lost and taken that veterans of all wars are forced to live with; stories that Dash would tell for himself, about himself, after he returned from Vietnam. But, in 1945, negativism and self-doubt were not yet a part of the public dialogue and veterans were not being criticized for the mistakes made by their political handlers. That would come later, when soldiers trickled home as individuals to a fractured public to be received as villains rather than being allowed to march home in mass as conquering heroes. The simple black and white, good or bad analysis Americans are so well known for allowed soldiers to become victims of a vicious media assault that painted all law abiding Americans with a broad criminal brush. To the growing numbers opposed to the war, soldiers were simply seen as part of the problem.

The negative publicity generated towards the military as a result of the Vietnam War only served to amplify any negative story in the ears of those who never went to Vietnam themselves. Many critics of the war voiced their objections to it by reliving the war vicariously through the words and deeds of those who had gone to Vietnam, often discrediting these men and women in the process.

The media characterization of Vietnam veterans then and now is not a fair portrayal of the soldiers who fought there. These men and women were not a collection of drug addicts and "baby killers" finding a release for their psychosis in Vietnam. Neither are Vietnam veterans appropriately represented by the beer bellied, beret and outgrown-jungle fatigue bedecked veterans who gather at the Vietnam Memorial telling anyone that will listen how unfairly Vietnam veterans were treated when they came home. These men do not speak for all of those who went on with their lives after Vietnam. The vast majority of Vietnam veterans are forward-looking men and women who refuse to wallow in the self-pity of those who want to continue to live in the past, commiserating and blubbering whenever a television camera shows up.

Vietnam was not something that any one who went there had asked for; it was just something they got. Where they fight and whom they fight is not a decision made by soldiers. For those veterans who still find greater pleasure in being seen parading around the Wall than they do in enjoying a quite moment of reflection there, you deserve no sympathy. Vietnam is over.

Nor is it right to hold Vietnam veterans accountable for actions required on a battlefield. Only those who have been there can even begin to describe and comprehend the split second responses combat requires. Short of what Lieutenant Calley did at My Lai, such second-guess pillorying makes soldiers much more a victim of the horrors of war than a willing participant to all that happens during a war. The very last thing any returning veteran needs or wants is to be criticized by some pointy-headed intellectual do-gooder for having gone to war; or to be held personally accountable for the political mistakes of those who sent them there.

Like most of the young men from Southern Idaho, Dash had been exposed to the belief that America was defending freedom, democracy, and hope for a better way of life for the people of South Vietnam. Many felt that the world was facing a communist threat in Vietnam that if not countered there would metastasize into a cancer that would spread throughout the free world. This seemed to be the opinion shared by most of the World War II generation, albeit reluctantly by the veterans. For this generation of Americans Communism had posed a very real threat, a threat that they saw quite clearly. In their lifetime millions of people had been killed and were still being killed by this evil they had learned to both fear and hate at a very young age.

Conversely, Dash also learned that not everyone felt that America had an obligation or even a moral right to intervene in what was felt by some to be a civil war in Vietnam. This was rapidly becoming the prevailing attitude among the young and was being encouraged in large part by the non-veterans teaching on college campuses across America. Ironically, because they had never served themselves and were simply repeating what they had read or been told by others, these professors, for the returning veterans, frankly didn't have much credibility, even if they were right.

As a result, during the late 1960's many young men of draft age were actively protesting America's involvement in the war. Some had already fled to Canada rather than report for induction. To Dash and others like him, the young men who had fled to Canada were simply cowards. Not because they had opposed the war. This was a right that they all had. They were cowards because they didn't have enough backbone to go to prison for their beliefs when others were prepared to die for theirs. Pussies always take the easy way out.

There were, however, other protestors to be openly admired. Dash had watched the boxer Mohammed Ali take a stand against the war that had cost him millions of dollars in lost revenue and gained him a public scorn that would hound him for the remainder of his illustrious career.

Dash remembered thinking at the time that Ali was the example of a true protestor. He never ran from trouble; he met it head on. If a man of his stature would stand up against the forces of government and knowingly risk a promising future, then how could anyone have respect for some eighteen-year old weenie tucking his tail between his legs and fleeing his own country? Statistically most educated draftees did not serve as enlisted combat soldiers in Vietnam, even fewer actually died there. Such facts were well known to anyone possessing half a brain and a spine upon which to mount it.

"No," Dash had thought in contemplating his own reaction to Vietnam, *"no way in hell would I want to be identified with those spineless jellyfish fleeing to Canada!"*

There were worthwhile as well as confusing arguments and rationales being expounded by high profile individuals in both camps. For young men just escaping the safety of the cocoon called high school, antennas were very much in the reception mode. Young eighteen-year old men had to make life-altering decisions based upon contradictory messages from both the pro-war and the anti-war camps. Compounding the confusion was the fact that there were very few absolutes in any of the messages, only opinions.

With the polemic surrounding Vietnam young men had to rely more than ever upon those closest to them for guidance. This was true in Dash's case and in discussions with his father he was told; "Self defense is nature's oldest law. War is about killing people and that if a cause is worth killing for then it has to be important enough to die for. If it isn't, then no one should wage war because they have lost the legitimacy of self-defense."

Though seemingly self-evident, the wisdom of this truism is unfortunately lost on young ears because they mistakenly believe that it will always be the other guy who dies in combat while they remain personally invincible to the effects of hot metal. So, at least in the minds of the young, the part about dying in war is dismissed as being non-applicable and the killing part is exaggerated, often even glorified; on television, in the movies, and regrettably, in the minds of old men who should know better.

This naïve, childish way of thinking about war has led to the death of countless young men over countless generations. Unfortunately, as Dash discovered in Vietnam, politicians of all ages, race, gender and nationality are all too frequently afflicted with this same malady of arrested development. For some inexplicable reason they seem to conveniently forget the reality of war when blissfully making foreign policy decisions that place young men and women in harm's way for reasons other than self-defense.

As an officer, Dash felt that he might be able to change this mind set. Instead, he would find out that following orders was something that went with the uniform; naïveté has nothing to do with it.

CHAPTER 5

Fort Bliss lies on the northwest corner of the city of El Paso, Texas, extending into New Mexico at Alamogordo and the White Sands missile range. It is a hostile environment for both men and equipment and for that reason it is a perfect training ground for newly minted Armor officers.

The post was originally established as a frontier cavalry post to provide protection for wagon trains and settlers living in and traveling through the bleak southwest Texas desert of 1800's America. Before the Army completed the National Training Center in the Mojave Desert at Fort Irwin, California, Fort Bliss was the Army's premiere desert training grounds. It was where the XM-1, soon to become known as the M-1 Abrams Main Battle Tank received an extensive evaluation before the Army adopted it to replace the aging M-60 series tank. And the huge maneuver area at MacGregor Range combined with the maintenance facilities at the Dona Ana range camp allowed armor units ample opportunity to both break and then fix their assortment of vehicles.

When Dash arrived at Fort Bliss, it was home to the 3rd Armored Cavalry Regiment and the Air Defense Artillery School. It was his first assignment as an Officer and like most second lieutenants, he was anxious to begin his new career. He reported early so he could get his wife and two daughters' quarters in the family housing complex at Biggs Field, a former Air Force facility that had been turned over to the Army. Once quarters were secured, Dash reported in to the squadron commander, a lieutenant colonel with Vietnam combat experiences similar to those of Dash's. Following this introduction and the sharing of several war stories with the squadron commander, Dash was assigned to E Troop, 2nd Squadron, 3rd ACR as a platoon leader.

Prior to reporting to their initial duty assignments all officers receive a rigorous branch specific education at their respective branch schools. Dash's school was held at Fort Knox, Kentucky at the Armor Center and School. The curriculum consisted of driving and firing the M-60 series tank along with the tactics and logistics associated with employing it. There were also several classes devoted to the maintenance of good order and discipline among the troops along with the development of interpersonal skills to be used when dealing with them. Most often, however, officers received instructions on how to fix their vehicles, as all were old, worn out, and in need of constant repair.

The duties of a platoon leader are considered to be the formative grounds for all aspiring officers. It is an introductory assignment designed to provide officers with a basic understanding of the organizational, tactical, logistical, and administrative requirements of a combat unit, some of which Dash had already learned as a former enlisted soldier. However, with almost a five-year break in service Dash had a great deal of catching up to do. He also had to master new skills he had not been forced to learn while serving in an elite marine unit, an assignment that had done little to prepare him for life in a conventional unit.

One of the first things Dash noticed was that the residual effects of Vietnam still lingered in the Army. Some of the troops still serving in the late 70's were people of questionable character and the Army would have been much better off had it put them in prison rather than in boots. But it was the beginning of the all-volunteer Army and like any new endeavor, it was going to take time before all of the kinks were worked out.

In the years immediately following America's complete withdrawal from Vietnam the United States Army was but a hollow shell of what it would become less than three years later when enlistment standards were raised and expeditious discharges had the desired effect. Prior to this however, the enlisted ranks were full of malcontents and never-do-wells of every stripe and color. Harnessing the energy of such an undisciplined mob and turning it into something positive is no easy job for anyone, let alone a lieutenant without any real experience under his or her belt.

Dash's previous military service had been in an elite unit, a unit that pretty much ran itself and required very little attention from the officers and senior NCO's overseeing it. Consequently, he was unprepared for what he found at Fort Bliss: soldiers who had to be told what to do and constantly checked on to insure that they had done it. Adding to the problem, unfortunately, some of the sergeants required constant monitoring as well.

Service in elite units does little to prepare an officer or NCO for military life in conventional units; a fact recognized and addressed by the Army. Elite units pretty much run on autopilot, so the army leadership forces soldiers to serve in assignments outside elite areas, rounding them into leaders with a better understanding of how to get the unwilling to do the necessary. Something Dash had not yet learned, but soon would; receiving his education from the other two platoon leaders, as well as both the executive officer and troop commander, all prior service enlisted personnel. And all of them had served in conventional units.

Although following Vietnam the Marine Corps had been better at hiding its warts than the Army had, the morale in both services was in serious need of repair, as was the requirement to enforce discipline. Black-on-white and white-on-black violence, drug abuse and lack of discipline had become so pronounced that the barracks was often considered to be more violent than the battlefield.

First Sergeants conducting barracks inspection did so wearing a sidearm for personal protection. In one tragic instance at Fort Bliss the body of a major fulfilling his duties as Field Officer of the Day was found in a Dumpster outside the K Troop barracks. Later evidence would show that he had walked in on a drug deal inside the E Troop barracks and had been killed as a result. Additionally, two cooks from the E Troop dining facility shot and killed a high profile attorney, Lee Chagra, in downtown El Paso Christmas Eve, 1978. Upon their arrest and subsequent conviction it came to light that they had been selling drugs for Chagra and rather than give him his share of the profits the two soldiers shot him instead.

On paydays prostitutes would be waiting in the parking lot to be pimped inside the barracks, having their soldier handlers pay the Charge of Quarters, known as the CQ, a token fee to simply leave his station at prearranged times. Such was the state of the post-Vietnam military. As a student of human nature Dash was not surprised that illegal activities took place and that the army had its fair share of criminals, but he had never had any personal experiences dealing with either.

Early during his Marine Corps enlistment a wise Gunnery Sergeant had counseled Dash that as dangerous as Force Reconnaissance was, it was even more dangerous to be a member of a rifle company. For as bizarre as it sounds, in a rifle company a leader had to fear being shot by his own people.

During the waning days of the war, marine rifle companies, like their army infantry counterparts were filled with people of questionable character. As a result, both morale and discipline were sorely lacking in conventional units. This is not meant as an indictment of all the many fine young men who served admirably in these units, but it is an acknowledgement that by the late sixties and early seventies, soldiers and marines were killing and wounding their own leaders with increasing regularity in Vietnam. Known as "fragging," this despicable act was a direct result of allowing criminals to wear the military uniform and suspending the necessary discipline required to compel the unwilling to do the necessary. It takes special soldiers to behave otherwise, and it was these special soldiers the wise sergeant counseled Dash to join.

Unlike typical line units, Special Operations Forces, or SOF, to which Force Reconnaissance belongs, consists of highly trained and motivated volunteers who are willing to accept the rigors and dangers associated with their job. Most special operations units are close knit, homogenous groups that shun both the spotlight and the conventional chain of command. Criminals avoid these units like the plague because they can't hide out in the crowd. Conventional generals despise them because they often appear to be operating outside the boundaries of their purview. Special Ops units are different, and the traditional, highly conservative military abhors those who are different.

Distrusted if not actually despised by the conventional military, Special Forces wasn't even a branch of the Army until the mid-eighties. Prior to it becoming a branch unto its own, junior officers were openly discouraged by senior mentors from seeking an assignment with special operations forces as they were considered to be a career stopper. "You'll be lucky to make major and you can forget about lieutenant colonel," was the career guidance given to those officers with an inclination to move out of the mainstream Army. "Besides," it was often said during this period, "the conventional Army is no longer a dumping grounds for criminals and derelicts. It is becoming a highly disciplined, professional force in its own right." Which was a declaration of fact difficult to argue against.

By the mid-eighties the quality of troops entering the military had greatly improved. Crime was down and discipline was up. In fact, by the mid-eighties the conventional military began displaying the same degree of intestinal fortitude and professionalism that the Vietnam era SOF forces had exhibited. This professionalism continues to this day. But it still wasn't quite the same for those who had experienced the unique camaraderie of special operations earlier in their careers. So, following his branch qualifying company command, Dash once again answered to the "call of the wild," as his wife would often remind him, returning to a life in special operations.

CHAPTER 6

After attending the Special Forces Officer Qualification Course training at Fort Bragg, North Carolina, followed by Arabic language training at the Defense Language Institute in Monterey, California, Dash received orders assigning him to the great Pacific Northwest at Fort Lewis, Washington. An unusual assignment, and one that he had not sought at the time because the only Special Ops unit then at Fort Lewis was the 2/75th Ranger Battalion. The rangers are a strike unit more dependent on youthful testosterone than intellect when called upon to perform its battering ram mission of forced entry into a hostile environment. Dash was seeking a more cerebral assignment than what the rangers could offer and he was apprehensive about going to Fort Lewis. But upon signing in he quickly understood why he had been sent there.

If the Army has a constant theme, it is change. The Army is painfully aware that the weapons, tactics and equipment used during previous wars quickly became obsolete as future enemies devise ways of defeating them. Consequently, emerging new technologies are constantly being developed and tested so that America maintains its superiority on the battlefield. This was what was taking place at Fort Lewis during the 1980's and it was a great place for any soldier to receive assignment orders.

Officially the unit Dash received assignment orders to was called the High Technology Test Brigade, or HTTB; technically the unit was the 3rd Brigade of the 9th Infantry Division. The commander, Colonel Barry McCaffrey, was at that time the most highly decorated officer serving on active duty, having been awarded the Distinguished Service Cross among other awards for valor during combat actions in Vietnam. The fact that a soldier with the stature of McCaffrey had been assigned to oversee the units conducting the tests of the emerging new technologies was a good indicator that this was to be no "dead" assignment.

It was while at Fort Lewis that Dash had the opportunity to command a company of Fast Attack Vehicles, or FAV's, as the soldiers would call them. Also, as his final assignment at Fort Lewis, he served as the battalion operations officer, or S-3, for the 2nd of the 1st Light Attack Battalion (LAB).

The high tech gadgetry being tested at Fort Lewis during this period was state of the art equipment and it was a heady time to be a soldier. Besides the FAV, a modified civilian dune buggy, the Army was also testing the Ground Launch Laser Designator, or GLLD, which would place an infrared beam of light on a distant target, painting it for a Ground Launched Hellfire missile being transported in the back of a standard ¾ ton pick up truck.

Helicopters would later carry these missiles and the laser technology employed by the GLLD would be refined and merged with Global Positioning Systems. This combination would allow missiles and bombs to be delivered with pinpoint accuracy from both rotary as well as fixed wing aircraft. These were the concepts that would later be refined and put to effective use a few years later in the deserts of Iraq during Desert Storm. But first the communications gear had to mesh with the bombs and bullets currently being developed and Dash was very fortunate to have been a part of this process. What was accomplished at Fort Lewis during this period would become leading film footage for CNN as it covered future wars.

The array of communications equipment being tested over twenty years ago at Fort Lewis was nothing short of amazing. In a tent in the middle of the Yakima Firing Center at Yakima, Washington, one hundred and fifty miles from Fort Lewis, digital text messages were being both sent and received using digitally secure FM radios. Messages, maps, overlays and computer-enhanced graphics were flying through space at the speed of light, being created and captured by computers at either end. Something now taken for granted, but email and attachments are both terms that were not even in the public lexicon in 1982. Yet the military had both the ability and the foresight to develop their use, spending tax dollars wisely at Fort Lewis instead of later spending blood foolishly employing outdated technology in the deserts of Iraq; a fact that should make all Americans proud.

***

It was while serving at Fort Lewis that Dash had the fortunate opportunity to work with a young Saudi Captain named Mohammed "Moe" Al-Assiri. Moe had been sent by the Saudi royal family to America to study the new equipment being tested by the HTTB. It was the beginning of a friendship between these two officers and Dash's company first sergeant, Todd Blackburn, that would lead to the three of them serving together again. The next time, however, it would be the Americans serving a one year unaccompanied (without family) assignment in Saudi Arabia working as advisors to Captain Assiri's Saudi Arabian National Guard unit.

Dash and Assiri first met while Dash was commanding B Company, 2/1 LAB. His company had been chosen to represent the battalion in a test of the LAB concept during the summer of 1983 at Fort Hunter Liggett, California. Assiri accompanied Dash to California as an unofficial observer, the two of them riding together in Dash's 1976 Volvo station wagon from Tacoma, Washington to Monterey, California. It had been Dash's idea to drive to California instead of flying down with the rest of the company. He knew that there would be time for recreation while conducting the exercise and he felt that when they had the time to relax, they should take advantage of it. Along with his platoon leaders and 1SGT Blackburn they did exactly that.

Dash and Assiri shared a room together that summer while at Hunter Liggett and became good friends as a result. The two became inseparable and Assiri shadowed Dash during virtually every mission at Hunter Liggett.

During the off duty hours at both Fort Lewis and Fort Hunter Liggett Dash and Assiri would go to the gymnasium and work out together in the martial arts; both being quite proficient in their respective styles. Dash had earned a 3rd degree black belt in the Korean art of Hapkido and Assiri was a 1st degree black belt in the Japanese style of Shotokan Karate. Their spontaneous sparring sessions were a main attraction for many of the weight lifters and aerobicisers, often causing them to interrupt their routines in order to enjoy the kicks and punches exchanged by the two officers as they wheeled and danced around the matted floor of the gym.

Like most soldiers, and especially those who come from a restrictive culture like Saudi Arabia's, Assiri enjoyed his American beer. Anytime that they had a chance he, Dash, and Blackburn would "pop the top" on a cool one while watching television in the Bachelor Officer Quarters (BOQ) lounge.

Assiri also enjoyed his American women, and with several good looking little hammers working for the Operations Test and Evaluation Command (OTEAC) at the post, he "popped the top" on a few of them as well. Often screwing them in the back of Dash's old Volvo station wagon, which Assiri had the unfettered use of. At other times he would bring them to the two-bedroom-quarters he shared with Dash, often awakening him to sounds similar to those made by fighting cats as the two lovers would tear at one another's clothing. Sometimes Dash had to put a pillow over his head to drown out the sounds of passion in order to get some sleep. Unfortunately, some of these women were married which precipitated a brief disagreement between Dash and Assiri one night.

During one night exercise, Assiri remained behind in the BOQ, telling Dash that he had other business to attend to and would not be accompanying them to the training area. When the exercise ended earlier than expected, Dash returned to the BOQ and upon opening the door to his room received a surprise when a naked woman sprinted across the living room floor and back into Assiri's bedroom. Not being a prude, Dash could have cared less if Assiri was banging someone and, after taking a shower, went to bed himself—alone. The next morning Assiri introduced Dash to his new girlfriend as she was leaving for work. Dash recognized her as being the wife of one of the sergeants working for OTEAC.

When the woman left, Dash carefully explained to Assiri that he was not to bring married women to the BOQ room the two of them were sharing; emphasizing that if her husband were to find her there things could get ugly in a hurry. Dash reminded Assiri that this was America, not Saudi Arabia, and in America *everyone* is armed. If the wayward wife's husband brought a gun with him, he would probably shoot everyone in the room, including Dash. A particularly unsettling thought for Dash as the evidence would suggest that she had been servicing both he and Assiri. Two officers banging an enlisted man's wife could be argued as the reason for the sergeant's temporary insanity. In the minds of the military jurors, some of whom would be sergeants, it would justify an acquittal in the aggrieved husband's murder trial. This would leave Dash's wife, Janet, believing that he really was a two timing son-of-a-bitch who deserved to be shot. Few women have a sense of humor about things like cheating husbands, Dash knew that Janet certainly didn't. In typical female furor, if he survived the gunshot, she would divorce him in a heartbeat, taking everything with her but his combat boots. Such a scenario did not seem to have a lot of positives associated with it for Dash, even if he had actually been banging the sergeant's wife, and he was careful to tell Assiri so.

Dash ended his lecture to Assiri by explaining that there would be enough opportunities in the future to be shot for something he had done that he wasn't really interested in being shot for something he had not done. Assiri silently nodded his understanding and they never had a problem with women in the room again, an activity that neither Dash nor Blackburn participated in, as both were happily married. Then again, so was Assiri; he already had four wives. One had accompanied him to the States and, at the time, was scheduled to give birth any day now at the Madigan Army Hospital at Fort Lewis. Three others were patiently waiting in Saudi Arabia for their husband's return. A fact either unknown or irrelevant to the many American females Assiri bedded that summer.

***

The test scenario that Dash's company participated in at Hunter Liggett called for them to operate deep in the enemy's rear area, inserted by sling loading FAV's beneath UH-60 Black Hawk helicopters. In this manner, with the vehicle crews safely inside the Black Hawks, the little vehicles could be inserted practically anywhere. Once inserted, the FAV's carried enough firepower to pose a mounted threat that was both difficult to locate and even harder to guard against. Known in the civilian world as dune buggies, the FAV's were in fact an off-the-shelf civilian desert-racing machine manufactured by the Chenowth Corporation.

In the early 1980's the United States Army Special Operations Command, USASOCOM, looking for a lightweight, transportable vehicle, decided to test the feasibility of using FAV's for special operation missions. Since Fort Lewis already had the HTTB testing all sorts of new equipment, it had only made sense to conduct the tests of these vehicles there as well; a fact unknown to Dash at the time, but one that sent him to Fort Lewis. He would be the Special Operation's representative testing these vehicles.

To decide which vehicle to use for the test, USASOCOM had simply reviewed the results of recent Baja desert races and purchased the machine with the most recorded wins. It happened to be the one built by Chenowth. The Skunk works at Fort Lewis then modified the machines for military use, adding stowage racks, radio mounts, and weapon systems. A later modification was an exhaust system that muffled the motor noise of its 1600cc Volkswagen engine to less than a whisper; allowing a two-man crew equipped with ANPVS-7 Night Vision Goggles to operate in total darkness, unheard and unseen in close proximity to dismounted troops. The inclusion of these modifications changed the center of balance on the vehicles and they would have fared poorly if they had been raced against their civilian counterparts. But these vehicles were not to be raced. They were to aid in special operation stealth missions requiring insertions, evasion, escape, and killing. With a well-trained crew they were very good at performing any or all of these missions.

Even when carrying a combat load totaling more than three hundred pounds, consisting mainly of extra fuel and ammunition, the vehicle with a two-man crew was capable of achieving cross-country speeds in excess of seventy miles per hour. A speed that when combined with its low silhouette and desert camouflage paint scheme practically made the FAV invisible, even in the daytime. As testament to how hard it was to identify the vehicle, a few years later, following Operation Desert Storm, Iraqi POW's who had seen them testified that they had such a brief glimpse that they thought they were imagining things. None of the Iraqi's ever reported anything unusual to their higher headquarters, allowing the FAV's to roam the desert in what virtually became an unchecked killing spree.

***

The exercise at Hunter Liggett required "Big Balls" Bravo Company to destroy a fuel refinery known to be supplying petrol to an enemy tank division. A cluster of tents and water trailers represented the refinery and were placed at the center of the maneuver box, fully instrumented and tethered like a lamb awaiting the slaughter by the FAV's. This would be no easy task as the refinery was protected by an enemy reserve mechanized infantry company as well as an enemy reserve tank company. The two companies portraying these forces, known as the opposing force, or OPFOR, were from the 7th Infantry Division, stationed at Fort Ord in Monterey.

Bravo Company had to destroy this refinery by direct fire, and then escape by driving rapidly from the area before the enemy reserve companies could react to the attack and block their escape routes. They were given a limited amount of time to escape and the time did not stop until all of the FAV's had exfiltrated through one of the two designated checkpoints.

All vehicles participating in the exercise were equipped with MILES (Multiple Integrated Laser Engagement System) and the range itself, called the box, was instrumented, tracking the real time locations of all vehicles the entire time that they were in the box. The box itself was simply an elliptically shaped mountain valley surrounded by steep ridges narrowing at the checkpoints located at either end. It was less than three miles wide and eight miles long at the extremes. For a vehicle like the FAV, which depended upon speed and maneuverability to survive, operating in such a small maneuver area was analogous to forcing them into a trap and offering them no way of avoiding it. The little dune buggies would be evaluated as assault vehicles fighting their way through a prepared position; something they clearly were not designed to do.

The test concept was extremely limited in both its objectivity and its design, skewing any analysis of the data collected and rendering it meaningless. The results of such an assessment would be similar to evaluating the capabilities of an attack helicopter by flying it around inside the Houston Astrodome. It was a typically canned scenario. In Dash's opinion, it was too damned canned. As the FAV's kept getting beat to the checkpoints by the tanks and APC's, regardless of how many mines or ambushes the FAV's forced them to fight their way through, he began complaining about the exercise design to the test directorate, a Signal Corps lieutenant colonel.

Dash, accompanied by Assiri and Blackburn, went to the colonel's office one morning, confronting him and other members of the testing board. Dash told them that unless an element of fear or confusion was injected into the scenario, delaying the reaction time of the "enemy," there would be no way that all of his vehicles could beat them through the checkpoint. He carefully explained that as designed the test was a waste of taxpayer money and that it would not validate the real capabilities of the FAV. A vehicle that the special ops personnel familiar with the FAV's true capabilities considered to be ideal for missions requiring speed and mobility. Yet they also understood that a less than stellar performance at Hunter Liggett would doom the funding for the vehicles acquisition.

At some point during his defense of the miserable performance by the FAV's, Dash casually mentioned that human beings did not react with such perfect efficiency as the opposing force of tankers and infantry soldiers were reacting. It had always been his experience that when people were really being shot at in surprise, as opposed to when they were just pretending to be shot at, there was always a great deal of confusion and chaos that accompanied response, regardless of how well trained the troops were. It would only be fair to take this into consideration when determining if the speed of the FAV was an asset allowing them to escape when other, slower vehicles couldn't. Dash sarcastically suggested to the colonel, "Sir, if you were to announce that half of the people conducting this exercise will now be using live bullets instead of blanks the OPFOR would begin to move at a snails pace."

When Dash finally finished offering his recommendations, the Signal Corps lieutenant colonel politely thanked him for his opinion. He was even so kind as to suggest that if Dash and company were really serious about "tweaking the scenario" they should write up their "excellent ideas" and submit them to his secretary. "Perhaps they could be incorporated into future exercises," the colonel said with a smile.

The colonel, who was aware of the many fights and pissing contests that had taken place amongst the troops, even went so far as graciously thanking the three of them. He seemed to be impressed by their responsiveness in controlling the "extracurricular activities" erupting almost daily in the box, thanking them for their, "gentlemanly behavior in helping to resolve many of the disputes that have been occurring between your men and the soldiers from Fort Ord."

"You know, Captain," he smilingly told Dash, "enforcing good order and discipline is a hallmark of an officer and a gentleman." It was the worst thing he could have said. When a commander is getting his ass kicked the last thing he wants is to be complimented on how graciously he is accepting his failure. It was a remark that did more to infuriate Dash than to placate him. Basically, yet patronizingly, the colonel had told all of them to "stay in their lane," take their limited knowledge of exercise design, and go pound sand with it.

Frustrated and furious the three left the test directorate's office angrier than when they had first arrived. As they walked across the hot asphalt parking lot to their vehicles, Blackburn turned to Dash and vented, "I don't know about you Captain, but I'm getting a little pissed off with the rules of this candy-assed game we've been playing. I think it's about time we injected a little realism into it ourselves. Tweak the scenario as it were."

"Why First Sergeant Blackburn, I'm truly shocked!" Dash replied in a false voice, still obviously upset by the colonel's remark. "Are you suggesting that I should conduct myself in an ungentlemanly manner?"

"No, Sir!" Replied Blackburn with a mocking tone of irreverence. "I would never suggest that an officer lower his standards to that of an enlisted man. It would tarnish the image of every self-respecting enlisted soldier who has ever worn a uniform. Besides," he continued, "most of you commissioned assholes are too anal to really be devious."

Blackburn's remark caused Assiri, who was still struggling with the nuances of the English language, to ask him the meaning of the word "anal" when used in this context. Blackburn smilingly replied, while pointing to the shiny captain's bar adorning Dash's soft cap, "any soldier who wears rank insignia that shines."

Assiri shook his head and smiled as if he now understood the meaning of Blackburn's words, but he didn't. Only Dash had this type of understanding with his First Sergeant, a self-deprecating understanding based upon the mutual experiences the two had shared over the course of their military careers. Neither considered themselves to be superior or inferior to the other in any respect and neither of them took themselves too seriously. They were just soldiers with a job to do. Yet both also understood that with the exception of Assiri, Blackburn would never speak this way about an officer in the presence of other troops. This would be a major indiscretion the consequences of which no one had to explain to either of them. They both knew who they were and were quite comfortable wearing their own skins.

As they approached their vehicle, Dash turned to Blackburn and asked, "Top, do you think you might be able to acquire some CS gas grenades from one of your buddies back in Monterey?"

Smiling, immediately envisioning what his C.O. had in mind, the burly First Sergeant answered, "Why, yes Sir, I believe I can. How many would you like?"

"I don't really know, First Sergeant. I haven't had much experience being devious. I would prefer to leave those details to a noncommissioned, professional asshole. You decide how much we need."

Turning to Assiri, Blackburn laughingly said, "Come on, Moe. We got things to do."

***

First Sergeant Todd Blackburn was an anomaly. He was better educated than most of the officers yet if the "F" word were taken out of his vocabulary, he would have had difficulty completing a sentence. He had graduated class valedictorian from Killeen High School in Killeen, Texas in 1966. While in High School he had excelled at playing football and had received a scholarship to play for the Longhorns at the University of Texas in nearby Austin.

His father had retired as the Command Sergeant Major, CSM, of the 2nd Armored Division then stationed at Fort Hood in Killeen. His father, like many other American soldiers his age had come to America after escaping the horrors of Hitler's Nazi Germany. His father's birth name had been Heimi Burkowitz, but he had changed it to Henry Blackburn while in England awaiting transport to the United States. In 1938 the elite of America didn't want any more dirty Jews washing up on America's shores.

Once here Heimi Burkowitz joined the Army because it was the only place in American society that didn't give a damn where he came from or who his ancestors were. The fact that he now got paid to kill Germans was just icing on the cake. It had been a good decision for both the Army and the future CSM. The Army had just been looking for young men who could soldier and CSM Heimi Burkowitz, AKA Henry Blackburn, could damn sure soldier. So could his son, First Sergeant Todd Blackburn.

Like most military dependents Blackburn had traveled extensively, following his father to postings throughout the continental United States as well as to Germany and Saudi Arabia. His strict but farsighted father had elected that Todd attend the local schools in Germany and Saudi Arabia instead of the DOD sponsored American schools. The Sergeant Major felt that the American schools did not present enough of a challenge for a boy of Todd's abilities. As a result of his school experiences, Blackburn spoke both German and Arabic fluently.

Despite this bright and promising future, Blackburn soon tired of the juvenile, grab-ass world of college athletics and dropped out after his freshmen year, enlisting in the Army instead of continuing his formal education. He then spent twelve months as a demolition man on a Special Forces A-Team at Lang Vei, just down the road from the infamous Khe Sahn Firebase that was under siege during the Tet offensive in 1968. He had been wounded twice and received both the Silver Star as well as the Bronze Star with "V" device for his bravery on the battlefield.

Returning from Vietnam, Blackburn accepted his discharge from the Army in June of 1970, returning to complete his studies at UT Austin on the GI Bill. Over the following four years he earned both a bachelor's degree in history as well as a masters degree in international relations. He secured a job teaching at a local high school in Austin, married his former high school sweetheart, Betty Lou Irick, and tried to live the normal all-American life. He succeeded for three years. Then, like his new company commander, Tom Dash, the "call of the wild" became too loud to ignore. Blackburn re-enlisted in the Army at his old rank of sergeant and followed in his now deceased father's footsteps.

With his experience and intelligence he easily could have qualified for Officer Candidate School and received his commission. Dash once asked him why he had elected to pass up this opportunity. Blackburn simply replied in his usual tongue-in-cheek way that, "a career as an officer is way too political for my liking." He chose instead to embark on a military career as an enlisted soldier that now had him planning a devious operation for unsuspecting soldiers at Fort Hunter Liggett.

A tireless prankster, Blackburn could often be overheard imparting his wisdom to young soldiers who both idolized and feared their First Sergeant. On one such occasion Dash had been close enough to hear Blackburn's answer to a young soldier's inquiry regarding the numerous ground squirrels found at Hunter Liggett.

Every day, during the cool morning hours, ground squirrels scampered about the training area. They were so numerous that they were pests. Some had become so accustomed to seeing the soldiers that they would eat crackers from their hand as the soldiers shared their meals. One afternoon the company was eating breakfast in the shade of an Oak tree grove when a young black soldier from Philadelphia, Private Roger Brown, humorously watching the frenetic activity of the ground squirrels, asked Blackburn a question. "First Sergeant, can I ask you a question?" Brown meekly asked. He had been in the Army for only four months and this was his first time in the field. As an inner city kid this was undoubtedly literally so.

"What you want, Son?" Blackburn roared back.

Blackburn addressed all of his young enlisted soldiers as son. In his booming voice it always sounded as if he were challenging them with his response. The effect of which served a very real purpose. It prevented them from asking him unnecessary questions and gave him an air of aloofness that belied the fact that both he and Dash would give their life's for each and every one of them if there ever came a time when they were asked to do so. Even though the troops had a healthy fear of their First Sergeant, they intuitively knew this to be true. Blackburn genuinely loved his young soldiers.

"What are those little animals called?" Brown softly asked, pointing to several squirrels running wildly about.

"Spams!" Came the bellowing answer, followed by a stunned silence and shocked expression on the face of Private Brown. Blackburn stared intently into a can of beanie weenies he had been wolfing down and waited for a response.

After a several second delay Brown asked incredulously, "That's a Spam? That's what the army feeds us?"

"Yep," replied Blackburn, stifling a chortle. He knew he had Brown hook, line, and sinker.

Stunned yet wanting to learn all that he could from his vastly more experienced First Sergeant Brown continued, quizzically asking, "What do they do with all the hair?"

"Goddamn son! They skin the sons-a-bitches!" roared Blackburn. "American soldiers are not a bunch of hide-eating animals!"

Every soldier within earshot listening to this exchange immediately spit what food they had in their mouth into the air in a fit of laughter. Blackburn even broke out in laughter as Brown looked around curiously, totally unaware that he had been the butt of one of his infamous jokes.

The hard-boiled First Sergeant also had a unique way of greeting new soldiers upon their arrival in the company, especially those new arrivals that had come from the softer side of American life. That side of American life where children are so protected from life's hard realities that they believe hamburger actually comes from a plant that is grown under cellophane. People who refuse to accept the fact, even after they should know better, that the cow that jumped over the moon in their childhood storybook landed on a McDonald's sesame seed bun when she came back down into the world of adults.

When a young, conservative and religious Mormon boy from Moab, Utah had first been assigned to the company back at Fort Lewis, Dash had overheard Blackburn instructing Sergeants McNabb, Thompson, and Anderson to immediately take the newly minted soldier down to the strip and get him drunk and laid. In Blackburn's opinion, "any man that won't drink beer and chase women can't be trusted. It ain't natural. He has a serious character flaw. Fix it!"

While Dash never heard whether the sergeants had complied with their tasking he had watched the new soldier blend seamlessly in with the other troops. He was even smoking cigarettes and asking about getting a tattoo. Problem was he asked First Sergeant Blackburn about the tattoo.

"What the hell you want to get a tattoo for, Son?" screamed Blackburn.

"I think they look cool," said the startled young trooper, not expecting to be attacked for asking a simple question. Defensively he asked, "Don't you have any tattoos, First Sergeant?"

"Yeah," roared Blackburn. "I got a whole bunch of tattoos. Nature's tattoos. The only kind of goddamn tattoo worth having."

Too scared to run away and too curious to give in to the impulse anyway, the young soldier simply stood stalk still, looking at his towering First Sergeant. "What exactly is a nature's tattoo First Sergeant?" he finally asked with a quivering voice.

"Scars, son. Tattoos that tell a story. Gunshot wound, knife wound, football injury, car wreck, rodeo wreck, or surgery. Even a knee that you skinned when you fell off your bicycle. There is a story that goes with every scar. Any other kind of tattoo is just make-up. And no man with a real pair of balls wants another man to know that he wears make-up. Now, get out of my office unless you have something intelligent to discuss. Get out! Get out! Get out!" To Dash's knowledge the young trooper never got a tattoo.

Blackburn also dispensed financial advice. Dash once overheard his conversation with a newly engaged sergeant who asked Blackburn about starting a savings account at the Fort Lewis credit union.

"It's good to see that you are taking your financial obligations seriously," Blackburn said in his best fatherly tone of voice. "But let me tell you about a rock solid, can't fail, no risk way of saving money."

"Great," said the young E-5. "I'd be interested in anything you have to tell me," he smiled.

"Well, since you will soon be a married man," Blackburn said in all seriousness, "what you need to do is put an empty coffee can in the bedroom you're going to share with your new bride."

"For what purpose," questioned the young sergeant?

"Now you're going to have to be diligent about this or it won't work!" warned the first sergeant, waving his finger in the air to emphasize the gravity of the advice he was offering.

"Sure, Top, I understand," responded the serious young man. "But I don't understand the significance of the coffee can."

"Oh, the empty coffee can is the key to the entire savings plan," winked Blackburn. "What you do is every time you want to have sex or even think of having sex with your wife, I want you to put a penny in the coffee can."

The young E-5 said nothing. Sitting back in his chair, he continued to look quizzically at his first sergeant, sensing something was amiss.

"Then," continued Blackburn, "every time that she lets you have sex with her, I want you to take a penny out of the can. Having been married for over twenty years myself, I can guarantee you that you will never empty that can of pennies. When you have been married for at least five years, I want you to start putting a dollar in the can each time instead of a penny. Hell, Son, before you know it you'll be a damn millionaire!"

For all his theatrical bravado First Sergeant Blackburn also had a soft side that he kept carefully hidden from his troops. Dash knew of one time when Blackburn had personally paid for an airplane ticket to send a soldier home to bury his grandfather. The old man had been a World War II veteran who had served in the Ardennes during the Battle of the Bulge with Blackburn's father. Since it was his grandfather and not his father, the young soldier did not qualify for emergency leave and a government voucher to purchase a ticket. When an Army Emergency Relief official heard about it through the grapevine, he attempted to chastise Blackburn for not having first used his chain of command. Blackburn told him in no uncertain terms, "go screw yourself! It's my money and I'll do what I want to do with it!"

There were other times when Blackburn and Dash had moved hell on earth to get Christmas gift baskets for their young married soldiers with children. Blackburn always made sure that it was the soldiers' squad leader or platoon sergeant that received the credit for this. Most of the recipients knew better. The troops loved their crusty first sergeant as much as if he were their own father. For some, he was the only father figure they had ever known. Except for his swearing, they couldn't have found a better one.

***

For the remaining three days of the exercise the FAV's continued to get their butts kicked. The soldiers of B/2/1 LAB were getting more than a little pissed off about it. They were good troops, hand picked by both Dash and Blackburn, all of them proud and highly competitive young men, as were their opponents. At every opportunity the tankers and their infantry buddies harangued the hell out of Dash's troops, calling them all sorts of names, laughing, taunting, and flipping them the finger as they passed by in their smoke belching, smelly tanks. There seemed to be a particularly vehement dislike between Dash's men and the tankers. Why he never knew. Had he asked he probably would not have wanted to hear the answer for fear of having to court martial someone, so he never asked. He had overheard one interesting story, however, involving his driver, Corporal Gary Floriddia, and a tanker's wife being caught by the Military Police performing some sort of bizarre mating ritual.

It was alleged that when the MP's had responded to a call of two people fighting in the parking lot outside the enlisted men's club, they arrived only to discover a naked, drunk and sweaty Floriddia in a passionate embrace with an equally naked, drunk and sweaty 250 pound woman. Sans a car to make love in the two were violently thrashing around in the sharp gravel of the parking lot. Floriddia had mounted her donkey style and was braying at the moon when the cops had arrived. The police had then dutifully hit the lovers with a beam of light from their high-powered spotlight, revealing to anyone watching a sight that would have scared the hell out of even the most hardened purveyor of pornography.

Allegedly First Sergeant Blackburn had been notified by the MP's to accompany them to the club. Dash had once inquired about the veracity of such rumors and Blackburn told him, "Sir, the very thought of what I saw that night still makes me sick to my stomach. Please don't force me to remember it."

Floriddia had come to Dash the morning after the incident allegedly had taken place and requested to go on sick call to have his knees bandaged. Dash asked him what had happened to his knees and Floriddia told him that he had fallen down while running during morning physical training. Dash told him to go ahead and go on sick call but to tell the first sergeant before going. Floriddia elected to go to work instead. Following that, Dash never asked Blackburn or Floriddia if the story was true; he didn't really want to know.

Regardless of whether the incident with Floriddia was true or not, something was creating a great deal of animosity between the tankers and Dash's soldiers. As the exercise drew to an end, the company NCO's in both companies frequently found themselves either breaking up or refereeing fistfights between the junior enlisted men. Eventually the final night of the exercise arrived. True to his word Blackburn had been able to secure several dozen CS gas grenades from his buddies at Fort Ord. With these nasty little devices in devious hands, Dash, Blackburn and Assiri soon hatched a plan.

Dash drew up his final company operations order requiring all of his FAV's to withdraw from the box through the same checkpoint, the one that just happened to be the responsibility of the Tank Company. Bravo soldiers had all learned from previous experiences that the tankers would race for this checkpoint just as soon as the ATWESS cartridges exploded, simulating that an attack had been launched against the refinery. There would be no delay, disbelief, doubts, or confusion. The tankers would simply drive as fast as they could to a spot on the map and await the arrival of the FAV's. But tonight would be different! Tonight the tankers would experience considerable delay, disbelief, doubt, and confusion.

While one platoon of FAV's went forward and initiated the attack on the refinery, Dash held the other two platoons in reserve near the checkpoint and slightly inside the instrumented maneuver box. This array of forces simulated to the observer/ controllers watching on their screens that this was where he was going to ambush and delay the Tank Company as it came speeding down the highway. Ostensibly providing the FAV's that had gone forward to launch the attack a rare opportunity to escape from the box.

Distant sounds of blank cartridges exploding in the hot summer night only briefly preceded the rumble of approaching M-60 tanks, closing in on the checkpoint well in advance of the arrival of the FAV's that had gone forward to launch the attack, just as the ambushers expected them to do. At the sound of the approaching tanks Blackburn and Assiri drove a FAV about 100 meters up the road and directly towards the tanks careening down it. As these tanks closed on their location, each man pulled the pins on one dozen CS gas grenades and scattered them about the road. Checking to make sure that their own masks were tightly sealed, the two of them pulled the FAV to the side of the road and patiently waited for something to happen. With a slight summer breeze blowing at their backs, they didn't have to wait long before seeing a reaction from the tankers as they blissfully sped directly towards them. Meanwhile, Dash and the remaining troops donned their night vision goggles, turned their radios to the tank commander frequency and, checking to make sure that their own gas masks were handy, moved forward to enjoy the show.

Since confusion had not been written into the scenario, none of the tankers had a gas mask with them. In a brilliant California full moon Dash clearly saw the lead tank commander, a second lieutenant riding in the cupola as if he were Patton himself, react to the gas as if someone had silently sneaked behind him and surreptitiously jammed a red hot poker straight up his butt. He disappeared, reappeared, disappeared and reappeared again in the commander's hatch. All the while trying to say something into his radio that sounded to those listening like, "Ga, SHIT! Ga, HOLY SHIT! Ga, Ga, OH SWEET JESUS! Ga, GAAAASSSS!!!" He finally screamed into his radio. Another tank commander, listening to his frantic call, responded with, "SAY AGAIN, OVER. AND SPEAK MORE SLOWLY."

It was also apparent to those watching that night that the lieutenant's driver suffered from the same affliction as his commander when he steered his vehicle in two complete 360-degree circles. With tank treads squealing on the asphalt, the lieutenant's tank finally left the road and disappeared from view, sliding down a nearby creek bed and ending up stalled on top of a very large oak tree that had graciously halted the tanks descent into the creek waters below. The remaining tanks, following closely on the heels of the lead tank, didn't fare much better. Before they realized what was happening all of them had driven into the cloud of CS gas. As the tanks came to a noisy, screeching halt the crews began abandoning them, emitting sickening sounds reminiscent of a two A.M. college kegger where someone poured formaldehyde into the beer. The awful retching sounds coming from out of the brush sounded as if they were throwing up every thing but their own anal cavity. It was a pitiful sight to both hear and behold. So much so that the troopers of B Company almost felt sorry for them.

Almost.

As the tankers fought for air and tried their best to flee the effects of the gas, they frantically ran back up the road they had just come barreling down. An understandable impulse but one that effectively kept them from escaping the cloud of CS that slowly followed their retreat. As this stampede of half-naked, hysterical tankers thundered back up the road looking more like escaping circus animals than soldiers, the remaining platoon of FAV's showed up.

Driving through a mob of men with snot hanging down to their knees is usually not considered to be a pleasant experience. But on this night the platoon of FAV's cruised through this despicable sight as if they were back on the block picking up chicks. Hooting and hollering while wearing their gas masks, the FAV troopers drove through the entire tank company as if they had just hit the lottery, weaving, yelling, and offering the one finger salute to any tanker who could keep his eyes open long enough to see it.

To their great delight the platoon finally crossed through the checkpoint without a single tank firing so much as one shot. The only difficulty the FAV's had experienced was in trying very hard not to run over some of the tankers who had elected to prostrate themselves in the road instead of running away with their friends.

With the entire company of tanks now stationary in the road, their crews running away from them in a disoriented race for safety, it was time to move in for the kill. Dash ordered his FAV's to attack the tanks by fire and with MILES gear blazing they set off the idiot light atop every one of them.

The observer/controllers watching these events on their computer screens from the comfort of their air-conditioned offices at Hunter Liggett could not fathom what was taking place inside the maneuver box. Not a single FAV had been destroyed, as represented by a red dot on their computer screens, yet all of the tanks had been destroyed. The FAV's still showed blue on their screens signifying that they were alive and moving.

Then, from the field, the radios began to come alive.

***

"What the hell did you think you were doing, Captain?" asked a highly irate

Signal Corps lieutenant colonel as both Dash and Blackburn stood at attention in front of his desk later that night. "Are you aware that hundreds of thousands of dollars have been spent on this exercise and that you two idiot's just skewed the data enough to invalidate the results. What do you propose to do about this, Captain?" Emphasizing the rank so that Dash was reminded that he was speaking to a superior officer.

"Well, Sir," Dash replied with more than just a hint of disrespect. "As far as I'm concerned, the only valid data you have is what you got on this last exercise. As you can tell, people don't behave like machines when you light their shorts on fire. They behave in predictable ways, but hardly ever in a way that is as sterile and inane as that written into this scenario. The idiot who wrote this crap should be fired." Dash knew full well that he was speaking to the author of the document.

Blackburn would later claim that he had actually seen the good colonel levitate from the effects of Dash's remarks. He reacted as if he had been slapped across the face, raising his ass from his chair as if by magic, without the aid of either his arms or his legs, just a severe clenching of his sphincter muscle that propelled him skyward.

The colonel then went on a tirade of personal attacks damning Dash, Blackburn, their ancestors, and the horses they had all ridden in on, finally ending with a comment about how he had been disappointed by the amateurish performance of two underachievers who were a disgrace to the uniform. He knew absolutely nothing about the combat records of Tom Dash or Todd Blackburn. While Dash could accept personal criticism, the comments about Blackburn clearly pissed him off. And the colonel could tell it.

"Bullshit!" hissed Dash through clenched teeth.

"Captain, I'm tired," said the effeminate voice, holding up his hands, palms out, as if he were surrendering himself. "And I have to assume that you are as well. I'm going to let your caustic little remark pass this time. We both need a little time to cool off. But I will see you in front of this same desk at eight o'clock in the morning and you had better have prepared some good answers for me when you show up. That will be all for tonight." Then, like a line out of a bad movie he continued in his squeaky little voice, "Now, get the hell out of my office."

"Yes, Sir." Dash responded as he saluted, brusquely did an about face and marched out of the office with Blackburn hard on his heels.

"Whooee!" exclaimed Blackburn when they were safely out of the building. "I haven't seen a man that pissed off since my brother's second wife told him that she was in love with another woman. It's kind of like watching a car wreck. You know you shouldn't gawk but you can't take your eyes off of it. Did you see the look in that bastard's eyes when you…"

"Top," interrupted Dash. "I hate to do this to you but there is no way in hell I'm going to report to that man in the morning. He is not in my rating food chain and I don't have to answer to him. I'm leaving tonight and going back to Lewis. I would like for you stay behind and push the Company out if you wouldn't mind."

Dash knew that he had no authority to order Blackburn to take what would surely be an ass chewing meant for him from the test directorate. But he also knew that he might say some things that would effectively end his career if he became confrontational with the colonel. The always-astute Blackburn knew it as well and replied, "Hell, Captain. I was just getting ready to suggest the same thing to you."

***

The trip back to Fort Lewis was anti-climatic as both Dash and Assiri shared the chore of driving the 600 miles of highway separating Fort Lewis from Hunter Liggett. Dash was not overly worried but he was concerned that his confrontation with the test directorate would follow him back to Fort Lewis where he would be made to answer for his behavior. Technically and legally the test directorate had been right in saying that Dash had no authority to modify the results of the test without his permission. In hindsight it had been a foolish thing for him to do. But as he drove the highway and reflected upon what he had seen when the tank company had reacted so chaotically to the CS he couldn't help by smile. As Assiri slept beside him he thought, *"Hell, no matter what happens it was worth it."*

Like good soldiers everywhere Assiri and Blackburn were taking care of their friend Tom Dash. Besides taking the ass chewing meant for Dash, Blackburn had called the 2/1 LAB Battalion CSM, Odell Hacker, back at Lewis and told him what had happened. Hacker, a Special Forces soldier himself, had laughed mightily at their antics. He then told Blackburn that he would smooth things over with the battalion commander first thing the following morning.

Likewise, Moe Assiri had called Dash's battalion commander, Lieutenant Colonel Dave Blodgett, and told him the same thing that Blackburn had told Hacker. Blodgett thanked Assiri for the call and went back to sleep. He would deal with it when it appeared as an official problem on his radar screen. It appeared on his radar screen the following morning when a highly agitated test director called him in his office.

When Dash finally arrived back at his Company Headquarters at Fort Lewis, he had a note on his desk stating that the battalion commander wanted to see him ASAP. "Well," Dash thought, "it didn't take long for this to follow me home."

Reporting to Colonel Blodgett's office Dash really didn't know what to expect. Following some small talk about how the exercise went, Blodgett finally brought up the phone call he had received from Hunter Liggett.

"Tell me about your problem with Colonel Smith, Tom. He called me yesterday morning and gave me all sorts of guidance as to why I should give you an Article 15 for insubordination. He was quite adamant that you and Blackburn were the two biggest derelicts he had ever met. So before I take the two of you out to have you shot at sunrise, I thought I could at least listen to your version of the events."

Dash carefully explained how the scenario had restricted the FAV's and made them appear to be worthless for insertions and raids, an opinion that neither he nor Blodgett shared. He explained how he had wanted to demonstrate the effects of fear, frustration, confusion, etc. in battle. As he described the effects the CS had on the tankers, he could see that Blodgett was trying hard not to laugh at the images being described. He then mentioned the personal attack that the test director had made on both he and Blackburn and that in all good conscience he could not stand by and let someone degrade a man of Blackburn's stature in his presence.

Blodgett, a former Vietnam paratrooper and Ranger Company Commander, listened intently to Dash's words and ended their conversation with some guidance. "Don't worry about it, Tom. If Colonel Smith calls you at your company, refuse to take his call and refer him to me, I'll handle it."

That was the last conversation Tom Dash ever had with anyone about LTC Smith.

He later found out about the phone calls that Assiri and Blackburn had made on his behalf when he and Blackburn drove Moe to the SEATAC airport for his return flight to Saudi Arabia. He thanked them both for their efforts. Moe Assiri replied that he would have paid good money to be a part of such a wonderful thing. It had been worth the price of admission just to work with both he and Blackburn.

As they shook hands in front of the Saudia Airlines departure gate, Assiri cryptically told both Blackburn and Dash that he would see them again in the not too distant future. He was right. Shortly thereafter both men were assigned to a one year unaccompanied tour of duty in Saudi Arabia as advisors to Assiri's Saudi Arabian National Guard Company. At the time both Blackburn and Dash would have dismissed Assiri's prediction as having been just a lucky guess. Even if someone had told them differently, neither would have suspected him of having the power to influence such a thing.

Neither knew it at the time, but their joint assignments together with Mohammed "Moe" Assiri had linked them to the forces of history that were about to be written in the bleak desert sands of Southern Iraq.

CHAPTER 7

As the C-141 taxied to a stop Major Tom Dash and the other special operations soldiers aboard began to collect their gear. They had arrived at the King Khalid Military City airstrip, KKMC, Saudi Arabia, with virtually every item of equipment imaginable. They brought it all with them because they had no idea what they were going to be required to do nor how long they would be there doing it. When the ramp of the plane dropped and the 130-degree mid-day desert heat hit them in the face, the soldiers all hoped that their stay would be short.

***

When Iraqi President Saddam Hussein launched his invasion into neighboring Kuwait in August 1990, Dash was on temporary assignment to Fort Drum, New York conducting a nuclear surety inspection. Assigned to 18th Airborne Corps current operations staff section of the G-3, Fort Bragg, North Carolina, Dash had only been back in the United States for two months following his one year unaccompanied assignment in Saudi Arabia with the Office of the Program Manager, Saudi Arabia National Guard, or OPM-SANG. Another lengthy and unaccompanied deployment was the last thing that either he or Janet wanted after having moved across the country from Fort Lewis, Washington, where the family had remained while Dash was in Saudi Arabia. But, as he sat in the lobby of the Bachelors Officers Quarters at Fort Drum watching the CNN news coverage of events unfolding half a world away, he had a bad feeling that once again his wants were about to take a back seat to his duties.

"Sergeant Blackburn, you been watching this?" asked Dash as his former First Sergeant entered the lobby.

"Yes, Sir," replied Blackburn. "What do you think it means?"

"For the Kuwaiti's or for us?" replied Dash.

"Both," came the reply.

"Well," Dash said, "for starters the Kuwaiti's can kiss their oil riches good-bye but I just saw President Bush give a statement to CNN declaring this to be an Arab affair. He has no plans of doing anything other than condemning the invasion and urging a peaceful solution. You know, standard political double talk when you're caught with your pants down."

"Good," the burly master sergeant replied in his customary irreverent tone. "It's too damn hot to fight in the Middle East in August. Besides, I'm too old to go to war." Dash detected a slight hint of disbelief, coupled with anticipation in his voice as he spoke.

At forty-one years of age Dash was two years younger than Blackburn. Both had taken a break in service following Vietnam to complete their college studies, and they had served together in stateside units as well as in Saudi Arabia. Even more important to the events to follow, both were fluent in the Arabic language.

It was precisely because of their familiarity with the region that the two men suspected the Bush administration of stalling for time with the announcement that America would not interfere. With the oil fields in the Eastern Province of Saudi Arabia and the port facilities at Ad-Dammam less than two hundred miles south from the Kuwaiti border, it would be extremely unlikely that Saddam Hussein did not already have plans for their capture as well.

America and her allies could ill afford to allow a demonic tyrant like Saddam to capture these oil fields. If he did, he would control the financial future of the world, not just the region. Such a scenario would be unacceptable to any legitimate administration anywhere in the world

Compounding Dash's disbelief of President Bush's statement was his awareness of American party politics. In a confrontational political system like America's it is unacceptable to be caught unprepared when an aggressor country like Iraq invades a neighboring oil exporting state and it is declared to be "only" an Arab problem.

"No," Dash silently thought, *"the President is blowing smoke, stalling for time to react militarily to the Iraqi invasion."*

Democratic congressional leaders smelled blood in the water and queued up for the CNN cameras, demanding an explanation from the Republican administration. As Dash humorously watched the pompous posturing accompanying the politicians "outrage," he turned to Blackburn and said, "Top, why don't you call back to Bragg just in case we've missed something."

Within the hour both men were back inside their rental car, driving the seventy miles of highway separating Fort Drum from Syracuse and a return flight back to Fayetteville, North Carolina, home of Fort Bragg, 18th Airborne Corps and the John F. Kennedy Special Warfare Center and School.

***

Upon arrival back at Fort Bragg, Dash and Blackburn were hurriedly cut orders reassigning them to the United States Army Special Operations Command, issued new protective masks, and given inoculations for overseas deployment. Both had just enough time to call home and have their wives bring them their personal sidearm, choosing their well-worn Sig Sauer .45 automatics instead of the new standard issue Beretta 9mm. The wives also brought several boxes of .45 caliber Black Talon and Hydra-Shock ammunition with them, along with several hundred rounds of Federal Supreme hollow points in .223 caliber.

When it came to actually having to use a handgun for self-defense, the soldiers knew from previous experiences in Vietnam and elsewhere that the standard issue full metal jacketed ammunition was a piss poor substitute for commercial bullets. They had the same low opinion regarding the efficiency of their M-4 carbine military issue ammunition. Dash and Blackburn had learned through practical application that when their lives depended upon knocking an opponent off his feet, not just poking a hole in his body, there is no substitute for a bullet that will blow a softball size hole in his torso. Neither of them was willing to believe the data that a platoon of PhD's had provided military procurement officer's showing that ball ammunition had the equivalent stopping power of a standard hunting bullet. They knew better, and all the charts and graphs in the world were never going to convince them otherwise.

Had there been such a thing available, both men would have requested that their wives bring them nuclear tipped bullets to vaporize the target while both the Law of Land Warfare and the Geneva Convention could go to hell. For soldiers accustomed to surviving in a world of sudden and extreme violence, war is not a sporting event. Those who fight wars do not do so under a gentleman's agreement to abide by supercilious rules written by people who have never experienced the harsh realities of life and death combat.

***

"Well Top, here we go again," Dash opined as the two arrived at the Green Ramp at Pope Air Force Base departure airfield later that same day.

"Yeah," replied Blackburn sarcastically. "And I'm afraid that this time the vacation is really going to suck!"

"You know Major," he continued, "I could have retired two years ago when I hit twenty. But no, the damn old lady penciled in the figures and said that we couldn't afford it. She wants me to stay in for thirty years and retire as an E-9. Now, as a result of Betty Lou's fiscal awareness, I get to go die in some goddamn desert inhaling God knows what from all the chemical crap Saddam has. Damn greedy women. They'll be the death of all of us."

Dash smiled at the remark as he visualized the fiery Betty Lou lecturing Blackburn on his financial responsibilities. Blackburn would have listened to her too. Or at least he would have pretended to. As near as Dash could tell Betty Lou was the only human being alive that Master Sergeant Todd Blackburn was afraid of.

But in the back of his mind Dash agreed with Blackburn's comment and thought that he just might be underestimating the difficulties they were about to confront.

***

About fifty kilometers north of the King Khalid Military City, nearer the Iraqi border, Hafar Al-Batin sits astride the pipeline road of northern Saudi Arabia as if it were a bad accident. Dilapidated adobe houses stand next to modern cement structures that had been prematurely aged and brown washed by the ever-blowing desert sands.

It was here, in the bleak surroundings of Hafar Al-Batin and King Khalid Military City that Dash, Blackburn and Assiri, a few short months ago, had molded a rag-tag SANG Company into a respectable fighting force. As Dash viewed the town now, approaching from the South, peering through his Scott ski goggles while sitting in the passenger seat of his Fast Attack Vehicle he thought, *"Welcome home, Tom, what a hell of a place to have to fight a war!"*

Adding to the disheveled look of the town a cluster of Bedouin tents had been placed at the intersection of the pipeline road and the highway leading to KKMC. It was here, in this hodgepodge of goat skin tents that Dash was to link up with his old pal, Captain Mohammed Al-Assiri. Mohammed "Moe" Al-Assiri had been Dash's Saudi counterpart when he worked for OPM-SANG the previous year. And, although unknown to him at the time, it was Moe Assiri's personal request through the Chief of the Saudi General Staff, General Atiah Hamas, that had precipitated the call from the American Ambassador in Riyadh to the Secretary of Defense inside the pentagon in Washington, D.C.

The Ambassador had presented the SECDEF with a by name request from the Saudi Royal family for a Major Tom Dash. He then further requested that Dash be immediately reassigned to the US Army Special Operations Command with subsequent duty in the Kingdom of Saudi Arabia. Major Tom Dash had then requested that Master Sergeant Todd Blackburn accompany him.

Still suffering jet lag following the eighteen-hour flight in the C-141 from Pope to KKMC, Dash viewed the array of tents quizzically and then told his driver, Staff Sergeant Gary Floriddia, to turn down the only visible street to be seen. The three other FAV's following Dash turned as well and it wasn't long before all four were ordered to halt by half a dozen well-armed guards.

They had arrived. But where and why they weren't yet certain.

***

Emerging from the tent with a Cheshire cat grin, Moe Assiri was obviously pleased to see his old friends. Although only a captain, it had become obvious to Dash while working in Saudi the previous year that Moe was not an ordinary captain. He had once watched a Saudi full colonel kneel and kiss the ring on Moe's finger before going to his own office in SANG headquarters. A clear indicator that Moe was a man of considerable influence.

And, as in the National Guard in the United States, rank did not always tell the entire story when dealing with guard troops of any nationality. Tom recalled his own experiences working with the state National Guard units at Fort Lewis wherein many of the sergeants employed the officers when working in their civilian jobs. Under these circumstances he found that it was always best to observe the unofficial protocol between people, ignoring wire diagrams and organizational charts when determining who was really in charge.

"Major Dash, Sergeant Blackburn," chirped Assiri as he extended his hand in friendship. "It is good to see you, my friends."

As soldiers who earned their pay in a foxhole and not in an officers club, both men had learned long ago that despite their difference in rank, salutes in the field during a time of war is a military courtesy best dispensed with. Unless, of course, the senior officer expecting to receive one is also curious to find out if there are any enemy snipers nearby.

"Likewise," replied Dash as he extended his own hand in friendship.

The two men then greeted each other in typical Arab fashion with kisses to the cheeks and a bear-hugging, backslapping embrace that caused the dust to fly from Dash's back.

Blackburn stood stoically by awaiting his similar greeting, following which, in his typically abrupt manner asked, "Moe, what the hell could be so important that you would interrupt our candy-ass peace time jobs and bring us back to this damn desert? I was just getting used to being laid on a regular basis."

"Well," joked Assiri, "I have obtained a harem of Bedouin whores and I wished for you to enjoy their pleasures with me. You can still get it up can't you, old man?"

"Listen, dickhead," came Blackburn's boisterous retort, "when I die it'll be thirty days before they can finally close the lid to my casket. I don't get it up; it stays that way."

Assiri roared his approval and beat the dirt from Blackburn's back in a chortling embrace of genuine affection that only those who have soldiered together can express.

As Moe Assiri tried to squeeze the life out of Blackburn, a Saudi soldier emerged from the tent and whispered something into his ear. Whatever was said to him, Assiri's facial expression immediately changed from one of joy to one of concern.

"I beg your forgiveness, old friends. But there is business that I must attend to," said Assiri. "Gentlemen, please, let us go into the tent and get out of this wind."

Following Assiri into the goat skin tent, Dash was pleasantly surprised by the opulence he encountered. Expensive Persian rugs and silk pillows were scattered about the floor of the tent and a large assortment of culinary delights from which to choose were dutifully carried about on large silver platters by the enlisted aides. However, once their eyes grew accustomed to the dim light, the American's were most impressed by the latest in military communications technology that sat at the rear of the tent.

Complete with radio operators wearing headsets, at least a half dozen TAC-SAT radios sat in a bank of communications gear alongside Vinson secure digital scramblers that gave Assiri the ability to communicate worldwide over a secure multi-channel network. At the push of a button Moe could speak in clear voice to his immediate commander, Prince Abdullah, in the Saudi Arabian National Guard headquarters in Riyadh, or directly to the Saudi Ambassador to the United States, Prince Bandar, in Washington, D.C. Or to both simultaneously, as he was apparently doing now.

However, what the American's found even more impressive than the communications gear was the fact that Assiri could speak directly to the Saudi centers of power in both countries. This would be the equivalent of Dash keying a radio and having both the President and the Secretary of Defense answer the call, not intermediaries, but the principals themselves. The way the American chain of command is structured Dash would have to wade through dozens of layers of bureaucratic parochialism before he could speak directly to a janitor in the White House, much less to the President himself. And if his immediate military superiors ever found out that he had broken the sacrosanct chain of command, they would have cut his balls off for doing so.

Obviously Assiri had an advantage in this regard. But such a streamlined command and control system was not unique to the Saudis. Just across the border, Saddam Hussein had a similar arrangement with his Republican Guard Commanders, as did Kim Jong IL in North Korea. In both Iraq and North Korea such systems exist because the leaders fear that sharing information with more than one person at a time weakens their ability to control events. And a perceived weakness, in any form, had the same effect as a real weakness. In the world of Saddam Hussein or Kim Jong IL this almost always ended with a bullet in the back of the head. In their worlds, paranoia and distrust of all but a select few kept them alive and in power.

As Dash listened to Assiri tell the voices on the other end of the radios that the Americans had arrived at his location, he couldn't help but wonder if what he was observing portended a similar fear on the part of the Saudi Royal family. He also wondered even more just who the hell Mohammed Assiri really was.

Dash knew that the Assiri tribe was so named because it originated from the Asir region of Saudi Arabia. The name itself means fruit in Arabic and signifies that Asiri's ancestors had established roots to the mountainous, fruit growing region of western Saudi Arabia. A rugged, isolated part of the country, the Asir region shares close ties with the centers of Islamic power in the not too distant holy cities of Mecca and Medina. Asir is also a region that shares a greater historical tie to the less cosmopolitan city of Jeddah than it does with Riyadh, the capital of Saudi Arabia, or to the oil wealth of the Eastern Province. Because of the remoteness of the region, it has often been a haven for the extremist sect of Wahabi Muslims who have so fervently objected to the Western influences America was bringing to their ancestral land.

Beyond these basic cultural facts, Dash also knew that Moe had been born in 1954, making him slightly younger than Dash, and that he had received his education in America, graduating from Harvard with a degree in mathematics. He knew that Moe had been involved with both the Afghan Mujahadeen and the Pakistani military intelligence service, the ISID, during the Soviet invasion of Afghanistan. While in Afghanistan Moe had been wounded twice, the last wound serious enough to require medical evacuation. He had subsequently recovered from his wounds in a joint Saudi/US military hospital at the Peshawar airbase in Pakistan.

Following his dismissal from the hospital, Moe had allegedly fallen from the CIA radar screen shortly thereafter for a period of two years. Only to surface once again to a hero's welcome in Saudi Arabia along with all the other Saudi "soldiers of God" who had fought the infidel Russians in Afghanistan. Assiri was then personally recruited by Prince Abdullah Bin Abdul Aziz Al-Saud, heir to the throne of his elder brother, the ailing King Fahd, to serve in the Saudi Arabian National Guard. Moe spoke English as well as any American and he understood Americans far better than the average American understood his or herself.

For Dash, all of this added up to nothing. For the time being at least, Moe Assiri was simply an enigma wrapped in a question mark. How all of this fit into what Dash was observing he wasn't really sure, but his survival instincts were warning him that something was amiss, he was going to have to be especially vigilant in any future dealings with his old friend.

***

Besides the Americans gathered in the center of the cavernous tent, Dash, Blackburn, Floriddia, and Air Force Sergeant Joe McNabb, the team's forward air controller, or FAC, there were two tea servers and two other Arabs. Or at least Dash assumed them to be Arabs; they may have been Persians or Turkmen, waiting for Assiri as well. All except for the servers were sitting silently on the rug-covered floor of the tent, cross-legged in typical Saudi fashion, sipping tea and waiting for Assiri to finish with his calls.

As they waited Dash discreetly studied the faces of the two men sitting across from him. It was obvious to him that the one sitting directly in front of him was a religious personage of some note. The deeply callused, bluish and bruised indentation in his forehead was a clear indicator of his devoutness to God. It also told Dash that he was probably a fervent and high-ranking Shi'ite Muslim. The indentation would have come from the Shia custom of placing a round stone on the ground and during prayer pressing, if not actually hitting, the forehead against it in a show of religious conviction.

Although Dash had met many Ayatollahs, Muftis, and other religious clerics of various standing while living and working in the Middle East he always found the indentation, a hole actually, in their forehead, to be rather distracting to normal conversation. It always appeared to him as if the person he was addressing had three eyes. In his candid ability to dispense with any political correctness or cultural sensitivities, Blackburn simply referred to all of them as a Cyclops.

Sitting next to the Shi'ite the other man appeared to be extremely nervous and greatly agitated by Assiri's lengthy conversation. He continuously stroked his mustache and fingered his tea glass as if in a hurry to get on with the proceedings. Dash supposed this man to be either an Iraqi or a Kuwaiti who had a great sense of urgency because either he or someone he cared deeply for was in grave danger with his being here. Probably both.

***

Assiri returned as abruptly as he had departed, his face and voice showing a new sense of urgency that belied his earlier cordial reception. Speaking in Arabic and looking at the two Arab men Assiri began. "Gentlemen, I believe that introductions are in order. You know of my friends Major Dash and Sergeant Blackburn. They are here to help us in our time of difficulty. Major Dash, if you would be so kind as to introduce your comrades."

Dash, also speaking in Arabic, introduced both Floriddia and McNabb, then returned the conversation to Assiri for further introductions.

"My friends," continued Assiri in a very business like tone, "may I introduce to you the Grand Ayatollah Ali Hussein Sistani, leading Shi'ite cleric for all Shia Muslims in Iraq and General Ali Talabani, Commander of the Iraqi 26th Division, currently headquartered at Al-Bussayah."

"Holy shit!" Dash refrained from saying, even though his thoughts were so evidently etched on his face that Assiri cracked a brief smile of recognition. Out of the corner of his left eye Dash could visibly see Blackburn's jaw drop as the shock of what had just been said sank into his brain as well.

"Dash," continued Assiri, "with your permission I want to jump right into this mission. You and your men are latecomers and much of the detailed planning of what I am describing has already been conducted. We don't have much time and going over old ground will not get us any nearer to the line of departure. So, please bear with me if I seem to hurry through this. But if you see some obvious holes that need to be addressed, then bring them to my attention."

Dash nodded his understanding and Assiri continued.

A map was seemingly produced from out of nowhere and quickly spread before the still stunned Americans.

"We are here today to conduct a mission of the greatest importance," Assiri stated with typical Arab flourish, as if trying to impress the Ayatollah and General Talabani. "As you all know, Saddam Hussein has successfully invaded Kuwait, and the Kuwaiti government, including the Al-Jabir Al-Sabah family, has fled into exile to Europe. Saddam is continuing to flow his forces south and at this time they sit on the border of Saudi Arabia, not far from here."

For emphasis Assiri produced a dagger and using it as a pointer slapped the map, tracing the boundary between the two countries and ending at Hafir Al-Batin.

"To our immediate north lies the great valley rift, Wadi Al-Batin, presently devoid of any large concentration of Iraqi troops or floodwater, and soon to be our route into Iraq," Assiri continued. "Once inside Iraq we will move to a hide position near Al-Bussayah then, ultimately, to Safwan where we will link up with resistance forces in order to assist with the accomplishment of our mission. Our mission is to establish contact with resistance forces to gain their assistance in the overthrow of the Ba'athist Regime of Saddam Hussein." Assiri paused for his words to sink in. It didn't take long.

"Wait a damn minute!" sputtered Dash. "Are you telling me that we're going to drive up the Wadi all the way to Safwan, through God only knows how many Iraqi Republican Guard divisions, conduct a link-up with unknown insurgents to incite a Civil War inside Iraq, and overthrow Saddam in Baghdad?"

"Yes. But first we will take a side trip to Al-Bussayah," smiled Assiri, seemingly humored by Dash's flustered response.

Before Dash could respond, Blackburn chimed in with his usual caustic remark, "Is that all? Gee, we may have brought too many men." Turning to McNabb he said, "Maybe you and Floriddia should just go back home. It won't take long for the Major and me to get killed trying to accomplish this mission."

Turning his attention back to Assiri his sarcasm was more direct. "Moe, a damn Armored Corps couldn't fight its way into Iraq right now. And you're expecting us to be able to drive in as if we're a bunch of gawking Japanese tourists looking for a shot of leg in Las Vegas? You can't be serious!"

"Hold on, Top," Dash said while gently placing his hand on the shoulder of the volatile Blackburn.

"I understand the mission, but where are these orders coming from? This is State Department and CIA responsibilities, certainly well above my pay grade," Dash said defensively.

"You're right," responded Assiri. "Not only are both the US Sate Department and the CIA aware of this but so too is your Department of Defense, including your

Joint Chiefs of Staff, as well as the Defense Intelligence Agency. And President Bush personally signed off on a finding from the CIA allowing American military participation in this effort. This request was then submitted to your Congress where it was approved in very short order."

"You must understand, gentlemen, that your country does not want a long and drawn out ground war with Iraq. It has become spoiled by the successes it has enjoyed with the small and inexpensive military operations conducted over the past ten years in Honduras, El Salvador, Grenada and Panama. For political as well as monetary reasons the Bush administration wishes to continue with the reduction in force, or RIF, of your military. Undoubtedly so it can then offer it as evidence of the so called 'peace dividend' during the upcoming elections. The fear in Washington is that an invasion of Kuwait will both delay these efforts and prove to be prohibitively expensive. It would also be embarrassing for elected officials to have to explain to their constituents that maybe the world isn't really all that peaceful following the end of the cold war," Assiri said in a matter-of-fact tone.

"A rather odd point to be making at a time like this," thought Dash while keeping his opinion to himself.

The American soldiers present inside the tent knew all too well that efforts were being undertaken by the Bush administration to reduce both the size and the costs associated with maintaining the current military force structure. The weekly edition of the Army Times was replete with stories of base closings and unit deactivations and in conversations with their counterparts at other bases, rumors of future reductions were proving to be more than mere speculation. It wasn't just the Army suffering from the draw down. Air Force, Navy and Marine Corps bases, ships and units were being rank ordered on a DOD decrement list that foretold of future mass reductions in order to save money and prevent politicians from having to increase taxes in order to pay for their upkeep.

From a dollar and cents point of view the RIF made good political sense in that critics of the cuts were having a difficult time justifying a robust military when no clear enemy could be identified. The cold war had been won and both China and Russia, America's old nemeses, were in the throes of reinventing themselves, posing little threat in terms of a possible challenge to American interests. But for the uniform wearers the RIF was much larger than a mere dollars and cents issue. For them the loss of ships, planes, troops, and new equipment was a simple matter of life and death. Assiri was quite aware of how they all felt about it.

"I am afraid that once again America's failure to remember history, combined with her four year presidential election cycle, is causing it to make some shortsighted decisions that will ultimately come back to haunt her, believing that there are no enemies left to fight." Assiri continued in a condescending tone of voice. "But, as your saying goes, ours is not to reason why, ours is but to do or die."

Dash noticed that the Ayatollah was nodding vigorously in agreement with Assiri and, sensing a challenge to his patriotism, he rose to the bait, responding with, "You didn't bring me here to talk politics Moe, so let's put it to rest."

Dash well remembered the many conversations that he, Moe and Blackburn had participated in while serving together at Fort Lewis and again in Saudi Arabia. Moe seemed to take a particular delight in ribbing the Americans on their short-sighted vision regarding world events. To Moe, America always seemed to dismiss global problems with a childish idealism that just because today was good for them, then it must have been good for everyone else as well, and so will tomorrow be. It reflected a vision of life that Moe felt required no personal effort to understand and no associated risk with failing to understand, since America did not have enemies on her borders. A condition not shared by most other nations. In other words, Assiri believed that most Americans wanted to avoid confronting the hard realities of a world beyond their borders, a world where many people are born, live, and die in uncertain fear of an aggressive neighbor and internal enemies. A world that an unsuspecting America was boldly signing up to adopt with its foreign policy of engagement, seeking to establish a presence in all nations in order to encourage the spread of human rights, equality, and democratic tendencies.

Some of the trio's previous political discussions would end with Blackburn, who because of his experiences growing up in foreign countries, threatening to punch Assiri if he didn't shut up and stop badmouthing America. Blackburn had a considerably shorter fuse than Dash when listening to an outsider's opinions on the American vision of peace and harmony. He often found Assiri to be abrasive and totally unrealistic in his analysis of the many sources of political discontent in various countries, particularly Muslim nations and their steadfast refusal to behave as if it were the beginning of the 21st century. Blackburn seemed to take a perverse delight in telling Assiri how screwed up Muslim nations were in comparison to European nations and was always quick to get in a little dig of his own by pointing out the many flaws found in the Middle East. Flaws such as the entitlement that went with a name or a particular religious sect at the expense of individual effort. Blackburn also knew, having spent considerable time in the Middle East, that Assiri was unusually vocal in his often anti-American didactic, political discourse. Other Saudis may have felt the same, but the vast majority of them were too polite to throw their arguments back into a guest's face.

"I am as concerned about the RIF as any other soldier," continued Dash. "But what Washington wants to do with the military force structure is being dealt with by much greater minds than mine. I personally have no idea what will be required from the military over the next twenty or thirty years or what the threat confronting my country might look like. But I do know that there are some very smart people working the issue and I have no choice but to go along with whatever it is they recommend. It is the way a democracy is supposed to work. Everyone, not just the rulers, gets a say in what their future is supposed to be. With that in mind, I find it very difficult to believe that my superiors have recommended or approved the mission you just gave to me. With your permission, I would like to delay this political discussion for a later time. Please forgive me but I'll have to confirm what you are saying with my higher headquarters," Dash apologized.

"Please, avail yourself of the INMARSAT or the STU-III," gestured Assiri pointing to the array of communications gear at the rear of the tent. "Both are encrypted, speak freely in any language you desire. Speak with whomever you want to but you might start with the American Embassy in Riyadh. You will discover that until this mission is completed, I am your higher headquarters." Reflectively he also added, "Tom you must come to grips with this as soon as possible because we have a great deal to do and very little time to get it done. We have forty-eight hours to get to Safwan."

Dash did not have to call any further to the rear than to the American Embassy in Riyadh to confirm all that Assiri had told him. The Ambassador told him that Moe was in charge and the Americans were along for the ride; their assistance necessary to coordinate fire support with the aviation assets rapidly flowing into the theater as Operation Desert Shield began to take shape.

For reasons that were never adequately explained, the Ambassador told Dash that this mission would not be command and controlled through traditional American military channels. The Saudis would run the show and the American Embassy staff; the Ambassador, the DCM and the Defense Attaché were his only authorized points of contact. In fact, the Ambassador had said, "It would probably be best for all concerned if you didn't deal with anyone other than the people I have just mentioned."

Dash had learned long ago that in the world of Special Ops strange and unconventional methods were often employed. Why should he expect this mission to be any different? He abruptly terminated his conversation with the Ambassador by saying, "Roger, Sir. We'll do our best." It didn't necessarily have to make sense; he just had to do it.

Back in the center of the tent, Moe Assiri continued to lay out the plan, not bothering to ask if Dash had been satisfied with the information received from the Ambassador or what that information might have been. He already knew the answers to both questions.

"Tom, the four FAV's that you have brought with you will be loaded into the back of some Iraqi trucks that we have marshaled in an assembly area closer to the Iraqi border near Al-Ruq'a. Iraqi Shia dissidents loyal to the Ayatollah Sistani will drive these trucks. I have personally vetted these drivers and I consider them all to be loyal to our cause of affecting a regime change inside Iraq. These trucks, with the FAV's loaded in the rear, will be driven to an assembly area near a large Republican Guard supply base currently under construction at Al-Bussayah." All eyes followed the tip of the dagger as Assiri deftly traced the route that would be followed from Al-Ruq'a into the assembly area near Al-Bussayah.

To the Americans the route appeared mundane enough but what the map did not reveal were how many Iraqi checkpoints and Republican Guard units were already established along the highway they would be traveling to the assembly area. Assiri sensed the question and answered it even before the Americans had to ask about it.

"We already have friendlies inside the assembly area. In fact, both the assembly area and the unit occupying it are fakes. They have been designed to appear to out-siders as a company size assembly area belonging to a corps support transportation unit, but it is in fact a unit comprised of soldiers loyal to General Talabani. We have also established our own Military Police checkpoints on the fringes of the assembly area as well as along the route we will travel to get there."

"But," Assiri continued, "I don't need to tell you that these conditions won't last much longer. As the fog of war lifts and Saddam consolidates his gains, our fake unit won't survive close scrutiny much longer. I estimate that we have no more than three days to get into Iraq, put all the necessary pieces into their proper places, and then get out of there before we are discovered. And that's where you come into play, Tom. If our window of opportunity closes before we can recross the border, then we will have to rely on American airpower to blow a hole in the Iraqi line here, near our crossing point at Al-Ruq'a." Assiri repeated with a quick dagger thrust at the map near the small border town. He then resheathed his dagger with dramatic flair. But he wasn't finished.

"Furthermore, we will need for your team to accompany us on our trips into Safwan," he continued. "This will be necessary for two reasons. First, of course, is the obvious advantage you Americans have to call in air strikes and, second, your FAV's will be used to transport the Ayatollah Sistani and General Talabani to their prearranged meetings with Iraqi resistance forces. These trips will always be made under the cover of darkness and your people already know the capabilities and limitations of your vehicles. We simply do not have the time it would take to train new people for the task at hand."

It almost sounded to Dash as if Assiri was apologizing for having dragged them into this mess.

"Questions?" asked Assiri.

As usual, Blackburn broke the ice. "Moe, it seems to me that we're being just a little too damn cavalier in accepting how much control your friendlies have inside Iraq. If just one of these little pricks changes his mind or doesn't get the word, our asses will really be hanging in the wind."

"Top," replied Assiri. "You have got to trust me on this. I have done my homework. All the pieces are in place. If you are asking me for a guarantee that nothing will go wrong then you know I can't answer in the affirmative. Wasn't it you who taught me the axiom that the next military operation to go off without a hitch will be the first one in recorded history. Things always go wrong. Murphy and all his laws live in the Kingdom as well as inside Iraq. If things can go wrong, they will go wrong. Frankly that is why I asked for your team to be here. To help me shoot my way out if this blows up in my face."

"That's always comforting to hear," smiled Blackburn. He knew Assiri was right. He also trusted his judgment. How events unfolded from this point on would determine whether he would be right in trusting him with his life.

Dash was a little more circumspect in his questions of Assiri, focusing on the task at hand and leaving the doubts he shared with Blackburn to be discussed at a later time. Despite his apprehensions, he knew that it was time to fully commit to the mission he had been given. How he felt about that was absolutely irrelevant.

CHAPTER 8

With their radio antennas tied down the FAV's backed into the rear of the Iraqi 5-ton trucks like bullets being loaded into a gun. The little vehicles would prove invaluable for the events that would follow.

The four FAV's were all equipped with the Mod 3, MK-19 40MM Automatic Grenade Launcher. The vehicles could have also been equipped with a TOW missile system that would allow them to engage tanks at a distance of 3000 meters. But this was not a mission where Dash felt he would have to shoot it out with tanks. Dismounted infantry troops were the most probable threat and the MK-19 would allow the team to quickly suppress any small arms fire it might encounter.

Besides, the best way for them to kill a tank was to laze it with the special operations laser marker, or SOFLAM, then bust it open with a Hellfire missile fired from an Apache Helicopter belonging to the 160th Special Operations Aviation Regiment. Dash knew from watching CNN that the SOAR had recently deployed to Saudi Arabia from Fort Campbell, Kentucky.

Barring the availability of SOAR helicopters, his second choice would be to laze a target for a Guided Bomb Unit (GBU) dropped from a fixed wing aircraft. Either way, Dash felt that he had a good handle on killing tanks. It was the simple turning of a corner and confronting an armed Iraqi soldier that he feared most. But the team had prepared and equipped themselves for this probable threat as well.

The vehicles also had an M-60D, 7.62mm machinegun mounted on the dash as an immediate self-defense weapon. The M-60D is the same weapon that a helicopter door gunner uses. Unlike the MK-19 or the TOW, both designed to engage hard targets at maximum stand off distance while stationary, the machinegun could be fired at soft targets, like thin skinned trucks and people, while sitting inside the vehicle and moving at a high rate of speed. The other weapon systems required the vehicle to stop and the gunner to stand up for an engagement, taking valuable time to accomplish and leaving the crew vulnerable to any return fire. By contrast, the M-60D could be fired in what was termed a "scoot and shoot" method while remaining seated and moving. The crews had become quite proficient at engaging close in targets in this manner while training at both Fort Lewis and Fort Bragg.

Besides becoming proficient in engaging targets the team had also learned, through trial and error, to leave the bipod on the gun. During one training exercise, as Dash was driving the vehicle over rough terrain, he had jumped a mogul causing Floriddia to depress the gun too far. As a result, Floriddia shot out the right front tire and sent three rounds through the hood of the FAV, narrowly missing his own feet and scaring the hell out of both of them. This close brush with injury taught them that if the legs of the bipod were extended three clicks and left locked in position, it would prevent the gunner from pointing the weapon at the vehicle, himself, or the driver as they sped down a road or jostled across country.

The soldiers training with the vehicles also learned that two combat loaded FAV's could be sling loaded beneath a UH-60 Black Hawk helicopter and that six of them could be carried beneath a CH-47 Chinook helicopter with the seventh inside. Use of a CH-47 allowed an entire platoon of the vehicles to be inserted with one helicopter. With the amount of firepower they carried it was a great asset for any special operations mission.

Tonight, both the men and the equipment were being asked to perform for the first time as a team operating behind enemy lines and the anxiety level increased with each passing moment. But first they had to get to the Iraqi lines, and Assiri was right about one thing so far; Murphy was alive and well in the Kingdom of Saudi Arabia.

Moving out from beneath the cover of the airplane hangar with the FAV's loaded inside, the four Iraqi 5-ton trucks merged with six more identical vehicles waiting along the side of the highway. All personnel (except for the Ayatollah) were wearing the Iraqi uniform of General Talabani's 26th Division. The Ayatollah Sistani chose to remain in native turbaned cloak and trust his fate to God rather than deception. Scorning any suggestion from Assiri to camouflage, he often looked at the Americans with unveiled contempt, refusing to dress as they were.

Once on the highway, the convoy of ten trucks drove north, following a British Land Rover belonging to General Talabani but now carrying Mohammed Al-Assiri. The convoy rolled slowly toward the Iraqi border, a mere fifty miles away.

The route they traveled would take them through the lines of the SANG border unit now defending Al-Ruq'a from any attack the Iraqis might make. Since it was a real mission and not a canned training exercise, things went well for the first forty-nine and one half miles, then, because people never behave as predictably as machines, all hell broke loose.

***

Saudi Private Hashim Al-Dori had arrived at his border guard post that very day. Like most of the SANG soldiers protecting against an invasion from the north, he was extremely nervous and uncertain what the future held in store for him. As a recent recruit, Hashim had only been in the SANG for three weeks, the standard length of time all Saudi personnel receive for introductory military training.

During his three weeks of training, Hashim was taught a basic familiarity with his G-3 German made assault rifle, and he received a short, perfunctory class that provided him with rudimentary instruction on Iraqi vehicle and uniform recognition. During this training a Saudi Lieutenant had flashed playing cards with vehicle and personnel pictures on them, asking the new recruits to identify the type of vehicle or uniform they were being shown. Hashim was very proud of the fact that he could recognize Iraqi vehicles as well as Iraqi uniforms when many of his fellow Bedouin tribesmen could not. It was a skill that he would proudly share with his father when he returned once again to the safety of his nomadic desert tribe.

But first he must perform his duties for his beloved King and for the sanctity of holy Islam, just as his father before him, and his grandfather before him had done. It was a tradition in the Al-Dori family to serve in the National Guard and Hashim was proud to continue with the tradition. His service would put him in good stead with the village elders and the unmarried girls would recognize him as the man he was becoming. Perhaps when he finally returned to his village his mother would help find him a wife.

He was lost in the grandeur of such thoughts when he heard the ten Iraqi 5-ton trucks approaching him from the south, the least likely direction he expected to see such vehicles. As he stared at what he correctly recognized to be Iraqi trucks, he did so with utter disbelief, then horror as the trucks rounded a corner and came straight toward his location.

In all the Middle Eastern armies, and the SANG is no exception, there is no NCO corps similar to that of western armies. In Arab armies one is either an officer or a soldier; there is no bridge of experienced professionals connecting the two. Consequently, although Hashim Al-Dori's Lieutenant knew that a convoy of "peculiar" vehicles would pass through his lines at midnight, Hashim knew nothing about it. Nor had he been told what to do in the event that something might happen on his first night of guard duty. He had simply been told to take his rifle and look north.

Hashim was sixteen years old, alone, and now, for the first time in his young life, scared beyond belief. So much so, in fact, that he returned his view to the north, staring at the dark desert highway leading into Iraq in the hope that what he had seen approaching from the south was just a mirage, hoping against hope that he really had not seen it. Wishing that it was a bad dream that would disappear as his mind awakened, yet all the while knowing that such would not be the case.

He hesitantly rubbed his eyes and slowly turned back around, looking south at the approaching Iraqi trucks. He felt a brief shame as he resisted the impulse to run away from the approaching danger, remaining frozen in place as his young mind recalled the fact that he was a Bedouin Warrior, the bravest of the brave. His father, his grandfather, and all of their fathers before them had been Bedouin Warriors, and a Bedouin Warrior knew no fear.

Hashim had often been reminded of such things as he bounced on his father's knee around the desert campfires, listening attentively to stories of bravery and sacrifice. The stories told to him often glorified the slaying of both infidels and invaders when they had been foolish enough to infringe upon the Kingdoms true believers. As a young Hashim listened to these stories, he soaked up the words of glory as if water from a desert oasis and dreamed of the day that he would have the opportunity to live such moments himself. With such a rich warrior tradition flowing through his veins Hashim did not openly fear death. At his tender age he could not really comprehend the finality of such a thing. For him, his own future tales of glory now rang in his ears as he fantasized telling his children and grandchildren about the night that he too had become a fierce Bedouin Warrior. Tonight, it was his turn to slay the invading enemy.

Swallowing his fear, controlling his racing heart as best he could, Hashim moved closer to where he had last seen the trucks and awaited their arrival. *"Allah Akbar!"* God is great, Hashim screamed as if the sound of his own voice would fortify his budding courage. Then, as the Land Rover carrying Assiri passed by, a vehicle he did not recognize as being Iraqi, Hashim fired on the leading 5-ton truck.

Assiri had heard the scream of Hashim as he drove past and he immediately ordered his driver to stop the vehicle. At Hashim's first shot Assiri keyed the radio and alerted Dash and the other Special Operators to stay in the trucks. He then raced towards the sound of the gunfire coming from behind a rock not one hundred feet away.

As part of their execution checklist Assiri and Dash had developed an evacuation plan in case they were ambushed. Called Plan Red, it was a quick reaction drill calling for the soldiers to drop the loading ramps behind the 5-tons and drive quickly away from the kill zone. This same plan would be implemented if they were compromised and had to exfiltrate back across the border from Iraq. With the sound of the gunshot ringing in his ears Assiri feared that the Americans might prematurely execute this portion of the plan. He need not have worried.

Traveling in the rear of the convoy, Dash wasn't even sure that what he had heard was gunfire. With the exception of First Sergeant Blackburn, the others hadn't heard anything at all. The motor noise inside the rear of the Iraqi truck was deafening. With the 5-tons exhaust barely five feet from their head anything short of tank fire or artillery would have been hard to hear. But, when the trucks quickly braked to a halt, Dash clearly heard Assiri's radio transmission through the earpiece on his helmet telling them to remain inside the trucks.

"Did we already cross the border?" Dash wondered aloud.

***

Startled but unhurt, the driver of the lead truck slammed on his brakes as shards of glass ricocheted around inside the cab. He had never been shot at before and wasn't entirely sure what was happening. He knew that they had not yet crossed into Iraq but his survival instincts were screaming that something had gone terribly wrong, telling him to get away from his truck.

Hashim moved forward to take a better aim, balanced his shaking rifle on another protruding rock, and fired again. This time the bullet shattered the left front black out drive light and the driver dove from the vehicle, taking cover behind the rear dual tires of the truck. Hashim shifted his feet to better balance the rifle, almost as large as he was, and prepared to take another shot when he heard a noise behind him, causing him to freeze in position.

"Qif!" Stop! Shouted Assiri in an attempt to get Hashim to stop firing. *"Qif!"*

Rising from his kneeling position Hashim turned toward the sound of Assiri's voice and in the full moon quite clearly saw an armed Iraqi Officer standing before him. He was as dead certain of this fact as he had been dead certain that the trucks before him were Iraqi as well.

Startled by the sight of Assiri standing before him, almost close enough to reach out and touch, Hashim hesitated for a brief second, then remembered his traditions as a warrior. He fleetingly relished the stories he would now share at the campfires of the time he met the enemy face to face and slew the beast with his own hands.

"Allah Akbar!" Hashim screamed once more as he brought the G-3 to his shoulder in the direction of Assiri. A move that he never completed.

With his Hechler and Koech MP-5, 9MM, submachine gun already held in firing position Assiri sent his first shot through Al-Dori's forehead from a distance of less than fifteen feet. His rapid follow-up shot hit Hashim under the chin as his head snapped back with the impact of the first round. Either bullet, by itself, would have been fatal.

All that Hashim Al-Dori was and all that he would ever be crumpled with a loud thud at the feet of Mohammed Al-Assiri. In the bright desert moon Assiri could clearly see the blood spurting from Hashim's massive head wound as it pooled in the sand near his feet.

"Allah Al-Raheem." God be merciful, Assiri whispered to himself.

Dash had clearly heard Hashim's second shot as well as both of Assiri's shots. Speaking through his Combat Vehicle Crewman's (CVC) microphone into the radio he ordered, "Drivers stay with your vehicles. Top, meet me on the ground in front of your truck!" With that he unplugged his CVC from the radio and leapt from the back of the truck, disappearing into the night.

Blackburn was waiting for him when he arrived.

"Goddamn!" Whispered Blackburn in English. "This is certainly going well. These are Saudi soldiers. We haven't even crossed the fucking border yet!"

"All right. Stay here with the vehicles and I'll see if I can find out what's going on," Dash cautioned.

As Dash walked towards the front of the convoy he couldn't help but feel self-conscious about being dressed as an Iraqi soldier. He knew even without being able to see them that all Saudi eyes were on him and that shooting could erupt at any moment. It was a feeling that no matter how many times experienced a soldier never got used to. It made the hair on the back of his neck stand straight up.

As Dash neared the lead vehicle, he could hear the excited jabbering of the driver as he spoke to another SANG soldier from Hashim's unit, describing how he had narrowly escaped death and but for the will of Allah, blah, blah, blah.

In the distance he could see Moe Assiri speaking quietly with a small group of Saudis representing Hashim's chain of command. He could also see the body of Hashim Al-Dori, now covered by a poncho, lying nearby.

Dash didn't need to ask what had happened. The hushed tones Moe was speaking to Hashim's Lieutenant told him all that he needed to know. Remaining at a distance, Dash thought it sounded familiar. It was the Saudi equivalent of something he had heard once before in a distant jungle far away, "Shit happens. Let's not dwell on it."

CHAPTER 9

O nce the convoy cleared Saudi airspace, the rest of the trip was indeed a piece of cake; just as Blackburn had sarcastically declared it would be. This is not to imply that there weren't any memorable moments, however. The first checkpoint being guarded by Assiri's inside help was not where it was supposed to be, requiring him to park the convoy in a holding area off the road while he went looking for them. After a thirty-minute search Assiri finally located them on the wrong road about three miles from their planned location. Like most military operations, complexity, coupled with human failings, caused everything to be close, but never quite right.

No sooner had this SNAFU been fixed than a large herd of sheep showed up walking the very trail the trucks had to use to get back to their original route. Bleating sheep delayed them for almost two hours as the wooly buggers wandered about attempting to eat everything in sight, to include the canvas tarps hiding the FAV's. Requiring the soldiers to get out of their trucks to protect the tarps from the four-legged plague that had descended upon them like a biblical swarm of locust.

There were about three thousand sheep in the flock and several Bedouin families accompanied them as herdsmen. In the dark of the desert they were orienting on the roads because Iraqi Republican Guard soldiers were planting minefields throughout the area, so the only safe place for the herd to travel was on or near the roads. Assiri showed the Bedouins a map and they pinpointed where these minefields were located. Dash marveled that it would have taken him two days to extract this same information from his own intelligence sources within the Pentagon or the CIA, proving once again that there is no substitute for eyes on the target or boots on the ground.

Once the sheep grazed away from the trucks they got underway and in short order arrived at the planned destination. As the convoy pulled inside the assembly area Dash peeked out from under the tarp of the 5-ton truck. In the early morning light he could see Assiri speaking with the guards manning the entry point into their perimeter. There was only one entrance, conspicuously located near the main supply route, or MSR. The rest of the 360-degree perimeter consisted of triple strand concertina wire, foreboding and threatening to anyone seeking entry anywhere other than the guarded entrance. Iraqi soldiers traveling the MSR could clearly see the guards, for there was no attempt to hide. Yet anyone coming to inspect them would have to get passed the guards and Dash was sure that Assiri was even now reconfirming that they were not to allow anyone to pass through without his permission. No exceptions!

Dash could also see past the guards and what he saw were the beginnings of what would ultimately become a massive Iraqi logistical supply base. Engineers were in the process of marking lanes that would later become streets when the facility was completed and slit trench latrines were being dug as far as the eye could see. It was being constructed to accommodate several thousand troops.

Trucks of all sizes and shapes, carrying huge amounts of ammunition jammed the road near their location, honking and waving at the guards. Some drivers even flashed the old Vietnam two finger peace sign, or "V" for victory sign, in the direction of the guards, who would return the hand gesture in kind, smiling as they did so.

Although a slight rise hid the final destination of the trucks, Dash would later use the INMARSAT to email the likely grid coordinates of the ammunition dump back to the target planners at 18th Airborne Corps Headquarters in Dhahran and USSOCOM headquarters at KKMC. His proximity to such a massive, vulnerable Iraqi build-up made his head swim with possibilities. For now at least, he thanked Assiri for presenting them with the opportunity.

***

At first the audacity of Assiri's plan concerned Dash, just as it had Blackburn. But the more Dash thought about it the more he believed that it just might work. The very simplicity of it was its real strength.

The anonymity enjoyed by a small unit operating in a Corps or Theater rear area is virtually foolproof. Even the planners that put the rear area plan together would find it extremely difficult to recall all the units assigned within, how many vehicles each had, and the exact unit location. It would take either an extremely bored or an extremely energetic staff officer to even slightly consider that a unit so obviously a part of the area didn't really belong there. Even if discovered, the unit would simply apologize, tell a believable lie, and then move on. No one would be any the wiser. Or so they all hoped.

Dash knew from personal experience that war is anything but a series of absolutes (it is in fact organized chaos) and that the likelihood someone would approach them to verify a unit location was practically nil. This knowledge comforted Dash simply because what they were doing was, well, simple. In the real world the only thing that counts is what is understood well enough to make it work. Assiri's simple plan contained no elaborate hoaxes that could be misunderstood, misconstrued, lost in translation, or otherwise, generally screwed up. There was no fluff. And in the simple mind of a dead-tired, harried soldier, nothing will work better than simplicity.

As Dash watched the activities from beneath the tarp, he began to appreciate

Assiri's intelligence regarding such matters. He also felt the nagging return of his unanswered question, "how was it that Assiri could be so well informed that Kings and Princes and others of stature consulted with him?" Dash once again began to run Assiri's profile through his mind; the results left him in a quandary.

First, how was it that Assiri commanded the attention of the Ayatollah Sistani and General Talabani? These individuals were not your ordinary guerilla insurgents he had been taught to work with back at Fort Bragg. They were both high profile, established individuals who might one day be in charge of Iraq. And there was little doubt that both of them entertained such notions. Second, Assiri seemed to be joined at the hip with the American Ambassador in Riyadh. He seemed to know before it was announced what units from the 18th Airborne Corps were being TPFDDL'd, or placed on the Timed, Phased Force Deployment Data List, for deployment to Saudi. Information that is not easy to come by even for those charged with developing the deployment schedule. Yet Assiri operated as if he had a direct line to the Pentagon planners, leaving Dash unsure as to the source of his information as well as how he was receiving it. He knew that the Ambassador could not request permission for troops to enter the Kingdom until after DOD had cut the deployment order. Leaving only Assiri to know who was coming to the party before it was officially announced. Why this was so remained a mystery.

Of one thing Dash was sure; the reason why Assiri had personally selected his team for the mission. They knew one another, and they were friends. They had trained together professionally, and they had socialized together as brothers. They knew one another's strengths and weaknesses and they knew how to either amplify them or compensate for them depending on the situation. But primarily Assiri had asked for his team because he was going to war and he feared death, just like everyone else. If war was necessary, then he wanted to go to war in the company of people he had confidence in. In the world of a soldier, nothing is more important than the confidence that comes with believing in the person standing next to them.

***

All four of the trucks carrying a FAV inside had been parked in the rear of the assembly area next to the concertina wire. Just outside this wire was a shale rock ravine that quickly disappeared into the desert. Although the concertina wire itself appeared to consist of an impenetrable barrier, a small portion of it was actually a gate that could quickly be opened or closed by one soldier. The gate was strategically located near the shale ravine so the FAV's could quickly and quietly enter and leave the assembly area under cover of darkness. Once they had disappeared into the ravine, the shale rocks would eliminate the tracks left by the vehicles so helicopters flying throughout the area would not be able to track them to their secure location inside the assembly area. A soldier was assigned to quickly sweep the small area between the ravine and the wire, perhaps fifteen feet distance, free of tracks before closing the gate, leaving behind no telltale reason for anyone to ask questions about tire tracks leading into the desert.

***

Moe Assiri parked his Land Rover next to the truck containing Dash's FAV and called for him to come outside. Having been cooped up inside the back of the trucks for over six hours, the Americans were happy to comply with Moe's request. Keying the radio Dash asked the rest of the team to join him and Assiri.

"Welcome to Iraq," began Assiri. The Americans nodded and stretched their stiff joints while surveying their new surroundings but remained silent, waiting to see what would follow.

"We have about ten hours of daylight remaining before we can safely remove the FAV's from inside the trucks," Moe continued in a very business like manner. "Tonight we will make our first run to Safwan to conduct an initial link up with the Ayatollah's resistance fighters. I intend to give the Ayatollah some money, perhaps four or five million in U.S. currency, to help in recruiting efforts," he continued, eyeing the Americans for any sign of interest in the amount of money he was describing. Assiri had learned in Afghanistan that large amounts of money was often a problem in itself as warlords fought each other instead of the enemy to get their hands on it. But the Americans all stood silently, as if they were unimpressed, yet each secretly wondered how in the hell Assiri planned on getting his hands on that kind of money inside Iraq.

"We will also accept the tribal leaders requests for support and begin coordinating for supplies and materials necessary to fight the war against Saddam's forces inside Iraq," he said, surprised that no one had questioned him about the money.

He took a deep breath and continued, "The Kuwaiti resistance fighters inside Kuwait, aided by the American CIA, have already initiated attacks to tie up Iraqi elements in and around Kuwait City. I do not expect any of Saddam's forces to be released to counter the Ayatollah's efforts on this side of the border. But you never know. The one thing you can be sure of is that the leaders you will meet with tonight will bring with them a shopping list at least ten feet long. Tonight, we will be expected to be a one-stop shopping center offering a blue light special on everything from ammunition to zebras. And once this list is accepted, we have to make sure that their needs, and maybe some of their wants as well, are met as expeditiously as possible."

Assiri paused to determine if what he was saying was registering with the Americans. He knew they were tired, having just completed an eighteen-hour flight that had taken them half way around the world, followed by a night road march to the assembly area. As a world traveler himself, Assiri knew that the effects of jet lag could often be deceiving, making it appear that people were wide awake when in fact they were virtually asleep with their eyes open, unaware of what was taking place around them. It was essential that the Americans understood their role in what was about to take place. After determining that they were still mentally with him, at least their eyes never rolled up into their sockets while he talked to them, always a good sign, he continued.

"Both your government and mine have had ample experience with this sort of thing during the Afghan war. In fact, many of the fighters you will meet tonight fought in Afghanistan and are members of the Afghan Service Bureau. For that reason, among others, they will be extremely suspicious of what you might promise to do for them. Some may even go so far as accusing you of lying to them. But not about the materials you claim to be able to acquire, they know that if they're willing to do the dying then America is willing to do the supplying, but lying regarding your commitment to their cause." Assiri paused to let his comment sink in.

Even in a state of being only half-awake, the American's knew to what he referred. When Russia invaded Afghanistan in 1979 America seized upon the opportunity to wage a proxy war, spearheaded by the Mujahadeen, at little cost to itself. American Special Forces personnel, along with CIA operatives provided equipment, logistical, and technical support in the form of advisors for the Mujahadeen, or soldiers of God, who actually fought the war. The Mujahadeen themselves were a collection of Afghan tribal warriors and Islamic fundamentalists from various Middle Eastern countries that sought the removal of the Godless Russian soldiers from a Muslim country.

According to the Mujahadeen part of the agreement America made to them for their assistance was that once the Russians left, America would use its considerable financial resources to help rebuild the country. So, in the conduct of the war no quarter was given and the cities were very quickly reduced to rubble. A consequence of modern war that the Mujahadeen expected America to compensate them for since, according to them, they would not have done quite so thorough a job of destruction had they known they would be stuck with the repair bill. But, since they did not expect to have to pay for it, a willingness to rip the country apart was a contributing factor to their success.

Another major reason for the Mujahadeen success during the war was their effective use of the American made and CIA supplied Stinger and Red Eye anti-aircraft missiles. American Special Forces personnel had trained the Arab and Afghan fighters how to employ these missiles and they had been used quite effectively by the Mujahadeen to shoot down the Russian Hind Helicopters, eliminating the technological advantage the Russians had previously enjoyed. With the loss of their helicopters, the Russian soldiers found themselves fighting a series of vicious infantry battles in the rugged, mountainous terrain of Afghanistan, often with a telling increase in the number of Russian casualties. Which of course upset the families of Russian soldiers dying in Afghanistan.

Like the public opinion in America regarding Vietnam, the Russian people didn't oppose killing for obscure reasons, but when it came to asking their children to die for those same obscure reasons they wanted concrete answers justifying the sacrifice. When called to task, the Russian politicians couldn't articulate any better reasons for being in Afghanistan than American politicians could for having gone into Vietnam, so they left. America's willingness to sleep with the devil in Afghanistan soon came back to haunt her when she began reneging on promises, real or imagined, made to the Mujahadeen. Assiri was right to criticize the American response to the Mujahadeen victory. As a fighter himself, Assiri's life had been put in grave danger when the west abandoned its "allies," leaving them holding the tribal quagmire that is Afghanistan. The resultant civil war left many thousands dead as the Taliban rose to power and various warlords partitioned Afghanistan into their own little fiefdoms. Like many of the Mujahadeen, Assiri felt fortunate to have escaped Afghanistan with his life.

When the war ended, America tried to quickly separate itself from the Mujahadeen by refusing to acknowledge their grievance. A political screw-up that was not appreciated by the Soldiers of God who just happened to still be in possession of a large number of these anti-aircraft missiles. When America demanded that the missiles be returned before any further discussion could take place, all accountability was lost. The Mujahadeen leaders simply refused to give them back. The refusal to return the missiles took the onus off American politicians, providing them with sufficient justification to dispense with any future discussions with the Mujahadeen. Something these politicians very clearly relayed to their voters back home because none of them wanted to be seen as being "friends" to backward Islamic fundamentalists less it cost them votes when they ran for reelection. But, unfortunately, these politicians traded the threat of losing votes for an even greater threat. The threat America then had was the same one it still has to this day, that it would get those same missiles back, one at a time, as they would be used by Islamic terrorists to shoot down commercial airliners.

Complicating this situation was the fact that the fundamentalist Mujahadeen were more closely aligned philosophically and religiously with Iran than with Iraq. With the recent seizure of American Embassy personnel in Tehran still fresh in American political minds, the Reagan administration was not about to be seen as siding with Iran in a war with any Middle Eastern country. So when Saddam attacked Iran, America supported his efforts in retaliation for Islamic fundamentalists not giving the missiles back, among other reasons. Though Dash knew that it was more complicated than this, the Arabs he had worked with always expressed a belief that America was throwing a temper tantrum because it was not getting its way. To them, the idea that Saddam was less of a threat to stability in the Middle East than Iran was absurd.

The stories that had come out of Afghanistan detailing the atrocities suffered by both the Russians and the Mujahadeen made even the most hardened American veteran cringe. Tales of mutilations, decapitations, homosexual rapes, and hangings seemed to accompany descriptions of every battle fought between the two forces. Underlying these stories were the Arab allegations that all of it was being supported, if not actually encouraged, by the American government.

Dash knew that blaming America for other people's ills was part of working in any foreign environment. Both America and Europe were often seen as the dog to kick when another couldn't readily be found. While some of the anti-American attacks were deserved, many were a result of simple misunderstandings and jealousies. He had grown used to such attacks while working throughout Africa and various Middle Eastern countries, but he was slightly surprised to hear Assiri mention that the Americans should be prepared to hear about these slights again, particularly on the eve of war.

Dash felt that whether or not America had lied to the Afghans or the Muja-hadeen was surely a moot point by now. The imminent threat Saddam currently posed would focus their attention on the moment and not on the past. Besides, he knew that neither the Russians nor the Mujahadeen needed any encouragement from America to be inhumane captors and fighters. Like mans inhumanity to man throughout the world, it seems to be a natural human trait that cannot be blamed on an outside force. However, he was about to learn that others felt quite differently about it being a moot point.

"Regardless of what is said tonight questioning Americas commitment to re-move Saddam from power," Assiri continued, "your response will always be that this time it is different. This time America herself has a stake in who ultimately controls access to the Middle Eastern oil reserves and President Bush has determined that it will not be Saddam Hussein. Politically it can't be. The Arabs understand this, even if some of your fellow countrymen don't."

"In fact," he surmised, "it would probably be best if you allowed me to do all of the talking tonight."

"Why in the hell is Moe lecturing us on U.S. resolve?" Dash wondered. *"We're just simple soldiers. We go where we're told and we do what we have been told to do when we get there. The Ambassador is in charge and he directed that my team take its orders from Assiri. That's all we need to know. If he thinks we will*

wobble when the going gets tough, then he is mistaken."

"O.K.," Moe said, interrupting Dash's thoughts. "In the back of the truck marked with bumper number 14 is a relief mock-up of the terrain we will follow to Safwan. There will also be recent JSTARS aerial photos faxed to me on the INMARSAT so we can confirm that there have been no recent changes. I would like to reconvene this meeting at the mock-up in two hours. Any questions before I go?"

"Yes," replied Dash, "but I will hold them until we have the terrain mock-up in front of us." As an afterthought he added, "I would like to know where you're off to though?"

"I need to make an office call on our gracious host, General Talabani." Moe answered, still wearing his trademark smile as he turned toward his Land Rover, entered it, and then sped away in a cloud of dust.

As Dash watched the Land Rover drive toward Talabani's headquarters, disappearing over a slight rise, he thought aloud, "I hope he is taking note of all the juicy targets being built enroute to Talabani's headquarters. In the very near future this is going to be a fighter pilot's dream come true."

Dash couldn't quite shake his disbelief that Assiri had been lecturing him on U.S. resolve. Of all the times and places, one hundred kilometers behind enemy lines is an unlikely place to be chastised for America's short attention span. But he knew from past experiences that when soldiers are under enormous strain their inner most feelings often surface. He had had several in depth discussions with American soldiers at times when it was expected that their focus would be on the task at hand, not on the politics of why they were risking life and limb for some ethereal cause. Understandably, when young men are mentally preparing themselves for possible death, there is a natural inclination for them to ask – "For what reason?"

Dash's personal experiences dealing with young men confronting death had reinforced his belief that on the eve of battle, combat soldiers do not need cheerleaders; they need honesty. He knew from having been a private himself that leaders make a mistake when they attempt to justify a soldier's pending sacrifice by ascribing it with certainty to some nebulous cause that no one really understands. The idea of risking death in defense of liberty and justice for a people that the average soldier could care less about, as was tried in Vietnam, is a vessel that holds little water. Confronting death is a personal matter that needs to be addressed on a personal level. Dash knew that soldiers would usually do what they were told to do regardless of how they felt about the politics surrounding it. But the stereotype of them as "Yes, Sir-No, Sir" mindless robots responding to a clarion call for motherhood and apple pie is the product of a Hollywood imagination. Soldiers fight and die for each other, not idealized beliefs spelled with four-syllable words. Consequently, when soldiers ask penetrating questions, leaders had better have a good answer for them.

In particular, when American soldiers begin to question their leaders those leaders have to have their facts straight or be prepared to have their words challenged. A belief in equality is a blessing of democracy, and regardless of the stature or rank of the person speaking to them, American soldiers will challenge anyone. Dash had witnessed this firsthand in Vietnam. Perhaps Assiri now felt like the Vietnam vets did when they knew they were supporting a lie, but felt compelled to do it anyway. He shook his head as he thought about it, then returned to the business at hand.

Like all soldiers the Americans took advantage of the two hours they had by crawling into the rear of the trucks and going to sleep, awakening just as Assiri returned from Talabani's headquarters in Al-Bussayyah with the general accompanying him.

CHAPTER 10

The sand table rehearsals the team conducted with Assiri basically confirmed the routes they had selected before crossing the Saudi border. The roads around both Al-Bussayyah and Safwan were crowded with military vehicles during daylight hours but were relatively unused during the hours of darkness. Perhaps in a misguided attempt to intimidate the Americans, the Iraqis were making no attempt to hide the fact that a massive military build-up was taking place along the border. In fact, the more visible their signature, the happier the Iraqi planners seemed to be. This audacity would soon come back to haunt them once the bombing started but for now the flagrant flaunting of military units and equipment was all designed to discourage the Bush administration from launching any sort of a conventional pre-emptive strike.

Even more important than the roads themselves, however, were the tank trails that ran alongside them. Dirt roads that ran parallel to, but at a distance from, the asphalt highway; highways that would disintegrate if the heavy tracked vehicles were driven over them in the hot summer sun. These tank trails were what the team would use extensively as they covered the seventy-five miles of empty desert separating Al-Bussayyah from Safwan, using the hardball roads only as a last resort to avoid encountering one of the frequent Iraqi mounted patrols. The IPAC pipeline road carrying crude oil north from the unoccupied zone along the Saudi border led straight into the heart of Safwan and to the meeting site. It would be an easy route to navigate even in a moonless Iraqi night, which tonight was anything but as a brilliant moon shined brightly in the star-studded desert sky.

As the FAV's crept through the concertina gate and began their descent into the ravine, Dash keyed the radio to alert those following to employ their red filtered flashlights so they could make better time. With the drivers wearing their AN-PVS-7 night vision goggles, or NVG's, the subdued light of the flashlights was magnified one thousand fold, lighting up the terrain around the FAV's better than headlights on a car. In many instances visibility was better with a 1/2 moon than it would have been in daylight. Tonight there was a 3/4 moon in a cloudless August sky, allowing the FAV's to travel at an average speed of forty-five miles per hour over the hard packed surface of the ravine. Once they struck the tank trails their speed would increase to an average of sixty-five miles per hour as they sped to the meeting site north of Safwan.

The trip through the ravine went like clockwork and when the FAV Dash was in hit the tank trail, he ordered Floriddia to drive slowly until the other three emerged from the ravine, and then strike for gold, meaning to floor it. Once the other vehicles had cleared the ravine, Floriddia put the pedal to the metal and the trailing FAV's responded in a similar manner. Within seconds all four were cruising along the tank trail somewhere between sixty and seventy miles per hour, speed that the vehicles were made for and the soldiers driving them were trained for; but a speed that was both exhilarating and dangerous none the less.

When traveling at such speeds, the FAV's were susceptible to floating, meaning that the driver had feathery control over the front end of the vehicle. This is not to imply that he could not steer it, but with most of the weight in the rear of the vehicle a more delicate touch was required than when driving the family station wagon. The slightest turn of the steering wheel could quickly catapult the vehicle off the tank trail and into the desert.

The team members had learned through trial and error at Hunter Liggett and the National Training Center at Fort Irwin, that only the driver should be wearing NVG's, or NOD's, Night Observation Devices, at times such as these. The NOD's impaired peripheral vision and if a soldier had to remove them quickly it took several precious seconds to regain his own natural night vision. Consequently, all of the passengers in the FAV's were staring into the dark, wind whistling through their CVC helmet, teeth clenched, virtually blind, holding the flashlight for the driver and praying like hell that nothing would pop up in front of them. Had anything done so they would have simply died wondering what had killed them because at that speed and without NOD's it was difficult to see beyond the front of the vehicle.

As it was, the many moguls on the tank trail often sent the vehicles airborne as they sped along, leaving the passenger wondering each time if they had just gone over the edge of a deep canyon, or if the driver had lost control of the vehicle. Such an experience was like riding in the world's worst roller coaster blindfolded. The drivers, of course, knew this as all of the team members had experience driving as well as riding in the passenger seat. It seemed to be a game that was played. The object of which was to scare the hell out of the passenger. Even in the enemy-controlled desert of Iraq, the American sense of humor played itself out that night as the sphincter muscles of those holding the flashlight clenched and relaxed, clenched and relaxed as passengers silently prayed that they wouldn't lose complete control.

Even for those used to it, the experience was intense, especially for the Ayatollah and General Talabani. Neither of them had ever ridden in a FAV before and the first ride of their lives was at high speed in total darkness. It had to have been one harrowing evening for the two Iraqis. Having two crazy Americans, McNabb and Blackburn, at the wheel couldn't have helped calm their nerves much either.

Blackburn, who had the privilege of chauffeuring the Ayatollah Sistani, had already complained to Dash regarding the Ayatollah's expectation of special treatment. Speaking to Dash over the radio in English, he complained, "the little weasel dick won't hold the flashlight for me!" Leaving Blackburn to both drive the vehicle and provide for his own illumination. Not an impossible task for the experienced Blackburn who only had to keep the FAV in front of him in view to stay on course. But it irritated Blackburn that the Ayatollah expected everyone to do for him those things that he should be doing for himself.

After almost one hour of blasting through the desert, Dash checked the latitudinal and longitudinal coordinates on his GPS receiver and realized that they were getting close to the link up site, a farmhouse north of Safwan. Ordering Floriddia to pull the vehicle over to allow the others to catch up Dash unbuckled the three-point harness and pulled himself from the vehicle before radioing the others to come forward to finalize their approach plan. Within minutes Assiri, Blackburn, and McNabb stood clustered next to Dash's FAV.

Now that they no longer had a sixty-five mile per hour wind blowing past them, Blackburn was the first to notice the smell.

"What the hell is that smell?" he whispered to no one in particular. "Something smells like sour owl shit. Gag a maggot."

"It's you, First Sergeant." said McNabb. "Looks like you've got mud or something all over your rain jacket. Christ, I've got it all over me too! Damn, what is this stuff?" he cursed, wiping his hand down the front of his rain jacket.

The others followed McNabb's gesture and soon all five men, including Floriddia, were pawing at the vile smelling stuff that was seemingly caked to every fiber of their being. The more they pawed the worse the smell became.

"My God!" hissed Blackburn. "Tell me it ain't so!"

During their training with the FAV's all of the soldiers had learned to wear their rain gear, pants and jacket regardless of the weather when driving at high speed, especially when doing so at night over unfamiliar terrain. With their low silhouette and all terrain tires the vehicles were known for picking up whatever refuse covered the surface of the road, depositing it in the occupant's lap, teeth, hair, ears, radios, personal gear, and the vehicle itself. The CVC helmet and rain gear afforded some protection but whatever foreign matter was being slung into the air still landed all over the occupants. Normal road debris like tar and sand usually stuck to a person's exterior and when the outer garments were removed the wearer remained relatively unscathed. Tonight was a little different!

"This is shit!" exclaimed Blackburn.

"Sure smells like it," replied a disbelieving McNabb. "Wonder what it could be?"

"Lick your lips, dumb ass. It's real shit. Sheep shit!" Blackburn said loudly enough for all to hear, causing everyone to freeze in place, staring at each other in stunned silence, regretting the fact that they had been smearing the vile smelling stuff all over their person by pawing at it. To the dismay of all those watching McNabb did exactly as Blackburn instructed, licking his lips and then going into a fit of spitting and gagging reminiscent of the tankers reaction to the CS back at Fort Hunter Liggett.

The best that Dash could surmise was that the Bedouin sheepherders they had encountered had recently moved their huge flock of sheep down the tank trail, probably just a few hours before the FAV's took the same road. Three thousand head of sheep leave behind a lot of smelly, sticky manure. That manure was now caked to the soldiers and their illustrious passengers, the Ayatollah Sistani and General Talabani.

"Christ almighty," Blackburn raved. "I would rather be covered with nerve gas than sheep shit! At least then I could just crawl off and die. It's going to be several days before we get a shower and we're going to be some rank S.O.B.'s by then."

"Well," announced Dash, trying to come up with some sort of solution for their current predicament. "We're ahead of schedule so why don't we take a few minutes and try to wash some of this stuff off. There are water cans on each vehicle so I suggest we use this water to give one another a quick shower. At least clean ourselves well enough that the people we are to meet with will be able to sit in the same room with us."

"Roger, Sir." answered Blackburn. "I'll put the word out."

Turning to Assiri, Blackburn continued. "Moe, I want to be with you when you tell the Ayatollah and General Talabani that they've been covered with sheep shit. Just make sure that their still harnessed into the vehicles when you tell them. I'd hate to have to spend the rest of the night looking for them if they run off into the desert with their head on fire."

"Why me?" Assiri mumbled to himself as he walked back to tell them, Blackburn respectfully following three steps to his rear, grinning like a little kid in anticipation of what he was about to witness.

To Blackburn's surprise General Talabani reacted to the news with typical soldierly humor. Telling Assiri that smelling like a barnyard was nothing new to him as he had grown up on a farm with camels and sheep. He had also listened to the soldiers when they told him to put on rain gear for the trip tonight. As a consequence he would clean up reasonably well.

The Ayatollah, however, reacted just as Blackburn suspected he would. With a "deer in the headlights" look plainly visible even in the dark desert, he reacted to the news as if Assiri had shoved his hands inside his robes, groping him in an unwanted sexual manner. He strained against the shoulder harness and lap belt as if they were snakes trying to squeeze the life out of him. Cursing, ranting, legs and arms flailing about inside the vehicle, he tried mightily to rid himself of the vile smelling manure and free himself from the harness at the same time. Neither task was accomplished and as he flailed about, Blackburn could hear Assiri apologizing profusely for having taken him through the sheep manure.

Unlike the General, the Ayatollah had refused the suggestion of putting on rain gear and was literally caked with the manure. His once salt and pepper beard now looked to be all pepper and his turban resembled a dunce cap as it was piled high with great gobs of sheep droppings, giving him the appearance of a wizard as he sat rigidly upright in the passenger seat of the vehicle.

As he was apologizing Assiri thought that he could hear the sound of muffled laughter coming from his rear, just about where First Sergeant Blackburn happened to be standing.

***

To the Americans the Ayatollah epitomized all that was wrong with the Middle East. A dead ringer for the late Ayatollah Khomeni who came to power following the fall of the American backed Shah of Iran, Rahzi Pahlavi, Sistani truly believed that God had chosen him to rule the Muslim world, at least this part of it. This insistence by clerics to rule dominated political thought in Iran and neighboring countries, thwarting the development of democratic tendencies in the region. The Ayatollah, and the many others like him, would die before they would ever agree to a separation between religion and politics to mirror the American experience.

For the Ayatollah, the idea that something written by man becoming the supreme law of the land, as the constitution is generally accepted to be by the vast majority of Americans, was beyond comprehension. In his world there could be only one source of law, that dictated by God to Mohammed centuries ago, the Holy Koran. Any other source of law was sacrilegious and an affront to God. God ruled the Ayatollah Sistani; it was only natural that Sistani should rule in the political arena of mere men.

Conversely, the American experience had put the soldiers in a secular world radically different from that of the Ayatollah. They had grown up in a compartmentalized social structure that saw no contradiction with viewing church as being separate from state. The educational experiences of the average American citizen, especially at the collegiate level, teaches that all religions, not just Islam, are an attempt to hold on to the past by portraying it as a blueprint for the future. Religion does provide rules to live by that, when not taken to extremes, provides much of the foundation for a civil society. In many cases, religion is the glue that holds men together and anything that can do that is certainly worth keeping. It is when extremists use religion to justify having personal control over the lives of others, demanding compliance, that a problem will arise. Something a modern, progressive society cannot tolerate. Acceptance of diverse beliefs and opinions are now required as the world becomes a much smaller place than when Mohammed lived and, so far, Mohammed's religion does not have a good record of being flexible enough to be so accomodating.

Most Americans are raised to believe that while the desire to remember the past is, in and of itself, not necessarily a negative concept, wanting to live in the past is. For this reason, as long as people like the Ayatollah are allowed to dominate the political scene in the Islamic world there will be limited progress made in Muslim societies. Especially distressing for the Americans was to observe the power that these religious Icons wielded in the Middle East. Radical fundamentalists were as attracted to men like the Ayatollah as a fly is attracted to manure, forcing the Americans to work with such people regardless of their own personal feelings, which were unanimously negative.

What people like the Ayatollah represent to the Arab world is a return to the glory days of the past. When Europe was locked in the throes of the Dark Ages, Muslim societies throughout what is today's Middle East experienced tremendous gains in the arts and sciences. Arabs, in particular, led the world in exploration and trade. Their collective gains ultimately ended in what became known as the Ottoman Empire. Though not exclusively Arab, the Ottoman Empire was certainly Islamic. It created a military, economic, and cultural power that stretched in all directions: north to the Crimea, east to Baghdad and Basra, south to the coasts of Arabia and the Gulf, west to Egypt and North Africa-and into Europe. At its peak, in the sixteenth century, the Ottoman Empire included most of the Middle East, North Africa, and what are now the Balkan countries of Europe. It stretched from the Persian Gulf to the river Danube; its armies stopped only at the gates of Vienna. Its population was estimated at between thirty and fifty million at a time when England's population was around four million; and it ruled twenty nationalities. The Ottoman Turks were a super power before there was any such thing as a super power.

Then came World War I and the British, French, and German partitioning of the old Ottoman Empire. The Arab people have never recovered from their losses, nor have they ever forgiven either the Europeans, or the Americans who assisted them, for stealing their past glories. The creation of Israel in 1948, carved out of what had been the Arab Palestine, simply added insult to injury. For a people surviving in a rear-view-mirror culture, one where adherents look to the past to predict the future, the Arabs see nothing but hopelessness and despair. The windshield cultures surrounding them, European and American, where the focus is more on where they are going than on where they have been, offer a stark contrast of progress and material wealth.

For people suffering the psychological impact of defeat with no accompanying

Marshall Plan to lessen the impact, and make no mistake about it, it has been a defeat, one hope for a better future for Islam is to grant the Ayatollahs and Imams their past powers. If Islam rose from the ashes under the guidance of Mohammed, then true believers feel that it can do so again under the guidance of an Ayatollah Khomenei or Ayatollah Sistani. It is frightening to know that such fundamentalist people as these possess almost magical powers in the Middle East.

Nor was religious fundamentalism something that the soldiers had encountered only in the Middle East, though it seemed to predominate there. An over zealous Baptist landlord in Radcliffe, Kentucky had once confronted Dash's wife, Janet, while he was a student at the Armor School at Fort Knox. The landlord, with a .357 pistol strapped to his hip, had demanded to see Dash's and Janet's marriage license after they had already moved into a small apartment that the landlord had advertised for rent. The landlord had waited until Dash was in the field before confronting Janet with his demand, scaring the hell out of her and cementing in her mind that she would never again go back to Kentucky. When she produced the marriage license, he had apologized with the excuse, "you can't be too careful with all of the sin going on today."

On another occasion Dash had brushed up against the effects of Christian fundamentalism when he attempted to buy a paintbrush from a local hardware store in El Paso, Texas while assigned to Fort Bliss. Ordinarily this is not a problem, but it was a Sunday and the Texas Blue Laws prohibited the merchants from selling anything indicating that manual labor would be performed on the Sabbath. When someone takes another persons freedom away from them, even if for their own good, it forces a belief on them that other less conservative Christians do not knowingly support. Such an attitude of superiority is blatantly un-American and belongs to a different time.

In conversations with other soldiers Dash discovered that his experiences had not been unique. It was understandable that soldiers often distrusted people who felt that they represented God, placing themselves above the laws of mere mortals. Laws made by man are not good enough for fundamentalists, nor are the differing opinions of others because unlike themselves, such people do not speak for God but only for their own selfish selves. For those who would prefer to think for themselves instead of having someone else do it for them, people holding such beliefs are in peril of being viewed as insane by those who disagree with them.

None of these beliefs are meant to suggest that the soldiers were not religious themselves. They certainly were not atheists. It is just that it had been their experience to note that when people carry their religion like a weapon no good ever comes from it. When zealots flaunt religion at every opportunity, preaching to people as if they couldn't possibly understand the complexities of God's grand plan without intervention from the knowing, essentially forcing their personal beliefs on a reluctant public, then those same people are living in a world of self-delusion. It is always best not to live there with them.

Blackburn, with his unique ability to synthesize the complex, had once proffered the following observation to Dash: "Imagine living in an America where the Pope was the President. Congress consisted of the likes of Jerry Falwell, Billy Graham, Jimmy Swaggert, and Jim Baker. Comrade Rush Limbaugh is the Speaker of the House charged with the duty of carrying their message to the great unwashed via his conservative radio talk show. In such a goose-stepping world you could cut off your dick and freeze your brain. Recreational sex and unapproved thought would both be illegal."

The inclusion of Rush Limbaugh in the above mix was not a misstatement on Blackburn's part. Although not known as a religious figure himself, by the late 80's and early 90's, Rush Limbaugh had become the darling of the Christian Coalition for his conservative stance on issues like abortion, the erosion of family values, and "get tough" law and order. As a conservative Republican himself, Blackburn, as were many of the soldiers at Fort Bragg, was a regular listener to Rush's three hour, five-days-a-week, daily radio diatribe railing against liberalism, communism, democrats, elitists, intellectuals, and anything or anyone else who differed with his version of the "truth." Blackburn had even met Limbaugh when he visited Fort Bragg, shaking his hand and encouraging him to "keep up the good work." But that was before Limbaugh's version of the anti-Christ, in the form of William Jefferson Clinton, arrived on the national political scene.

With the arrival of Clinton Limbaugh's criticism of liberalism went beyond challenging ideas to become personal attacks on individuals that he did not like. Blackburn had once confessed that although he continued to listen to Rush's radio program he felt that Limbaugh's particular brand of conservatism was a little too radical even for him. Commenting that, "I don't necessarily disagree with all that Rush says. But when someone openly brags about not having gone to college and possessing a mind closed tighter to differing opinions than a duck's ass is to water, I can't help but wonder if this is someone who should be seen as a role model for other conservatives. The man is getting downright vicious!"

With his background, especially those memories associated with his father, Blackburn absolutely despised those with an air of superiority about them. To him they were nothing but bullies and like bullies everywhere if confronted with sufficient force, they would fold their hands like any other spineless bluffer. As a radio talk show host viewed only as an entertainer, it might be acceptable to be viewed as a bully. But in a country like America, where even children are taught to dislike a bully, for a political party to project an image of being a bully is a guaranteed recipe for failure.

Blackburn was ahead of the political curve in his analysis of Limbaugh's attacks on Clinton during the campaign, telling anyone who would listen, "If the Republican Party allows itself to become identified with the likes of Limbaugh and his supporters, they are dead meat come November!" Sure enough, Clinton defeated George H.W. Bush for his first term in office then soundly trounced Bob Dole to receive his second term in office. During the entire eight years of the Clinton presidency, Limbaugh and his supporters, known as "dittoheads" for their unquestioning support of virtually all Limbaugh's positions, were like people possessed, criticizing the Clinton's for even breathing.

Like most listeners Blackburn had no way of knowing the credibility of the many outlandish accusations Limbaugh made against Clinton, ranging from adultery to murder. But he intuitively knew that there was no way an inquisitive American media would ever give any high profile politician a pass and not cover a legitimate story. There would have been far more money and prestige associated with covering such juicy stories than hiding them.

It wasn't just President Clinton that Limbaugh attacked; his wife Hillary, according to Limbaugh, would have made Hester Prine of Scarlet Letter fame appear the moral equivalent of a Blue Bird or Brownie. But the final straw came for Blackburn when Limbaugh attacked the Clinton's daughter, Chelsea, during his short-lived television show.

One evening following a parachute jump Dash, Blackburn, and several of the company NCO's were gathered in the orderly room reviewing the next day's training schedule when Limbaugh came on the television. It was the first, and last time, that Blackburn ever watched his show, which must have been the viewing norm across America since the show was shortly taken off the air.

"Did you hear that they now have a dog in the White House?" Limbaugh asked his audience. Then he put up a picture of twelve-year old Chelsea Clinton wearing braces and the audience roared its delight. Blackburn's response was both immediate and audible.

"My God!" he gasped. "It's like a scene from 'Krystalnacht,'" referring to the initial Nazi onslaught on the German Jews in 1938. "That audience would do any Brown Shirt proud."

"I'm glad you said that and not me," Staff Sergeant Eddie Lopez, a Mexican national remarked. "If I had said that, one of these crackers would throw me out the window," he smiled in jest as he looked at the White sergeants sitting beside him.

"Who you callin' a cracker, boy?" staff sergeant Dennis Cahill, from Knoxville, Tennessee roared, causing everyone in the room to laugh except Blackburn. He sat mesmerized by what he was seeing on television.

"Don't those dumb bastards realize what they are doing?" he fumed. "Any adult who would publicly ridicule a child is an adult in name only. Limbaugh has to have piss poor judgment and be completely devoid of conscience. How can any thinking human being respect the opinion of a man like that! If this is where the Republican Party is headed then republicans are screwed. Hell, even I wouldn't vote for a candidate that someone like that supports!"

Which is a shame for even though the messenger might be off target, Limbaugh's message is often worth listening to. He just needs to work on his delivery because it does offend many conservatives whom otherwise agree with what he is saying.

As historical footnotes validating Blackburn's comment that Limbaugh had become offensive, more people voted for Al Gore than George W. Bush during the 2000 presidential election and Chelsea Clinton has since matured into a beautiful, intelligent, delightful young woman. The jury is still out on what Rush Limbaugh may yet mature into. The last any of the soldiers knew of his career was he was being investigated for violating federal drug laws and busily frequenting the Manhattan singles scene searching for his fourth wife. Incredibly while still being promoted as a law and order conservative concerned with the erosion of solid, Christian, family values by his followers, proving to anyone willing to learn that like ideologues everywhere, a dittohead's hypocrisy knows no limits.

Unlike either Limbaugh or the Ayatollah, General Talabani exhibited a down to earth realism that the soldiers quickly identified with. Besides the obvious fact that he was a General Officer, the soldiers respected him because, unlike the aforementioned two notable individuals, he didn't look down his nose at people. Smiling and shaking hands, General Talabani had immediately blended into the American's world, a world where everyone carried their own weight and entitled slackers would not be tolerated.

***

Though none of the soldiers knew it at the time, General Talabani had his own reasons for wanting to see Saddam dead. Assiri later explained to Dash and Blackburn over tea that the General had been blessed with two beautiful daughters, Haifa and Iftakar, but no sons. The two girls were the delight of the General. He had sent both of them to the prestigious Wellesley College in Boston where Haifa, two years older than Iftakar, graduated twenty years to the day after another famous Wellesley Alum, Hillary Rodham Clinton.

The General had chosen the all girls' school for his daughters because he had heard of the decadent lifestyle enjoyed by the young in many of the American coed schools. It was his hope that his girls could complete their studies without succumbing to the many American temptations.

The girls had enjoyed their time in America, with all its freedoms and opportunities for women, but they told the General that Iraq was their home and as long as the General and their mother remained, so would they. Upon their graduation both had returned to Baghdad to be near their beloved father. Besides, as young women of privilege, they enjoyed the opulence that their father, an Iraqi General, enjoyed as a member of the elitist Ba'athist Party and a confidant of Saddam Hussein. The many gala balls and black tie parties they were privileged to attend were luxuries that would turn any girl's head. It was while attending a social function at one of Saddam's many palaces that Haifa had caught the eye of Saddam's son, Udai. A man well known for his many excesses, but still a man possessing enough charisma and panache' that he could capture the attention of two very naive young Iraqi women.

When Udai Hussein, like his father Saddam, saw something he liked, he took it. And Udai Hussein liked what he saw when looking at the beautiful Talabani sisters. Enticing them to follow him downstairs with promises of excitement, Udai led them into a room in the basement of the palace, into what he would kindly call his sex room. It was actually a rape room complete with the latest in ingenuous restraint devices, where he closed and locked the door behind them. Once inside he produced a pistol and forced the girls to snort cocaine and perform any manner of sexual acts with him. Satiated after several hours of drug-induced sex, he surrendered them to his four bodyguards. Each of the guards then dutifully had their way with the beautiful Haifa and Iftakar.

Of all the many kinky sex acts that Udai Hussein was known to perform on his victims — they could not possibly be called lovers — possibly the worst was the act of asphyxiation. To perform such an act Udai had fashioned a leather strap with a large knot in the center. While mounting the girl from behind, he would tighten this strap around her neck, pressing the knot tightly against the trachea, preventing her from drawing a breath. As she began to run out of oxygen the girl would thrash wildly about, enhancing the moment for Udai.

The bodyguards had watched Udai perform asphyxiation many times in the past. They had even done it themselves when Udai had tossed his victim's aside, beckoning the guards to do as they pleased, as he had done tonight with the beautiful Talabani sisters.

As one of the guards, the largest of the four, mounted Haifa for perhaps the third time, he slipped the leather strap around her neck, drew it tight, the knot firmly pressed against her trachea, shutting off her air. As Haifa fought wildly for oxygen her movements excited the guard, already high on Udai's stash of cocaine, and he squeezed the strap even tighter around her neck. Because he had already achieved multiple orgasms during a short period of time, the guard could not ejaculate as quickly as he had before. Yet in his frustrated efforts to achieve satisfaction, he continued to squeeze the strap tightly around her neck, prolonging Haifa's tortured gasping and his own desires. By the time he reached a final climax the beautiful Haifa Talabani was dead, the leather strap twisted so tightly around her neck that it had cut through her flesh, bulging her once beautiful blue eyes from their sockets.

Later, when Udai led the sobbing Iftakar back into the room where the General was socializing, he simply walked away from her as if he had never seen her before in his life. The General, noticing his daughters' tears rushed to her side, asking her what was wrong. Iftakar described for the General all that had transpired in the basement of the palace, ending with the painful acknowledgement that Haifa, lying motionless in a pool of her own blood, could not arise from the bed. She was probably dead, or at least Iftakar had heard the men laughingly say such a terrible thing.

As the General listened to Iftakar's recounting of the rape, he went through a series of emotions. First was disbelief, then anger, followed by rage. Still he continued listening to the soft sobbing of Iftakar and his rage was replaced with a feeling of remorse for Haifa, pity for Iftakar, and then a bone chilling fear for the both of them as reality seeped through his overwhelming grief.

The General was suddenly struck with the ugly realization that if he confronted either Saddam or Udai with the truth that they would have both he and Iftakar killed, taken out and shot that very night. For even though Udai was known to be an animal, he was still Saddam's son and no father would want his son to go to prison for rape and murder, not if a father had the wherewithal to secretly intervene, preventing it from occurring. Saddam certainly had the power to help his murderous son, Udai. More importantly, General Talabani knew beyond doubt that Saddam would do whatever was necessary to protect his son, no matter how horrendous the deed.

General Talabani and his one remaining daughter, Iftakar, left Saddam's residence that night without saying a word to anyone about what had happened. There was a pronounced sadness clearly etched on the General's face as the last memory of his beautiful Haifa that night was that she lay in a pool of blood not twenty feet below where he was now standing. He had swallowed such thoughts and shaken the hand of both Udai and Saddam before leaving the palace. His graciousness towards the Hussein family had been the most difficult act he had ever performed, but his fear for Iftikar's safety compelled him to behave as if nothing was wrong. But in his heart General Talabani knew that he must kill Saddam and his son Udai if he were ever to have any peace of mind.

It was that very same night, while his emotions were still at a fever pitch, that he had been contacted by a former Afghan Mujahadeen freedom fighter from Saudi Arabia named Mohammed Al-Assiri. Moe had also been at Saddam's party and had heard what had happened while drinking Champaign and laughing with the bodyguards as they recounted for him how they had ended the life of the beautiful Haifa Talabani.

This had all occurred two months ago. Finally, tonight with Assiri and the American's help, General Talabani was starting to get even with the Hussein family.

***

After Assiri had calmed the Ayatollah and washed him as best he could, he and Blackburn returned to Dash's location. Though the water can shower had helped somewhat, there was nothing any of them could do about how they smelled. Besides, they had bigger worries to deal with anyway.

With Assiri now taking the lead, they cautiously approached the farmhouse, flashed their recognition signal with the flashlight, and pulled into the yard, parking beside the dilapidated building away from the road. There were no other vehicles around. As the Arabs greeted the guards outside in typical fashion, with kisses to the cheeks, Blackburn made sure that the drivers conducted preventive maintenance checks, PMS, on the vehicles. He also had them draw fuel from the jerry cans they carried in the FAV's bustle rack and refill their water cans from a nearby well. It appeared to all of them that the guards were a little taken aback by their smell, diluted as it was because of the strong aroma of the adjacent onion fields, but detectable none the less. Then again, perhaps they were simply being polite in not mentioning it. Since they didn't, neither did anyone else.

While McNabb, Floriddia, and Assiri's driver remained outside to guard the vehicles, the others went inside, first the Ayatollah, then General Talabani, Assiri, Dash, and last, Blackburn. As their eyes became accustomed to the candle-lit room, Dash surveyed the scene inside and could see that six Arab men were present. All looked to be soldiers and as hard as woodpecker lips. They were a collection of Iraqi Shi'ites, Kurds, Sunnis, and Coptic Christians. All professed to have an intense hatred of Saddam and his Ba'athist party. All were guns for hire. They were here representing the so-called "Marsh Arabs" that Saddam had tried so diligently to exterminate over the course of the past twelve years. They were also the very people that America had unwittingly helped Saddam try to exterminate during his eight-year war with neighboring Iran. And all of them were staring intently at the Americans sitting before them.

Besides the six Arabs in attendance there were two Caucasians, probably Europeans Dash initially thought, sitting in the back of the room. It was to the supposed Europeans that Assiri first approached, an unusual *faux paux* for the sociable Assiri. Until tonight it had always been the custom of Assiri, as well as any other Arabs present, to greet each other with great deference before acknowledging the presence of outsiders. But as Dash watched Assiri approach the two Caucasians, it was obvious that they knew one another. It was also obvious that a financial transaction was taking place as the two of them each handed Assiri large duffel bags presumably filled with cash.

As Assiri dragged the large bags into the center of the room, the two Caucasians followed and they, along with everyone else in attendance, squatted and took a cross-legged seat on the dirt floor. A blue-light special had just started blinking in Safwan.

"Gentlemen," Assiri began. "I bring with me tonight the good wishes of King Fahd, keeper of the two Holy Mosques in Mecca and Medina, and those of the American President, Mister George Bush. They thank you in advance for all the assistance your people will provide them in our efforts to rid ourselves of this plague, Saddam Hussein."

Dash found it strange that Assiri had not made introductions. But as he scanned the room, it slowly dawned on him that Moe didn't know who these Arabs were either. That was why he had brought the Ayatollah and General Talabani, to have them verify that these people were who they were claiming to be and that they were capable of doing all that was about to be asked of them. As Assiri looked around the room, making eye contact with the six Arabs, Dash could see out of the corner of his eye that the Ayatollah and the General were nodding ever so slightly to confirm for Assiri that the six men present were worth the trouble of dealing with. And they were trouble. It was just going to be a question as to what degree they would be trouble.

"I have brought with me tonight money so that you may reward your warriors for leaving their farms and families. These are difficult times and family matters must be attended to." With that Assiri reached into one of the duffels and withdrew several stacks of American one hundred-dollar bills, handing them to the Arab sitting directly across from him. The Arab didn't even flinch, never even looked at the money, actually. Instead he stared straight at both Dash and Blackburn and said in a voice dripping with contempt, "Why did you bring the Americans here? They smell bad. So does their money!"

If Dash ever doubted that America had burned its bridges in this part of the world by abandoning the Mujahadeen in Afghanistan and supporting Saddam in his war with Iran, he didn't anymore. As the words of the Arab hung in the air, he could see the other five Arabs, as well as the Ayatollah, nodding in agreement. He also felt Blackburn's hand slip down to the forty-five pistol on his hip just in case this turned into something other than a finger-pointing contest as everyone in the room was heavily armed.

"Gentlemen," responded Assiri, holding his hands in front of him, palms out, as if he were trying to hold back a tide of emotions. "We cannot allow our past differences to poison our future. Tonight we have but one enemy. He sits now in Baghdad and Kuwait. He is the killer of your women and children. The Americans are here to help you in your efforts to rid yourselves of this tyrant."

Then, in an effort to convince them otherwise, he offered a reason for them to let the Americans help.

"This time it is different. This time the Americans have an interest in seeing that Saddam is removed from power. This time access to oil is at stake and the Americans will pay attention."

Assiri had looked directly at both Dash and Blackburn as he said this, ensuring that neither of the two took it as a personal affront to their vision of American foreign policy. He need not have troubled himself, as both men were well aware of the fact that American foreign policy had always been about promoting American business interests in foreign countries. In their minds there was nothing wrong with this philosophy. Money is the lifeblood of capitalism and capitalism is the lifeblood of America. Always had been; probably always would be. Besides, both men had served in enough foreign countries to know that the real problem in most of them was the government that ruled the country, not the American businesses that operated there, though admittedly it is often hard to distinguish between the two. But, if a country had an honest, caring government, regardless of whether it was a functioning democracy or not, the quality of life for the people always improved with the injection of American money. Conversely, if a country was controlled by a ruling elite bent on personal enrichment at the expense of the governed, the quality of life for the people never improved. It was not the responsibility of the American business interests to tell the rulers how to spend their profits. Maybe it should be, but such a caveat is clearly not written into American foreign policy.

With Assiri's announcement that oil would serve as the great magnet for American resolve, the Arabs seemed to accept the soldier's presence and tensions lessened, slightly. Seizing upon the opportunity Assiri attempted to further lessen the animosity being displayed by the Arabs, announcing to all present why those he had brought, himself included, smelled so bad.

With the telling of the story Dash could physically detect the tension being reduced in the room. The Arabs began laughing as Assiri described Blackburn's reaction to the smell and McNabb's bravery when he had actually tasted the manure to confirm its existence. Assiri mentioned that the General, who quietly chuckled with the others, had grown up with such conditions and that it had reminded him of his childhood.

Dash noticed that Assiri never mentioned that the Ayatollah had also experienced the same fate with the sheep manure. Instead he spoke in general terms and carefully avoided mentioning the Ayatollah by name. He was still highly pissed off about it and Assiri knew it. So did Blackburn, and he quietly whispered to Dash, "Look at that tight assed prick Cyclops. You couldn't drive a ten penny nail up his ass with a twenty pound sledgehammer."

Now that Assiri had captured the assembled Arabs attention he began doling out stacks of money like a blackjack dealer doles out playing cards. What little Dash could decipher from the Marsh Arabs excited jabbering was that all six of them had a multitude of men available but they needed cash to entice them to brave the dangers ahead. Dash and Blackburn watched Assiri and the two Caucasians pass out five million dollars in Uncle Sam greenbacks before the blue light special came to an end with Assiri promising that more money would be available if it were needed.

"What are the odds that more will be needed?" Dash thought as he watched the now departing Arabs filing from the room with Assiri shouting instructions for them to assemble their men and wait for his orders of when and where to begin their attacks.

As the last Marsh Arab departed the room with Assiri following him out the door to continue their conversation outside, Dash turned his attention to the Europeans now standing in the rear of the room, approaching them and offering his hand.

***

"Hello, I'm Major Tom Dash, U.S. Army."

"Yes Sir, we have been waiting to meet you," said the taller of the two, taking Dash's hand and shaking it vigorously. "My name is Larry and this is Mike. We heard that there would be four other Americans with Moe."

"You must be First Sergeant Blackburn," Larry said as Blackburn moved up beside Dash. "It is a pleasure to finally meet you two," he continued as he shook Blackburn's extended hand.

Mike did likewise and as the four of them stood there Blackburn asked, "What do you mean, finally?"

Dash was taken aback. Not just because the two were obviously Americans themselves, but that they knew their names and apparently worked for the Agency. Although it hadn't been mentioned yet, in previous encounters with people who introduced themselves by using only their first name, and a false one at that, they had always been CIA. Larry and Mike were no exception. This was why they had access to so much money and why Assiri had asked them to the farmhouse. More to the point however, the two evidently knew enough about the mission to get them all killed should either one of them fall into enemy hands, a fact that both Dash and Blackburn were quick to pick up on.

"We heard through the grapevine that there would be some dune buggy racers with Assiri and since he had told us about his previous exploits with you two, we just assumed that it would be you," Larry said with a smile.

"Obviously you have us at a disadvantage. You seem to know who we are but how did you two get whickered into all of this?" asked Blackburn.

He knew it would be a waste of his time to ask the two men any direct questions. They would either refuse to answer or lie about it if they did answer. His general questions always left maneuver room for them to concoct a believable story. Like Dash, Blackburn had dealt with his share of "spooks" before; he hadn't been very impressed by them. In his military mind they ranked slightly above politicians, the lowest backstabbing scum on earth.

In his previous dealings with either the CIA or FBI Dash had usually found the agents to be very parochial and enamored with their own abilities. Briefly recalling his last confrontation when four FBI agents had come to his office in the Ministry of Defense and Aviation building while he was TDY (temporary duty) serving as the ARCENT G-5 in Saudi Arabia. They were investigating a recent bombing that had destroyed the OPM-SANG headquarters in Riyadh, killing seven Americans and wounding many others. The agents had wanted Dash to accompany them, serving as translator since none of the four spoke any Arabic, as they knocked on doors and asked questions of Saudi civilians living near the destroyed OPM-SANG complex. Dash asked them if they had cleared this with the Saudi Intelligence Chief, Prince Turki bin Al-Faisal, since the Saudi police and security personnel had already done, several times, what the FBI was now planning on doing once again.

With the usual air of pomposity the senior FBI agent told Dash that it would be best if the Saudis were not informed of their efforts. The agents then justified their secrecy by claiming that the Saudi intelligence apparatus, as well as Prince Turki himself, couldn't be trusted. Shaking his head in disbelief Dash asked the agents what the questioning would concern, pretending not to know. The senior agent present told him that he wasn't at liberty to discuss it.

"Wait a minute," Dash said. "You want me to go with you to ask questions of Saudis, translate their answers, and you won't tell me what this is about?" As an addendum asking, "Since none of your agents speak Arabic how will you know if the questions I am asking are the ones you want me to ask? Furthermore, how will you know if I am giving you an accurate interpretation of the response?"

The senior agent, failing to note the tone of condescension in Dash's voice caused by having been told that he too could not be trusted, answered in all sincerity, "Hey, we're all American's here. There is no reason to believe that we can't work together on this thing."

Dash refused to do the agents' bidding, choosing instead to report their intended efforts to the American ambassador who quickly put a stop to such nonsense. To Dash, Larry and Mike were simply caricatures of the inept FBI agents.

"We were in Basra posing as French oil men when Saddam launched his invasion," continued Larry in answer to Blackburn's question. "We immediately went to ground and contacted the embassy in Kuwait before it fell to the Iraqis. The defense attaché there contacted my station chief in Riyadh, relayed the message to meet with Moe tonight and to bring plenty of cash. The rest you saw."

"How did you come up with this kind of cash on such short notice?" Queried Dash. "And how did you get to this meeting site? I didn't see any vehicles parked nearby."

"I'm not at liberty to answer those questions, Major. They are on a need to know basis and you simply don't need to know," Larry smiled. "Don't be concerned about it though. I can tell you that it was no surprise when Saddam invaded Kuwait. Christ, they had been massing troops on the border for several weeks before they finally invaded."

"Listen, damn it," Dash replied in a tone that left no doubt that he had heard this type of circumspect bullshit before. "When people I don't even know are here on the ground possessing intelligence that can get my entire team killed, then I am very concerned about it. No one has mentioned to me that you two would be here tonight and I do not like surprises like this. What am I supposed to do if one of you gets caught and I don't find out about it until it's too late?"

"We don't intend to get caught, Major," the little one, Mike, shot back.

"No one ever does," replied Blackburn. "But the Major is absolutely right. You two know all about us, yet we don't have a string on you. If you're caught, you will talk. And you know too damn much about us already."

"We are not going to talk," Larry said defensively. "Besides, even if the Iraqi's.."

"That response alone tells me that you will talk," Blackburn fired back. "This isn't a game we're playing, and neither are the Iraqis. How many times have you done this before?"

"I've been around," Mike answered defensively. "Besides, if I am caught…"

"How do you know Moe?" interrupted Blackburn, refusing to listen to any more of their macho bullshit.

"That really isn't important now is it First Sergeant?" replied Mike.

This attitude was what both Dash and Blackburn disliked about working with agents. They always played a little game of one-upmanship; discretely letting you know that they had information you weren't privy to. Like little children singing, "I know something you don't know." Such an attitude told the soldiers all that they needed to know about the agents; they wouldn't trust either one of the bastards.

The soldiers knew that both the FBI and the CIA rated their agents statistically. The more successful they were in compiling impressive statistics, the greater were the rewards. As a result, ambitious agents were attracted to fields like computer crimes, counterfeiting, blackmail, and extortion; or other areas where an agent could quickly rack up impressive statistics. Conversely, in the world of counterterrorism and clandestine service, a field agent could work for years and never be able to show any statistical success by compiling arrests or amassing a library of classified publications. Especially a CIA field agent who, in order to be effective against terrorism, essentially had to become a terrorist themselves in order to break into their operational planning cycle. Consequently, because of rampant careerism in both the CIA and the FBI counterterrorism was the dumping grounds for burnt out agents and newbies. People at the end of, or the beginning of their careers. Both men could tell by talking to them that Larry and Mike were two agents who had long ago suffered career burn out.

"It may not be important to you," hissed Blackburn. "But if I didn't want to hear the answer, I wouldn't have asked the goddamn question!" He then took a threatening step in Mike's direction.

"Hold on, First Sergeant," Larry interrupted, stepping between Blackburn and the rapidly backpedaling Mike. "We've done some work with Assiri before. That's all I'm going to say about it. The rest has to come from Assiri himself."

"Fair enough," replied Dash. "But at least tell me what the long range plan is from America's perspective. Killing Saddam is one thing, replacing him will be something else again. Who does President Bush have in mind for replacing Saddam and the Ba'athists in the Sunni triangle around Baghdad? Where is that man or those people right now? How do Iran, Jordan, Syria, and Turkey feel about this? I have to assume that something as vaunted as the American CIA isn't just making up things as it goes."

"Well," stammered Larry. "That's the kind of information I'm just not privy to. It is well above my pay grade. The two of us received orders to meet Assiri here to assist him in his efforts to get the Marsh Arabs to overthrow Saddam. What comes next I haven't a clue. And that's the honest to God truth."

"What happens if your efforts fail?" asked Blackburn.

"Then we are all dead men," answered Larry.

"Or at least the Marsh Arabs will be," winked Mike.

Stunned and frustrated, Dash simply stared in disbelief at the two operatives and slowly shook his head.

"I would like to stay here and discuss all that is wrong with your vision from a strategic point of view, but I don't have the luxury of having that kind of time tonight. I am afraid that we've got to pull pitch ," Dash said.

Then, turning to Blackburn he said, "Top, we've only got three hours of darkness left. Find Moe and tell him we will leave in ten minutes."

"Yes Sir," responded the First Sergeant. "And you two make damn sure that you don't get caught!" Blackburn said, thumping his index finger in Larry's chest.

CHAPTER 11

The return trip from Safwan was uneventful. A good thing because Dash's mind had been elsewhere during the entire trip.

The two-hour drive had given him the opportunity to run through the many incongruous variables and players that he had observed at the farmhouse. As he reviewed what he had observed things began to appear totally out of concert with what he felt to be the realities of the Middle East. Beginning with his own personal belief that once these disparate groups of resistance fighters had successfully tapped into U.S. and Saudi coffers there would be a never-ending request for money, with few lasting results. Such a technique of bribes always carried with it the risk of unbridled greed being a poor substitute for loyalty of purpose. To his knowledge, despite the enormous sums of money that had passed through CIA hands in Southeast Asia, the agency had never gotten all that it had paid for. To put this in perspective, the CIA's refusal to believe that America was losing in Vietnam could only be matched by their later surprise when the agency, despite many thousands of "spies" being on their payroll, failed to predict the collapse of the Soviet Union.

As a professional soldier Dash knew that loyalty came from the heart, not from the pocketbook. Although anyone will take money, a true willingness to risk physical injury is not something that can easily be bought and sold. Though it can be reasonably argued that the "quick fix" of throwing money at it is a problem solving approach that still has many die-hard adherents in the CIA, if not in American culture itself.

Dash remembered a point that he had argued while in graduate school working on his Master of Science degree in International Relations. The class was a joint class being taken by MBA students as well as political science students. The class dealt with the business, economic, and developmental aspects of third world development. Based upon previous discussions the two had enjoyed, the professor asked Dash that if only one could be chosen, in his opinion, would national pride or riches be most important to poor people in developing nations. Dash, without hesitation, answered that national pride was more important than money in such countries, mentioning that he had personally observed this phenomenon first hand in his travels around the globe.

Dash firmly believed that the size of people's bank accounts could never be a substitute for either self-respect or national pride. Emphasizing his point by stating that the government of North Vietnam could have made billions by striking a financial arrangement with the United States rather than confronting it on the field of battle. Yet the North Vietnamese had chosen nationalism along with the personal precepts of duty, honor, and country over riches. Other countries like Cuba, Libya and North Korea could succumb to a natural desire for riches and feed from the American federal treasury any time they so chose. Yet all three remain as virulently anti-American today as they ever were in the past. Like all good teachers, rather than invoking his own opinions the professor asked the students to agree or disagree with Dash's comments.

The MBA students were naturally aghast at what they were hearing and vociferously argued that money was more important than national pride. In their world, a world where the pursuit of profit is both a means as well as an end unto itself, they simply refused to believe that the American dollar could not be used as a salve for ailments worldwide. The fact that history is replete with examples of where this had been tried and failed to work was simply disregarded by them as relics of the past. In their world, the modern world where free trade zones and cheap labor were seen as substitutes for national pride, it would work if for no other reason than their generation was so much "smarter and prettier" than all of those preceding it. The MBA students defended their position by stating that the problem in countries like Cuba and North Korea was the government, not the people. "If the impediments of government could be removed," they unanimously agreed, "the people living there would welcome capitalism." Usually ending their rebuttal with, "the world has changed and all those refusing to believe in the power of money need to change with it."

Dash then trumped their statement with an example a little closer to home. "If you truly believe the desire for wealth is a common denominator for all people, then explain why Native American Indians choose to shun what is obviously a life of greater financial opportunity off the reservation by knowingly and willingly staying on the reservation?" To no one's surprise, none of the MBA students ever had a satisfactory response to this question. None of them ever understood the concept that remaining Red — even if that means limited opportunity — would always be more important to an Indian than being seen by other tribal members as having turned White. Native Americans, like people around the globe, are not opposed to wealth; they just want it to be their wealth.

What Dash had witnessed tonight at the farmhouse told him that this MBA mentality still dominated the American political psyche. As a country America had still not come to grips with the fact that everything and everyone could not simply be bought and sold by the highest bidder. America steadfastly refuses to believe that such a tactic is more a matter of short term political expediency than it is of long-term nation building, a concept that must come from the heart, not the bank, if it is to have any chance at being successful.

In Iraq, no amount of money would be enticement enough to hold such a grouping of tribal fighters together if they should be fortunate enough to actually kill Saddam. In the ensuing power vacuum following Saddam's death there would be a rush for control of the country's oil wealth reminiscent of the California gold rush of 1849, but with much more violence accompanying it.

Saddam's death would appear as a loss of power by the ruling Ba'ath party. Whether real or perceived, a loss of power would immediately be answered by the Kurds seeking to reestablish their ancient country of Kurdistan in northern Iraq, a possibility that Turkey would vehemently oppose with its formidable military. Simultaneously the Iranian backed Shi'ites, possibly the Iranian military as well, would fight for control of Southern Iraq, which the Americans and Saudis would oppose. In the West Jordan and Syria, along with remnants of the Ba'ath party would have to safeguard their own access to oil from the oilfields and pipelines in central Iraq. No Middle Eastern nation would be immune from the events that would transpire in an unstable Iraq. Implying that the potential for a full-scale Mid-East war was the most likely scenario for an Iraq without a strong centralized government, even if that government was a tyrannical dictatorship consisting of criminals and murders. The only other alternative to civil and regional war erupting with Saddam's death was for America to occupy Iraq to keep the wolves at bay, a position that the Bush administration was reluctant to take.

As Dash ran these dismal possibilities through his mind, he couldn't help but feel a slight pang of sympathy for the State Department foreign policy wonks working inside the Washington D.C. beltway. As a part of his Special Operations training Dash's class had spent a month at the State Department reviewing U.S. policy options and participating in the development of future policy proposals with the many young people working there. Many were no more than two years out of graduate school. Most of the analysts were professionals; dedicated to doing the best job they could in the uncertain, confusing world of international relations. Yet there were some analysts who were titled, pampered, mostly Ivy League men and women, who had clashed with the ethics of loyalty and sacrifice valued by the soldiers. These analysts were the ones who would adamantly deny that they had achieved their station in life by virtue of name and wealth rather than by the sweat of their brow. Yet everyone who met them immediately knew that they had earned their position the old fashioned way — with Daddy's checkbook. Unfortunately, too many of them ultimately ended up in positions of power, seeing the world as their own personal oyster to be devoured whenever the time was right.

For all these reasons as well as for others to come, in his opinion, what Assiri was trying to accomplish by working with the CIA — who hopefully had consulted with the State Department — simply would not bear fruit. The American body politic does not like uncertainty, nor does Wall Street. If Larry was telling the truth, that no one had the answer for what comes next following Saddam's removal from power, then there was too much uncertainty for the Bush administration to decapitate the Ba'ath party by removing Saddam.

The next presidential election was slightly more than one year away. Meaning that the Bush administration would not have enough time to implement a military coup with General Talabani, nor, given America's recent history with Iranian fundamentalists, would it want a successful political/civil uprising spearheaded by the Ayatollah Sistani coming to power.

Dash now knew that General Talabani's anger was a personal matter, understandable, but still a matter concerning few people. The more Dash thought about it the more clearly he could see flaws in promoting Talabani as the future for Iraq. First, Talabani would need to recruit several thousand more Iraqis to accomplish an actual coup, and he did not appear to be trying to do that. Besides, Talabani's focus was on killing Saddam and Udai, as a long standing member himself he had no vision of destroying the Ba'ath party. Second, the General did not display that burning desire to rule that always surfaced in the personality of other military officers contemplating a coup. He was no egomaniac with a burning desire for power. He was just a father with a hole in his heart, hoping to heal the wound by exacting vengeance on his daughter's killers.

Conversely, the Ayatollah Sistani, as a religious personage known to many, had the popular support for a civil uprising. But America would not support the creation of another radical theocracy next door to Iran. Such a thing would be political suicide for any western democracy to support. It would be hung like an Albatross around their political necks in the upcoming presidential elections. Even the Saudi Royal family would not welcome an additional, aggressive Shi'ite theocracy on their northern border. *"No,"* Dash thought, *"Moe is too smart to sign onto such an amateurish mission. Then again, maybe he knows much more than Larry and Mike. Maybe the Saudis have planned this thing all the way through. Maybe they have identified a reward for their country that is worth all of these risks they are willing to take."* Obviously they were being proactive for a reason, an observation that Dash was curious about. As was Blackburn, who shared his doubts.

The only way to know for sure was to ask him. Which is exactly what he and Blackburn did when Assiri returned from having delivered General Talabani safely to his divisional headquarters.

***

When Dash heard Moe's Land Rover pull into the assembly area later that day, he and Blackburn stepped outside the truck containing the sand table mock-up and waited for their friend to approach.

"Moe," Dash called out, "May we have a word with you?"

Assiri had expected this moment. Having lived and worked with American soldiers he knew that they always asked questions, refusing to comply with the common stereotype of soldiers being mindless robots doing simply as they were told. He knew that, sooner or later, he would have to explain to them not only the methodology of this mission, but also the philosophic and strategic reasoning behind it. Something he would never be required to explain to his own troops, who had grown up in a culture accepting the decisions of leaders as being the natural order of things. The Saudi culture of entitlement and stratification is radically different from the individual responsibility emphasized in American culture. In most Arab cultures there exists an almost starstruck worshipping of royalty and privilege while in American culture there is an obsession with challenging the status quo by perpetually asking, "Why?" of our elected leaders. The average American does not consider a President to be royalty. Only those who work for him do that. Instead, those Americans with such an inclination withhold their starstruck mentality for rock stars, movie stars, athletes or other people who earn their position in life through personal effort and God-given talent. The only thing that separates an American politician from the average man-on-the-street is that he or she got elected. Hardly any reason to elevate their stature since they now work for the average man-on-the-street and can be fired by them at their discretion.

When he had first visited an American military post, Assiri had been shocked to see privates questioning the orders of their superiors. Something that he had not expected, nor had he been trained to expect. In most militaries, including his own, challenging authority was not something that was routinely done. But in the American military he found it to be a fact that the lowest ranking individual will openly challenge both the credibility and the orders of the President of the United States, the highest ranking individual, without so much hesitation as the blinking of an eye. Something no Saudi soldier would dare do in public to the King.

The questioning of decisions was a character trait that he both admired and feared. He admired the willingness of each American soldier to think and accept responsibility for him or herself, yet he retained a native, inborn fear because challenging authority in most countries meant chaos and civil war as each group fought for control. Something America had experienced during its own civil war, but something the nation had been able to control since, at least inside its own borders.

This habitual questioning of authority by Americans was a trait that often led other cultures and countries to erroneously believe that America was incapable of taking decisive action. Assiri had often participated in discussions with Arab friends wherein Americans had been likened to a group of school girls squabbling over the latest in fashion, fighting amongst themselves with neither logic nor purpose, leaving them vulnerable to the whims of passion at the expense of calculated reason. It is a common yet inaccurate stereotype of Americans often reinforced by the American media's seemingly divisive reporting. Ironically a role most informed Americans demand the media perform. By democratic design, the media is not supposed to be co-opted by either the left or the right, but to simply point out to the public the differences between the two sides so informed choices could be made by them. Unfortunately, for people living in a repressive society, this role played by the media is misunderstood. The media is often seen by them as the antagonist to government, leaving people living in repressive countries to wonder who is really in charge of America. People in countries like Iraq and North Korea can not even imagine a newspaper being openly critical of leaders. It is something that simply does not happen in their country, making an American President appear weak and uncertain to them. But Assiri knew better, having lived for several years in America. He knew full well that all of the family squabbling masked a fierce desire on the part of Americans to both understand and shape the environment surrounding them, allowing them to take personal control of their own destiny, rather than allowing destiny to control them. Assiri felt that this attitude stemmed from the American belief in equality, a concept taught to schoolchildren in public schools at the earliest of age, and that because of their strong belief in equality, no American ever felt inferior to another human being, regardless of that persons rank or title. Assiri knew that despite America's history of racism that organizations like the NAACP and programs like affirmative action had been created to erase feelings of inferiority among the black population. How well it had or had not worked was not really the issue in his mind, the fact that they existed told him that every American is expected to consider themselves the equal of any other and to never accept decisions simply because someone supposedly in charge told them to. As a result, he was now uncomfortably aware that neither Dash nor Blackburn could simply be ignored when they felt a need to ask a question.

In preparation Assiri had taken his time at Talabani's headquarters, spending most of the afternoon there before returning to the assembly area, collecting his thoughts for just such an occasion. He dreaded having to confront his friends questions with what he knew would have to be cryptic responses, making him sound like Larry and Mike. As fellow soldiers sharing the dangers with him he felt they deserved better than this. The Americans were his comrades in arms; they had a right to know the overall plan. As he slowly drove from Talabani's headquarters, he made up his mind that, within reason, he was prepared to answer their questions as honestly as possible. Within Saudi reason.

Moe took the initiative and began the conversation by addressing their questions before either Dash or Blackburn asked them. A reaction that slightly surprised his audience because both Dash and Blackburn had been taught that volunteering information without first being asked for it often meant that there was something the person volunteering the information was trying very hard to avoid having to talk about.

"I apologize for springing the CIA operatives on you like that," Assiri began. "I would have told you about them sooner but I wasn't sure that they were going to make the meeting. I know that this is not a good excuse, loose ends can get us all killed, but I didn't want to burden you with things beyond your control. Neither you nor they will voluntarily surrender to the operational control of the other, so it wouldn't have made any difference anyway. For the time being, I am in operational control of your team as well as the CIA operatives. That is simply the way it has to be for now."

Dash and Blackburn nodded their head in agreement without saying a word. It was obvious to them that Assiri was nervous and uncomfortable with having to explain his actions. The Americans knew that Assiri's discomfort was the result of one of two reasons, either because he was inexperienced with having to explain his actions to others, or because he was lying through his teeth.

The two Americans had conducted enough interrogations, even if this wasn't really an interrogation, to know that when someone starts volunteering information without having first been asked for it the best thing to do was to keep their own mouth shut and let them talk. It was a technique that had often left them pleasantly surprised when people provided detailed responses to questions that they weren't yet knowledgeable enough to even think of asking. This had usually occurred when the respondent believed that their interrogators knew more than they actually did, hoping that their answers would show how open and honest they were being. It was also a way for them to stall for time, wishing to avoid having to answer questions that they did not want to be asked. Or, such forthcoming "honesty" happened when the respondent was delivering a well thought out lie in the hope that he or she could lead the listeners down a false but believable path. Where Assiri fit along this spectrum, they weren't yet sure. Regardless, they had him right where they wanted him, speaking quickly and defensively, their own desire to ask questions could wait until after he finished.

"Also," continued Assiri, "I overheard part of your discussion with the operatives regarding the end state we are trying to achieve by assassinating Saddam and disassembling, or at least reorganizing the Ba'ath party. I can only tell you that this is an objective my country wants to achieve. The operatives probably don't know what the final end state is projected to be. Your government simply wants Saddam's forces to withdraw from Kuwait. Whether Saddam himself remains in power is really not a concern for them. At least this is what your politicians are saying publicly. Though I suspect that they would not be disappointed if he were killed."

Assiri briefly paused, expecting the American's to respond with questions of their own. But both stood silently, staring directly into his eyes, increasing his anxiety and forcing him to continue with his recitation.

"However," he continued, "the Saudi royal family believes that if Saddam remains in power he and his regime will become such an obsession with the Bush administration and the American Congress that they will refuse to remove American troops from Saudi soil as long as he remains in power. To prevent this from happening my government very much wants Saddam's regime destroyed. As you know, stationing ground troops in the Gulf has long been a foreign policy objective of your Departments of State and Defense. Up to now, the people most opposed to doing this has been the American public, seeing it as putting its soldiers in a den of terrorist snakes where it will only be when, not if, they are bitten. Using the invasion of Kuwait as a pretext for doing so your electorate feels that the American public will now readily agree with a policy of coalition troops, all of whom will be American, British and French, remaining in Saudi Arabia for an indeterminate amount of time. This policy will essentially force the Saudi government to agree with being occupied; requiring them to convince the Saudi citizenry that Saddam will invade as soon as they leave. This may or may not be the case, but Saudi Arabia's military is in no position to forcibly eject an Iraqi army from its soil, despite the fact that Saudis are asked to participate in and fund our rather expensive military. Now that it is time to see what they have been paying for there is little to show to them, having to hire westerners to stay and protect us." He again paused, casting a fleeting glance at the Americans, awaiting their cross-examination. But none came. They simply continued to look at him with well-trained blank expressions on their faces, leaving him feeling uncomfortable and keeping him talking.

"For regional, political, cultural, and religious reasons, a western army occupying Saudi Arabia is simply an unacceptable option for the Kingdom to openly agree with. Our biggest fear is that the presence of American troops on Saudi soil will incite a fundamentalist revolt throughout the entire Middle East. The focal point of that revolt will be my own country. From my personal point of view it would be much better to overthrow Saddam and remove the one compelling reason America has for occupying Saudi Arabia. With him gone, it would be very difficult for the United States to convince the UN Security Council that a military occupation of Saudi Arabia is necessary. They would view it simply as a desire for America to control the oil, and every other nation in the world would object to it."

Pausing briefly to collect his thoughts, being swept away by his own emotions, no longer waiting for a response, Assiri continued. "Killing Saddam is a scenario that would be best for all of us in fact. As you already know, there is a growing resentment against the Royal Family and their overseeing of the declining wealth of the Kingdom. These political differences are something that will have to be worked out by the Saudis with no outside interference."

He nervously shifted his weight from side to side, obviously deep in thought.

"The perception of having western infidels as a palace guard to help King Fahd retain power will not go over well with any Arabs, especially those who achieved a certain degree of autonomous pride by having kicked the Russians out of Afghanistan. These people, the Mujahadeen, are too proud to be seen as western "lap dogs" and they will fight against what will appear to them to be an occupation. Even if that occupation is being done ostensibly for the right reason, to protect Saudi Arabia from an Iraqi invasion. These Arab fighters firmly believe that it is their duty, not America's, to protect Islam from its enemies, foreign and domestic."

"The term "lap dogs" was one Dash had heard many times before. And each time he had heard it people with an extreme dislike of America's aggressive foreign policies had used it. People like the Mujahadeen. In an attempt to keep Assiri with the same vein of thought that caused him to use this term, Dash softly said, "but the world is not forcing its will on the Saudi government."

"Try to see this through Saudi eyes, my friend." Assiri quickly responded, pointing at the ground beneath his feet. "As we stand here today Saudi Arabia is being invaded by a coalition army that will exceed one half million foreign troops. The western powers will all say that it is requested military assistance, not an invasion, but for the Mujahadeen who fought the Russians the results will be very much the same thing. All of you will be viewed as infidel invaders, especially since Saudi Arabia has not done anything deserving of a military invasion. The Kingdom never attacked anyone and she is not a regional threat to any of her neighbors. Yet she and Kuwait are the only two countries that have already lost their autonomy to a foreign army. This is an indefensible position for the Royals to attempt to convince the Saudi citizens to accept. Billions of dollars have been spent buying equipment in order to protect ourselves and now that it is time to do it, we have to tell our people that it cannot be done without outside help."

"But…," began Blackburn.

"Please! Let me finish!" interrupted Assiri, holding his index finger to his lips as if he were shushing a child.

Now they had him. His emotions had completely taken over and opinions were coming out of him in a rapid-fire rate like bullets fired from a machinegun.

"Yes, Sir!" smiled Blackburn. "Please continue."

"If this occupation of the Kingdom is viewed by the Mujahadeen as being anything more than a temporary blip on the radar screen of life, it will ignite a fire in the Muslim world that will take generations to extinguish. I want to make sure that this fire doesn't erupt by killing Saddam Hussein, then allow the Arab League and the United Nations to assume control of Iraq through an interim government to negotiate a complete withdrawal of Iraqi troops from Kuwait and all foreign troops from Saudi Arabia."

As an afterthought he quickly added, "You also know that I am one of those Arabs who fought in Afghanistan. I know that I am speaking for a large number of Muslims when I say these things, even if I am speaking only for myself right now. We want our country back." Taking a deep breath and exhaling loudly, Assiri looked as if a huge weight had been removed from his shoulders. He looked at the Americans, asking expectantly, "Does this help to explain my actions?"

"Damn," Dash thought. *"You were really on a roll. Don't stop now!"* Instead of answering the question, in hopes of keeping him talking without limiting him by questions, Dash pointedly challenged Assiri's beliefs by caustically replying, "Thanks for the history lesson. Do you really believe everything you just said or are you going political on me and just saying whatever happens to pop into your head?"

"Yeah, Moe," Blackburn chimed in, following the same tact as Dash. "You're a soldier, not a politician. Stay in your own lane and leave the politics of this to all of those milquetoasts that put on a tie or a dress when they go to work."

The fiery ex-Mujahadeen soldier pounced on the challenge like a cat pouncing on a mouse. Just like they hoped he would.

In a soulful tirade Assiri exploded in protest. "Don't you understand that in this part of the world it is not the milquetoast politicians representing their constituents who determine policy? There are no democracies in the Middle East! These countries are all run by a ruling elite that may or may not reflect the beliefs of their country-men. Most of them don't; they could care less what the people they govern think about them. Unlike your political system, which is more of a popularity contest every four years, it certainly isn't a priority for Arab rulers to have to be liked by the public they lord over. The problems we have in the Middle East are Muslim problems, and it is best to leave the solutions to those problems with us. Islamic beliefs guide us, not American foreign policies. What we determine to be solutions may or may not be of benefit to non-Muslims, but it will be of benefit to Islam."

"You know," he continued in a manner too well thought out for it to have been spontaneous improvisation. It was obvious that he had spent many hours thinking about this subject before. "If we were to have democratic elections today, throughout the region, America would not welcome the results. Pro-western rulers would most likely be voted out of office. But, since there are no presidential elections every four years, accountability for their actions is the last thing Middle Eastern leaders are concerned with. Their decisions are always centered on maintaining power, by whatever means is necessary. This is true in your country as well but with your multi-party political system it is much harder for deceitful leaders to remain hidden from public scrutiny. Your politicians keep tattling on one another, and your inquisitive media makes its living by making sure that they continue to do so. If they stop tattling then that same often overzealous media will create its own version of the truth, just to keep the heat on your elected leaders."

Then the less thoughtful, fiery Mujahadeen within him reappeared as his emotions quickly vacillated between rehearsed reason and spontaneous emotion.

"Do you know what Arabs call leaders whom they dislike?" he fumed. "Americans! But it is always said behind their backs because here in the Middle East open, honest political dissent is kept out of the public rhetoric, always subject to censorship by either your government or mine. Except for the all too frequent bombings, an uninformed person might actually believe that all Arabs live in peace and harmony, blissfully reading from the Koran, lighting candles, and merrily singing 'Koom By Ya' to one another."

Then, with the telltale glimmering eyes of a man who fervently believes in what he is saying, Assiri continued venting. "But, I personally know from having lived several years in your country that most Americans actually believe Arabs to be a bunch of crazy bastards who would rather die in an explosion of self immolation than enter the 21st century. Regrettably, as a Saudi Arab myself, I can understand how westerners might form such an opinion, mistaken though it is."

Assiri paused in his political litany to the Americans, drew a deep breath, composed himself then reflectively continued, but in a much calmer voice. As the words fell from his mouth, it was immediately obvious to both Dash and Blackburn that this was not something that he had intended to share with them; a personal moment from his own life.

"You know," he began, "I have an uncle who I have enjoyed having many conversations with regarding this very matter. He also believes that it is better to die a true believer in Islam than to succumb to the greed of modernity that places a greater importance on the creations of man than those created by God. For him, there can be no acceptable blending of the past with the present without first making the present more closely resemble the past. And there are many more Muslims than just my uncle who feel this way. He has a large and growing group of followers in the Islamic world. It is not so much the material progress of modernization that they object to, after all, they enjoy money and the creature comforts it brings with it as much as anyone else does. It is the accompanying spiritual decline of mankind — often referred to as western decadence — that seems to go with the pursuit of wealth that they so oppose."

As he spoke his eyes began to tear, as if he were recalling moments of sadness.

"They have a valid argument, you know, whether you agree with it or not. A world economy based on conspicuous consumption requires sacrifices to be made that some people simply do not want to make. But the requirement to make these sacrifices is being forced upon them daily with the encroachment of modernity in their ancient world; a world where God, community, and family are still more important than material things. A world being sacrificed at the altar of modernity where American and European businesses dominate many local economies, having a negative impact on the regional belief systems which are vastly different in scope than the western belief that money can buy peace of mind right along with family pride."

Then came what Dash and Blackburn had not expected from a man with Assiri's education and experience, the anti-American vitriol that so captures the emotions of the Middle East.

"In your country for instance, newborn babies are placed in day care centers with perfect strangers so that the mother can return to work as quickly as possible. After all, time is money. The mother has been taught to mistakenly believe that this money can compensate for the time she will miss with her own children, nurturing and educating them with what she and her husband believe to be important. Instead, she places them with people who may be radically different than her family, allowing complete strangers to raise her children. These strangers often teach her children their first formative lessons on life by allowing them to watch *Big Bird* on *Sesame Street* television, along with all of the 'buy-me-now' commercial advertising accompanying such shows. Later, when these children become teenagers, they are allowed to entertain themselves with violent video games where people kill one another. And all of this is viewed as being normal behavior in America!"

Dash carefully looked into Assiri's eyes as he spoke, noticing that they seemed distant, lost in a world far away. But a world he had obviously visited many times before, a world of absolution and denial. A world occupied by well over half of the people on this globe.

"Divorce often follows," he ranted, continuing with his sermon. "Parents point accusatory fingers at each other when their son or daughter spends far more money than they think they should, or when the children end up on drugs or in jail. The parents argue against each other defensively in court that it was the other parent's fault that the kids ended up this way; it couldn't possibly be a fault of their own making. Neither realizes before it is too late that all of the additional money made working the long hours is the root cause of many of the problems and they don't even get to keep it. All of the money ends up in a lawyer's pocket. The parents have gained nothing, yet they have lost a great deal."

He was really on a roll now, animating with his arms as if he were trying to take flight, waving them about as if to help emphasize all of the important points he was making.

"At the other end of life's spectrum in America," he preached, "grandfathers, grandmothers, mothers and fathers approaching the end of their lives are placed in retirement homes where, like the newborn's first days, their last days are spent in the company of strangers. The people who should care the most for them are simply to busy making money to properly care for them. Of course the extra money they are making now goes toward paying someone else to take care of their ailing family member. This self-destructive behavior is done for one reason and one reason only, the pursuit of the almighty dollar. Yet the real irony of money is that people seek wealth so more of what isn't actually needed can be purchased while the real meaning of wealth, the family, the community, the tribal network, the belief that a man should worship God more than wealth, is ignored."

Then he brought his sermon full circle by introducing other, simpler cultures and emphasizing the beauty of them while still denigrating American culture, as if pointing out to the Americans that there is another way to live.

"Any Arab man, or Asian man for that matter, would be dishonored in admitting that he is treating his family members in such a manner. Yet in the West such selfish behavior is viewed as progress. America's expectation that other peoples and cultures should adopt such materialistic lunacy so that they too might one day have two cars in their garages does not have many adherents in the Middle East. For Muslims, people believing that the past is just as important as the future, such ideas do not make the future look to be all that promising. In fact, for the true believers in Islam, it makes the future appear to be almost frightening. I mean, how much money and how many things is enough? Is it really possible to ever have it all? Are you even supposed to? We all know that if having ten dollars in our pocket makes us happy, having one hundred dollars won't necessarily make us ten times happier. We instinctively know that there is a point of diminishing return with money yet we behave as if there isn't, always wanting more of it in the pursuit of something we can't even describe."

"Greed is like drug addiction," he fumed. "Nothing seems to matter except for the next fix, the ultimate high, the lifestyle of the rich and the famous. Yet if the world's children are raised to believe that money can buy happiness, while at the same time the vast majority of them will never have all the money they want, then the vast majority of young people will never be happy. This would seem to be a fact that any sane person would seek to avoid, not encourage. And if personal freedom is what we want from wealth, then purchasing material things actually takes our freedoms away because we are left with having to work in order to pay for them.

People are actually more free with less than with more, yet it is the rare person who can determine where necessity ends and wants begin."

"No," he surmised, "I fear that this blind pursuit of profit and its encouraged squandering is a self-defeating philosophy that will one day have dire consequences for all of us."

Assiri paused, as if he were suddenly aware that his vulnerabilities were showing, wishing that he could stop talking. But he was at fever pitch and couldn't refrain from continuing with his lecture to an attentive audience of non-believers. All he would have needed to make his sermon even more convincing would have been a pulpit.

"Now, couple my uncle's beliefs with that of the widely held Muslim belief, as written on the flag of Saudi Arabia, 'there is no God but God and Mohammed was his messenger', and you have the recipe for conflict. Anything conflicting with this belief is an affront to both God and Islam. The American belief that a human being can find the same sense of perfection and self-satisfaction with money as they can with God is an affront to all religions, or at least it should be."

"What my uncle has done," he proudly proclaimed, "is take his anti-western, anti-capitalist sentiments and co-mingled them with the Koran, making anything modern appear to be in conflict with God's true desires. Whether he is right in doing this only God Himself can know, but for the true believers, any affront to God, as explained in the Koran, will simply not be tolerated. It goes without saying that Saudi Arabia is the home of the true believers. Edicts and fatwahs emanating from the Kingdom resonate loudly throughout the Muslim world. I fear that having American troops here will serve no real purpose but to light the fuse connected to the powder keg of emotions that is the Middle East."

As Assiri continued speaking, Dash tuned out his words; he had already heard similar versions of this same speech many times before. Instead he concentrated on running through his mind a list of known Islamic fundamentalists with the name of Assiri and kept coming up with a blank. Yet he had clearly heard Moe say that he had an uncle who had a large and growing following of true believers.

The always-astute Blackburn, on the other hand, never skipped a beat and asked, during a brief pause in the lecture, "Moe, what was your mother's family name?"

"Al-Laden." He answered. "Her father was a Yemeni named Mohamed Avad bin Laden. Her mother was the tenth wife of my grandfather and she bore him eleven children, the last of which was the only son the two ever had. All the other children were girls, of which my mother was the eldest. As happens often with Arab families, I am slightly older than my mother's only brother, the uncle of which I speak. His birthday is on June 28, 1957, in your Christian calendar; mine is the exact same day, but in 1954. Ironic, isn't it?" He asked with a smile.

Assiri seemed pleased to be able to speak of his family. The mental escape it offered him from the strain of the present moment caused an almost blissful look to appear in his eyes. Like all Arabs, Moe had a virtual encyclopedic knowledge of his heritage and seemed more than proud to share it with his American listeners. Dash thought that the look in his eyes that came with remembering his relatives made him look serene and peaceful, at ease with himself and all those around him. He almost envied him. At the same time he felt foolish for not having noted the obvious, as Blackburn had.

For Dash, when Blackburn asked Assiri his mother's family name, it was one of those seminal moments in life when the answer to a puzzling question was so obvious that after hearing it he wanted to slap his forehead and say, "DUH!" But he was being too hard on himself. He had forgotten the wisdom of noted philosopher George Santayana when he had written the following pearl of wisdom: "Those who receive their education only from books are the truly uneducated in life."

Unlike Blackburn, who had attended two years of Saudi high school while living with his parents in Riyadh, Dash had never really "gone native" in the same sense that Blackburn had. Although he had lived and worked throughout the Middle East Dash had received most of his education on the family side of Arab life from books he had read while in graduate school. All of them had emphasized the paternal side of Arab culture and only briefly explored the maternal side of the Arab family.

Blackburn, because he had actually lived with the Saudis, having spent many nights and weekends sleeping over and partying with his Saudi classmates, intuitively knew better than to focus only on the father's side of the family. He knew from first hand experience that educated Arabs like Assiri could not only trace seventeen generations on their fathers' side of the family, but that they could also trace seventeen generations on their mothers' side as well.

With Assiri's brief recitation of his maternal lineage it was apparent that he had learned his lessons well. Dash marveled that a similar endeavor for the average American would require a Ph.D. in genetic research, yet most Arab children can routinely accomplish this by the time they are ten years old, never forgetting or leaving out a single person.

"What is your uncle's name? What does he do for a living?" asked Blackburn.

"His name is Osama bin Laden. He is an Islamic soldier of God," he proudly answered.

***

In August 1990 the name Osama bin Laden did not have the same infamous notoriety that it would achieve eleven years later when nineteen of his followers flew airplanes into the World Trade Center Towers, the Pentagon, and an empty farm field in Pennsylvania. The combination of which killed over three thousand Americans. Still, both Dash and Blackburn had heard the name before.

Two years earlier, in 1988, both had been assigned to an anti-terrorist task force working the Olympics in Seoul, South Korea. During this assignment they had worked closely with the CIA and had helped develop a list of potential terrorist groups that might seize the opportunity to make a big splash upon the world scene. Such an attempt to garner the media attention of the entire world was not unprecedented. The Palestinian terrorist group Black September had accomplished it when attacking the Israeli athletes during the Olympic games in Munich, Germany in 1972. If, for no other reason, Seoul was believed by many to be the next target for a similar attack because terrorist groups always followed up one successful operation with another similar one.

As it turned out the Seoul Olympics were not attacked but both Dash and Blackburn remembered the name of Osama bin Laden as being a probable financier for terrorist groups with such an inclination. He was known to have access to the family construction fortune and he was known to have both bank rolled and soldiered with the Mujahadeen during the war against Russia in Afghanistan. He was also a Saudi and with their natural interest in the Kingdom, the Americans made a mental note to keep a watchful eye out for Osama as well as any of his Al-Qaida followers.

***

"I will also tell you that my uncle feels that Iraq's invasion of Kuwait is an Arab matter that can be resolved by us without the world going to war over it," Moe continued. It was obvious to him that with the announcement of his uncle's name he had captured the undivided attention of his audience.

"If a war is necessary he feels that the Mujahadeen will evict the Iraqis just as they evicted the Russians. Either way, my uncle is preaching to his followers that King Fahd is looking to America as his savior because he knows that he has already lost the faith of his own people."

"Although I personally disagree with his assessment," he shrugged, "it is easy to see how those with a more jaundiced eye can easily be co-opted to believe it. This is why it is so very important for America to support our efforts to destroy Saddam's regime. It is the only way it can regain the credibility it lost in the Arab world when it abandoned the Muslim cause in Afghanistan and supported Saddam in his war with Iran."

"As even you must admit," he said, slipping back into his role as an ad-lib history professor, "promises of American developmental aid, assistance, and interest seems to have departed Afghanistan right along with the Soviet troops. It seems that once America no longer had any use for us they severed all ties and abandoned the Mujahadeen just like they earlier abandoned the South Vietnamese. Like the Mujahadeen, the Vietnamese had foolishly allied themselves with America's paranoia against communism; even though the average Vietnamese could have cared less if either Saigon or Hanoi were communist or capitalist. When your life revolves around hand to mouth existence, what the hell difference would it have made to them?" he asked rhetorically.

"Now," he continued, "here we are fifteen years after Vietnam and America is making the same promises to the Marsh Arabs. If they assist with the destruction of the Ba'ath party and Saddam Hussein, then American money and know how will help them build a nation from the ashes. Which we all fear to be just another lie of political expediency. Yet we welcome your money!" he confessed.

"I can personally tell you that if America does not honor her commitment this time," he threatened, "that if she ever has to go to war with Iraq in order to destroy Saddam's regime then she will have to do so all by herself. It will be American blood that will be spilled because no Arab will believe anything America tells them, not unless you do it right this time, seeing it through from start to finish."

Looking at Blackburn Assiri calmly stated, "How is it your saying goes? Fool me once, shame on you. Fool me twice, shame on me. Well, there won't be a third time."

"Do you really believe that Saddam will peacefully withdraw from Kuwait if the Arab nations ask him to?" asked an intrigued Dash.

"Yes, I do," answered Assiri. "Saddam Hussein knows that he cannot stand up against an American army. Your forces will pass through his Republican Guard forces like crap through the proverbial goose. It will be suicide for his Army to actually engage in a conventional war against western forces. Don't for a minute believe that he doesn't know this; his generals certainly do. The last thing Saddam can afford to have happen is to have his army destroyed, leaving him to the mercy of his enemies. Of which he has many, as you saw last night. Even now he is making back channel overtures through Syria, Jordan, and Saudi Arabia, seeking a way out of this mess."

Then Assiri reverted back to his anti-American diatribe.

"It is your President with his insane macho posturing that is backing Saddam into an inescapable corner, threatening that if he doesn't leave then he will be forcibly evicted. This attitude may play well with the American media and help get Bush reelected; but for a man like Saddam, capitulation to such bullying is a sign of weakness. Regardless of what the back channel messages are saying, the only thing the Arab public sees is your President threatening to kick Saddam out of Kuwait. Of course, Saddam is never going to be seen as having backed down to anyone, let alone an American."

"It's like two jackasses running head long into one another," he cautioned. "Neither will take a step backwards, but both will squeal loudly in the hope that they can force the other to. In the uncertain world of Middle East politics Saddam cannot afford to appear weak and step back from threats or danger. Image is everything to a man like Saddam. Anyone who understands this mindset knows that public threats will have just the opposite effect from those intended. Kind of makes me wonder who is advising President Bush to do such a stupid thing. How about you?" he asked with a smile.

There must have been about one million questions that Dash and Blackburn would have liked to discuss with Assiri just then. But who the idiots were that were advising the President to take such a stupid, boisterous position was not one of them. Unfortunately, as events in a combat zone often have a way doing, they wouldn't even have the chance to discuss this mundane question, much less all of the others. The only comment either of them had the opportunity to make was Blackburn's closing one, "Moe, Karl Marx would be proud of your speech, but I couldn't disagree with you more."

To which Assiri replied, "Karl Marx didn't believe in God. Neither was he willing to die for his cause."

CHAPTER 12

As the two Americans stood silently, each of them wondering where to begin yet both anxious to respond; they were in the process of formulating coherent questions to Assiri's unexpected diatribe when one of the five-ton trucks came careening through the gate. The gate guard, recognizing the truck and its driver was in the process of opening the concertina wire gate when the large vehicle simply burst through the narrow opening, causing the guard to jump out of the way to avoid being run over. In a cloud of dust the truck braked to a screeching halt directly in front of the three men. The driver, who had been making a supply run near Talabani's headquarters, leapt from the vehicle and excitedly announced, "The Mukhabaret have just arrested General Talabani!"

All that transpired in the first seconds following the driver's announcement that Saddam's secret police had arrested Talabani couldn't clearly be recalled, except to say that it was one of those moments in life that defied explanation. Like an orgasm, it had to be experienced to be understood because words alone are inadequate. But the effect of the driver's words was about the same as if someone had walked up to the three of them and poured a bucket of ice water over their heads. They immediately shifted mental gears from one of political disagreement to that of the hardcore reality of soldiers trying to survive what they knew was about to happen. The men instinctively knew that at any minute the same Iraqis who had arrested the general were going to speed toward their assembly area. It didn't take a rocket scientist to understand that it would be best for all concerned if they were long gone and far away when they arrived.

"Top, drop the ramps and unload the FAV's," ordered Dash. "Get the men ready to get the hell out of here ASAP."

"Yes, Sir!" replied Blackburn, already running to accomplish just that task.

Even though it was not quite dark enough to safely unload the FAV's they really had no choice but to run the risk of being seen from the nearby highway. Dash took solace in the fact that, as the light slowly drained from the desert sky, it was dark enough that it would take a dedicated effort for someone passing by to notice the formidable little vehicles parked among the trucks and wire inside the assembly area. He was not yet overly concerned about an aerial search for them by helicopters, which would be taking place nearer to Safwan, where they had last been seen.

In the gathering uncertainty none of the team members, to include Assiri, yet knew what events had transpired leading up to the general's arrest. At the time, none were even thinking about it. The answers to their questions would have little bearing on what they had to do tonight. But it would have been right, and ultimately proven to be correct, for them to assume that someone who had been at last night's meeting had been caught leaving the farmhouse.

It would later come to light that this is precisely what had happened. In fact, two people had been arrested while still at the location of last nights meeting —Larry and Mike. The two CIA agents had actually been flown by helicopter to the farmhouse and were waiting idly by when it had returned to pick them up for their return flight back to Basra, accompanied by two truckloads of Republican Guard infantry soldiers from the Medina Division. The Iraqi soldiers then dutifully beat the hell out of both agents, threatening to shoot them if they could not come up with a good reason for keeping them alive, finally getting them to claim diplomatic immunity as American, not French citizens. Realizing that they had a "good catch," the Republican Guard Captain surrendered them to Saddam's Fedayeen forces in Basra, a professional para-military force experienced in prisoner interrogations. Once they had finished peeling away the layers of machismo and CIA deceit there was little left to tell.

The Fedayeen interrogators had stripped the agents naked, tying their hands over their heads and around water pipes hanging from the ceiling of a shower room in a Basra police station. The floor drains had been plugged and water flooded the floor; just enough water so that their toes were covered by it. An electrical probe had been inserted in each agent's rectum and each probe had been connected to a 5 kW, hand crank generator. The agents had held out as best they could, but it had not taken long for them to break. Use of such a method doesn't take long to break anyone.

The decision to fly a helicopter to the farmhouse had been an incredibly stupid one. Even an army as unprofessional as Iraq's doesn't allow unauthorized aircraft to fly over battle positions without questioning the pilot. The pilot, with a pistol firmly pressed against his temple, had quickly told the Iraqi officer about the French oilmen he transported to a farmhouse near Safwan. The information leading to General Talabani's arrest had to have come from either Larry or Mike when their captors questioned them.

The soldiers were angry that someone had been caught after only one night in Iraq, but they didn't really hold any grudge against the agents for talking. They knew that everyone who is caught eventually talks. It is only a matter of time and method to get them to break down. If the speed of General Talabani's arrest was an accurate indicator, the method used on Larry and Mike must have been particularly painful. The macho attitude Mike had displayed that if caught he would only provide name, rank, and serial number had most assuredly been revealed to him by now to be a Geneva Convention fairy tale written by people far removed from the reality actually found on a battlefield.

Now that General Talabani was undoubtedly in Fedayeen custody as well, he might not break as easily as the agents had, but he would break. He knew far too much about the team for them to be wasting valuable time waiting around inside the assembly area. But the who, what, when, where and why of the information leak mattered little to the soldiers as they hurriedly prepared to depart the assembly area. Their focus was on getting back across the Iraqi border and into Saudi Arabia with their body parts still attached. Survival was the only remaining measure of success that had any real meaning.

Assiri's delay in returning from Talabani's headquarters had one positive effect on immediate events; it had given the team the opportunity to spend the afternoon updating target folders and getting some sleep. Allowing them to conduct detailed planning for just this sort of contingency. They even had the opportunity to walk through actions on contact if they had to abort the mission and exfiltrate tonight. An occurrence that, at the time, seemed to be a rather remote possibility. Now, with updated JSTARS and satellite imagery containing enemy troop movements and dispositions along their planned route, the Americans felt like kissing Assiri for making them wait all afternoon for his return.

All of this latest planning information had been placed in a target folder and emailed to the 160th Special Operations Aviation Regiment (SOAR) at KKMC. As a result of this planning they felt reasonably confident that with the updated information and the SOAR's aviation assets, they could make their way back across the border. It was while enjoying this temporary feeling of confidence and conducting final equipment checks on the FAV's that Assiri approached them with news that immediately deflated the Americans budding hopes.

Speaking as if in a state of shock himself Assiri told the assembled team, "there has been a change in mission from Riyadh. They now want us to be airlifted out. They have given me some pickup zone (PZ) coordinates near Rafha, one hundred and fifty kilometers southwest from here. We are to immediately go to this PZ and coordinate pickup from there. A Saudi Special Forces Aviation detachment will fly four Black Hawks in from Ar'ar to pick us up. Pickup time has been set for 0400, giving us a little more than six hours to get there and rig the FAV's for sling load operations."

As usual Blackburn was the first to explode. "What the hell do you mean Riyadh changed its mind!" he hissed through clenched teeth. "It was those dickheads in Riyadh that wanted American SOF involvement in this abortion in the first place because of our firepower. Now you're telling me that we just came along for the ride? Get those bastards back on the phone, I want to talk to them!"

"These orders didn't originate in Riyadh," continued Assiri apologetically. "They came from your Ambassador."

Now it was Dash's turn to explode. But he knew that it would accomplish nothing to take it out on Assiri. Turning to Floriddia, he calmly said, "Get me the American Ambassador in Riyadh on the INMARSAT."

In less than one minute Floriddia announced, "Sir, the Ambassador is unavailable but the DCM (Deputy Chief of Mission), Mister Anderson, said he would speak with you if you would like."

"Sir," Dash said, taking the receiver from Floriddia, jumping straight to the purpose of his call. "We've been compromised and are prepared to execute Plan Red," pretending not to know about the change in mission Assiri had announced. "Do you have any updates for us before we depart the assembly area?"

"Uh, well, uh, I believe there might have been a few adjustments," he stammered.

"Like what, Sir?" Dash questioned.

"Well, I, uh, is Mohammed Al-Assiri there with you?" asked the DCM.

"Roger."

"Well, uh, did he mention that there might have been a slight change in mission? Nothing you guys can't handle, just a few recommendations I made to the Ambassador. But I would like to take this opportunity to hear your feelings regarding the matter as well."

"Listen, damn it," Dash finally fumed, losing control of his temper. "I didn't call you just to be asked a bunch of questions myself! We're in a pretty tight situation here. If you have mission guidance for me spit it out. I don't have much time to spare."

"Well, uh, Major, I can only speak with you if you calm down. We have to be civilized about this. You must understand that we are working very hard here to put together a UN coalition. Some of whom we hope will be Arabs. It wouldn't be of much help to us if you folks were found to be killing Iraqis when we aren't even in a shooting war yet, now would it? Mister, or rather, Captain Assiri can fill you in on all the details. Don't forget sir, that the Saudis are in charge of your mission. Have a nice day!" he cheerfully cried out. With that there was a loud click in Dash's ear and the call was terminated.

For several seconds Dash did not move. He simply stared dumbly at the dead receiver clutched in his white knuckled hand. "He hung up on me!" a stunned Dash finally yelled out. Incredulously rotating glances between the phone in his hand and the eyes of an even angrier First Sergeant Blackburn.

"We are a hundred miles behind enemy lines running for our lives and that son-of-a-bitch hung up the phone! Call that prick back, Floriddia!" Dash vented, walking in a tight circle, boiling inside and trying to sort out in his own mind what had just happened. He was still holding the receiver, slapping it against the palm of his hand as if he were beating the life out of it. Floriddia stood silently, wanting to comply with his instructions but he needed the receiver and didn't want to ask for it back. Stunned by the look in both he and Blackburn's eyes he was uncertain as to what to say.

"No, wait," Dash eventually said, restraining his desire to yell, but still waving his arms in the air as if he were punching demons. "Screw it! I'm just wasting valuable time. Moe, show us what you've got so we can get the hell out of here."

***

As the realization that they were working outside military channels with people more concerned with process than product settled in they dismissed it and went back to work. What else could they do?

With this change in attitude it took less than five minutes before Assiri's new overlay was transposed onto their maps, radio checks made, and weapons function checks completed. It was going to be another long night. To survive it they would need to stay focused and forget about those things beyond their control.

The route that they were to follow to the PZ took them through the desert, carefully avoiding the roads. It was much too dangerous for them to follow roads now that Iraqi troops would be searching for them. They knew from having watched the Iraqi units occupy positions along the main roads that the likelihood of running into one of them in the featureless, empty expanse of the desert would be unlikely. Their most immediate problem would be in traveling a great distance at high speed, in the dark, over unfamiliar and uneven terrain, having a limited amount of time to reach the PZ before the lift aircraft arrived. If they weren't there when the helicopters showed up, they were going to be out of luck, having to exfiltrate by whatever means they could. Something they would prefer not to do since appearing unexpectedly in front of a Saudi border unit could prove to be as deadly as being caught by the Iraqis.

Traveling at high speed over uneven terrain was exactly what the little vehicles were made to do and the soldiers were experienced and confident in their ability to complete the mission. As much as anything, they were just angry with having to do it. It would have been much more certain, faster — and admittedly more exciting — to simply blow a hole through the Iraqi line near Al-Ruq'a. They were disappointed that they were not going to get to put their previous target planning to good use.

It was also frustrating for the soldiers to know that those far removed from the action could so cavalierly announce a change of mission at the last second, expecting the soldiers to behave as if they were characters in a video game. A fine-tuning, or tweaking of every military mission is expected, but a total change is unusual and fraught with loose ends. It seemed as though those making changes didn't always understand the danger this placed soldiers in. The soldiers were convinced that planners in the White House, DOS and DOD, to include uniformed personnel inside the Pentagon, felt as if they could simply restart the game whenever they disliked the results. Seemingly unaware that they were unnecessarily risking soldiers' lives and squandering critical military assets as they stumbled and fumbled around experimenting, looking for the perfect solution. Perfection is not something field soldiers demand; close enough is usually good enough but it needs to be done before placing them in a hostile environment, not after.

Offsetting their misfortune with the State Department was one fortunate coincidence. The driver of Assiri's vehicle had grown up along the border with Iraq and knew of an ancient camel caravan trail that crossed the Southern desert. He had traveled this trail many times in his youth helping his Bedouin grandfather as they moved sheep back and forth across the invisible border North of Rafha, confirming Dash's belief that no matter how desperate the situation, there is always hope. A person just has to look hard enough to find it and it can usually be found in the most unexpected of places.

As the driver traced his recollections of this trail on Assiri's map it appeared as though it might go near, or even through the proposed PZ. Whether it did or not, didn't really matter. All the soldiers needed was to get close to the location, avoiding all road traffic and guiding themselves through the desert with their GPS guidance system. A mission that may not be easy, but it certainly wasn't one that was impossible. In any event, they now had a destination and a route to follow; the rest would require simple hard work and an abundance of good luck, something that seemed to be in short supply at the moment.

***

As the FAV's slowly exited what had once been the perimeter of the assembly area the air was heavy with apprehension, and not just from those departing; those staying behind were concerned as well. And they were right to be concerned. Not only did they have to fear being apprehended by the Iraqi military, they were well aware of America's less than stellar track record in support of unconventional, indigenous warriors. Which, with their professed allegiance to Talabani, they had signed up to be.

These people, the truck drivers and guards, had already removed the concertina wire and marshaled their trucks for a road march into Al-Bussayah to be lost among the hundreds of similar trucks already there. They would then be left to their own devices as to what they would do next. One would ride as a passenger in Blackburn's FAV, holding the flashlight for him so he could keep pace with the other crewed vehicles. Most would return to their guerilla groups scattered throughout the countryside and help tie up Saddam's combat forces by forcing them to defend against the Marsh Arabs increasing attacks when the war kicked into full gear, exactly as the American taxpayer had recently paid them to do.

As a consequence of these attacks, most would later be executed by Saddam's returning forces when America abandoned them. Those who had helped in the coalition efforts to overthrow the Ba'ath party were simply left to the mercy of a vengeful Saddam Hussein following the Iraqi withdrawal from Kuwait when American politicians followed precedent and replaced interest in their cause for votes back home. Just as previous American politicians had left their South Vietnamese allies to the mercy of the North Vietnamese, the Cambodians to the mercy of the Khmer Rouge, and the Afghans to the mercy of the Taliban following America's loss of interest in these respective countries. These acts of abandonment would result in what historians now identify as being the killing fields in South East Asia and the recreation of a brutal tenth century regime inside Afghanistan. The latter spawning the creation of a new, growing threat to the United States, a base of operations for Osama bin Laden's terrorist group Al-Qaida, leading directly to future attacks on American interests around the globe.

America, the richest, most powerful country in the history of the world has deliberately chosen not to simultaneously achieve both a political and a military victory since World War II, almost fifty years earlier. Being content instead to wage wars of containment, not victory, always leaving in its wake antagonistic political and military infrastructures in control of a repressed people, virtually guaranteeing that those peoples hope for a brighter tomorrow would end up a repeat of a dismal yesterday. When those same repressed people are recruited to side with America during wars of containment and then left to the mercy of a brutal government they had knowingly opposed, it should come as no shock to the public when they are killed in large numbers after their protective "friend" leaves. Such disloyalty makes the United States a fickle sponsor to choose for an ally, making it very difficult for either the CIA or SOF to recruit new "suckers" willing to die for America's promises. Leaving America to fight future wars by itself.

With such a disreputable track record only the truly desperate will ever side with America more than once. This reluctance is not based purely on desire; it is also a matter of numbers. An unconventional guerilla alliance with America during a war of containment may result in there not being enough indigenous survivor's left to form an alliance more than once. A fact not lost on those whose doors are knocked on when America attempts to form regional coalitions.

A continuance of such a bad precedent often leaves soldiers wondering where the hallowed virtues of duty, honor, and country fit into America's foreign policy.

It is a politician's duty to conduct foreign policy; as Americans, it is certainly their country. But how can there be honor in telling people that America will help them achieve their own objectives if they help America achieve hers, then abandoning them for votes at home? Votes cast by people who usually don't understand or care about what is going on anyway since only half the people in America actually vote.

Then again, politicians don't have to look the families of the dead and missing in the eyes. Soldiers do. Most soldiers have never read articles on foreign policy, even fewer have ever written any. They simply implement those policies, leaving the talking and writing of such heady matters to the politicians and their academic clones. But it is soldiers who deal with the aftermath of those policies, and it is soldiers who are the first to know if those policies have benefited those affected by them. Thus it is the soldiers, not the policy makers, who first see the blossoms of hate when people begin to realize they have been lied to. And it is the blood of soldiers that prevent those same people from exacting their vengence on those responsible for those lies. Proving once again there is a big difference between talking about doing something and actually doing it.

CHAPTER 13

With Assiri taking the lead, the FAV's shot from the assembly area as if they were late for happy hour at the club, disappearing into the darkness with both a sense of purpose and resolve. Any lightly armed force unfortunate enough to catch up with the FAV's would have their hands full, like catching a tiger by his tail. Once accomplished it is the tiger, not the pursuer who gets to decide when they can let go.

As the vehicles hit the release point, a well-worn animal trail directly across from the assembly area, they turned southwest and immediately spread out into combat intervals. A distance of fifty to one hundred meters between vehicles was the standard for night movement in an uncertain environment. The critical measurement was not so much determined by distance, but by the drivers' ability to follow the black out drive lights on the rear of the vehicle immediately in front of it.

With the aid of their night vision goggles the rule of thumb defining distance between vehicles was an appropriate dispersal had to always ensure if the lead vehicle blundered into something, or someone, the following vehicles would be in an overwatch position to support by fire. Again, with the assistance of the AN/PAS-4 night sight mounted on the MK-19, targets could be seen well enough at two hundred meters distance to be engaged in total darkness.

Even in a worst case scenario, such as being caught in a sandstorm, no two vehicles were ever to be moving so close together that they would both be caught in a hasty ambush. The most likely kind of ambush they would encounter.

Since speed was the first priority, both the vehicle driver and the passenger/gunner remained buckled into their three-point harness, dictating that the crew would rely on the quick cover fire afforded by the hood mounted M-60D machinegun, also equipped with a night sight. Any engagement would be a "scoot and shoot" with speed, not firepower, being relied upon to break contact. With a concept built around speed it was more likely to wreck a vehicle than to drive into a prepared ambush.

In the empty desert, without the aid of GPS or night vision devices, the Iraqi army was limited to road movement, especially at night. This meant that the FAV's would move cross-country over unfamiliar terrain once again. In so doing the real danger was that the driver would roll one or, worst case, drive over the edge of a cliff, disappearing in a cloud of camouflage paint and desert dust when they hit the bottom. For safety reasons it was necessary for the soldiers to remain buckled into their vehicles.

For the first twenty kilometers the trail recommended by Assiri's driver was little more than a path meandering through the scattered scrub brush surrounding the northern end of the great valley rift, Wadi Al-Batin. Movement was slow and tedious. At times such as this, when clock watching becomes a nervous habit, it seemed to Dash that for every ten minutes on his watch, an hour had elapsed. Each soldier wondered to himself if they could make it to the PZ by 0400. They also began to suspect that Assiri's driver had been blowing smoke up their butts when he had told them about a well-traveled trail.

After one hour of bumping and thumping along at no more than twenty miles per hour, each soldier cursing Assiri's driver under their breath, the terrain eventually opened up into a compact desert landscape as flat and smooth as a billiard table. The speed was immediately increased to seventy miles per hour, allowing the group to travel at this speed for about thirty minutes, then the terrain returned to rivulets of sand and scrub brush, forcing them to slow down considerably, but not as slow as before.

The ancient caravan trail they were driving on was beginning to show the effects of centuries of use. Beneath the loosely packed three inches of surface sand covering the trail, the innumerable camels, sheep, horses and people that had walked its length since before the time of Christ had tightly compressed the desert floor, turning it into a surface as hard as any modern asphalt highway. This hard surface allowed the FAV's to maintain a consistent speed somewhere between forty and fifty miles per hour as they sped through the dark desert, subdued flashlights lighting up the terrain for the NVG's as if it were broad daylight.

The troops made such good time that they were near the PZ coordinates by 0200, allowing plenty of time for the thirty minutes that it would take them to rig the vehicles for sling loading, an observation that left them all pleasantly surprised. Unfortunately, as in most military operations, it was a pleasant feeling of satisfaction that did not last for very long. As rapid and uneventful as their night move had been, it had not been rapid enough to beat the large vehicles currently parked in the center of the proposed pickup zone.

***

As Assiri's vehicle topped the rise overlooking the PZ, he stopped, shut off his engine, and quickly called for Dash to halt the march and come forward on foot. Something below him had caught his attention. From a distance of over one half mile, Assiri couldn't really be certain that what he was looking at through his NVG's were vehicles or sand dunes. But whatever the large lumps were, they appeared conspicuously out of place in the flat desert terrain spreading out below him.

Although it was still dark, Assiri had removed his NVG's and replaced them with his Swarovski binoculars, holding them to his eyes as he scanned to his front. He was intently scanning the desert floor when Dash silently approached his vehicle.

"What have we got?" whispered Dash.

"I think I see vehicles parked on the PZ," Assiri whispered in response.

"I knew things were too good to be true," Dash whispered as much to himself as to Assiri. "If the powers that be would have just let us go through with the original plan, we would already be back across the border by now."

"Yeah, but it could be worse," Assiri reminded him. "We could have driven straight into them."

Handing Dash the binoculars so he could look for himself, Assiri explained what had to be done.

"I can't tell exactly what they are from this distance, but I think they're tanks. I haven't seen any troops though. We need to get closer."

"Roger," whispered Dash, unable to discern the identity of the distant lumps either. "Let's do it."

With that Assiri unbuckled his harness and pulled himself from the vehicle, directing his driver to back down from the ridge and pull into an overwatch position to cover the reconnaissance mission he and Dash were about to conduct. Quickly returning to his own vehicle Dash keyed the radio and directed the other FAV's to do likewise, providing everyone with a cursory, verbal fragmentary order, or FRAGO, explaining the situation. When the others acknowledged receipt of the FRAGO Dash removed his CVC helmet, replacing it with his beret. He needed to be able to listen to the sounds of the desert and the CVC would only make it harder to hear. Dash then checked to verify that both his M-4 carbine and .45 pistol had a round in the chamber. Although he knew they were loaded, it was always reassuring to double check such things.

He also put his hand held Motorola Saber radio into the breast pocket of his Kevlar vest so he could maintain voice contact with the vehicles. Ordinarily he would not have worn the heavy vest but having crawled through the desert before, he knew that it would afford him some protection from the thorns, sharp rocks and scorpions he was likely to encounter. For these same reasons Dash also removed from his bulging rucksack a pair of knee and elbow pads, slipping them on and pulling the straps tight. The pads were the type that bricklayers and cement finishers wear while working on their knees. Usually he wore them only for airborne operations, protecting his limbs from the unintended consequences that went with parachuting. Something he would not be doing tonight, but the hard exterior of the pads worked equally well for protection when lowcrawling over the sharp surface of the desert.

Satisfied that he was as prepared as he was ever going to be, Dash conducted a radio check with Blackburn over the Motorola, then turned and sprinted back up the hill to Assiri's vehicle. Blackburn would remain behind to direct the vehicle covering fire should it become necessary.

Dash and Assiri moved to the top of a slight ridge to their front, knelt down and, using Assiri's binoculars, scanned the terrain to select an approach route. The binoculars worked almost as well in the darkness of the desert night as the NVG's did, collecting the light from a star lit desert sky and magnifying the effect much better than the human eye can. In addition to helping them select a route, the binoculars powerful ten-power optical lenses, cut with typical German precision, slowly brought into focus four Russian-built T-62 tanks; all parked in the open with no appearance of having been camouflaged or placed in a defensive position. They were simply lined up like beached whales, apparently unguarded.

Choosing a slight, brush-covered ravine for their approach, the two sprinted towards the nearest cover and concealment, a small clump of bushes near its mouth. They began moving towards the tanks in a low, crouched position and worked their way down the small ravine; cautiously placing their feet to avoid stepping on any of the dry branches scattered about.

By all appearances the proposed PZ was an ancient lakebed surrounded by slightly higher terrain. The many small ravines leading into it indicated that the winter rains still flowed into it periodically, filling the small basin as if it were a shallow soup bowl. By late summer, long devoid of any significant amount of water, its crusted surface had sun baked into a hardstand that made it ideal for parking heavy vehicles, like these tanks. Yet the nearest road was at least twenty miles further to the west, connecting the small Saudi town of Rafha with the Iraqi village of An-Najaf, one hundred and fifty kilometers to the north. Someone had intentionally placed them here, in the middle of the desert, as if they were parked in a motor pool. But where was that someone now?

As Assiri and Dash got closer to the tanks, the two soldiers dropped onto their stomachs, low crawling the remaining thirty meters through the ravine and stopped directly in front of the tanks, behind the last cluster of brush affording concealment. Dash took up a position where he could provide cover fire as Assiri crawled even closer, hoping to hear or see a crewmember before they saw him.

***

As Assiri began his slow, methodical approach it seemed to Dash as if it was taking forever for him to crawl the final one hundred feet. He would move quickly for about ten feet, then lay perfectly still for a couple of minutes, listening and looking. Dash wanted to yell out at him, encouraging him to hurry, reminding him that they were running out of time. But he knew better. Assiri was the one in danger if he were detected. He would be the first to die if a wrong move was made now. Dash would probably be the second. Under such circumstances it was only logical to allow Assiri to choose the methodology and timing of his approach, this was no place for a critic.

His brief introspection reminded him of Blackburn's often-repeated saying to new Second Lieutenants arriving from the service schools full of "book learnin" and opinions, but having no real practical experience to draw upon. With his no nonsense manner, the crusty Blackburn would curtly tell the inexperienced lieutenants, "Leave the how of doing to the doers, Sir. Then roll up your own sleeves and help them, or simply get out of the way and let them do it by themselves. Never criticize others for how they are doing something that you have never done yourself. It's a sure sign of ignorance!"

***

As Assiri drew closer to the tanks, Dash could see him lift his upper torso off the ground, as if he were looking at something beside the tank on his far left. After several seconds he raised himself to one knee and continued scanning the area near the tank. Then, dropping back onto his stomach, he scurried to the tank on the far right and repeated the procedure. Finally, after what had seemed to Dash to be an interminably long time, Assiri hurried back to his location.

"There are four people sleeping on the ground near the tank on the left," he breathlessly whispered to Dash. "There may be more inside one of the tanks but in this heat I doubt it."

"Did you see their weapons?" whispered Dash.

"No." he puffed. "They're either still in the vehicles or lying on the ground beside them where they can't be seen. I would suspect that there still in the vehicles. This doesn't appear to be a very observant group of soldiers."

During a brief pause as they thought of what to do next, Dash could hear Assiri's labored breathing. A combination of the physical exertion the crawling had required, coupled with the laborious mental effort he was expending searching his mind for a solution to their predicament were taking their toll. Assiri's ass was literally dragging as he sucked in great gasping gulps of air. Dash felt slightly guilty, realizing that he was relishing the mental and physical anguish his partner was experiencing being the man in charge; a position that is always more taxing than just following another person's lead.

"Well, boss, what's the plan?" Dash finally whispered, taking further sadistic delight in surreptitiously reminding Assiri of his previous declaration that he, not the Americans, was in operational control.

"I'm thinking!" he responded, catching his breath but still blowing like a winded mule.

Killing the four men where they slept would be an easy task, but it may not solve the problem. If there were four tanks parked here, it was logical to assume that others were hidden nearby, certainly near enough to the PZ that gunshots or the arrival of a package of UH-60 Black Hawk helicopters would not go unnoticed. If there were other tanks out there, they would shoot the choppers down or at least force them to abort the mission, leaving the soldiers up the creek without a paddle.

There was another problem with killing the Iraqis lurking in the back of Dash's mind. If it were ever discovered that he had killed them he would have the political problem of explaining the purpose for it once they returned to Saudi Arabia. Something that Assiri would not have to deal with as second-guessing is not an Arab trait. A disconcerting fact often lost on an American public that mistakenly believes that the decision regarding when to kill and who to kill rests with soldiers. Soldiers, however, are well aware that others have been court martialed by back seat drivers for deaths occurring on their watch when twenty-twenty hindsight is used to evaluate split second actions taken by scared young men doing whatever it took to stay alive. America had not officially declared war yet, something the Deputy Chief of Mission pointedly mentioned. Technically, killing these four men would not be a self-defense killing. Dash knew with certainty that there are too damn many DCM's in the world that would be glad to conduct an inquiry into second-guessing his actions.

A quick barracks conversation with American soldiers recently having returned from the battlefield will reveal that more than one leader has been forced to concoct a lie to keep him or his troops from going to prison for murder, a consideration that no soldier should have to ponder. But an attitude closely in keeping with the "you cover my back and I'll cover yours" mentality of combat soldiers.

It was while Dash was lost in such thoughts that Assiri shocked him by announcing a solution to their dilemma.

"We are going to take them prisoner," he whispered.

Dash's initial response to his announcement was to stare at his friend in disbelief! But as Dash stared at him through the green glow of his NOD's he could see that Assiri wasn't smiling.

"Seriously," continued Assiri, "I don't think that killing them is necessary. We need to ask them some questions before we can clear the PZ for aircraft arrival. I am still dressed in the uniform of an Iraqi Colonel. We are all still dressed in the uniforms of Iraqi soldiers. I doubt that these people know anything of an American SOF team operating across the Iraqi border near Rafha. Even Talabani can't tell anyone that we have moved all the way to Rafha for evacuation, he only knew of the plan to blow a hole in Iraqi lines near Al-Ruq'a. Besides, if they behave suspiciously then we will kill them. We certainly don't have the available manpower to place a guard on them."

Dash, shaking his head in disbelief, simply replied, "It makes as much sense as anything else I've seen on this operation. But, technically we can't take prisoners yet. We're not at war. They would be more like hostages."

Words that even as he whispered them left him amazed that such an irrelevant thought would enter his head at a time like this. But his thoughts of having to legally cover his ass had so dominated his mental processes that this politically correct thought had simply slipped out.

"I don't give a damn what we call them!" hissed an irate Assiri, shocked that Dash would say such a thing. "I just want to get some information from them."

***

It was while the two of them were mentally massaging these immature thoughts that the decision to act was made for them. One of the Iraqi soldiers awoke from his slumber and stood erect beside the tank, yawning and stretching his stiff muscles. He then began walking directly towards where the two soldiers were hiding, causing both Dash and Assiri to cease all conversation and bury themselves even further into the desert sand.

As he approached their position, both men silently withdrew a Randall trench knife from a scabbard strapped to his leg. If they were forced to kill, then they would have to do so silently. They did not want to fire a weapon because they did not yet know what else lay hidden in the darkness of the surrounding desert. Fortunately for the Iraqi he stopped about twenty feet from where they were hiding. He would have been killed had he stumbled into them.

As the two of them intensely watched the Iraqi he scratched, unzipped his trousers and began to relieve himself. The sound of his urine splashing on the hard desert floor as if he were pouring water onto cement. It was while Dash was watching the Iraqi pee, wondering what to do next that, quite unexpectedly, Assiri resheathed his knife, removed his NOD's, stood erect, and began quickly walking toward the peeing soldier. Loudly greeting him with *"Sabbah Ilxeer,"* Good Morning.

Dash was stunned, completely unprepared for this action. He felt the impulse to charge forward and take into custody the other Iraqis before they awoke; yet he was so unprepared for Assiri's tactic that he continued to remain motionless, unsure of what to do except cover Assiri's impromptu approach with his rifle.

Assiri's greeting was even more startling to the peeing Iraqi than it had been to his American partner. Through his NOD's Dash saw the startled Iraqi soldier yank his penis as if he were trying to rid himself of the offending appendage. Urinating all over his hands and feet as he recoiled from the sound of Assiri's voice, causing him dance around like a thoroughbred racehorse in the starting gate at the Kentucky Derby.

In a loud and commanding voice Moe spoke without pause, rousing the remaining three sleeping Iraqi soldiers, causing them to noisily leap to their feet. "I am Colonel Mohammed Al-Assiri, Chief of Staff of the 26th Iraqi Division. Who are you?" His voice boomed through the quiet desert air like the concussion from an artillery shell.

"Sir!" replied the meek little voice of the Iraqi as he tried to put what remained of his well-stretched manhood back into his trousers while simultaneously saluting with the same hand, alternately swapping it between his forehead and his groin. "I am Private Mazen Darwish, proud Iraqi soldier."

"What unit do you belong to Private Darwish?" demanded Assiri.

At first there was nothing but several seconds of silence in response to Assiri's question. Then, from one of the Iraqi soldiers standing nervously in the background an answer was shouted. "We believe we are soldiers of the Tawalkana Division, Sir."

"Christ Almighty," Dash thought to himself. "These aren't soldiers. They're kids, forced at gunpoint to be out here by Saddam's henchmen."

"The Tawalkana Division is in Kuwait," boomed Assiri, his voice rising two octaves. "What the hell are you doing so far away from your command? I should have you shot as deserters." At the thought of such a prospect, the boys responded to Assiri's threat exactly as he hoped they would. In a rush of servility the four approached him and dropped to their knees. In a passionate wailing they began denouncing all infidels as cowardly dogs, pledging that they themselves would fight to the death for their brave leader, Saddam Hussein.

As Dash watched the proceedings, he hoped that Blackburn, watching from a distance through his night sight, would not make the mistake of thinking Assiri was being attacked and open fire on the pleading mob. Although he had his Saber radio with him, Dash did not yet feel comfortable enough to give away his location by calling Blackburn and explaining to him all that was taking place in front of him. Besides, he really didn't know himself just exactly what was taking place in front of him. There would simply be no way that he could adequately explain it to the inquisitive Blackburn. Who, even at a distance, would later acknowledge that he could hear the sound of Assiri's command voice reverberating across the desert and had wondered what was taking place on the PZ.

"Where is your Commanding Officer?" roared Assiri. "Where are your weapons and other troops?"

"Sir, please! Mercy be to God!" pleaded the loudest voice. "We were trucked to this location from An-Nasiriyah and told to protect these vehicles from thieves. We do not know who these tanks belong to or where any other troops are. We ourselves have been here for five days now and have not seen another soul during that entire time." Quickly adding, "Until your esteemed arrival, Sir."

"What were you given to protect these tanks with? Where are your weapons? Is there any one else inside the vehicles?" demanded Assiri, repeating himself, keeping the pressure on the Iraqis by asking questions, not allowing them time to think about asking any themselves.

"Sir! There is a rifle and ammunition inside this tank," the loudest voice proudly announced, pointing to the tank immediately behind him. "There are no other soldiers or rifles here."

"You have no pistols or grenades?" queried Assiri.

"No Sir!" Came the chorus of replies. "Just the weapons on the tanks and none of us knows how to fire them."

"Who brings you food and water?"

"Sir! No one has brought us food or water since we have been here. The drivers who brought us here gave us ten gallons of water and twenty pounds of rice. They said they would return in three days to resupply us and retrieve these broken vehicles. That was five days ago. I fear that they may have forgotten about us." Then, without thinking, he asked, "Do you have food and water for us?" Followed by a deafening silence as the four conscripts, quite literally, stopped breathing.

Realizing that he had committed a major indiscretion by asking a question of an Iraqi officer, the loudest voice quickly crawled forward on his knees and began kissing Assiri's right hand. Breathlessly exclaiming, "Sir! With God as my witness, I beg your forgiveness!"

This pitiful display went on for several seconds when, with typical Arab aloofness, Assiri beckoned with his left hand for the soldier to arise, which he did, humbly returning to his position among his comrades. Then, the Saudi Captain/Iraqi Colonel, Mohammed Al-Assiri calmly called out in English, "Dash, would you come out here, please."

As Dash had been both listening to and observing Assiri's performance, he knew that these conscripts were telling the truth. They would have been too frightened not to be telling the truth, certain that Assiri had the power to have them shot if he thought they were lying to him. They all sounded young and were literally scared to death. So scared that as Dash rose from his hide position in response to Assiri's request his sudden appearance was more than a little unnerving for the Iraqi conscripts, it was the proverbial bridge too far.

Wearing his beret, Kevlar vest, NOD's, elbow and kneepads, Dash must have appeared to them as an apparition from Hell itself. Adding to the ambience, Dash had fashioned a metal loop on the back of his flack vest that allowed him to affix the Saber radio to his back as he crawled. When crawling, the radio was near enough to his mouth that he could speak into it without removing it. When standing however, the radio's location made it appear as if it were growing out of the side of his head. The sight of him rising from behind the bush had about the same effect on the young conscripts that an electrical shock has on a cat. One of them simply collapsed to the ground and fainted. The other three screamed, *"Allah Al-Raheem,"* God be merciful, and took off running into the desert, disappearing in the blink of an eye, apparently convinced that this weird-looking apparition had somehow silently killed their faint-hearted friend.

Assiri's commands of, "Halt! Or I will shoot!" did little to stem the speed of their departure.

"Let them go. They're not going to bother anything." Assiri shouted to Dash, fearing that he would shoot the fleeing Iraqis.

Dash hadn't even thought of shooting them. He hadn't had time. He was so stunned by the collapse of the Iraqi, coupled with the speed with which the others had departed that he hadn't even shouldered his carbine. But Blackburn wasn't shocked. He was ready to end the lives of the three running Iraqi conscripts. Dash heard his voice over the Saber radio announcing, "I've got three people running away from your location. Do you want me to engage?"

Quickly pulling the little radio from his back Dash responded, "Negative. But watch them for a few minutes to see where they go and if any others join them. Then send two of your vehicles on a mounted reconnaissance around the perimeter of the PZ. I want you to push out at least six clicks beyond the perimeter, beyond the effective range of any other tanks that might be out there. When you're done, come on down here and prepare the vehicles for sling load operations. Once the vehicles are lashed together for lifting, we become just as immobile as any other foot soldier. Make sure there are no surprises hidden out there."

The time was now 0230, leaving ninety minutes before the aircraft commander entered their radio net.

"Roger,' replied Blackburn, "good copy."

"Well," smiled Dash as he approached Assiri. "That certainly went well. Got any other good ideas?"

CHAPTER 14

With Blackburn reconnoitering the perimeter, the two officers quickly searched the tanks, verifying that no one else was hiding inside and that the only weapon, a rusted AK-47 with one magazine, was in fact the only one they had to render incapable of being fired. They accomplished this task by placing the barrel of the rifle inside the main gun of the tank, using it as an ad hoc vise, and bending the barrel ninety degrees.

Assiri then returned to the Iraqi conscript who had fainted, splashing his face with water, reviving him in the hopes of getting any intelligence information that he might have. As he suspected, it wasn't much. The prisoner/hostage simply repeated what Assiri had already been told by the loudest voice, who was now somewhere in the desert, hiding, shaking like a small dog passing a cockle burr through its bowels.

The prisoner/hostage appeared to be about fourteen years old and did not have a clue where he was or who these people were that he was talking to. While Assiri was questioning the young Iraqi, Blackburn arrived at the tanks, followed by the other three FAV's.

As the vehicles approached Dash felt that he could have taken a stick and knocked the eyes off the young Iraqi conscript as they bulged from their sockets. What a strange night it must have been for him! First monsters from outer space, and now the spaceships they had flown. Mama had certainly never told him about things like this! The shocked look on his face almost made Dash laugh.

"The perimeter is clean, Sir," Blackburn reported to Dash. "We didn't see any other people or vehicles out there."

"Your three track stars are about six hundred meters from here," Blackburn said, turning to Assiri while pointing in the direction they had run, north into the desert. "Alone, squatting behind a rock and looking as if the devil himself paid them a visit tonight. When I was watching them through my night sight, I thought the weapon was shaking. Then I realized that it was the three stooges who were shaking. You could almost feel their fear. It was palpable. We don't have to worry about any foolish bravery from them tonight. The shock of what they experienced knocked ten years off their lives. When the helicopters show up, it'll finish scaring the hell out of them. Those guys won't stop running until they get to Baghdad," he emphatically summarized. Then, turning his attention to the young Iraqi sitting in front of Assiri, Blackburn asked, "What about this one. What are we going to do with him?"

"I was wondering the same thing," Dash chimed in, knowing full well that Assiri didn't know what to do with him either. "We could just tie him up and leave him here. Surely someone will come along and untie him. Wouldn't you think?"

"Well," Assiri responded, "they've been here for five days and no one has come back to retrieve them or the tanks. I agree with Blackburn; the three that ran away will just keep on running. If no one comes to help free him, it would be a hell of a way to die, tied up in the desert."

Then, just to prevent anyone else from mentioning it, he added, "We can't shoot him! He's just a boy."

"No!" confirmed Dash. "We're not going to shoot him."

"Maybe we should turn him loose, to rejoin the others?" thought Assiri.

"That might be a mistake," cautioned Blackburn. "Three cowards will remain three cowards because one brave man cannot change the hearts of two cowards. But four cowards together risks the possibility that of two of them, ashamed by their actions, will return as one brave man. That's a risk we need to avoid."

The three stood silently for a moment, weighing their options.

"Well, now that we've settled absolutely nothing, just what the hell do you two college educated officers propose we do with him?" challenged Blackburn, breaking the pensive silence.

"You've got a couple of college degrees yourself," responded Dash.

"Yeah," answered Blackburn. "But I ain't no damn officer. I don't get paid to think. You two do."

"Thanks for all the help, First Sergeant," grinned Assiri. "We couldn't do this without you."

Again, the three stood and reflected on what to do with their charge.

"Look, gentlemen," Blackburn finally said, growing tired of watching the two officers cerebrally avoid the obvious solution. "Why don't we just take the little prick out with us. There's plenty of room on the choppers. If they want to, Saudi Intel can then suck his brain dry for information. Who knows what they might find? Besides, I know just what to do with him if we can get him back to Riyadh."

"What's that, Top?" Dash asked inquisitively.

"I can't tell you, Sir. Not yet anyway." Blackburn smiled. "You'll find out if we can make it back to Riyadh."

"We get him across the border I guarantee you that I can get him to Riyadh," boasted Assiri.

Thus a plan was hatched that night that would consume the efforts of both Blackburn and Assiri over the next several months. But in the end, it would all be worth it.

***

With a solution now found, the three left the tanks and drove the remaining two vehicles out to the middle of the PZ to rejoin their teammates. Floriddia and McNabb had continued to the PZ while Blackburn and the officers weighed their options concerning the Iraqi captive. By the time the three arrived the sergeants had already completed rigging two FAV's for sling loading.

With the Iraqi captive sitting in the passengers seat of Blackburn's vehicle he didn't need to put on his NOD's for the short drive to the PZ. The young conscript's eyes were shining as brightly as streetlights, certainly enough to illuminate the path to the PZ.

Because of the constant training the American soldiers had undergone, sling load operations had become as routine to them as parachute operations had, though both entailed a certain degree of risk if done incorrectly. More than a few experienced parachutists, for instance, becoming blasé about jump procedures had injured themselves during training jumps. This was usually the result of a carelessly routed static line that went unnoticed by the jumpmaster. The consequences of which would rip a biceps loose as the force of the airplanes prop blast, combined with the opposing force of the jumpers' weight, worked in tandem to pull the biceps down to the elbow. Sometimes it would rip the arm completely off, tearing it from the shoulder as if the paratrooper were made of paper. At best, the unintended consequences of a carelessly routed static line would leave an arm a mangled jumble of muscle tissue and blood, scarring the soldier for life. On any given day at Fort Bragg soldiers with "Popeye" arms and telltale scars could be seen drinking beer in the club or sodas at the snack bar. No one had to ask them how they had been injured because as experienced jumpers themselves they had seen it all too often before.

Sling load procedures were similar in that there were risks, even if the risks were less dramatic than those resulting in parachute injuries were. But anytime a soldier had a helicopter hovering two feet above his head as he attempted to hook the doughnut ring connecting the lifting straps to the clevis on the belly of the aircraft, there was danger involved. Though none of the soldiers had been injured while performing this feat, there existed the constant possibility that one would. As a consequence, safety never took a backseat to realism during training.

Sling load operations were taught the way all good military training is taught; it is taken to the point where someone might get killed and then backed off a notch. When aircraft were involved, it is sometimes backed off even further than one notch, often to the point of having the helicopter land next to the vehicles so that the soldiers and the aircrew could rehearse the necessary procedures.

But this was during peacetime training, not during an actual combat mission behind enemy lines. Tonight the aircraft would show up with the express purpose of getting in and out as quickly as possible. Avoiding detection and escaping back across the border, not safety, was everyone's first priority now.

Tonight's lift would be standard operating procedure (SOP). It required the aircraft to home in on the strobe lights marking the pickup point after having first establishing radio contact with the ground commander, Assiri, through his vehicle mounted radio. Once on station, following a brief coordination conversation between the lead pilot and the ground commander, all radio conversation is terminated. Any subsequent commands come from the soldiers on the ground utilizing hand and arm signals. The purpose of radio silence is to prevent listening posts from triangulating a specific location by locking in the electronic signature made by a radio transmission. Even if the message being transmitted is through a secure network and cannot be monitored, the source of the transmission can still be located and killed. Radio silence is a surveillance avoidance technique that soldiers from all armies are trained in as anyone broadcasting over the airwaves is most assuredly being listened to by unfriendly ears.

Once contact is made and identities confirmed, the aircraft is guided into position above the vehicles by following chemical lights held in the hands of the soldiers on the ground. These soldiers, called hook-up men, then place the doughnut ring, a small circular strap connected to the four lift straps, into the aircraft's lifting clevis. Once hook-up is completed the aircraft then touches down next to the vehicles, and the soldiers jump on board, conducting a quick head count once inside. The senior ground person aboard each aircraft gives a thumbs up to the aircraft crew chief, who in turn relays this message to the pilot, and the aircraft lifts off, speeding away carrying two FAV's underneath and four FAV crewmembers inside. The entire process, when performed by well-trained air and ground crews, was not to take longer than two minutes from the time the helicopters arrived until the lift was completed.

Conceptually, the sling loading of vehicles is simple and fast. And when rehearsed as often as the Americans had rehearsed them, they became quite routine. However, complicating tonight's mission was the fact that the Saudi Special Operations Aviation crewmembers tasked with the mission had never done it before, a fact Assiri reluctantly shared with everyone, making them extremely apprehensive as they awaited the arrival of the helicopters.

This is not to imply that the Saudi Special Operations aircrews were inexperienced. They had airlifted their own V-150 armored cars, as well as an eclectic variety of gun vehicles belonging to the Saudi Arabian National Guard many times. But they had never picked up a FAV before, nor had they ever worked with an American SOF team. Tonight's mission would be the first time they had done either. If they screwed it up, it might be the last time as well, for all of them.

***

Blackburn was the first to hear the helicopters, turning to Dash and giving him a thumbs-up gesture, shouting "Inbound" as he did so, precipitating a flurry of activity on the briefly dormant PZ. Blackburn and Dash sprinted for the infrared (IR) strobe lights in preparation for activation when they received the order from Assiri over their Saber radios. Floriddia and McNabb sprinted for their vehicles as well, climbing on top of the roll cage, doughnut ring in hand, prepared for the arrival of the lift aircraft.

As the noise from the choppers grew louder Assiri keyed the SINGARS radio and began transmitting, "Delta Three Yankee Zero Six, this is Alpha Two Oscar Zero Six, over."

"Alpha Zero Six, this is Delta Zero Six, over, " came the immediate reply, a comforting response indicating that the aircraft knew why they had been sent here; presumably they had also been told what they were supposed to lift.

"I've got your approach about three clicks west of the PZ, over," continued Assiri.

"Roger, that would be us. We are activating strobes now. Activate your strobes, over," said the lead pilot.

Assiri then keyed his Motorola radio and had Dash and Blackburn turn on the IR strobe lights. Once completed, they then turned and sprinted back to help Floriddia and McNabb guide the aircraft over the top of the vehicles. The soldiers felt conspicuously vulnerable working under the light of the IR strobes, which seemed to light up the PZ for the NOD's as if it were a mall parking lot.

From his approach altitude of two hundred feet the lift commander could clearly see the ground strobes. "I've got visual," he transmitted. "We're three minutes out, over."

"Roger," responded Assiri, "I've got visual on you as well. You will be picking up two lifts with nine passengers, over."

"Roger, Alpha Zero Six, understand two lifts with nine passengers, over," replied the pilot.

"Affirmative. Except for an emergency all radio communication will now be terminated. All further commands will come from the ground, over," said Assiri.

"Roger, Alpha Zero Six," replied the pilot. "Good luck, over."

"Roger, Delta Zero Six," said Assiri. "Same to you. Out."

The entire radio transmission had not lasted longer than thirty seconds, giving any communications intercept equipment that might be lurking in the dark desert very little time to get a fix on their location.

As the four Black Hawk helicopters arrived over the PZ the anxiety was somewhat alleviated when two of them flared away to provide security and the other two headed straight for the FAV's. Dash watched their aerial maneuvering realizing that they had done this before, maybe with different equipment, but the principle remained the same. The pilots were demonstrating that they were seasoned professionals.

Both Dash and Blackburn had a yellow chemical light in each hand, marking the location of the vehicles and ground guiding the helicopters to a position directly above them. The soldiers were positioned in front of the aircraft where the pilot could see them. Floriddia and McNabb each had a white chemical light that the aircraft crew chief, peering through the inspection plate in the belly of the aircraft, would focus on until hook up was completed. He would then announce over the aircraft intercom for the pilot to move to the side of the vehicle so the soldiers could scramble aboard.

Dash could see through his NOD's that the pilot picking up Blackburn's package was having very little difficulty. He had already come to a hover directly above the vehicles and McNabb was completing the hook up, slapping the doughnut ring against the clevis until he forced it through the yawning gap. The crew chief had already electronically closed the clevis as the pilot was positioning the aircraft to the side of the vehicles in order to load the crew.

The pilot picking up the FAV package that Dash and Floriddia had was just as professional, floating it into position above the vehicles as if it were a hawk preparing to pounce on a mouse. Through his NOD's Dash saw Floriddia reach up to attach the doughnut ring to the clevis, extending his arms as high as he could reach when the ring slipped from his hands, falling back into the vehicle. Dash watched with a sense of increasing dread as Floriddia jumped down from the roll cage to retrieve the doughnut ring. The crew chief, not knowing what had happened, continued to direct the pilot to lower the aircraft in an attempt to guide him closer to Floriddia's chemical light, now on the floor of the FAV as he reached down to retrieve the doughnut ring. When Floriddia attempted to pull himself back onto the roll cage, placing one foot on the ground outside the vehicle, his head touched the skin of the much lower than expected aircraft.

It was as if lightning had struck the vehicle. Like a flashbulb on a camera, it lit up an area twenty feet across. Had he not been watching the proceedings and been prepared for what he saw, Dash would have thought that a mortar round had hit the FAV. But he had been watching and as a result he knew exactly what had happened; Gary Floriddia had been electrocuted.

***

A helicopter is a marvelous invention. It has much greater versatility than any fixed-wing aircraft, allowing it to get into places and do things that cannot be duplicated by anything except for another helicopter. It deserves a great deal of credit for these capabilities. It also has to be given respect for something it is not generally considered to be; a flying generator capable of producing a tremendous amount of static electricity. With its whirling blades a helicopter can produce several thousand volts, usually discharging them harmlessly into the air through the skin of the aircraft. But sometimes, for unexplained reasons, a helicopter will retain its charge. To aid in discharging this electricity many helicopters have a ground probe on the under carriage.

In Floriddia's case his head had just served the same purpose as the ground probe. Initiating a stunning and vivid electrical explosion that had rendered him unconscious and convulsive, erasing his mental tapes, leaving him upside down in the driver's seat of the FAV kicking like a dying chicken.

***

When Dash saw Floriddia get blown into the air and land back inside the vehicle, he immediately rushed to his assistance, taking his chemical lights with him and leaving the pilot confused. The pilot automatically and rightly resorted to standard operating procedures, aborted the lift attempt and increased his altitude to several hundred feet above the PZ, awaiting further instructions from the ground.

Dash reached Floriddia and pulled him from the vehicle, immediately giving him mouth-to-mouth resuscitation, alternately smashing his chest with the heel of his hand to get his heart beating. At the time, with the sound of the helicopters and the effects of the rotor wash, Dash could neither hear nor feel a pulse, nor did he attempt to. Under such circumstances he started with what he expected to be the worst possible results of being electrocuted, such as stopping the heart and breathing, and hoped for it to get better. Floriddia may well have had a heartbeat and been breathing on his own, but Dash wasn't going to take the time to check for either.

As Dash labored away, looking for all intents and purposes as if he were beating the hell out of his patient, Floriddia began to show signs of life, moving his arms and legs, thrashing around in a failed attempt to regain his feet. With each try he would simply collapse back to the ground, rolling around as if he were an injured snake, slithering in circles, using his legs like rudders.

As Dash watched Floriddia writhing in pain, he noticed something unusual about his feet, or at least the foot that had grounded Floriddia outside the vehicle. It was gone. All that was left of it was a glob of burned rubber from the sole of his boot with oozing flesh protruding from the wound. The electricity had blown Floriddia's foot off just as certainly as if it had been a mine, requiring Dash to tie a tourniquet tightly around the stump, just above the ankle in order to staunch the bleeding. Floriddia's duty as a soldier was finished.

***

Like Dash, Assiri immediately recognized what had happened. Rushing to where Dash was providing first aid to Floriddia, he watched the proceedings, noticed that Floriddia was still alive, and turned on his radio to reestablish contact with the hovering Black Hawk. Assiri explained to the pilot what had happened, directing him to follow ground commands and return for pickup. He also alerted them to the fact that they now had a MEDEVAC to contend with.

Picking up the yellow chemical lights, Assiri moved to the front of the vehicles and began directing the helicopter back to the waiting FAV's. By now Dash had stabilized Floriddia, laid him beside the vehicles, and taken his position as hook-up man on the roll cage. Hook-up was completed without any further incident and Assiri, his driver, and Dash, carrying an unconscious Floriddia, scrambled aboard the aircraft.

During the short flight to Rafha Floriddia, now breathing on his own but looking as if he was in another world, would drift in and out of consciousness, babbling incoherently about a dog that he had owned when he was a child. A big yellow mongrel that had killed his sister's cat. The significance of Floriddia's story concerning the dog was lost on all capable of hearing his ranting but it seemed important to him, and his ability to speak was all that mattered.

The Black Hawks landed at Rafha just long enough to draw fuel. But it gave Blackburn enough time to retrieve a local doctor to evaluate the extent of Floriddia's injury. The doctor honestly admitted that he was incapable of doing so. He did, however, volunteer to accompany the aircraft to KKMC in the event Floriddia became worse, a gesture of kindness and professionalism that was much appreciated by the soldiers.

Upon arrival at KKMC Floriddia was evaluated by a team of doctors and immediately MEDEVAC'd to the Landstuhl Medical Center, in Landstuhl, Germany. He would spend Desert Storm drinking good German beer and watching the war on television. Floriddia would later be fitted with a prosthetic foot and go on to a life teaching history at the University of North Carolina in Chapel Hill. Dash, Blackburn and Assiri all would return to Riyadh for further duty. In tow was an Iraqi captive that no one but Blackburn had any future plans for.

CHAPTER 15

oth Dash and Blackburn received orders assigning them to the Central
Command (CENTCOM) staff with duties as host nation liaison personnel, working in the Ministry of Defense and Aviation building (MODA), on
Abdul Aziz Street in the capital city of Riyadh, Saudi Arabia. They would
become part of a CENTCOM host nation liaison team responsible for coordinating
Saudi logistical support for the growing number of coalition forces flowing into the
Kingdom. Their jobs entailed receiving requests for food, water, fuel, transportation
and lodging from the support elements charged with taking care of the basic needs
of the many thousands of foreign troops then pouring into the Kingdom. The host
nation liaison section would then take these requests to the Saudi General Staff
where they would be massaged and managed by various Saudi staff officers. Once
accepted by MODA, the host nation liaison section performed all follow-up actions
tracking the status of the various requests through the labyrinth of the Friendly
Forces Logistical Support section of MODA.

It was a typical staff assignment, complete with the many frustrations that go
with being a "staff weenie" with no real authority. However, it was anything but boring as MODA would inevitably question the amount of supplies and services being
requested, then refuse to accept them until they were reduced to a less expensive
amount. Something none of the foreign forces were inclined to do. In allied minds,
whether the Saudis liked it or not, the Royal family was going to pay the costs of Desert
Storm one way or the other. Those responsible for paying the many foreign soldiers
being sent to the Kingdom were convinced that the Saudis were now going to have
to pay them to fight their war. They certainly were not going to fight it for free.

Predictably, whenever cost is an issue, there is another nuance that quickly
raises its ugly head—greed. Since the Saudi Royal family was getting stuck with the
bill, they also had the right of first choice in determining who would benefit from
all of the contracts being let to provision the armies. Bidding, as is the common
practice in the west in order to determine the lowest cost provider was not supposed
to be a part of the process, at least not for the Saudi Royals. Consequently all of the
contracts initially let went to companies owned by members of the Royal family. So,
in a circular motion, the Royal family members were actually paying themselves to
fight their own war. This of course angered the foreign contractors, most notably
the American ones, as they fought for a piece of the action.

Principal among the American companies vying for a piece of this action was a firm named Halliburton, a Houston based multi-national conglomerate once headed by the then current Secretary of Defense, Dick Cheney. With an entourage of lawyers that would have put to shame the American invasion of Normandy in 1944, Halliburton stormed the commercial section of the US Embassy demanding that they receive equal access to the enormous amount of money that this war promised. These same lawyers also began running articles in the various Arab newspapers claiming that their subsidiary companies, Brown and Root and Tamimi Global, among others, could perform the same functions at less cost than could their competitors who just happened to be owned by friends of the Royal family. It was an international brouhaha of the first order and provided great entertainment for all of those watching. But it also angered many people from all of the nations involved. Then, to break the loggerhead of Saudi nepotism, America played its trump card. She sent so many troops to fight the war that the Royals were forced to share the contracts. The Saudi owned businesses couldn't keep up with the demand created by such a huge influx of foreign troops.

The Royals antics also angered many Saudis, Mohammed Al-Assiri among them, who were astute enough to see what the family was attempting to do. Eventually, after giving themselves innumerable contracts, the Royals planned on passing the costs of the war down to the taxpayers and businessmen working and living in the Kingdom with an exorbitant rate of return attached. In effect the Royal family intended to pay themselves twice for a war designed to keep them in power, creating an atmosphere of distrust and deceit among all involved. Standing right in the middle of all this distrust and deceit, like a dam holding back the flood tide of outrage, was the host nation liaison section of CENTCOM.

Obviously, such a competitive arrangement was a constant source of consternation to the Saudi staff officers and their relationship with the host nation liaison personnel suffered as a result. The many conversations held between the two sides often bordered on downright hostility as both fought to have their voices dominate. Complicating all this were the many American contract lawyers rushing into the Kingdom in support of their favored sugar daddy. Dash and Blackburn were often as bedazzled by the legalistic contractual mumbo-jumbo being spewed by the high priced Ivy League lawyers as the Saudis were.

Assiri, on the other hand, would return to a real soldier's job. He would command a unit of the Saudi Arabian National Guard and participate in the battle of Khafji when Iraqi forces launched an unsuccessful invasion south across the Saudi border. His unit would acquit itself with courage and bravery, a characteristic gleaned from their commander.

It was while serving in the liaison position that Blackburn executed his promised plan for the young Iraqi conscript they had brought with them to Saudi Arabia.

Assiri had initially kept the boy with him, allowing him to do odd jobs around one of the four villas that he shared with each of his four wives. As it became more evident with each passing day that a ground war was imminent, he was forced to find a Saudi family the young man could stay with when his Army duties required him to take his SANG unit north to the Iraqi border. He had kept Blackburn informed as to the location of the Iraqi, telling him that the family watching over him expected to have to do so for only a short period of time, providing the only impetus the devious First Sergeant needed to finish preparing his plan.

Before Assiri deployed north Blackburn asked him to assist in contacting all of the appropriate Saudi agencies, including the two of them personally visiting the heads of these organizations to begin laying the foundation for the great game that would follow. Assiri happily complied, escorting Blackburn through the maze of offices that are the Saudi Ministries of the Interior, Labor, Health, Religion, and Customs.

As a side note, Assiri also introduced Blackburn to some "friends" of his who could produce any sort of official documentation that might be required to lend an air of legitimacy to his plan. Documents like Igamas, or work permits, passports, immunization and medical records, and a birth certificate that made the young man a Saudi by birth, making him legally eligible for adoption and satisfying a critical requirement that fit neatly into Blackburn's overall scheme.

These "friends" of Assiri's worked in a two-story warehouse in the Ba'atha district of Riyadh. Not far from the clock tower market, the new gold souk and "chop-chop" square, a place of Muslim repute where every Friday night following prayer call a public execution would be held to enforce the strict legal and moral codes of Wahabi Islam. All three were places frequented yearly by thousands of westerners seeking the baubles and beads of Middle Eastern culture or the thrill of a lifetime by watching some poor luckless bastard get his head cut off for some real or supposed violation of Saudi law.

The building Assiri's "friends" worked from advertised itself to be a book publishing company. It was, at least the bottom floor was. On this floor neatly bound and gold inlaid Korans stocked the many shelves along with religious writings, wedding and photo albums. But upstairs, on the second floor, the real business was conducted.

Behind a heavy metal and bullet proof door leading into a cavernous room filled with the latest in computer technology was a counterfeiting and forgery operation on a scale that would have put the New Jersey Mafia to shame. This was where Assiri's "friends" worked, busily providing high dollar customers with the latest in identity fraud and the type of supporting official documentation that would allow them to come and go anywhere in the world with minimal risk and a brand new name. Even if any number of countries these customers passed through were seeking them on Interpol, the chances of them being identified by carrying suspicious documents were practically nil. When he had first visited the site, Blackburn also made the observation, based on the large piles of American Dollars and Saudi Riyals stacked in a corner of a small adjacent room, that they were capable of producing their own currency as well.

Blackburn, a man not easily impressed, had been amazed at the efficiency of these forgers and counterfeiters. They were very, very good. Capable of, at least on paper, turning a man into a woman or a woman into a man. It would take a pelvic exam to prove that the documents they were carrying were fakes. Yet, at the same time, he was also uneasy when around Assiri's "friends," which he never was unless Assiri accompanied him. Blackburn sensed that they shared his uneasiness with being required to be near an American as well. They were good at what they were doing and, for the time being at least, Blackburn needed their help. They in turn were assisting the American only because Assiri had personally asked them to. It was, at best, an uneasy alliance and both Blackburn and the forgers were grateful when their business transaction was finally completed.

***

In discharging his duties as the host nation liaison support NCOIC Blackburn had a requirement to conduct routine business with the American Embassy, traveling to the diplomatic quarters several times a day. During his frequent visits he had become friends with many of the civilians working in the Political and Military (Pol/Mil) section of the embassy, often taking requests for support directly to them that required the signature of the Ambassador.

Proper protocol before these requests could be acted upon would have had him take them to the many Arabic translators working in the Embassy first, before taking them to the Pol/Mil section, so that the translators could ensure that the Arabic correspondence matched the English version accompanying it. But proper protocol was not at all the type of thing that Blackburn was concerned with. As an Arabic linguist himself, he was the author of many of these documents and he already knew that they in no way mirrored the English letters they were attached to. Of great assistance to him was the fact that, with Assiri's help, all of the Arabic correspondence had been typed on official ministry letterhead paper, complete with the requisite Saudi stamp verifying authenticity of the many agencies required to affect his ruse.

Taking official fake documents to the Embassy for signature was not something that he did on a daily basis for he had no reason to deceive the Ambassador, but he was in a hurry to expedite the process. As long as the Ambassador was in, legitimate requests moved expeditiously through the system. When the Ambassador was unavailable, as he often was, those same duties fell to the Deputy Chief of Mission (DCM), a Mister Anderson, the same Mister Anderson who hung up the phone on Major Dash as the team was escaping from Iraq.

When the DCM was left in charge requests moved through the system with the speed of molasses, often taking several days to be signed. Coincidentally appearing signed and undated just as the Ambassador was returning to his duties. The guy was a slug. Even the State Department civilians despised him, and that's saying a lot.

Most of the requests that Blackburn took to the Pol/Mil section were written only in English. But, lately, many had been written in English as well as having the fake Arabic version attached to them. Both the Arabic and the English version required the Ambassadors or DCM's signature on it. At least this was what Blackburn had told the Pol/Mil personnel. Had the Pol/Mil personnel been more observant they would have noticed that multi-lingual correspondence appeared for signature only when the DCM was placed in charge. It would have also served them well to remember that the DCM could neither read, write, nor speak Arabic. Since he had the annoying habit of waiting until the last possible moment to sign the requests, he didn't have time to have anyone translate them, naively assuming that it was an Arabic duplicate of the English correspondence it was attached to. This was exactly what Blackburn had expected he would do.

Following three months of this subterfuge, Blackburn approached Dash one morning and proudly announced, "Sir, I've finally found a sponsor for our Iraqi prisoner."

Blackburn always used the word prisoner when he spoke of the young conscript. Unlike the wishful thinkers in the State Department, he had no qualms about admitting that America was already at war with Iraq.

"Not only is this man going to sponsor him," he continued. "He has agreed to adopt him as well."

"That's good news, Top," said an admiring Dash. "Who is the lucky family?"

"I'd just as soon surprise you with that, Sir," he smiled mischievously. "All that I can tell you is that he is a high-roller in the American Embassy."

Failing to make the connection, Dash simply nodded his approval, smiling, and shaking his head.

"What do you say you and I take the young man over today and introduce him to his new stepfather?" Grinned Blackburn.

"Sure, why not? Go get him."

Later that same afternoon Dash received a phone call from the American Embassy. It was Blackburn.

"Sir," Blackburn's booming voice came over the phone. "I took the liberty of bringing our young man with me to the embassy. I've scheduled an office call with his new daddy for 1530. All three of us personally request your attendance at this joyful event. Can you make it?"

"Sure," answered Dash. "I just need to rewrite a couple of support requests I received from the French and I'll be right there. Should be there by 1500. That'll give us enough time to have a soda in the embassy cafeteria before we meet the man."

"Yes, Sir. I hear that." Blackburn said. "We'll meet you in the cafeteria at 1500." Ending the call with, "Oh yeah, you may want to bring a little whiskey to mix with that soda."

"I wonder what he meant by that?" Dash thought as the phone in his hand went dead.

Arriving in the cafeteria early at 1445, Dash found Blackburn and the young Iraqi sitting at a table by themselves, each of them quietly sipping a Root Beer float. Looking up and seeing Dash standing in the doorway, Blackburn smiled and motioned for him to join them. After he had ordered a Root Beer float for himself — they looked too good to pass up — Dash asked the young Iraqi a few simple questions like where he had been living, what he had been doing, how did he like Saudi Arabia, etc. Basic small talk. He didn't dislike the young boy, but he didn't feel that he had anything in common with him either.

Blackburn, however, could talk the legs off of a grasshopper and was anxious to demonstrate his young steeds growing proficiency speaking English. He kept asking the boy to repeat in English a phrase that he had been teaching him. It was, "Daddy! I am so happy to finally meet you. Can we go home now?" The young boy's English was getting much better. Dash could tell that Blackburn was proud of the work he had been doing with him. Like an animal trainer teaching a dog to sit up and bark, Blackburn seemed thrilled to have the opportunity for his pet to repeat the trick before any willing audience.

"Major," Blackburn said somewhat apologetically during a lull in the Iraqi's recital, "as D-Day, H-Hour rapidly approaches, I suppose I should tell you what is about to happen. You can then choose for yourself whether or not you want to participate. There may be some fall out from this and I want you to be aware of it before you sign up."

"Oh, sweet Jesus!" Dash thought, wanting to end the conversation before he knew too much. He hated it when Blackburn began a conversation this way. He had been involved in enough of his shenanigans over the past several years to recognize the signs. But, intrigued, against his better judgment, he said instead, "Keep talking; I'm listening."

Blackburn explained what he had been doing over the past three months. How with Assiri's help and his points of contact in the Ministry of Labor, Interior, and Muslim adoption agencies, he had managed to complete both sponsorship and adoption paperwork on the young Iraqi in the name of a Mister John Anderson. A Mr. Anderson who just happened to be the DCM in this very embassy. He told Dash how difficult it had been getting the various agencies to agree to let an American adopt a Saudi child. In the Kingdom, Saudi families take care of their own; rarely, if ever, allowing someone else to accept responsibility for a child carrying their name, especially a male child.

It had been a long and hard fight between Assiri and the many agencies involved, Blackburn continued, and Assiri had been forced to draw an ace from his deck of cards in order to break through the recalcitrance that is a part of any large bureaucracy. Somehow, in a way and manner unknown to him, Assiri had persuaded the King of Saudi Arabia, King Fahd himself, to issue a Royal Decree legitimizing the adoption. "When that happened, the whole thing kind of mushroomed," admitted Blackburn, an admission that caused the hair on the back of Dash's neck to stand erect.

Dash asked Blackburn to explain what exactly the word "mushroomed" meant and the canny first sergeant explained with his trademark grin that the local Arab media was going to cover the story, beginning with a dinner at Prince Sultan's palace tonight to celebrate the unusual event. Al-Jazeera, an Arab television network broadcasting regionally from Qatar would also be in attendance, meaning that the event would be announced throughout the Arab world. And, last but not least, CNN was planning to carry the story around the world as well, making the entire blessed event an international story.

Dash, who never carried a personal grudge for any length of time and did not think the way his mischievous first sergeant did, was beginning to lose interest with Blackburn's lengthy explanation, turning his attention back to his melting soft drink. He had still not yet made the connection between Mr. Anderson and his phone call from the desert. Simply replying in response to Blackburn's long-winded recitation, "That's wonderful, Top. I don't see any problems with it so far," as he slurped the sweet contents of his Root Beer float.

Blackburn never told him about the nefarious characters Assiri had introduced him to in order for the necessary documents to be forged. After all, Blackburn reasoned, Dash was an officer. And there were just certain things that sergeants did not share with officers. One being that the sergeant had been consorting with Saudi criminals who, in all probability, are also members of a Muslim terrorist cell. Such an admission is usually not something that is considered to be career enhancing.

As Blackburn rambled on about all the difficulties he had been forced to overcome Dash, having finished with his Root Beer Float, followed along listening attentively to detailed explanations of how he had procured the proper documents, gotten them signed, then returned to the various agencies. Dash still did not comprehend what the fall out might be other than it had been a lengthy and difficult process that had more than likely resulted in a few ruffled feathers.

As Blackburn continued to complain about the numerous bureaucracies he had been fighting with over the past several months, Dash finally stopped him, slowly piecing together in his mind what was happening, and asked, "And of course Mister Anderson doesn't know anything about this, does he?"

"Oh, Christ no!" replied a shocked Blackburn. "That would take all the fun out of it!"

Then, more pointedly, he asked, "You in or out, Major? And before you answer that, let me remind you of one small fact. This Mr. Anderson is the same uncaring dickhead that refused to talk with you when our ass was hanging in a sling inside Iraq. He is also directly responsible for the team losing the services of a fine young soldier like Floriddia."

"I'm in!" Came the immediate answer.

***

At precisely 1530 Dash, Blackburn, and the young Iraqi — Dash never did learn his real name — were sitting in the spacious waiting room of the Deputy Chief of Mission, Mister John Anderson. They didn't mind waiting, really. The DCM's secretary, a twentyish looking long-legged, buxom blonde, was wearing a mini-skirt and low cut blouse that left little to the imagination. Having been separated from their wives for over four months, it didn't take much to fire up that part of their imaginations either.

The nameplate on her desk said "Marsha," but to Dash she looked more like a 1-900-BIMBO girl to him. She was nice to look at though. So nice that they almost forgot why they had come, flirtatiously being reminded when a sultry voice purred, "Mister Anderson will see you now, gentlemen."

Blackburn, who had been pleasantly fantasizing about how good her underwear would look wrapped around his neck with her still wearing them, startled at the sound of her voice, causing Dash to smile, something he wasn't certain he should be doing at the moment. Angering a Deputy Chief of Mission was not something that was generally considered to be a boost to a career, officer or enlisted. But it was too late to back out now.

With Marsha's announcement Dash and Blackburn stood up from their chairs and walked into the DCM's office, closing the door behind them. They weren't worried about the Iraqi wandering away. The way he had been staring at the leggy secretary and her bouncing breasts, they doubted that he could even walk.

"Gentlemen, how may I be of assistance," asked the smiling, squeaking voice of a bespectacled Mister Anderson as he extended his hand in greeting. Blackburn would later remark that with his thick framed glasses, pointy nose, balding head, and bulging belly the DCM had looked like Woody Allen on steroids.

Following the initial handshake both soldiers took a seat in front of the rather large desk that the rather smallish DCM sat behind, scanning his office walls as they did so. The walls were covered with "I am a Hero" awards. Plaques and pictures from everywhere he had ever served and everyone of note that he had ever met were stacked from the floor to the ceiling, like a wall full of "Salesman of the Month" awards in a one-employee used car dealership. The guy was a legend in his own mind.

"Sir," Dash began. "This is First Sergeant Todd Blackburn, Noncommissioned Officer In Charge (NCOIC) of the CENTCOM Host Nation Support office in MODA. I am Major Tom Dash, Chief of that same section. We don't have a lot of time and I would like to come directly to the point, if you don't mind, Sir?"

"Certainly not," came the reply. "I'm a busy man myself," he said, waving his arm over an inbox full of paperwork.

"You and I spoke to one another once before, Sir," Dash continued, "three months ago when my SOF team was stuck behind Iraqi lines and looking for a way out. I have an unconfirmed suspicion that you hung up the phone on me that day. Hopefully you will be a little more receptive to my being here today."

As the sound of Dash's words and their possible implications registered the DCM's face went ashen, his eyes flashing the fear of a caged rat, fearing that these two very violent men were about to beat him. A thought that reinforced his stereotype that all military people were uncouth, illiterate barbarians incapable of civility, driven only by their insatiable desire to kill. Dash continued, delighted that he could see fear in his eyes. "Because I don't actually know with any degree of certainty if you could have even been of assistance to my team or not, I have withheld my judgment concerning how our phone call was cut short. I believe that a man in your position would move hell and earth before denying assistance to American soldiers performing a dangerous mission. I would like to think that it was electrical interference that ended our call and that you didn't really hang up on me. No diplomat with an ounce of character would refuse to help a fellow American in need."

Dash briefly paused to gauge the DCM's reaction. There was none. He simply stared at Dash open-mouthed, wheezing as he breathed, as if he were having a mild heart attack. So he continued, "And I have recently been told that you have a great deal of character, having volunteered to sponsor and adopt a young man in need of fatherly guidance, no easy task for a busy man like yourself. The idea that you would wish for the responsibility of raising a kid during such busy times melts my heart. Which is why we are here today, Sir. To finally make your wish come true."

"What are you talking about, Major?" The little voice squeaked. "I haven't volunteered to sponsor anybody. And I'm certainly not going to volunteer to adopt someone. I've been divorced from my third wife for over three years now. What the hell would I want with a kid? In answer to the phone call, it was interference. I would never hang up on a soldier in need," he lied.

"Yes, Sir." Blackburn interjected. "You did agree to sponsor and adopt a child, a young man, actually. He's fourteen, sitting outside the door having fun ogling your secretary at the moment. Would you like to meet him? He's a hell of a nice kid."

"This is preposterous," the little voice squeaked once again. "I should call security and have you escorted from these grounds at once! Adoption indeed!"

"You might want to think about that, Sir," countered Dash. "There is something you should know about the phone call I placed to you. It was bounced off a military satellite, which means that it was recorded. I have a copy of that recording with me. I think the Ambassador might enjoy listening to it."

Dash produced a cassette tape from his blouse pocket that contained *"The Eagles Best Hits,"* quickly flashing it in the air before putting it back into his pocket. He had been listening to the music during the drive to the embassy and had absent-mindedly put it in his pocket out of force of habit. In the hot sun of Saudi Arabia cassette tapes often melted if left in a car. He hoped that the little weasel would be intimidated by it. Hell, he didn't even know if satellite phone calls could be recorded. But it seemed like a good thing to say at the moment.

Taking the bait, the little voice squeaked again, but this time with much less authority. "What do you two want?"

"Sir, we don't want anything except to participate in this joyful occasion," Blackburn quipped. "And to present you with your file copy of the official documents you signed requesting sponsorship and adoption."

With that Blackburn produced a seventy-three-page document he was carrying and handed it to the DCM. Adding, "If you try to renege on your legal responsibilities, we'll see to it that the Saudi Royal family requests that the Ambassador remove you from your position and bar you from reentry into this country. A piece of paper like that won't look very good in your official file."

Dash, noting that the DCM was beginning to wobble, went for the kill. "When we leave here today the Public Affairs Officer is going to inform you about a party you will be attending tonight, thrown in your honor by Prince Sultan I might add, where you will be allowed to give your version of this adoption to the Arab media. I would suggest that you carefully consider what it is that you tell them because it actually took a Royal Decree from King Fahd himself to allow you to adopt this young man. If you no-show this party or in any other way embarrass the Royal family you can kiss your career in the Foreign Service good-bye."

"I've already bought me some popcorn," added Blackburn. "Gonna have my feet propped up tonight watching you on the boob tube. Should be quite a sight; gala event and all."

The DCM was loudly wheezing with every breath now. As Dash looked into his eyes he feared he might actually be having a real heart attack, but he pressed on, thinking "*if the bastard dies he deserves to.*"

"This party will not only be covered by local media," Dash continued, "but Al-Jazeera and CNN as well. Making you somewhat of an international celebrity. Hell, it might even be a boost for your career or, if you dick it up, a real career killer. As would any negative publicity you would get if you simply dump the kid after your big television debut."

Then, knowing that he had captured the DCM's total attention, Dash ended with a threat. "I mean it. One phone call from Saudi authorities telling me that you are abusing or neglecting this kid and I'll fry your pointed little ass. You'll never work in a Muslim country again."

Satisfied that the DCM was as confused as he was ever going to get, Dash concluded with, "Now, what do you say we meet your new son."

Without further prompting Blackburn went to the door, opened it and called out, "Young man, your father would like to meet you now." As he spoke he motioned with his hand for the Iraqi to come to him, a necessary hand gesture because the young man had no idea what Blackburn had just said to him in English. Nor was he expected to. Blackburn had made the statement for Marsha's benefit and it had produced the desired result. Out of the corner of his eye he noticed that the secretary's mouth had fallen wide open when she heard his words, leaving her looking as if she were preparing to give a blowjob to Goliath.

At the sight of Blackburn's beckoning hand motion, the young Iraqi conscript gleefully leaped to his feet and bounded through the DCM's open door, performing exactly as Blackburn had coached him. Smiling, with an obvious youthful erection that made him look as though he had a banana stuffed inside his pants, he shouted his well-rehearsed line, "Daddy! I am so happy to finally meet you. Can we go home now?"

As the two soldiers walked from his office they heard the DCM shout, "I don't goddamn believe it. Marsha, come in here, and I mean now!" Quickly followed by a repeat of, "Daddy! I am so glad to finally meet you. Can we go home now?"

In keeping with the SOF maxim, they had struck fast and they had struck hard, leaving the enemy confused, dazed and off balance. Now it was time for them to get the hell out of Dodge.

CHAPTER 16

With Operation Desert Storm looming on the horizon, the work pace of the CENTCOM Host Nation Support staff section began to gain speed. As a component of the J4/7 staff they dealt not only with the logistical requests from the American, British, and French forces preparing to go to war, they also had the staff responsibility for smoothing over any cultural, social, political, legal, or religious indiscretions as well. With an army of over a quarter million American infidels occupying the Holy Land of Islam there would be no shortage of indiscretions, making it a very busy time for both Dash and Blackburn. So many incidents occurred, in fact, that it was hard to remember all of them. But a few of them stand out for no other reason that it clearly shows the difference between the American and Arab cultures. Most, but not all, of the problems arising from this massive collision of cultures centered on the most visible difference between the two—the treatment of females.

***

In Saudi Arabia women do not drive. This rule applies not only to Saudi women, but to western females living and working in the Kingdom as well. Under strict Saudi Islamic law all females are forbidden to drive—period—break—end of message—no discussion follows! Unfortunately, in the modern unisex military that is America's, many vehicle drivers are female. The American Army, Marine Corps, Navy and Air Force units being deployed to the Kingdom had a large number of females assigned for exactly that purpose; to drive trucks, HMMWV's, sedans, even combat vehicles such as the Patriot Missile Carriers. These American females had deployed with their units expecting to perform their job to the best of their abilities. They ultimately did, but not without first putting the J4/7 staff and the Kingdom of Saudi Arabia through some cross-cultural growing pains.

As far as the American military commanders were concerned, some of whom were female themselves, the laws prohibiting females from driving were not only archaic, they were mission stoppers. Commanders could not accomplish the missions they were assigned unless the female soldiers were allowed to do their jobs. That commanders were required to develop plans denying women the right to perform their jobs was simply unacceptable to all but the Saudis. The American solution to this problem was that the restrictive culture of Saudi Arabia could go to hell; they were simply going to ignore the laws prohibiting females from driving. After all, they reasoned, if America was there to save the Saudi's butts, then the

Saudis were just going to have to bend a little. As usual, the State Department didn't see it quite so clearly.

In an attempt to prevent American soldiers from offending Saudi sensibilities the State Department intellectuals and other people who had nothing better to do with their time put together classes and materials to "educate" the less enlightened, barbarian American soldiers on local Saudi customs. After all, the State Department elitists righteously felt, most of the soldiers had not been to college so those who had received a higher education felt obligated to hold the hand of the less enlightened at this critical juncture when the American "can do" attitude collided with an ancient culture. Surely, these elitists reasoned, something as complicated as working and living in a foreign environment required an education program to minimize the many "misunderstandings" likely to occur. These elitists failed to remember that soldiers have been doing such things longer than politicians and academicians have.

As point men for this "train the trainer" program both Dash and Blackburn were required to endure hour after interminable hour at the Embassy sitting through "cultural sensitivity" sessions. These sessions were equally divided between classes and seminars where some pointy-headed intellectual would decry America's latest and most blatant violation of Saudi sovereignty. Presenters would show dozens of supporting power point slides detailing the latest indiscretion, then offer a remedy to prevent it from happening again. Discussed were thoughts as earth shattering as the illegality of females driving or male soldiers "hitting" on Saudi females, something that seemed to be occurring with increasing regularity the longer the troops were deployed. Other items for discussion were such cultural *faux paux* as using the left hand, or "toilet hand," to eat or pass written correspondence to your Saudi counterpart; or showing the soles of your feet or interrupting the Saudis during prayer call, etc., etc. All items of monumental importance to be sure. Items that once learned Dash and Blackburn were to take back to the American units where these lessons would be taught and distributed down to the user level. None of the soldiers could have cared less about learning any of it.

It seemed as though everyone in the state department who considered themselves to be important had an opinion on something. Since it was *their* opinion, it was essential that it be heard. Most of these opinions never seemed to have any logical beginning and certainly never a logical end to them. But the many points all had one thing in common — they had absolutely nothing at all to do with fighting and winning a war. They were all just touchy-feely mumbo-jumbo with pretty slides and graphics, always accompanied by an exaggerated sense of urgency and a lot of whining and complaining.

CENTCOM required Dash and Blackburn to attend these sessions to give the

American media and the pointy headed state department intellectuals the impression that the U.S. military was concerned with Saudi sensitivities. In all honesty, no American male soldier gave a damn how the Saudis treated their own females, and they had already decided to simply ignore Saudi complaints regarding how Americans treated their female soldiers. Commanders were going to give the females the same freedoms and responsibilities that they gave to the male soldiers, not listening to any contrary hogwash from either the state department or the Kingdom of Saudi Arabia. The many sensitivity sessions were pointless and a complete waste of time for American military personnel. The soldiers weren't in Saudi Arabia to make friends or to change a culture, theirs or the Saudi's. They were there to kill Iraqis then go home; nothing else mattered to them.

The Mutawah, the Saudi Religious police, on the other hand, were absolutely incensed that American females were given such liberties on Islamic soil. Such freedoms for a woman were viewed by them and other like-minded religious bigots as being tantamount to challenging God.

The Mutawah are essentially civil service workers, hired and trained by the government of Saudi Arabia to enforce the moral codes of Islam. Because of the presence of American female soldiers in the Kingdom, the Saudi governmental bureaucrats were in a quandary. The religious clerics and their foot soldiers, led by the Mutawah, were being denied the legal right to enforce the strict moral codes of Islam and the very people who had hired them to enforce these codes were now denying them this right. Many Saudi religious figures began complaining through the media that it was the Saudi government's complicity in granting infidels permission to occupy the Kingdom that was the root cause of the "female problem." These same religious figures also began demanding that the Royal Family take action supporting them in the performance of their official duties.

The Mutawah solution to the "female problem" was to demand that all foreign troops not in the Kingdom prior to Saddam's invasion of Kuwait be immediately evicted. Barring this, the Mutawah demanded that all foreign female troops be evicted, and, lastly, they demanded that any females remaining in Saudi Arabia comply with Saudi laws.

On the surface, for the weak kneed diplomats and their complicit media lap dogs, it appeared to be an insurmountable problem. It certainly received an undue amount of media coverage in the States and throughout the Arab world. But for the American soldiers working with their Saudi counterparts, it wasn't even a topic of discussion.

The Saudi soldiers knew that American intelligence, especially the satellite photos showing Iraqi troop dispositions, had convinced the Saudi Royal Family that Saddam Hussein had planned to invade the Kingdom. They also knew that Saddam's army would kick the crap out of anything the Saudis could put in the field. If the Royals wanted to remain in power and the Saudi soldiers wanted to stay alive, there was no choice but for them to get in bed with the American infidel devils, proving that politics do indeed make for strange bedfellows. Then again so does a soldier's desire to stay alive when staring down the gun tubes of an invading army.

But, as is the custom in Saudi Arabia, the rulers would never publicly defend their position because it was so controversial with the civilians. People not serving in the military who were blissfully unaware that a fellow Muslim leader wanted to kill them; a fact not lost on the Royal Family. They were acutely aware of the danger they faced, going to great lengths to ensure that Saddam did not invade the Kingdom. King Fahd's reliance on outside protection as a guarantee that he remain in power effectively left the Mutawah in the impossible position of trying to do their job but having neither the political backing nor legal authority required to do it. While at the same time the average Saudi citizen demanded from them that the Mutawah earn their pay and stop all of this feminist nonsense before it got out of hand and their own wives and daughters demanded driving privileges as well.

As this dilemma percolated through both the Saudi and the American hierarchies, a salient incident occurred that quickly clarified the Saudi government's position regarding coalition female personnel as juxtaposed against their desire to enforce the moral codes of Islam — not to mention saving their own asses in the process. The Mutawah attempted to arrest an American female soldier, not for driving, but for the way she was dressed.

***

One morning in early December Dash was quietly sitting behind his desk when Blackburn burst through the door and announced, "An American female soldier just shot a Mutawah!" eliciting a flurry of questions from Dash concerning the who, what, when, where, and why of the incident. Questions that Blackburn could not satisfactorily answer. He had simply been drinking morning tea in the office of Prince Faisal, Chief of MODA Security, when a MODA guard had burst into his office claiming that an American female soldier had just shot a Mutawah. He was simply repeating what he had heard. Now, it was up to the two of them to verify the story.

Like most initial reports, the story had been greatly exaggerated. The American female soldier had not shot a Mutawah, but she had pointed a gun at him, threatening to shoot him if he didn't stop harassing her. The gist of the story was that two American female soldiers from the U.S. Army Military Police Company (MP's) assigned to help provide security for MODA had entered an elevator inside the MODA building when a Mutawah, along with a Saudi Air Force Captain entered it.

The Mutawah became offended that the females were not wearing the Hijab, or headscarf, required of all Saudi females. Making the mistake of vehemently telling them so by yelling at them in pigeon English, demanding that they immediately cover their hair, threatening to have them arrested for breaking Saudi law if they failed to comply with his dictates. The Mutawah became so enamored with his perceived powers that he ultimately made the mistake of reaching out and tugging on the hair of one of the females, emphasizing to them the indiscretion he wanted to see addressed. The woman whose hair the Mutawah pulled was a rather large and muscular black woman named Sonya Sylvester, an Army Specialist born and raised in Selma, Alabama.

At the time of the incident, Sonya Sylvester had been in the Kingdom for less than three days and wasn't exactly thrilled that she was there at all. Like most Reservists, she had a civilian job and family life that had been interrupted when her unit was activated in response to Saddam's invasion of Kuwait. She was a long-term employee of the Alabama state prison system, employed as a prison guard in charge of male prisoners at the Limestone Correctional Facility near Huntsville, Alabama. Sonya Sylvester was a thirty-five-year-old reservist who had been selected as an Individual Replacement (IR) augmentee to assist the American MP's charged with providing security for MODA. In Dash's interviews with her he discovered that she also had a nineteen-year-old son back home who was attending the University of Tennessee on a football scholarship where he was an All-SEC Conference defensive tackle. As she explained her background to Dash, he took the liberty of noting that Sonya looked as if she could have taken a few snaps from center herself, or maybe even have played center. She certainly didn't look like she was a woman who could be intimidated. Why a Mutawah would pick a fight with someone like Sonya was a clear indicator to Dash that he was not only overly zealous in the performance of his duties, he was also a crazy son-of-a-bitch with a death wish as well. As a White American male Dash was instinctively afraid of a woman like Sonya. Why a Mutawah hadn't been scared of her as well would always be a mystery to him.

Growing up in 1960's Selma, the hot bed of the civil rights movement, Sonya was also well acquainted with her personal civil rights. She was already angry about the prospects of spending Christmas in Saudi Arabia and was not about to take any crap from a strange looking Arab man dressed like a woman, wearing Thobe and Guttrah, telling her to cover her head. She damn sure was not in the mood to let him touch her without her permission. Because of all the emotional highs and lows she had experienced when ordered to Saudi Arabia against her wishes, Sonya Sylvester was far beyond a PMS mood swing — she was a large package of black dynamite just waiting to explode. When the Mutawah pulled her hair, she did explode, punching him in the face hard enough to knock him to the floor of the elevator, where he remained, lying on the floor, looking up at her through glassy eyes. Sonya then turned her attention to the Saudi Air Force Captain accompanying the now prostrate Mutawah, shaking her ham sized fist in his face and screaming, *"You want some of this too, faggot bitch?"* The frightened Captain flattened himself against the wall, profusely apologizing on behalf of the Mutawah and wishing that he had taken a different elevator. Then, thinking that maybe the Mutawah had not understood why she had decked him, cultural "misunderstandings" and all, Sonya pulled her Beretta 9mm pistol from the Bianchi holster strapped to her hip. She then carefully aimed the pistol at his crotch, closing one eye as she squinted down the barrel at the sights, telling him in no uncertain terms that if he didn't shut up and keep his hands to himself she was going to shoot his dick off.

The deeply religious, dyed-in-the-wool Muslim Mutawah had a limited command of the English language. It is doubtful that he understood a word that the very large, very angry American black women standing over him, pointing a big pistol at his crotch, had said to him. Then again, he didn't have to. Her body language and Beretta pistol were a universal language that spoke volumes. When the elevator door opened the Mutawah scrambled to his feet and burst through it as if his life depended on it. It did! He disappeared running around the nearest corner, the sounds of robes flapping and sandals slapping, knocking a group of Saudi soldiers out of his way as he did so, secretly hoping that if she shot at his back she would hit one of them instead of him. This incident was the final straw for the Royal Family. They ordered all Mutawah out of Riyadh until the Americans left before one of them really did get shot.

***

A similar incident occurred in Dhahran when a group of American soldiers, some of whom were females, were playing volleyball near enough to the highway that gawking drivers could see them. The soldiers had been told to comply with Saudi sensitivities concerning dress and for the most part they did, always having at least a T-shirt covering their torso. However, as reserve troops poured into the Kingdom a few of them had fallen through the cracks and had not yet received instruction on proper "etiquette," particularly female "etiquette," while living and working in the Kingdom.

A group of soldiers assigned to a reserve transportation unit were playing a rousing game under the hot Saudi sun when one of the females, a well-endowed brunette from Raleigh, North Carolina, removed her T-shirt, revealing a multi-colored halter-top that almost covered her ample mammary glands. The colorful blue and orange mini-cloth, coupled with her large, well-tanned breasts, proved to be a major distraction for drivers speeding down the highway as their eyes locked on to the sight like a Patriot Missile locks on to an incoming Scud. Unfortunately diverting their attention from the chore at hand, which happened to be controlling a three thousand pound automobile traveling in excess of eighty miles per hour.

The unexpected yet titillating sight (no pun intended) resulted in a fourteen-car pile up that killed several people and generated a flurry of letters from the Emir of the Eastern Province demanding that MODA do something about this shameful exhibitionism before anyone else got killed.

Some of the letters given to Dash by his Saudi counterpart contained the phrase *"kabeera lahama,"* meaning a lot of meat could be seen. In American vernacular the females were showing too much skin, distracting the fragile Arab male mind while driving his car, resulting in them losing control and driving over the top of the vehicle in front of them.

The Commander at Lucky Base, where the incident had occurred, simply moved the volleyball court to the far end of his perimeter where it couldn't be seen from the highway. Solving the problem, but no doubt disappointing the drivers of the many vehicles now driving past Lucky Base to get a good look at such a despicable sight.

***

Living in a culture so repressive for females also afforded some of the American male soldiers living at Eskan Village, South of Riyadh, an unexpected benefit. Dating is not allowed in Saudi Arabia. The Saudi mothers and grandmothers do all of the matchmaking because they are the ones who know when some other mother's son or daughter comes of age. This is necessary primarily because Arab men, like their American male counterparts, usually aren't even aware who has a son or daughter, much less how old they are. The Saudi females take this duty quite seriously. So seriously in fact that they allow their daughters to go on shopping trips to the mall where they meet with their friends and discuss who knows some boy who is looking for a wife. In much the same manner that American teenage girls gather to discuss such heady matters. Unlike America however, in a strict Islamic country like Saudi Arabia, such excursions to the mall are usually chaperoned, but not always.

By chance or design, a group of Saudi females acquired an Eskan phone directory, sharing it with their friends, and had begun to call the soldiers living there. Since English is a part of the Saudi school curriculum, most could converse well enough to get their message across. Especially when that message was stated in a sultry voice that caused the male listener to pay very close attention to what was being purred over the telephone. A sultry voice telling them that the caller would be at the Al-Rashid Mall, which was across the street and two blocks down the street from where many of them worked in MODA, on a certain date and at a certain time, essentially making a blind date with them. Young men being young men it wasn't hard to get the Americans to agree to meet with them.

Inside the Mall was the usual number of clothing and record stores with the occasional soda shop where most of the unchaperoned females would gather to cluck and cackle like all teenage girls do. But with increasing regularity, some of these girls were coming to the Mall to do more than just gossip with their friends. Some were coming to the Mall to practice international relations in the purest sense. Assisting them in their efforts, just down the hallway from one of these soda shops was a dark corner where a shop had recently closed. Adding to this ambiance of solitude someone had either broken or removed the ceiling lights from this part of the Mall, leaving it quite dark and a place naturally avoided by all of the older people shopping there.

Because of the lack of customer activity in this particular corner of the Mall, it quickly acquired a reputation amongst the Saudi females as being the "in" place to be seen by one another. It was even more "in" if they could be seen by their friends returning from the dark recesses of the Mall in the company of a smiling American male soldier.

American soldiers would meet their "dates" in the soda shop and with a guard posted to prevent any interruption, the two of them would go into the darkened corner and have sex. There must have been hundreds of American soldiers who got a shot of Saudi leg while standing vertical, leaning against the wall at the Al-Rashid Mall, always with a girl whose face they never even saw, proving once and for all that looks mean nothing to a horney soldier. A girl can cut her head off and he will still find her to be attractive as long as she will lift her skirt.

**

The incident described above is not really an example of how different the two cultures are, but how alike people really are. Regardless of culture or country, any time that young men and women are placed in close proximity to one another, they will seek out the opposite sex to fulfill their biological purpose in life, propagation of the species. Even if procreation is not the goal, casual sex is always good practice in preparing for the day when it is. If nothing else came from these romantic dalliances, the fact that many young people were now well trained for that day when they finally met Mister or Miss Right was sufficient enough reason in its own right. Young people instinctively know how to get along with each other by fulfilling one another's desires, which is the purpose of relationships; personal, domestic, or international. Dash found it odd that young people with no ulterior motives except to enjoy one another's company could practice effective international relations without training and diplomats with years of research and experience behind them couldn't. Maybe more diplomats should be put against the wall and screwed!

There was one other incident worth noting that occurred prior to the commencement of hostilities that also indicates how alike people are. But this incident had a more sinister component to it than just casual sex, it involved fundamentalist religion and offers a clear example of how great ideas can be used to divide rather than unite people.

***

One day Dash received a phone call from the Saudi General Staff liaison officer informing him that Saudi Customs officials had seized a rather large shipment of books at the Dammam seaport, a port facility in the Eastern Province where all of the materials shipped into the Kingdom arrived. He requested that Dash, or someone from his office, fly to Dhahran and investigate these findings. Dash and Blackburn dutifully did, arriving at the seaport two hours later via Black Hawk helicopter.

After being greeted by the custom officials and drinking the requisite glass of tea, Dash and Blackburn were taken to a receiving warehouse stacked to the roof with all sorts of packages, crates, and paraphernalia that had been shipped into the Kingdom from civilians back in the States. The bulk of these items were care packages from loved ones who were trying to make their soldiers lot in life as comfortable as possible while they were enduring the hardships of a combat deployment. The remainder were commercial products wherein some enterprising entrepreneur was trying to capitalize on the tremendous financial opportunities available during any war. None of the crates, packages, or paraphernalia was official military goods. Military items all arrived duty exempt, through different channels, always handled exclusively by American military personnel.

As Dash and Blackburn marveled at the abundance the "land of the big PX" could produce, they were shown a box opened by customs officials that contained books inside. The customs officials had become suspicious as to the contents when they noticed that the return address on the upper left corner of the box was from the Samaritan's Purse in Boone, North Carolina. This in and of itself was not suspicious, but there were several hundred of these boxes marked with this same return address which made it suspicious.

Accordingly, the custom officials had opened one of the boxes and found it to contain a large number of New Testament Bibles. Written in Arabic, the bibles had allegedly been sent to the troops as a Christian gesture of camaraderie and support, as well as a textbook for them to learn the Arabic language. Proselytizing, the attempt to convert from one belief or faith to another, is illegal in Saudi Arabia. In the Kingdom, by codified law, there is but one religion allowed to practice the tenets of its faith and that religion is Islam, a fact well known to the good folks from the Samaritan's Purse in Boone, North Carolina.

For a country like America, having a religious system based upon a plurality of competing religions, it is understandable that an honest mistake of sending Bibles into the Kingdom could be just that, an honest mistake. But this was larger than a mere honest mistake, or even proselytizing. It was a counterattack against Islam by the loving Christian folk back home.

The 24th Infantry Division, based at Fort Stewart near Savannah, Georgia, had arrived in Saudi Arabia in early September as a part of the 18th Airborne Corps deployment. One of the lesser-known facts about an Army post is that the majority of the soldiers assigned there are from that, adjacent, or nearby states, meaning that most of the Divisions soldiers were from Georgia, North and South Carolina, Florida, Alabama, etc., states with a large Southern Baptist population.

Commanded by Major General Barry McCaffrey, a no nonsense warrior and highly decorated Vietnam veteran, the Division arrived in Saudi Arabia and immediately deployed deep into the desert, shunning any effort at civility, such as living in buildings and crapping in flush toilets. McCaffrey reasoned that since war is a nasty, brutal, physically and mentally demanding endeavor that it would be counterproductive for his soldiers to become accustomed to a softer, gentler side of life when, any day now, they would be ass deep in Iraqi soldiers, fighting, capturing, and killing them. When that day came, he wanted his soldiers so angry at the Iraqis for causing them to have to live like animals that they would attack them the way a Pit Bull attacks a small Chihuahua.

In the meantime, in addition to a constant training regiment, McCaffrey allowed his soldiers a modicum of civility by granting permission to conduct worship services in the Division's desert base camps. To include Muslim worship services, a concept of "cultural sensitivity" that quickly spread throughout the Corps area of operations to other base camps. As a result, for reasons known only to the converts, a "statistically significant" number of American soldiers were converting to Islam, especially the black soldiers, who would then write home and tell their parents what they had done, touting the appeal that Islam had for them. Unfortunately, Mom and Dad did not share in their son or daughter's joy in finding a home in Islam. In fact, they became downright angry and demanded that the Southern Baptist leadership do something to put a stop to it.

Dash never learned how the Bibles had been produced but the reasoning behind them was made apparent by a letter written in English and placed inside the front cover of each Bible. It read:

> *Dear Fellow American:*
>
> *Now that you are in the Persian Gulf, you may find that you have some spare time. Don't waste it! Instead, why not try learning a little Arabic?*
>
> *Enclosed is a copy of the New Testament in the Arabic language. You may want to get a Saudi friend to help you read it. Arabic is a difficult language, but once you learn it, you'll never forget it.*

We're very proud of you and pray that God will protect you and bring you safely home to your loved ones. Meanwhile, have fun learning Arabic, using God's Word as your textbook.

Sincerely,
(S)
Franklin Graham

Franklin Graham is better known to less religious Americans when announced as being the son of his more famous father, Billy Graham.

The purpose for Mr. Graham's letter was self-evident. If the Saudi friend Franklin Graham referred to was busy reading the Bible to an American soldier, then he or she could not be reading the Koran to them as well. This meant that the soldier was being kept in the Christian camp and the Muslim was being exposed to Christianity, hopefully converting him or herself in the process. Legally this was a clear attempt at proselytizing but rather than making an issue of it the Saudi custom officials simply sent the boxes of Bibles back to North Carolina. Which is why the American press never had the opportunity to embarrass the Saudis by making a major issue out of it, as they had done with the Saudi treatment of females. The last thing that any Saudi official wanted was to have to defend their "backwardness" against another onslaught from "enlightened" Americans, especially religious Americans who were just as bigoted as the Saudis were.

Having lived and worked throughout the Middle East, Dash and Blackburn were well aware of the deleterious effects of religious fundamentalism. Yet no matter how many times they encountered it, they were left amazed that people living in a country as free and open as America could demand that the rest of the world be just like them. Such people literally reek of insecurity and a desire to dominate. Naively reasoning that if there were more people believing as they believe that there would be an end to war, poverty, hunger, disease, and any other number of human ailments. Completely dismissing the history of America's creation, one where Christians killed other Christians by the hundreds of thousands. An incontrovertible fact that any serious student of European and American history can recite in great detail. Just ask the Christian British what their experiences were in fighting American Christians during the American Revolution. And what Southern Christian could ever forget what their Northern Christian brothers and sisters did to them during the American Civil War; not to mention the stories of atrocities that the Native American Indians could tell detailing their experiences with Christianity. In light of historical fact, Christianity has been as aggressive, if not more aggressive, than any of the other major religions. A statement not meant to indict any religion at the expense of another, but one meant to enhance a greater understanding of all religions when religion is offered as a panacea for the woes of mankind.

Nowhere in the world has religion ever trumped the effects of nationalism, greed, sex, freedom, politics, or economics. It won't in the Middle East either, no matter what flavor it comes in. Solutions to world problems will require more effort than the simplistic belief that everybody holding hands and singing hymns from the same good book, Billy Graham's or Mohammed's, will provide an answer for them. The world, thank God, is a much more complex place than that.

CHAPTER 17

When the bombing campaign initiating Desert Storm began in January, Dash and Blackburn found themselves still sitting behind desks in MODA. For warriors, nothing can be as disgruntling as being a "staff puke" when there is a war going on. They were both champing at the bit to get in on the action, as were all the other "staff pukes" in CENTCOM headquarters. But somebody had to do it, and this time it was their turn. Despite the fact that staff work is unglamorous, and nobody really wants to do it, it is essential that it be done well if the overall effort is going to be successful. Good staff personnel are just as hard to come by as good troop leaders. In fact, any good commander or first sergeant is also a good staff officer or staff NCO. Both positions require attention to detail, integrity, personal courage, and an almost obsessive desire to do what is right.

Still, when the guns are pounding, it is difficult to admit, after the guns go silent, that the most dangerous thing faced as a staff weenie was that a suspense was missed and an ass was chewed by some irate colonel or general. A soldier has a tendency to feel a little guilty about it years later. Especially when bouncing a grandchild on a knee and he or she asks, "What did you do in the war, Grandpa?" And the only answer he can come up with is that he once shot himself in the thumb with a stapler and suffered a nasty paper cut that same day. Such an honest admission doesn't exactly reinforce the saying that "war is hell."

Fortunately, or unfortunately, depending upon your perspective, the ground campaign was about to kick off and both Dash and Blackburn would get to participate in it. This time as 18th Airborne Corps liaison personnel attached to the Saudi ground force leading the attack into Kuwait. Once again they would be with their old friend Moe Assiri.

Before joining the unit Dash and Blackburn had watched with great interest the battle for Khafji and the performance by the Saudi units participating. One had been the company commanded by Assiri. They were proud of the fact that they had been a part of training these same forces one year earlier while assigned to OPM-SANG. Based on the Saudis performance, they had obviously done something right.

Still, both men knew that the Saudi Arabs were not U.S. soldiers. Not to take anything away from them, but they were no way near the equivalent of an American combat unit. Individually there were some fine, brave soldiers in the ranks but, collectively, they always seemed to fall short of meeting the expectations that an American commander would have for his own troops. Then again, in their defense,

Saudi troops had not had the decades of war fighting experience the European and American armies had either. Their combat deficiencies may have been there because of a lack of experience, not necessarily desire. And, conversely, these deficiencies may have been there precisely because the Saudi soldiers had no burning desire to prepare for the hardships of war, preferring instead that someone else do the fighting and dying while they cheered from the sidelines. Consequently, going into combat with the Saudis had both Dash and Blackburn nervous. They really didn't know what to expect from them.

As it turned out, they were worried about nothing. Assiri had predicted that the coalition forces would pass through Saddam's vaunted Republican Guard like crap through a goose. And they did, except for a few minor skirmishes, none of which were significant enough to cause extensive coalition casualties. With the exception of one Scud missile that unfortunately escaped the Patriot missile umbrella protecting Dhahran, hitting a warehouse and killing several American soldiers sleeping there, the greatest danger front line soldiers faced was from fratricide, being killed by their own forces. The real killing that was taking place was Iraqi on Iraqi killing. Before, during, and after Desert Storm, Saddam cleaned his political house, ridding himself of anyone and any group that sought to affect the regime change that America was not so quietly supporting.

When Iraqi forces withdrew from Kuwait and were caught on the "highway of death" by coalition aircraft north of Kuwait City, it was seen as a signal by the Iraqi resistance fighters that now was the time to launch their final attacks against Saddam. They fatefully reasoned that with Saddam's army clearly on the run, and the coalition army clearly assuming control of both Kuwait and southern Iraq, there would never be a better time. After all, with the coalition forces in position to prevent Saddam's Republican Guard forces from interfering, a political uprising would have a very good chance of succeeding. America had encouraged the resistance forces to plan such a thing, paying and equipping them. It was now time for them to earn their money and execute the long awaited attack against their arch nemesis, Saddam Hussein. The Marsh Arabs were prepared to hold up their end of the deal. They mistakenly expected America to do the same.

***

North of the Kuwaiti border, near the Iraqi towns of Basra, Umm Quasar, Safwan, extending all the way to the gates of Baghdad itself, resides a large population of predominately Shia Muslims. Politically different from the Sunni Muslims represented by the Ba'ath party in that Shia political, cultural, and religious allegiance is more closely aligned with that of Iran's than that of Iraq's. In 1991, even more so than today, Iran was vehemently anti-American, which created a problem for the Bush administration who, along with the current crop of congressional leaders, were left with the political "hot potato" of seemingly supporting an Iranian backed insurrection in Iraq or leaving Saddam Hussein in power. They opted for the latter by invoking the rationale that it is "better to deal with the devil you know than the one you don't know." Performing a complete political one-eighty from what the strategy had been before and during the war, a time when the CIA and SOF forces employed in southern Iraq had been actively fomenting a revolution designed to topple Saddam Hussein from power utilizing indigenous forces.

In the minds of the Americans fomenting and conducting this revolution there was no legitimate reason not to topple Saddam from power. There was no effort on their part to attempt to deceive anyone. Even a fool could see that if left in power Saddam would continue to be a festering sore on America's body politic. But the CIA and SOF people were looking at long term problem resolution. They were not considering the fact that a presidential election was slightly more than one year away. But half a world away, in Washington D.C., the Republican party campaign planners knew that if the Bush administration succeeded in removing Saddam from power, it would not leave them enough time to put a stable government together to replace him in Baghdad, certainly not one that was not anti-American. And in election year politics opening up a can of worms like Iraq and not being able to close it would prove disastrous to political ambitions.

The end result of this thinking was that, for reasons of politics rather than humanity, tens of thousands of Iraqi Shia Muslims were allowed to be put to the sword by Saddam while American soldiers were boarding aircraft less than two hundred miles away. Immediately being sent home after the "televised" war was declared over for a much-appreciated "Miller Time" and a clean uniform. To be welcomed home and congratulated for a job well done by a proud and grateful nation with parades, picnics, and interviews with home town newspaper reporters. It was a proud moment for America and for its returning soldiers, just as it should have been. But, lurking in the background of these festivities, all of which were attended by local political representatives, was the awareness that even though Desert Storm had ended, the civil war inside Iraq certainly had not ended.

***

The first shots in America's current war against Islamic terrorists were fired immediately following the declaration of victory in the desert sands of Iraq following Desert Storm. Saddam's forces fired these shots and their targets were other Iraqis who had allied themselves with America in order to satisfy their own political desires. But since these shots did not kill Americans few Americans were told about them. Stories of Iraqis killing Iraqis do not sell magazines and newspapers in America so the media elected to cover other stories instead, like the surging political popularity of George Bush following his recent "victory" in Iraq.

Several other shots had previously been fired in America's war against terrorism, most notably the attack on the marine barracks in Lebanon in 1983, killing 243 marines President Reagan had foolishly placed there in a weak attempt to show resolve in combating Middle East violence. He then clearly demonstrated a lack of resolve by ordering the marines to get out of Lebanon before any more of them were killed. A foolish and cowardly political act that sent a message to terrorist groups around the world that it was open season on American military personnel wherever a suicide bomber could find them. Certainly no American politician was rattling his saber demanding that Americans overseas be protected from such attacks, even if it meant going to war in order stop them.

Finally and regrettably, a shot was fired in America's war against terrorism that all Americans heard because it killed over three thousand of them, mostly civilians, driving home the fact to the general public that America was at war, and had been for several years. It was no longer just soldiers, sailors, airmen, and marines serving in remote locations overseas that were in danger. Suddenly, what had been happening to uniformed and state department personnel for years had now happened to civilians inside the no longer safe confines of the United States of America. Now America itself had a problem, leaving the politicians dutifully vowing to hunt down and kill whoever had done this terrible, incomprehensible thing. The politicians feigned surprise that someone wanted to kill Americans more than they themselves wanted to live. Never admitting to their constituents that they had known for years that people were conspiring to bring war to the American homeland for indiscretions that the American government had personally been a party to. This complicit silence on the part of the electorate left most Americans in a fog of uncertainty wondering what these crazy Arabs were so angry about.

Sadly, as Dash watched the events of 9/11/01 unfold across his television screen, he had to acknowledge a firmly held conviction, gut wrenching that it was. He believed that if it had only been the Pentagon that had been attacked, and if it had been overseas instead of in Washington, D.C., killing only military and civil service personnel, America probably would not have demanded retribution. He also silently prayed that he was wrong in feeling this way. A real American should get fighting mad anytime one of their countrymen is killed in an act of terrorism, military or civilian, and they should demand that their elected leaders do the same.

***

For Dash and Blackburn the period immediately following the war was particularly troubling. They had represented 18th Airborne Corps at the peace accords signed by American General Norm Schwarzkopf, Saudi General Prince Khalid, and a host of Iraqi Republican Guard Officers. Ironically, the accords were signed in a tent north of Safwan not far from the farmhouse where they had taken General

Talabani and the Ayatollah Sistani to meet with the resistance leaders. Assiri had been present in the tent as well, as a representative of SANG and as an honored guest of General Khalid, son of Prince Sultan and grandson of Abdul Aziz Al-Saud, a legendary figure who is generally considered by most Saudis to be the political equivalent of George Washington.

Following the signing of the peace accords, Assiri remained in Kuwait assisting in the recovery efforts to get some of the Kuwaiti riches returned from Iraq. The invading Iraqis had stolen everything they could get their hands on and were in no hurry to return any of it, including the Kuwaiti prisoners they had taken with them.

After the war both Dash and Blackburn remained in Iraq assisting in the establishment of a refugee relocation and repatriation camp along the Iraq and Kuwait border south of Safwan. They remained in Iraq for three months after America had declared victory, a time that had the media overcome its short attention span and responsibly covered it would have proven very enlightening for all those who mistakenly believed that Saddam had lost the war. During this three month period Dash, Blackburn and Assiri often got together and went for drives through the country side, a simple event not without its own risks as they had to carefully navigate around tons of unexploded ordinance remaining from the coalition air strikes. But trips worth the risk as the three comrades would stop and talk to the villagers as well as to stragglers in the continuing stream of refugees trying to make their way back across the Kuwaiti border. All of these people, without exception, told tales of beatings and mass killings that were taking place throughout the area.

When the coalition forces left Iraq Saddam's forces returned and exacted a fearsome toll on the inhabitants. Dash and Blackburn watched as Assiri became more livid with the telling of each survivor's story, often verbally attacking the Americans for allowing this to happen, at the same time realizing the three of them were powerless to stop it.

Compounding Assiri's anger with America for abandoning the resistance forces, was his growing awareness that the American military was not going to leave the region anytime soon. A plan had been implemented that would leave an American armored brigade in Kuwait in case Saddam changed his mind and invaded again. In Saudi Arabia a Patriot battalion would remain to protect the Kingdom from any Scud missiles Saddam might fire and Operation Southern Watch, the American, British, and French enforcement of the no fly zone in southern Iraq, would be conducted from Saudi Airbases. All of which was being done, allegedly, to prevent the massing of Saddam's forces on either the Kuwaiti or Saudi border. Rightly or wrongly, by circumstance or design, this plan validated Assiri's prediction that America would use Saddam's invasion of Kuwait as a way to legitimize its own invasion of Saudi Arabia.

Assiri firmly stuck to his belief that had Saddam been killed and the ruling Ba'ath party apparatus been dismantled, followed by a mandate granting the United Nations to establish an interim government in its place, such actions could not have been justified to the American people. For men like Assiri, every action now being taken to protect Saudi Arabia and Kuwait from invasion was a direct attack on Saudi sovereignty and the world was standing by and allowing it to happen all because Saddam Hussein was still alive.

The longer the three of them remained together, the angrier Assiri became, especially about the worlds lack of concern for the Muslims who had agreed to support American efforts being killed by Saddam. When Dash or Blackburn would remind him that these people were being killed by other Muslims and not Americans, that it was now an Iraqi civil war, he would launch into a tirade about how it wouldn't be happening at all if America had honored its original commitment.

There was no doubt that America could have done more to protect the dissidents and their families from Saddam's retribution. Dash and Blackburn were as outraged by the killings as Assiri was. But to lay the entire state of Iraqi affairs on America's doorstep was not entirely fair either. The Iraqi Government had a long history of brutality against its own citizens, as do all of the other countries in the Middle East. Neither they nor their citizens needed any encouragement from America to go after each other's throat. America cannot be the world's policeman. The experienced SOF soldiers knew all too well what has happening. Assiri manifested the classic signs of falling into the familiar pattern of an insecure, confused, angry people blaming everyone but themselves for their lot in life, a pattern Dash and Blackburn had seen repeated time and again throughout Africa, the Middle East, Latin America, and Southeast Asia. Places where residents had conveniently forgotten that life is not fair anywhere on this planet, and that it never has been. Places where people routinely blame all internal problems on an external source in order to avoid having to fix these problems themselves. Beginning with a look into history's mirror and honestly confessing to what they saw, putting an end to the fabricated lies describing what they wished they had seen, then standing on their own two feet and doing something about it themselves.

Some of Assiri's complaints were legitimate, but most were not. That the Marsh Arabs had been lied to is irrefutable. But even if they had killed Saddam there was no way America was going to protect them while they stabilized the country. It would take years before they could accomplish such a task and Assiri knew full well that the western powers would not wait years for a stable, oil-producing Iraq to emerge. He also knew that if the world suddenly lost its appetite for Iraqi oil that it would be the people, not the politicians, who would suffer the most.

The real complaint of people like Assiri was that they wanted to live the way their ancestors had lived, with power and privilege in an isolated Islamic world immune from 21st century problems. But modernity has already overrun that world and change is required if Islam hopes to keep pace with the rest of the world. Unfortunately, the only efforts many poor Muslim nations are willing to make in order to catch up with the modern world is to complain about it. They steadfastly refuse to make any cultural, educational, political, or economic adjustments to help themselves, expending an enormous amount of time and energy avoiding reality, preferring instead to remain locked in the mythical grand illusions of past glories.

Too many intellectuals who should know better often fall victim to this argument by the poor and downtrodden as well. Mistakenly agreeing with their rhetoric, justifying their self-pity, carrying the torch for them by arguing their position in governing bodies, perpetuating their plight by failing to suggest to them that maybe, just maybe, they could do a little more to help themselves out as well. Honest intellectuals should encourage these people to spend a little more time peering through the windshield of their future to see where they are going, and less time fixating on the rearview mirror of their past. Carefully explaining to them that the highway of life in the 21st Century does not allow a people to make U-turns simply because they fear what is ahead of them. Reminding them that life's highway in the tenth or fourteenth century did not allow for U-turns either, which is why the world looks the way that it does today. It was a dirty, miserable place then as well for a lot of people. Intellectuals need to take the time to remind them that the very people now complaining about the unfairness of the modern world were in charge of it during the tenth and fourteenth century. They hadn't done any better with it than America is. In fact, they had done far worse. It is time that the intellectuals around the world stop perpetuating myths and remind all disgruntled people of one uncomfortable historical fact: dwelling on the greatness of times long past holds far less promise for their children than does a willingness to change for the dream of a brighter tomorrow.

What America saw in an unstable Iraq was a return to factional fighting that would spread throughout the Middle East, interrupting oil supplies and destabilizing the entire region. In a world of *Real Politic*, where all nations operate on a principle of selfish self-interest, it would have been counterproductive to American interests to allow the return of a civil war inside Iraq, spreading outside its borders and fanning the flames of hatred throughout the region. Instability is bad for the pocketbook, and what's bad for the pocketbook is bad for the politicians and people in any democratic, capitalist country.

Assiri's desire that America simply continue north to Baghdad without coalition agreement was not a good idea either. Under international law, if you break it you bought it. America did not want to have to buy Iraq. The Bush administration had clearly articulated that the objective of Desert Storm was to evict Saddam from Kuwait, not necessarily remove him from power. Assiri was smart enough to know that no matter what was being said behind the scenes, once Saddam withdrew from Kuwait America would declare victory and end its participation in the war. This was what the American people and the opposing Democratic Party would demand happen. And without America there was no coalition. What Assiri had done was gamble that it would take long enough to defeat Saddam's forces that the Marsh Arabs would have a chance of being successful. He had simply made a tragic error in judgment. Either by omission or commission he disregarded the fact that killing Saddam would only be of benefit to Saudi Arabia and the Marsh Arabs. He must have forgotten that neither has a vote in American elections. To a large extent both he and the Marsh Arabs were victims of their own making and his growing awareness of this made him even angrier.

***

As a result of his frequent tirades, both Dash and Blackburn were beginning to fear their friend and his growing resentment of all things western, especially when the three of them visited the growing number of graves around the area. They had visited many of these sites and found them to be covered with fresh graves, graves dug by the very hands now buried within. Their existence confirmed the rumors of mass executions were true, taking place right under the noses of the United Nations and coalition forces, an awareness that made Assiri even more livid.

Dash would find it ironic, when in 2003 the 43rd President of the United States, George Walker Bush, would use the existence of these same mass graves as justification for invading Iraq. Ironic because he knew full well that his father, the 41st President, George H.W. Bush, had been in charge of American foreign policy when most of them were dug and filled. At the time of their occurrence these massacres had not been a secret. CIA files are full of documentation detailing that these killings were well known to western governments. It is only slightly less well known that none of these governments lifted a finger to put a stop to them. If such knowledge made him feel uncomfortable, and it did, Dash often wondered how it must have made those feel who had loved ones buried inside those graves.

Because of the growing anger displayed by Assiri, Dash and Blackburn stopped associating with him. Suddenly, one day Mohammed "Moe" Al-Assiri simply disappeared. Neither Dash nor Blackburn had any inkling of where he might have gone. They knew he had not been reassigned because the Saudis were asking both of them if they had recently seen him. Assiri had simply fallen from the face of the earth, Absent Without Official Leave, AWOL. But he hadn't fallen far. They would meet him again, two years later, on the mean streets of Mogadishu, Somalia, where, as an Al-Qaida soldier he had found a new line of work as an Islamic freedom fighter, employed by his uncle, Osama bin Laden.

CHAPTER 18

I magine the characters in the book by Herbert Asbury or the Martin Scorsese movie by the same name *"Gangs of New York"* with automatic weapons, Rocket Propelled Grenade's (RPG's), mortars, and mines and you will have an accurate image of what Somalia was and still is to this day. It is *Mad Max* in the extreme. Yet somehow Somalia was determined to be a place where America should try to promote the image it was seeking to cultivate as a caring, compassionate country, genuinely concerned with starving Africans. This despite the fact that if the entire African continent were to slip beneath the Ocean, and CNN was not there to film it, most of America world would never know that it was gone.

The poster child for Africa's troubles is Somalia. If ever there was a place not worth trying to save from itself, it had to have been the gang infested-civil war pro-moting-terrorist haven on the horn of Africa named Somalia. A place where even those fighting and dying could not articulate all of the reasons why they were doing so. Yet America knowingly and willingly sent its sons and daughters there to save the Somalis from themselves.

The American military arrived in the small African nation full of good intentions, wearing their hearts on their sleeves. The Americans arrival in a Black nation for humanitarian purposes provided the Washington cocktail circuit politicians reasons for toasting one another at the latest black-tie social event as they gathered in droves to take advantage of the photo opportunities while congratulating each other for their latest magnanimous gesture of humanity. Unfortunately these same politicians were never asked by the multitude of reporters why they were refusing to admit to the growing 21st century awareness that in many impoverished places on the globe, like Somalia, tyrants and dictators do not rule over decent, honest, caring, hard-working people yearning to be free. Such a question would have forced the politicians to justify their willingness to place American soldiers in harm's way knowing that people become tyrants and dictators precisely because they *do not* rule over decent, honest, caring, hard-working people yearning to be free. They rule over people cut from the same cloth as themselves and freeing them is not worth the life of a single American soldier. Had this question been asked and the politician's answers properly scrutinized by a reluctant public, America would have never gone to Somalia. Even a first year journalism student would have seen that the answers were full of emotion and wishful thinking. Nowhere would a journalist have found logic or rational thought for wanting to take sides in an African civil war.

The decision to intervene in Somalia's civil war was made for two overriding reasons. First, America was just beginning to flex its muscles as the lone super power capable of spreading its influence around the globe. Because the decision to intervene in Somalia was made during the twilight zone transition period of a lame duck Bush administration and an incoming Clinton administration, nobody bothered to ask whether America *should* be spreading its influence around the globe. Naively assuming that just because America could stick its nose in other people's business then it should. Second, it is always easy to be gracious with someone else's life. After all, the politicians and their supporters who wanted to save the world didn't actually go to Somalia themselves. They didn't have to. It was easier for them to send someone else in their place — the American military. The military would leave Somalia fifteen months later with its tail tucked firmly between its legs and the blood of several thousand people on its hands. Too damn much of which was American blood.

***

Following their return to the States after Desert Storm, Dash and Blackburn would go their separate ways. Dash would go to Fort Leavenworth, Kansas to attend the Command and General Staff College, which he had been scheduled to attend prior to receiving Assiri's personal, by-name request for him to return to Saudi Arabia. Blackburn would go back to Fort Bragg, North Carolina, with an assignment to the United States Army Civil Affairs and Psychological Operations Command (USACAPOC) to assume duties as the First Sergeant of Charlie Company, 96th Civil Affairs Battalion (Airborne). They would be separated for only twelve months when in May, 1993, Dash would also return to Fort Bragg to command that same company.

***

The 96th Civil Affairs Battalion (CAB) (Abn) is a unique organization. It is the Army's only active duty airborne Civil Affairs Battalion in the Army inventory. The bulk of all Civil Affairs (CA) personnel reside in the United States Army Reserve (USAR) force structure and are called to active duty when they are needed, which, lately, has been quite often. So often in fact that the distinction between active and reserve has no real meaning anymore since there is no longer any such thing as a part-time soldier.

The unit can trace its lineage back to the Office of Governmental Affairs, created during World War II, which in large part was responsible for orchestrating the implementation of the Marshall Plan in Europe. The primary mission of today's CA troops remains much the same as it did following World War II: to provide an interim government to help stabilize post-conflict regions, eventually creating an indigenous government to replace themselves. Successful CA operations are designed to work the CA personnel out of a job by returning control of the government back to the people it had helped.

The Battalion is organized in five Direct Support Civil Affairs Companies (CAC) that share an affiliation with regional Combatant CINC's, EUCOM, ATLANTCOM, PACOM, SOUTHCOM, and CENTCOM. The soldiers assigned to these CAC's undergo a rigorous academic training curriculum involving language, regional studies, U.S. regional foreign policy objectives, and a never ending update on current regional issues and players. All of this is in addition to their normal requirements of being trained, combat ready, airborne qualified, super soldiers.

The initial mission given to the 96th CAB (Abn) is to deploy early to regional "hot spots" to make an assessment of how many of these USAR soldiers will be needed and in what specialties to accomplish the mission of creating a stable environment for diplomats to work in. Termed stability and security (SASO) operations, it requires putting an end to violence, gaining stability, rebuilding infrastructure, and reestablishing essential services before returning control of the country back to the indigenous people. In the interim, before a large number of reservists can be brought on board, the 96th CAB (Abn) soldiers assume the responsibility for that mission, performing administrative, construction, logistical, health and welfare, police and last but certainly not least, combat functions required during SASO operations.

The assessments performed by CA personnel often become missions in and of themselves. Lasting far longer than they should as politicians and UN officials grapple with the complexities of nation building and individual responsibilities, then, like spinsters, fight over who is going to pay all of the bills. Leaving the soldiers stuck in a hostile environment as the reality of promises and expectations become deep disappointments and the anger reaches a boiling point. In a place like Somalia, where the desire for people to get off their lazy asses and help one another is not a cultural trait taught to the young, these missions become quite hazardous.

Growing up in a war torn country, the young Somali males, in particular, have been taught that might makes right and that the only way to achieve any measure of success in this world is to take it away from the other guy. The soldiers and marines that went to Somalia on a humanitarian relief mission quickly learned that there is nothing in this world as unpredictable and dangerous as a teen-ager with a gun, no conscious, and no hope.

To perform their mission CA personnel have to rely heavily on diplomacy to get all of the indigenous combatant commanders, warlords, gang leaders, government leaders, clerics, and other centers of influence (COI's), such as business people and teachers, to sit together to resolve disputes. Civil Affairs operations are very much a nation building enterprise, relying in large part on the decisions of political bureaucrats back in Washington and New York regarding what the end-state is supposed to look like. CA operations can be both a peacemaking as well as a peacekeeping endeavor.

To be effective in either mission tasking, however, basic policy questions must be answered before CA commanders can implement any sort of coherent support programs. Questions such as: "What are America's interests in the region? Who does America want in power in the region? How much time, effort, and money is America willing to spend to get what it wants?" A question that is never asked of the politicians, but probably should be, is "How many lives is it worth to get all that you are asking for?"

A very poor policy to follow is one that seems to be the norm for nation building: let the people decide for themselves how they want to run their country and who will be in charge of it. Such a policy begs the question: "Isn't this the root cause of the current problem?" And if not, if the people are truly capable of deciding for themselves then, "Why the hell are we here?"

The soldiers, sailors, marines, and airmen who were unfortunate enough to be deployed to Somalia would have very much liked to have heard the answers to the above questions before going there. It would have helped them narrow their focus. It would have certainly told them if they were achieving any measure of success or when they were exceeding the requirements of the mission. Instead, they received guidance to the effect of, "feed the people and fix the problem!" Not exactly the kind of mission guidance that is quantifiable, measurable, achievable, or in the case of Somalia, even worth doing.

The "problem" in Somalia was that there was a multi-factional civil war taking place. There was never a famine resulting from a shortage of food as the media portrayed it to be. Food was being withheld from certain groups but that was only because they were enemies of the group with the most guns and most power in their region. Starvation was simply an inexpensive and effective way to kill them.

Adding to Somalia's problem of a civil war was about to be added another. When any country attempts to assist a group of people during a civil war, that country, well meaning though it may be, just chose sides in their war. Unofficially, America, at the behest of America's congressional Black caucus, demanded that the lame duck Bush administration do something to put an end to the horrible pictures CNN was showing of walking Somali cadavers. Hitting Bush below the belt by suggesting to the press that if it were White people starving instead of Black people that there would be no reluctance to commit troops. The official effect of this criticism was the congressional Black caucus shamed Bush into declaring war on some warlord faction inside Somalia and the troops being sent there had no clue who the enemy was supposed to be.

In fairness to the politicians, there were two Somalia missions. The first, Operation Restore Hope, or UNOSOM I, was an international effort to feed the starving people who had fallen victim to the savagery of various warring clans. The U.S. military was initially sent to Somalia to assist the relief agencies by riding shotgun for their food convoys, providing protection for both their workers as well as the foodstuffs they were transporting. During their "free time" American military forces dabbled with stability operations by creating police forces, rebuilding schools, and trying to establish a modicum of civility in an otherwise extremely hostile former nation that had imploded from within. For all intents and purposes the first part of Operation Restore Hope went reasonably well, especially the joint military and humanitarian relief agencies' attempts to reduce the so-called famine. Though the long term effects of this success was like putting a Band-Aid on a broken leg. It might have looked pretty but it did little to solve the real problem of Somalis wanting to kill one another.

The second Somalia mission was conducted under the auspices of the United Nations Operations Somalia (UNOSOM) and was dubbed UNOSOM II to differentiate it from UNOSOM I, which had the limited mandate of feeding the people and avoiding being sucked into a Somali civil war. Tasked with providing stability to the region, and not just feeding people, the UNOSOM II mission quickly became more than a "meals on wheels" program because for stability to be achieved, heads had to be busted. Something the American military is very good at doing but something that is also at odds with the United Nations and its many attendant humanitarian groups' view of themselves as neutral, avoid-violence-at-all-costs, organizations. Unfortunately, the Somalis did not share this self-congratulatory and highly idealized view of the humanitarian groups as they routinely raped, robbed and murdered many of the relief agency workers. But UNOSOM II really began to unravel when a Somali warlord named Mohammed Farah Aideed ordered his forces to attack a group of United Nations Pakistani soldiers, killing several of them, challenging the United Nations for supremacy in the capital city of Mogadishu.

This attack left the United Nations with an identity crisis. The generally pacifist United Nations was now at odds with its own belief system. With the implied threat of violence contained in the provisions of UNOSOM II, the UN now had to put up or shut up, neither of which it is very good at doing. With a challenge to its authority, the UN was now experiencing what every parent experiences at some point in their own child's life; a recalcitrant child calling the bluff that Mom or Dad won't really spank him or her. Unfortunately, like too many spoiled children, Aideed would be proven right in believing that the UN didn't have the stomach to spank him, choosing instead the threat of violence without actually having to endure all of the negative feelings that goes with employing it. America, on the other hand, had no qualms employing violence as a solution to Aideed's aggressive behavior. After several months in Somalia the American military was getting more than a little tired of all the clan fighting and other pettiness in Mogadishu and volunteered to unilaterally go after Aideed, a plan that by itself, even had it been successful, was foolish from the very beginning.

* * *

Though Blackburn and the entirety of C/96th CAB (Abn) would participate in both UNOSOM I and UNOSOM II, Dash would only participate in UNOSOM II. The one where America went from feeding the starving Somalis, albeit being forced to occasionally shoot some for major indiscretions, to killing a large number of them one fateful night in Mogadishu. When Dash assumed command of Charlie Company virtually all of the unit's personnel were still serving in Somalia. Blackburn and selected Team Leaders had returned to Fort Bragg for the change of command ceremonies and, as they so succinctly put it, "a roll in the hay with the old lady." Three days later, Dash accompanied all of them back to Somalia where he would serve as the Civil Affairs Direct Support Company Commander to the United Nations Logistical Support Command (UNLSC).

Headquartered in the former University of Somalia compound, the UNLSC was responsible for providing logistical support for all the forces under its command, consisting of forces from America, Pakistan, Malaysia, India, Egypt, Saudi Arabia, Bangladesh, and Tunisia, to name but a few. It was an eclectic, ad-hoc organization if there ever was one, but it functioned relatively efficiently, keeping the peace, by various means, in their assigned sectors.

One of the most often employed means for keeping the peace for many of these forces was to simply barricade their troops inside a compound and never venture outside it. Especially at night and never in Aideed's sector in the vicinity of the Black Sea neighborhood of central Mogadishu, a place in the center of the city, ostensibly under the control of Pakistan, not far from the American controlled air and sea ports. The Black Sea neighborhood also contained the Bakarra Market, a virtual arms trading bazaar where the most indiscriminate buyer could easily purchase weapons of any sort along with any sort of legal supplies or illegal contraband. Effectively allowing the most powerful warlord in Mogadishu, Mohammed Farah Aideed, to virtually do as he pleased.

Unlike America, the other nations participating in UNOSOM II felt that becoming embroiled in a Somali civil war was akin to lighting their own asses on fire. They knew their efforts would not make a bit of difference in resolving the internal strife of Somalia, employing the same logic of avoidance that Dash had seen employed as a young marine in Vietnam. This time, the entire country of America was about to learn the same lesson that experienced troops in Vietnam had first learned. Regrettably, the country would learn this lesson the same way that the young Vietnam era marines had learned it — by counting their dead.

***

"Damn it's hot here!" said a dripping wet Dash to an also heavily perspiring Blackburn following their three-mile morning run around the inside perimeter of the university compound. A once teeming college campus on the edge of Mogadishu now as devoid of students as it was of hope in the slowly dying African nation. The two men were there as a part of a Civil Affairs Special Operations Task Force that had been hastily pieced together to support United Nations efforts to reestablish the fine threads of civility that had once held Somalia together as a unified nation; a noble but fruitless task. They were discovering what others before them had discovered: the threads of civility holding any nation together are tenuous at best. In Somalia they had been torn asunder by a group of ruthless warlords vying for control of the once beautiful Capitol City of Mogadishu. God himself would have had trouble pulling the country back together and neither the United Nations personnel nor the soldiers stuck in Somalia considered themselves to be on a par with God. Though some of the self-absorbed UN staffers, aid workers, and career politicians probably would have argued against this observation.

The Special Operations soldiers would have preferred running on the nearby beautiful beaches bordering the Indian Ocean while enjoying a cool breeze to running on the hot, hard asphalt of the now defunct university. But it was much too dangerous; too many snipers, too many mines, and too many angry teenage males looking to "make their bones" by killing an American. Surrounded by a city seething with anger, the heavily guarded university compound was the only place secure enough to allow soldiers the freedom to exercise.

"Yeah," replied Blackburn in a despondent voice, "and it isn't going to get any better for awhile."

"Well," Dash said in a voice reflecting his own unhappiness with being in Somalia, "I guess we'll just have to take whatever Mother Nature throws at us."

Blackburn knew what he was talking about. Even though it was only June he had already spent one Christmas in Somalia and his awareness that the political situation inside the country was getting worse instead of better served as a prescient indicator that he would probably spend another Christmas in this hell-hole. A dismal thought that he and all the other American soldiers serving in Somalia dreaded. The despair in Blackburn's voice accurately reflected how everyone felt.

As a late arriver Dash had been in Somalia for only two weeks and wasn't as dismayed with the futility of the mission as the other soldiers were. His self-pity was simply the result of not having recovered from the effects of family separation that goes with a deployment. It usually took him about three weeks to a month to get over the feeling of being homesick, missing Janet and his two daughters. The girls were now teen-agers attending Pine Forest High School in Fayetteville, North

Carolina and were staying busy by becoming involved in all sorts of extracurricular activities. They were typical military brats who would tell their civilian friends that they really did have a father, even though he was never home to meet them. They didn't have to make such a claim to their military friends attending the school; they knew the score because their own fathers and mothers were often gone as well. Janet had secured a job teaching at Westover Middle School in Fayetteville, so he wasn't concerned that the three of them had nothing to occupy their time during his absence. Yet he missed them so, just like all the other soldiers missed their families.

Dash had left the family at Fort Bragg while at Leavenworth, knowing that he would be coming back to Bragg following CGSC. They had purchased a house in the new development community of Pine Valley Estates in the hope that they would be stabilized in one spot long enough to build a little equity. Something they hadn't had much luck with during Dash's thirteen years in the Army. Their frequent moves had only meant that the realtors and the taxman walked away with any profit from the sale of a house, leaving them with nothing but memories.

Like most of the men in the Special Operations community, Dash had spent very little time with his family during the past several years. With a one year unaccompanied assignment in Saudi Arabia, followed by nine months there during Desert Storm, followed by one year at Leavenworth, and now Somalia, he had once added up the number of months he had spent with his family over the past three years and it had totaled three. Three months in three years! He wondered what Doctor Laura would recommend as a solution for that. Still, Janet had accepted his life as a soldier and like Blackburn's marriage to his wife, Betty Lou, their marriage was as strong and solid as ever. Something many of the two, three, and four times divorced Special Operations soldiers could not brag about. It took a special kind of woman to tolerate the frequent deployments they had gone on, and they both knew that they were lucky to have found a woman who would do it. Though in a form of retribution both Janet and Betty Lou gave their husbands hell for volunteering for Special Operations when they hadn't had to by reminding them that so-and-so's husband in a conventional unit was always home.

But truth be told, the entire Army was operating on fumes, not just the special units. Several combat divisions along with their support units had deployed to Desert Storm. A Task Force from the 10th Mountain Division from Fort Drum, New York, TF 2-87 and 2nd Brigade, had deployed to Somalia during the first phase of Operation Restore Hope and another Task Force, TF 2-14, was still there now. Bosnia was looming on the horizon as a major deployment, as were Haiti and Rwanda. It seemed as though the last place a soldier could be found these days was in the States. With the Clinton administration foreign policy position of granting the UN more incentive to request American troops by routinely rubber-stamping the request, it didn't look like the deployment train was going to slow down any time in the near future.

But feeling sorry for themselves was not something that accomplished anything worthwhile, and all of the soldiers knew it. The fact that Somalia was beyond repair was not their fault. That could be laid at the feet of the average Somali because it was no exaggeration to claim that the Somalis themselves were beyond repair. They seemed quite content to live in the squalor and despair of a war torn country, adamantly refusing to make any adjustments in their own miserable lives to better themselves, a typical third world attitude that is far beyond the ability of the American military to fix.

Yet here they were, America's finest, stuck in a hellhole like Somalia because CNN had filmed a civil war there and made Americans feel guilty. What a hell of a deal for the soldiers! The sights and sounds of war didn't unduly sicken them. Nor were they overly anxious to jump into the middle of one they did not have a dog fighting in. But, since they were there, they figured they might as well do something to make the time pass more quickly.

***

"Top," said Dash, "let's hit the shower, grab a quick bite to eat and go over today's missions with the team leaders."

"Yes, Sir." Replied Blackburn. "I'll alert the team leaders and meet you in the mess hall."

After showering with sun heated hot water in the makeshift shower, eating breakfast in the heat of the mess hall, and walking uphill in the humid ninety-degree morning heat to the G5 section, Dash and Blackburn were sweating almost as much as they had been following their morning run. Somewhat defeating the purpose for having showered in the first place. The G5 section of the United Nations Logistical Support Command was in the "doughnut" section of the university compound. A name derived from the "doughnut" appearance of the many classrooms and administrative offices that were arranged in a circular design with a small courtyard in the center, like a hole in the middle of a doughnut.

Today's missions would have one of Dash's teams escorting a truckload of school supplies to a school on the fringe of the city recently reopened under the auspices of an Islamic charity group from Pakistan. The mission could only loosely be described as being a doctrinal civil affairs' mission. Getting kids off of the streets and into a classroom aids in stability efforts but since it was only going to effect the "little people" and not the teen-agers the opening of the school would do little to stem the growing threat of violence. It did, however, provide one of the teams with something to do that would get them off the compound and away from the self-induced "light your head on fire" mentality of being near the flagpole. It seemed to the soldiers that no request ever went through the UNLSC headquarters that did not emerge with an "immediate action required" routing slip attached to it. The other three teams comprising C/96th CAB, along with Dash and Blackburn, would drive to the port to check on the arrival of two additional HMMWV's being shipped from Fort Bragg. The vehicles belonged to a CA Headquarters attachment from the 351st Civil Affairs Command (USAR) headquartered in Riverdale Park, Maryland, just outside Washington D.C., near the campus of the University of Maryland.

The Commander of this USAR unit was Colonel Mike Degan, a fine officer, and an experienced CA expert. Having served in Grenada, Panama, Desert Storm and now Somalia, his expert counsel would be greatly appreciated by Dash in the months ahead, as would the counsel of his Executive Officer, Lieutenant Colonel Bill Dean. Dean was a former active duty Special Forces Captain who had been a part of Colonel Charlie Beckwith's Delta Force mission to rescue the hostages being held in Iran following the Ayatollah Khomeini's seizure of the American Embassy and all its personnel in Tehran.

An addition to the staff of these two very capable officers was Major John Whidden, one of the most intelligent, farsighted officers Dash ever worked with. Whidden's attention to detail and vast experience in CA missions around the world complemented the experiences of all the other CA members, making the unit fit together like a well-oiled machine.

Accompanying the USAR Officers was a contingent of superb NCO's. Many of them had extensive experience with CA missions during Desert Storm and their unit's participation in hurricane relief efforts, such as those with Hurricane Andrew in 1992, when it had decimated the area around Homestead, Florida.

The CA personnel assigned to the UNLSC certainly had the training and experience to execute any doctrinal mission received. Therein lied a small problem; there really were no doctrinal CA missions to conduct. There were no governmental officials with which to coordinate. Those that had been in power prior to the start of the war had either been killed or had fled to Europe or the United States, leaving in their wake a motley assortment of bandits, warlords, thieves, the sick, lame, and lazy. Many of whom weren't even Somali, they were Ethiopian and Sudanese refugees who had fled their own country in the hopes of finding a better life in Somalia. A discovery that gives credence to the old saying about trying to improve one's lot in life by jumping from the frying pan straight into the fire! As interlopers themselves none of these people could be used by the CA teams to create an interim government, much less be used as seed stock for future development.

Yet the soldiers had been ordered to Somalia to conduct CA support for the United Nations because America wanted to give the appearance that it too had become a kinder and gentler nation. What they would do, how they would do it, whom they would do it with, and even the why of what they were to do was essentially being left up to them. Which was all right with Dash, who felt that you couldn't screw up something that had no beginning, no middle, and no end. Important considerations for someone with career aspirations. It was becoming more obvious with each passing day that nation building in Somalia was going to end in total failure. Causing heads to roll when the idealists began looking elsewhere for the cause of their own failed ideas, refusing to admit that caring too much about dysfunctional people only delays the inevitable. The Somalis had no intentions of changing their self-destructive behavior. Dash knew that as this realization began to sink in, many of these idealists would go through a finger pointing and backstabbing exercise designed to deflect criticism away from them. Whom those criticisms wounded as they ricocheted around the international community was of very little concern to them. Knowing that this was what the future held, Dash wished that he could distance himself from the entire process. Then something happened that changed the entire focus of UNOSOM II; Mohammed Farah Aideed ordered his Habr Gidr clansmen to kill some UN soldiers. And the UN Secretary General, Boutrous Boutrous-Galli, an Egyptian who had crossed swords with Aideed earlier in his diplomatic career demanded blood atonement using American blood.

***

"All right, guys," Dash began. "Listen up. Today's missions will have Alpha team accompanying the Pakis to the newly opened school on Medina Street, around the corner from, and just behind Binti's camel market. The rest of us will go to the port to pick up the Hummvees with our blood brothers from the 351st." Colonel's Degan and Dean, sitting in the back of the room, simply smiled at Dash's reference to the USAR folks as being blood brothers.

"First Sergeant Blackburn will go over the march order and route with you," Dash continued. "I want all weapons function checked, two frags per man, radio checks conducted, and vehicles topped off before we SP." Then, turning to Blackburn, finished his speech with, "Top, go over actions on contact with them as well."

"Roger that, Sir," replied the crusty NCO. "Listen up, Dickheads...."

Thus began another day in Somalia, a repeat of yesterday and a rehearsal for tomorrow. Since the killing of the Paki soldiers by Aideed's forces there had been a not so subtle change in the demeanor of the Somalis; they were becoming far more aggressive than they had been. Two days earlier, while conducting a courtesy call on the commander of a Saudi compound they often traveled through, the soldiers were confronted by an angry mob of Somalis demanding blood money for a child who had been run over and killed by a relief agency truck. The crowd refused to take no for an answer and when one young teen-age male grabbed Major Whidden's web gear, Whidden pulled his K-Bar knife and slashed the Somali's arm with it. Leaving the young man writhing in pain, thrashing around on the ground with blood spurting into the air and an even more enraged crowd screaming its disapproval. Dash ordered PFC Mike Brown, a young Black soldier from Delmar, Mississippi, to fire a burst of machinegun fire over their heads to disperse them. It failed, but it had the effect of momentarily stopping the mob and allowed the soldiers to withdraw without further incident. Another thirty seconds of turmoil and Dash would have ordered Brown to shoot into the crowd itself; something he really did not want to have to do.

The events that day were really not that unusual for a place like Somalia where hostile mobs were something the soldiers dealt with on an almost daily basis. But it had been different than previous mobs because this time the mob showed no fear of the soldiers, taunting them, daring them to open fire. When Brown fired over their heads, the mob did not run away as they had always done in the past. This time the mob actually surged forward and it was the soldiers who had been forced to hurry away. As Dash walked to the back of the room to talk to Colonel Degan he heard Blackburn begin his briefing on what to do if they ran into trouble with, "and remember, no one gets left behind. No one!!" A fitting harbinger for things to come.

***

The Hummvees pulled through the heavy metal gate of the university compound with Dash in the lead vehicle, exiting the compound and turning east on Afgoy Road, away from town and towards the empty desert. The soldiers returned the smiles of the Tunisian gate guards who were flashing them the old Vietnam two finger "V" peace sign as they drove past. As usual, Blackburn would bring up the rear of the convoy to ensure that the four Hummvees between them would always be where one of the leaders could see them. They did not want any vehicles taking a wrong turn only to find itself isolated in the hostile city where it would be ripped apart by the Somalis in much the same manner that a pack of Jackals rips apart a lone antelope.

Once all of the vehicles had cleared the gate they would make another left hand turn on 21 October Road and travel south for four miles until they reached Jalle Siad Road, commonly referred to as Medina Road since it ran through the Medina district of Mogadishu. They would turn east on Medina Road and follow it through the city to the airport. At the airport they would travel a hastily constructed military highway meandering along the edge of the Indian Ocean and to the gateway of the New Sea Port terminal on the eastern edge of Mogadishu. The entire trip would take approximately one hour.

Medina Road had become the favored route for the soldiers, even though it was technically off limits to U.S. personnel following an ambush where two American

MP's had been killed. Since the ambush all military traffic was supposed to travel around the city, following a military highway carved through the desert that made a long and sweeping turn before ending up at the airport. Medina Road led directly to the airport, saving the soldiers an additional hour of travel time under the hot African sun.

Even though the Special Operations soldiers were traveling on a restricted road, they weren't really violating any direct order for them to stay off of it. Because of the nature of special operations, the CA troops were required to interface with the locals throughout the city and the tribes living along Medina Road were no exception. The soldiers had cultivated a civil relationship with most of them, often taking the elders a case of Israeli beer, or several cases, and then helping them consume it. As a result, they had never had any trouble in this part of the city and the chain of command simply turned a blind eye whenever they left the compound. The chain of command never knew about the beer; none of the soldiers would ever tell them about it either since it would have been in direct violation of General Order Number 1, DOD's attempt to suck the pleasure out of life.

Even though befriending the Somalis with bribes of beer was the safest thing they could have done, the fact that they were consuming alcohol in a combat zone was reason enough for them to receive a courts martial for the offense. Drinking and fraternization were both offenses that the highly conservative, almost puritanical conventional commanders seemed obsessed with preventing, an anal restriction that did not begin with Somalia.

Following the signing of the peace accords ending Desert Storm hostilities, Dash had purchased a gallon of Wild Turkey whiskey from a Marine gunnery sergeant working in the American Embassy in Kuwait City. Evidently the Gunny was as much an entrepreneur as a patriot because the whiskey cost Dash one-hundred American dollars. But it had been worth the inflated cost when he shared a celebratory drink with the soldiers belonging to a nearby tank company assigned to the 1st Infantry Division from Fort Riley, Kansas. When the company commander announced over his radio for the soldiers to come to his location for a shot of whiskey, it had been as if lemmings had been released into the desert. From as far as a mile away soldiers could be seen running across the desert, canteen cup in hand, to receive a small taste of the "demon rum." The smiles on their grimy faces made each and every one of them forget about the recent horrors and reminded all of them of how proud they should be of who they were and what they had accomplished. When a brigade commander found about it, he threatened Dash with a court martial if he ever caught him in his sector again.

Largely as a result of the discipline problems the military had experienced in Vietnam, the Department of Defense decided that the root cause of many of these discipline problems was alcohol, and not a flawed foreign policy. The current military leadership sees General Order Number 1 as a cure-all for many of the discipline problems they had experienced while junior grade officers. As a result, admirals and generals who were lieutenants and captains in Vietnam have forbidden the consumption of alcohol during all deployments. Of course this is only for American troops as the French, British, Canadians, Israelis, etc., deploy with cases of the stuff. Much of which ends up in the hands and bellies of American troops.

As the unit Commander Dash was the one most susceptible to punishment if one of the frequent puritanical witch-hunts revealed that he and his men were drinking beer with the Somalis. A fact that Dash was well aware of, but keeping himself and his men alive was something that seemed of greater importance than being burned at the stake by some overzealous field commander. What they were doing with the Somalis made good sense. Dash, with wise counsel and encouragement from Blackburn, had discovered that Muslims, just like "real people" everywhere, enjoy beer, whiskey, and wine. This made alcohol a handy bartering tool for soldiers in a hurry to get things done. The two of them often used alcohol with good results in every Muslim country they previously served in and Somalia was now proving itself to be a virtual treasure trove for alcoholics in training. Because they usually brought beer with them, many of the Somalis welcomed the soldiers anytime they saw them coming and on occasion even volunteered to repay them for the cost of the beer. The locals desired to escape the misery of Somalia's civil war and the soldiers spent many nights in convivial song with some of the meanest bastards in Mogadishu, drinking beer and howling at the moon. As a result, they pretty much got to go where they wanted when they wanted, making it much easier, and safer, for them to do their job. Collectively, the special operations soldiers felt that complying with some of the provisions of General Order Number 1 made their jobs more dangerous, not less dangerous.

However, alcohol wasn't a commodity that guaranteed unfettered access everywhere in the city of Mogadishu. Some areas were so anti-American as to be virtually immune from the powerful attraction of alcohol. The Black Sea Neighborhood of central Mogadishu, controlled by Mohammed Farad Aideed, never did belly up to the bar the way all of the others had. Proving to the soldiers just what an asshole Aideed really was, causing many of them to comment that, "the son-of-a-bitch thinks he's a general already!"

***

As the convoy passed the open-air market on Medina Street about half way to their final destination, it was apparent that the daily supply of "Khat" had arrived from Kenya. Either that, or it was what remained from yesterday's supply, usually sold and consumed shortly after it had arrived. It was unlikely that the greenish, alfalfa looking plants piled high on the tables was leftover merchandise. The drug being there in the open wasn't unusual; it could be bought on virtually every street corner in Mogadishu, but it was early in the day, before noon in fact, and the Khat usually arrived later in the day.

A mild narcotic, Khat was the drug of choice in Somalia. Virtually everyone chewed it and as a result virtually everyone in Somalia was high every afternoon and evening, making it a dangerous time to be in the city. When Dash saw the piles of Khat in the market, he radioed Blackburn and alerted him to the fact that they needed to be especially vigilant because the daily party had started earlier than expected, leaving them in a potentially precarious position. They even discussed aborting the mission and turning back, but elected instead to continue to the port, where they would spend the night, returning to the university compound early the following morning while the Somali males were sleeping off the effects of the drug. The problem with that decision, however, was that to get to the port they had to go through the area of Mogadishu where Major Whidden had slashed the Somali with his K-Bar knife. They seriously doubted that the sight of them so soon after the confrontation would be welcomed by any of the people who had participated in the nasty little affair. The emotions associated with that brief encounter, coupled with the effects of the Khat, offered a promise of high adventure that the soldiers would have just as soon done without. But neither Dash nor Blackburn felt that a confrontation was something that should be avoided.

"No one said that this was going to be easy," Dash told the soldiers. "We are not looking for a fight, but neither can we afford to let the Somalis dictate what we do and when we do it. We're going on to the port. If they try to stop us, then we will do what we have to do in order to continue with our mission."

The six Hummvees in the convoy, as well as the soldiers sitting in them, were loaded for bear. This was standard operating procedure each and every time they left the compound. There was an M-60 machinegun with one thousand rounds of ammunition mounted on every cargo Hummvee in the convoy, giving them a total of three 7.62mm (.308 cal) rapid-fire guns capable of penetrating most of the cement walled houses along the street. Additionally, each soldier carried an M-16 with two hundred rounds of ammunition and either a .45 cal or 9mm-hand gun along with two fragmentary hand grenades. Both Dash and Blackburn carried a demolition bag in their vehicles containing forty-seven, thirty round magazines, along with one in their weapon and two in the pocket of their Kevlar vest. Supplying each of them fifteen hundred rounds for their M-16's, two hundred of which was Federal Supreme commercial hollow point hunting bullets.

The soldiers presented a formidable opponent for any of the Somalis wanting to pick a fight with them and when they weren't stoned on Khat most of them recognized danger when they saw it. Sober teen-agers simply gave the soldiers a dirty look when they drove past, often flipping them the bird as a parting gesture. But such displays of insolence were tolerable and largely ignored by the soldiers. Blackburn said it reminded him of his years as a high school teacher where American teen-agers actually believed they were in charge of their world while simultaneously being clueless to how insignificant they really are. Their insolence a display of innocent, self-centered arrogance that was annoying to watch but relatively harmless unless they were mentally impaired. Once a teen-ager is drunk or stoned their demeanor takes on a whole different dimension. Teen-agers high on alcohol or drugs are a danger in any society and it was the stoned ones who concerned the soldiers the most. With the early arrival of the Khat the likelihood of encountering armed teen-agers, already high on the drug, was a good possibility.

As the convoy approached the airport looming on the edge of the Indian Ocean a short distance ahead, they all breathed a collective sigh of relief. There would be a brief period of safety as they drove through the airport enroute to the seaport as it was considered to be a secure compound, much the same as the university and embassy compounds. Except for occasional sniper and mortar fire, it was as safe as one could be and still be in Somalia. It would be after they left the airport and reentered the city that they would be in the greatest danger of an ambush, a prospect that Dash quietly prepared a contingency plan for.

Between the airfield and the seaport were two UN compounds, one secured by the Pakistanis, the other by the Saudis. Between these two compounds was a shantytown of makeshift huts occupied by a group of Eritrean refugees, who, like their Ethiopian neighbors, had fled to Somalia for a better life, a fact which, by itself, should describe to even the most casual observer what a desperate place Africa really is. That aside, it was in this shantytown where Whidden had the altercation with the young Somali who, with several of his friends, had forcibly moved into the Eritrean refugee camp.

Inside the Paki compound five hundred meters south of the shantytown was an American Special Forces sniper team from 5th Special Forces Group, Fort Campbell, Kentucky. The two snipers, SFC Russ Baker and SSG Steve Bleigh, had been there for several weeks and had observed these young Somalis living with the Eritreans smuggle several boatloads of weapons, mostly RPG's, from the beach into the city. They had also been watching when Whidden cut the Somali with his knife and Brown fired a burst of machinegun fire over the head of the crowd. It had taken great restraint for the snipers not to fire on the crowd for had they done so it would have compromised their mission. Since they hadn't fired on them, none of the people living in the makeshift shacks separating the two compounds knew that they were there. The snipers had been put on the Paki compound only to collect intelligence and so far their repeated requests to engage the Somalis smuggling in RPG's had been refused by UN bureaucrats, despite the fact that the possession of RPG's was strictly prohibited according to the united nations.

Both of the snipers had worked with Dash and Blackburn before, Baker as a former member of C/96th CAB before returning to life behind the fence with Delta Force. Bleigh had attended Arabic language training with Dash where, although he never really got the hang of speaking Arabic with any degree of proficiency, he developed a reputation of being a super soldier and a hell of a shot. Exactly the qualities Dash was looking for before entering the Eritrean camp.

The convoy stopped inside the Paki compound and Dash and Blackburn coordinated covering fires with the sniper team in the event they encountered difficulties inside the camp, exchanging radio frequencies and leaving a Motorola Saber radio with them. The Paki compound, an abandoned warehouse and storage site surrounded by high, cement walls, was perched on a rise overlooking the Eritrean camp and provided an excellent firing platform from which the snipers could see almost the entire length of road passing through the refugee camp. The entire camp was well within the range of the Barrett .50 caliber Sniper Rifle they had with them. The only portion of the road they could not observe was the last two hundred feet where the road made a slight turn, disappearing behind a large Acacia tree. For some inexplicable reason the tree had been allowed to grow to a ripe old age and was now being used by the Eritreans for shade.

Part of Dash's discussion with the sniper team centered on their awareness of the fact that if they fired on the villagers their mission would be compromised, leaving them to explain to USSOCOM their reasons for violating their written orders. Both Baker and Bleigh responded as all good soldiers are expected to respond, with an "up theirs" attitude.

"Before I stand by and watch these dirt bags spring an ambush," Baker stated while Bleigh nodded in agreement, "I'll blow up this whole damn city!" It was a good thing both felt that way, for they were about to get kicked off the Paki compound.

Satisfied that they were as prepared for trouble as they would ever be, the convoy rolled through the gate of the Paki compound and began a slow approach toward the Eritrean camp. The first sign of trouble came when Dash noticed a young male with a large white bandage tied around his arm emerge from a hut, look in their direction, and quickly duck from sight, running around the corner of a tin shack. The second sign of trouble, noticed by both Dash and Bleigh, who alerted Dash with a call over the Motorola, was when all of the Eritrean children, who moments before had been playing outside in the streets, immediately disappeared from sight. A disappearance that left the entire camp looking like a ghost town; always a bad sign in an otherwise congested and busy area.

Now Dash had a decision to make; he could guide the convoy around the camp, taking it near a built-up area that didn't appear to be much more promising, or he could continue with the plan he had discussed with the sniper team. He chose the latter for two reasons. One, allowing the Somalis to prevent them from passing through the village would be like leaving a poisonous snake where someone else could step on it. They weren't the only Americans who traveled this road and the thought of the Somalis later killing an unsuspecting traveler was too hard for Dash to live with. Two, all of the soldiers were growing tired of this chicken-shit macho game the young Somalis had been playing recently and, knowing that an eventual showdown was inevitable, figured that now was as good a time as any for it to run its course. Dash keyed his radio and told the convoy members as much, warning all of them to double-check their weapons to ensure that they were loaded and to remember to put on their Kevlar helmets and button up their Kevlar vests.

As Dash led the convoy along the dusty street passing through the camp, they were greeted by an eerie silence, the kind of silence where you can hear the sound of your own heart beating. As he rounded the Acacia tree, out of sight of the Snipers, there in the road, straight ahead, stood a young Somali male with a large white bandage covering his left arm. About the same time that Dash ran into this Somali, Blackburn, bringing up the rear of the convoy, was entering the camp. The entire convoy was now in what was undoubtedly intended to be a kill zone. Then a thunderous explosion broke the eerie silence.

The boom of the Barrett .50 caliber rifle fire echoed through the camp as if an F-16 just scraped the deck above their heads. A quick second round sounded just as loud. Now the white bandaged Somali who had run around the corner stood no more than thirty feet in front of his Hummvee, straddle-legged in the middle of the street as if he were Gary Cooper in the Movie *"High Noon."* Dash, who already had his M-16 outside the vehicle using the mirror as a rest, never waited to see a weapon. The look in the Somali's eyes and the aggressive body language told him all he needed to know and he shot him in the head.

The .223 caliber hollow point bullet exploded through the Somali's skull as if it were a melon, splattering hair, bone, and brain tissue all over the dusty street. Lifting him off his feet, hurling him backwards through the air and giving Dash a good look at the AK-74 carbine he had hidden behind his skirt. Then, as quickly as it had started, it was over. The entire incident had not lasted longer than two or three seconds. During that time the sniper team had killed two Somali gunmen on the roof of a building overlooking the camp and Dash had killed the probable leader of the small gang. The Eritreans never even came out of their huts, being either relieved that the Somali gunmen had been killed or afraid that if they appeared the Americans would shoot them as well. Either way, except for his now racing heart, the only sound Dash could hear were the Seagulls squawking high overhead.

After retrieving the Somalis' weapons, the convoy continued on to the port. They would leave the bodies for the seagulls to ravage or for the Eritreans to bury. It mattered little to the soldiers which one occurred first. The only thing that mattered to them was that this shooting was the last time they were ever confronted in an aggressive manner while passing through the Eritrean camp.

***

Over the course of the next several days there grew a growing crescendo of voices demanding justice for the killing of the three Somali gunmen. All had been members of the Habr Gidr clan headed by Aideed and neither they nor many of the relief agency workers employed near the port and airfield felt that Americans should simply be shooting Somalis as if they were vermin and calmly driving away. To the soldiers, the relief workers reluctance to see and feel the growing animosity developing between the UN forces and Aideed's clansmen was a chink in their otherwise impervious armor, providing Somalis with a glimpse of the dissention developing within UNOSOM. This chink was adding fuel to the growing fire of clan versus UN resentment developing inside Mogadishu.

The day of the shooting Dash called the legal affairs office in the embassy compound from a telephone at the port, explaining what took place and why it was necessary to kill the three gunmen. He had already put the incident out of his mind when, four days later, a large entourage of Somalis marched to the embassy compound demanding that blood money, to the tune of fifty-thousand dollars for each Somali killed be immediately paid to them, or else.

The concept of blood money is somewhat unique to the Muslim world. It revolves around the principle that everything and everyone has a monetary value. In the event of a loss of life, such as the killing of the teen-age gunmen, someone or somebody had to pay the grieving family for their loss. Blood money is both a legal as well as an economic principle contained in the Koran and is not without merit. Throughout history many Muslim families have recovered monetary damages for crimes against them or their property by invoking the principle of blood atonement, in much the same way that a western court fines a criminal. Under Islamic law the criminal pays the fine to the victim or his/her family rather than to a court. Judges and lawyers don't get to pocket the money, which is probably why it was never adopted by the western legal system. But in a place like Somalia, where the intrinsic value of human life was virtually nonexistent and a gullible benefactor could be found, it was a source of an underlying problem; dead children were seen as a means of extorting money from the UN.

The incident involving Whidden and the now very dead Somali gunmen would never have taken place had the UN lawyers not agreed to pay blood money for the first child run over and killed in Mogadishu by a relief agency truck. Even though the unfortunate accident fit the requirement for blood atonement, it established a precedent with unintended consequences. Mogadishu, like any other war torn city teeming with refugees, had many unwanted, uncared for children wandering the streets. When the UN had agreed to reimburse the genuinely grieving family for the loss of their two-year-old little girl, gunmen, like those encountered in the Eritrean camp, had simply rounded up several of these unwanted street children, forged birth certificates for them, and begun throwing them in front of speeding UN trucks. Afterwards, with a large entourage of fellow gunmen in tow to play the part of grieving witnesses, they would tearfully demand they be reimbursed for the loss of their child.

Even though the killing of children in this manner was a well documented fact, and the three dead Somali gunmen were known to have participated in it, it was amazing to Dash and the other soldiers how willing many of the UN workers were to comply with the request to reimburse the grieving families. Something the soldiers were adamantly opposed to doing, telling those in favor of it that the color of compassion in Mogadishu was red — blood red — and that paying for dead children was only going to lead to more dead children. As a result of their contrary position Dash or any of the other CA personnel attending humanitarian relief effort meetings in the Civil Military Operations Center (CMOC) felt as if they were viewed as pariahs or serial killers, a Charles Manson or Jeffrey Dahmer in desert camouflage.

Fortunately, this time, the lawyers refused to pay blood money for the death of the three teen-age gunmen and the emotions surrounding the incident eventually died away. But the rift such occurrences were developing between the soldiers' response to Somali aggression and the expectations of the "feed the poor Somali" crowd of UN relief workers was not going unnoticed by Aideed or any of the other warlords in Mogadishu. People like Aideed were going to exploit this growing chasm between the realists and the idealists to the maximum extent possible in order to destroy UN cohesion from within, forcing it to withdraw from Somalia, one of the reasons why Aideed had ordered the killing of the Pakistani soldiers.

***

America's response to the attack on UN soldiers was to send in more Special Operations troops to capture or kill Aideed. It will forever more be argued by critics and supporters alike whether or not this was a good idea. But the soldiers living and working in the growing hostility of Mogadishu were just glad to see more Americans with guns. Like a B-grade western movie plot, Mogadishu was no longer large enough for both Aideed and the UN; one of them had to get out of town.

Like two large dogs hiking their leg to see which one could pee highest on the bush, UNOSOM forces, especially the Americans, and Aideed's clansmen were circling one another for a fight. Unlike the UN idealists, the American soldiers living and working on the mean streets of Mogadishu watching the rising anti-UN anger, had a natural sense of how world involvement in Somali affairs was going to ultimately end — people were going to die. The soldiers wanted all the firepower they could muster before the killing finally exploded in their face.

***

Until that fateful day arrived however, the CA soldiers would continue to perform missions that allowed them to:

1. collect intelligence
2. establish and maintain rapport with the Somalis
3. establish and maintain rapport with the UN (often more difficult than 2)
4. have as much fun as possible under the circumstances

The most important of all these missions was the last one: to have as much fun as possible under the circumstances. The other three were simply weak attempts at kicking an already dead horse back onto its feet.

During the long, hot, summer months the CA team wandered about Mogadishu like young teen-age boys on first dates, knowing what they wanted to do but worried about getting their faces slapped for trying to do it. The tension between Aideed's forces and the UN was so thick that it could have been cut with a knife. CA missions inside Aideed's sector were now officially put on hold. With the American Delta Force, or D-boys, and Rangers escalating attempts to capture or kill him, Aideed had turned up the heat on UN efforts in those parts of Mogadishu under his control. Making it far too dangerous for the CA soldiers to wander around inside the center of the city. With the UN focus now almost exclusively on killing or capturing Aideed, the CMOC was temporarily out of business as well, meaning that no CA missions were being developed, leaving the soldiers to entertain themselves.

***

"Major," began an excited Blackburn, "have I got a deal for you!"

As much as Dash would have liked to not respond to Blackburn's declaration, he couldn't resist that large grin. Besides, there were just the two of them in the G5 office.

"And what might that be, First Sergeant?" Dash asked with more than a slight hint of reservation.

"I just came from the beach, down by the salt plant, where we delivered some cots for Doctors Without Borders. You wouldn't believe the size of the lobsters the Skinnies were pulling out of the lagoon!"

Blackburn, as well as all the other CA personnel had taken to calling the Somalis Skinnies simply because most of them were. It was also a more politically correct way to describe them. The other, equally common appellation applied to them had been "Sand Niggers." Since several of the American soldiers were Black it was not only more acceptable for a White soldier to call them Skinnies, it was also safer. Using the other might rightfully get their head shoved up their ass.

"I made a prospective deal with one of the fishermen. For a couple cases of beer he and some of his friends will catch some lobsters for us, cook them up, and prepare a real seafood dinner," continued the exuberant Blackburn, like a little kid on Christmas morning. Thus began an unlikely friendship that developed between the CA soldiers and the villagers in Jesira, a small fishing village on the southern tip of Mogadishu, outside the influence of the Habr Gidr clan and their leader, Mohammed Farah Aideed.

Jesira had a population of about one hundred people, though none of the soldiers really knew the actual population for sure. It was small enough, however, that they would immediately notice an increase in the headcount, especially if that increase consisted of young Habr Gidr males, the only group that the UN leaders had essentially declared war against.

Within diplomatic circles, Boutros Boutrous-Ghali, the UN Secretary General, and Mohammed Farah Aideed had a long-standing reputation as being antagonists. Earlier in their careers they had crossed swords over the control of Somalia when a young Egyptian diplomat, Boutros-Ghali, had opposed Aideed's revolutionary forces in the attempted overthrow of the diplomatically recognized leader of Somalia, Siad Barre, in 1991. Now, two years later the Habr Gidr still had not consolidated power and Aideed believed that Boutros-Ghali was using the power of the UN to accomplish what he failed to do earlier, destroy him and his clan's power base in Mogadishu. Aideed was also convinced that Boutros-Ghali had co-opted Admiral Jonathon Howe, an American leading the UN mission in Mogadishu, to support his UN efforts with American guns. In so doing the Americans were playing right into the hands of Aideed by appearing to be the biggest, bad-ass warlord on the block, but no more than that.

Following the killing of the Pakistani soldiers both the UN and the United States were convinced that killing Aideed would somehow bring peace to Somalia, or at the very least a lessening of hostilities. Their reasons for believing this were as varied as the people who held them, but one overriding factor existed in all camps; the willingness to believe that lesser warlords, such as Ali Mahdi, would cooperate with UN efforts in Mogadishu once Aideed were removed from power. The soldiers who had been working the streets of Mogadishu knew that this diplomatic analysis was pure and simple bullshit but, since they were mere soldiers and not seasoned diplomats, no one sought their opinion.

Ali Mahdi and all the other lesser warlords had sidled up to the UN only because they saw it as a way of getting a piece of something they could not achieve by themselves, the removal of the Habr Gidr from power. Had Mahdi or any of the other warlords been in Aideed's position they would have behaved just as he was behaving, thumbing their noses at the UN and the world for attempting to tell Somalia how Somalis should behave. They too would have died before prostrating themselves to Boutros-Ghali and his gang of hired killers.

The American mission to kill or capture Aideed was causing far more problems than it was solving, which was why the CA soldiers had to abandon their missions in central Mogadishu. On July 12, long before the Special Ops mission to find or kill Aideed had even been launched, American Cobra Gunships fired sixteen TOW anti-tank missiles into a Somali meeting house, hoping to kill Aideed who, as it turned out, wasn't even there. Oops!! Instead, the missiles killed several dozen Somali clansmen who had come to the meeting to develop a plan to reduce the growing hostility between the UN and the Somali people. This failed effort single-handedly painted the face of war on every Somali inside the city. Now they not only had one another to hate, they could all simultaneously hate the Americans as well. For the proud Habr Gidr clansmen, America had declared war on their clan leader and if war was what America wanted then so by God be it. To the young Somali gunmen American soldiers from the land of the free and the home of the brave were just the latest enemy in a lifetime of enemies. "Welcome to the Motherland and all its glory, brother," Somalis would begin saying to the American Black soldiers. They meant every sinister word of it.

Adding insult to injury, the Americans now seemed to be playing some sort of macho game with the Somalis as well. The Joint Task Force (JTF) operations were wreaking havoc on the civilian populace, swooping in and out of areas in the city with Black Hawk helicopters, literally blowing Somalis off their feet with the rotor wash, doing little to endear the pilots to the average Somali citizen. Not that the pilots were there to make friends, but their methods left much to be desired even for the other American soldiers watching their cowboy antics. As a result of these cowboy antics, the Somalis were getting genuinely pissed off at all Americans, not just the ones blowing roofs from their houses with their low flying helicopters.

As Dash and Blackburn watched the efforts of the Joint Task Force ebb and flow throughout the city, they developed a certain degree of misgiving. Not because they cared about the inconvenience this was causing the Somalis, but because they had a deep feeling in the pit of their stomach that somehow, someday, one of those low flying helicopters was going to get blown out of the sky. The people it landed on would not greet the occupants with open arms. But, until that day came, Dash, Blackburn, and all the other CA soldiers were intent on enjoying life as much as they possibly could.

CHAPTER 19

"**D**amn, Major," smacked Blackburn, "this is some fine Lobster. Don't you think?"

And indeed it was fine Lobster, as was the fresh tuna and calamari as well. All caught and prepared by their new Somali friend Mohamed-Mohamed, or Moe-Moe, as he came to be called, and his fellow Jesira villagers.

This was the third or fourth time that the soldiers had enjoyed a seafood buffet on the Jesira beach, a small fishing village twenty kilometers south of Mogadishu. Each time they had come to Jesira they had brought with them several cases of Israeli beer to both share and consume with Moe-Moe and his friends as an enticement for them to venture forth into the frothing surf to catch lobsters. For some unfathomable reason the soldiers had been unable to catch the lobsters themselves, having to rely on the Somalis to do it for them. A reality that did not sit well with the "can do" attitude of the typical Special Operations soldier who believes himself capable of doing anything that another human being can do. Yet the more often the soldiers attempted to capture a lobster the greater became the mounting toll documenting their failures. The soldiers suspected that it had to have been technique, rather than intelligence, that allowed the Somali divers to catch the lobsters when they couldn't. At least they secretly hoped that was the case. However, after observing one particular episode by the Americans Dash suspected that the Somalis would claim just the opposite. To the good folks of Jesira these Americans were some of the silliest people they had ever met.

On one bright, sunshiny Friday afternoon, Sergeant First Class Mike Gerard, a reservist and member of the 351st CA Command, decided that he had seen enough failed attempts by the Americans to catch a lobster, and determined that he was going to break the curse. Gerard was a Fairfax County police officer when not playing army and was an interesting character. A French linguist, he was slightly overweight and also a bit of a hypochondriac, always complaining about aches and pains that interfered with his ability to do anything strenuous, things like exercise, which he avoided like the plague. Quick with criticism toward others he had a thin skin regarding any criticism directed his way and generally considered himself to be above the fray of sweating, hard work, danger, and accepting personal responsibility for completing a task. But he was harmless enough and when the soldiers began going to the beach for their weekly seafood buffet, he had been quick to sign on. The other soldiers simply tolerated his presence and guarded their beer whenever he was around since he could suck down the suds faster than a flushing toilet.

Over the course of the past several months the soldiers had made many attempts to catch the jittery little beasts but had not had even a sliver of success. The only exception being one time when Dash threw a hand grenade into a pool of water and stunned several lobsters, allowing him to retrieve one of them from the calm waters of Jesira bay. On this particular day, however, they were further down the beach and in deeper water, making the feat more difficult for Gerard to repeat. But he was determined to do so and with everyone on the beach already full of lobster and beer, he had a rousing cheering section to urge him on, overcoming whatever inhibitions he may have harbored.

***

"Major Dash," said a naked and shockingly white Mike Gerard as he prepared for his dive into the Indian Ocean to catch a lobster; wearing only a pair of tennis shoes to protect his feet from the sharp coral rocks and clutching a hand grenade. He, like all of the other soldiers had learned that the heavy salt water of the Indian Ocean had a deleterious effect on clothing so soldiers would always strip before entering the water. Since they never exposed their bare skin often enough to the hot African sun to darken, none had anything that remotely resembled a suntan. The white-skinned soldiers looked like gobs of mayonnaise as they splashed around in the surf or laid on the beach in their birthday suits. Gerard, even whiter than the others, undoubtedly looked like a ghost to the dark-skinned Somalis gathered on the beach with them.

"Since you're the only one still sober enough to shoot straight," Gerard continued, slurring his words as he spoke, "would you be so kind as to provide shark watch while I swim out to get us some more dinner?" Technically this was an overstatement by Gerard as it was an unwritten rule that no one was to get drunk during these events. A mild buzz was acceptable, but an intoxicated soldier in Somalia was still a risk that Dash and Blackburn were not willing to accept. Accordingly, no more than two beers could be consumed in one hour. Of course some soldiers drank these two beers in a matter of a few minutes, leaving them temporarily blitzed for a short time as Gerard was now.

Seeing Gerard standing in front of him in all his natural glory reminded Dash of the old joke about cops loving doughnuts. Gerard certainly did not look like he had ever seen a doughnut that he hadn't liked. As Dash looked at his flaccid muscles, he silently wondered if Gerard could even swim the thirty yards out to the middle of the pool.

"No problem," replied Dash. Then, noticing the glassy eyes of Gerard, he added, "I'll even throw the frag for you."

Gerard climbed atop a large rock overlooking the pool of water and waited as

Dash pulled the pin on the frag, released the spoon, counted to four, and threw it into the water. A few seconds later there were two loud explosions, one from the exploding frag and the other by a thunderous belly buster as Gerard flopped into the water.

Along this particular section of beach a coral reef separated the shore from the deep blue water, allowing the high tides to wash sea life over the reef, then trapping the creatures in deep water pools during low tide, as it was now. But in so doing the tide wasn't too particular about what type of sea life it washed over the reef. An occasional shark could be seen patrolling near the shoreline waiting for the tide to return, allowing him to escape back to the open ocean.

Sharks had never really been a problem before but on those rare occasions when a frag had been thrown into the water, the soldiers noticed that the shock waves caused by the explosion seemed to attract them. To prevent anyone from being attacked it had become standard operating procedure that anytime a diver was in the water, frag or no frag, a shark guard had to be posted to protect him. Today Dash would be that guard. He watched Gerard swim out into the middle of the fifteen-foot deep pool of water, his bright white butt cheeks undulating across the surface like headlights on a bouncing pickup truck, saw him stop, draw a deep breath and dive for the bottom. When he disappeared from sight Dash quickly scanned the surface for any sign of sharks. Seeing none he continued to watch the bubbles rise to the surface where Gerard had disappeared. Surfacing a few seconds later, Gerard yelled out in surprised delight, tightly clutching a large lobster in his right hand, proudly holding it above his head and cheering his accomplishment as if he had just hit the lotto. Joining Gerard's cheers were all those of the soldiers and Somalis gathered on the beach watching his performance.

When Gerard surfaced holding the lobster above his head, Dash quickly jumped down from the rock on which he had been standing and started toward the crowd of cheering soldiers and Somalis, wanting to be among them to congratulate Gerard for a job well done. However, no sooner had his feet hit the sand than he heard a loud groan similar to that made by a bull calf when he is being castrated. Having grown up working on an Idaho cattle ranch, Dash recognized the sound, and it had come from where he had last seen Gerard. The immediate thought of "SHARK!" flashed through his mind and he leapt back atop the rock, looking down at the now frothing water where Gerard had slipped beneath the surface.

As soon as Gerard had let loose with the sickly groan and went under for the first time, the always alert Blackburn, along with two other soldiers, dove into the pool and began swimming towards the frothing water. As they raced towards him Gerard reappeared and groaned again, but this time not quite as loud, before once again slipping beneath the surface. Dash continued to scan the water for blood and shark fin, wanting to help Gerard but there was nothing to shoot at.

Streaking through the water like an Olympic swimmer, Blackburn was the first to reach him and with one massive arm literally jerked Gerard to the surface, allowing the other two soldiers to get their hands on him as well. The three of them swam for shore, dragging Gerard with them as if he were a dying albino seal, curled tightly in a fetal position and doing nothing to assist his struggling rescuers. Who appeared to be having a hard time dragging his dead weight out of the water. Blackburn would later remark that swimming while pulling Gerard behind him had been like trying to pull a tank out of mud with his bare hands. When the four of them reached the shore, the three rescuers collapsed in a heap, sucking loudly for air as the crowd rushed forward to drag Gerard further up on to the beach. One by one, they began collapsing in fits of hysterical laughter, especially the Somalis, who did not have a restriction on their beer consumption and were completely blistered.

One quick glance explained all the levity to Dash. In his exuberance to bring his catch back to shore Gerard had employed the elegant, yet fashionable, Esther Williams' sidestroke, reaching out with his left arm and sweeping his right arm in front of his body, gracefully gliding through the water as if he were a water ballerina. Unfortunately his catch had a different opinion of his graceful sidestroke. When Gerard swept the nasty little critter in front of his body, it had reached out with a rather large and powerful pincer claw, firmly securing a grip on the only portion of Gerard's anatomy it could reach, his protruding manhood and its two dangling attachments. With one quick grab the lobster threatened to remove a branch from the Gerard family tree. As Gerard maintained his death grip on the lobster to prevent it from threshing about Dash noticed that the creatures other claw was securely attached to his rather ample, round, bright white stomach. Making it appear to Dash as if the lobster was snow skiing over a large white mogul while holding only one ski pole.

After the mostly drunken mob of would be rescuers had finished dragging Gerard's motionless body back to shore, those with clearer heads quickly assessed the situation and took what appeared to each to be the appropriate action.

"Stand back and I'll shoot the damn thing," Dash posited, standing ready with the rifle.

"No!" responded Blackburn. "Don't shoot it, for God's sake, the impact might rip his dick off."

Gerard, now being prostrated over the hood of Dash's Hummvee as if he were a side of beef seemed to be in agreement, weakly muttering, "Please, no gunfire."

"Doc, damn it man, get your butt up and get over here," Blackburn roared. Doc Adams, the team surgeon, was one of those still rolling around laughing hysterically, as was the team veterinarian, Captain Miller, whose particular expertise was also going to be required as the soldiers sought to come up with a solution to end this bizarre pornographic liaison between man and beast.

"Gerard," said Blackburn, "you've got to uncurl your legs so we can get in there and work."

Gerard remained tightly curled in a fetal position and was quite reluctant to change his posture. Every time that he straightened his legs the lobster would flap its powerful tail as if it were swimming, trying to return to the surf and threatening to take Gerard's family jewels with him, eliciting the sound of a freshly castrated calf each time.

"Brown!" shouted Blackburn. "Get over here and hold on to this damn lobster." "You two," the First Sergeant shouted to two of the 351st personnel, "get over here and grab his arms. Relax Gerard, we'll get this thing off of you, no problem," he lied.

For the first several seconds Blackburn looked at the sight like a hog looks at a wristwatch. It caught his attention, but he had not a clue what to do with it, periodically tugging here and there, always resulting in a cry of pain from Gerard. Finally, the two professional medical men of science had collected themselves enough to be of assistance and dutifully approached to lend a helping hand.

"Shall we cut its pincer loose, Doctor?" Doc Adams asked his colleague Doc Miller. The two professionals staring at the strange attachment as if they were back in medical school preparing to dissect a cadaver.

"I'm afraid that it wouldn't do any good, Doctor." replied Doc Miller. "It might relieve some of the pressure but the pincer will simply lock down into position." Then, making sure that Gerard clearly heard every word, loudly whispered, "I am afraid that we're going to have to amputate."

Gerard didn't appreciate their sense of humor and told them so by weakly saying, "It's not funny! It hurts." Then, in an even weaker attempt to add a little drama hoarsely mumbled, "I can't feel my legs."

Dash, who had been quietly observing this comical exchange between the doctors simply replied, "If it has to come off, then it has to come off. We can't very well take him to the hospital like this."

"Yeah," chuckled Blackburn, "besides, it ain't like you've never used the damn thing Gerard. What have you got now, four kids? In fact, weren't you the one talking about having a vasectomy a few years ago? Hell, we'd be doing you a favor by removing all this dead weight."

Gerard, the intoxicating effects of the two beers now completely worn off, continued to hoarsely murmur, "No kidding, guys. My whole body is going numb. I can barely breathe."

"O.K.," said Miller. "Doctor, if you would be so kind as to assist, I'll prepare a medicinal cocktail for the lobster and we'll separate these two love birds."

As they were walking away Gerard whispered, "Could you give me a little something for the pain too, Doc?"

"No," came the reply. "I want you alert and awake in case the cocktail has just the opposite effect and excites rather than relaxes the lobster."

"Oh, my God!" Gerard moaned.

As the two doctors retrieved their medical bags and prepared the cocktail, a mixture of Demerol and Acetylpromazine, Blackburn and Dash had an opportunity to evaluate the extent of the damage caused by the lobster attack. Since it wasn't attached to their manhood, it didn't appear to be all that extensive. Still, the large roll of belly fat being squeezed by the lobster appeared bright red and was hot to the touch. Gerard's genitals had the ghostly gray-black look of dead flesh and neither Blackburn nor Dash would touch the area to see if it was hot. But they did offer encouragement to Gerard by telling him that he would probably live.

Arriving with a syringe and a wide smile Doctor Miller inquired of his colleague Doctor Adams, "Where shall I inject the cocktail, Doctor? I can't ever recall taking a course in vet school on stoning a crustacean."

"Well, Doctor," replied Adams, continuing with their exaggerated formality, "it is my professional opinion that you should insert the needle here, where the appendage protrudes from the body." Pointing to where a layman would call the armpit under each clawed front leg.

"I concur with your opinion, Doctor," responded Miller as he lifted a flap of shell and deftly slipped the needle beneath it, repeating the procedure on the other side.

Instantly the lobster visibly relaxed. The injection had either killed it or made it very, very happy and when Blackburn raised its tail and let it drop, he got no response in return from the once hyperactive lobster.

"Well," said Blackburn, I don't think we'll ever have a better opportunity. Let's pull the little bastard off of this great American soldier."

Grabbing the left claw, the one attached to Gerard's belly, Blackburn gave a slight tug, followed by a moan from Gerard, and absolutely nothing happened. He then grabbed the pincer itself and tried to forcibly pry it apart. Again nothing happened except for the constant moaning from Gerard. The lobster continued to retain its death grip on Gerard's now purple dick.

"Major," a puzzled Blackburn asked, "would you hand me your Randle and I'll see if I can wedge it between the pincer?"

Dash reached inside his Hummvee and pulled the razor sharp knife out of its scabbard, passing it directly in front of Gerard's eyes as he handed it to Blackburn.

"What the hell are you going to do with that?" asked a wide-eyed Gerard as he tried to pull himself back into a fetal position. An endeavor he couldn't complete as Blackburn was straddling his legs.

"I'm going to try to slip the blade between his pincer and pry it loose," answered an exasperated Blackburn.

"Jesus Christ, be careful," moaned a heavily sweating Gerard.

There must have been thirty pairs of eyes gathered around the Hummvee watching the large hands of First Sergeant Blackburn slowly forcing the knife blade between the lobster's pincers. As Dash watched he noticed sweat rolling down Blackburn's forehead, flowing to the tip of his nose, briefly hanging there before finally dropping with a splash on Gerard's stomach. It was about as incongruous a sight as he had ever witnessed. One large semi-naked man — the soldiers were only wearing PT shorts — holding a large knife straddling another equally large man wearing only tennis shoes while being restrained by two other individuals, defied imagination. Throw in the vision of a lobster holding onto a man's genitals as if they were the Holy Grail, and it completes the picture. But, like the sight of a monkey attempting to mate with a coconut, it just didn't look quite right to normal eyes.

After several seconds of slowly twisting the blade side to side, Blackburn finally worked it between the pincers and in one deft motion turned the blade on its edge, prying the claw loose, eliciting a boisterous session of hooting and hollering from the onlookers. Then, without pause, a now smiling Blackburn quickly switched his efforts and the very large, sharp knife, to the other claw, the one holding the family jewels, and Gerard went ballistic, wildly thrashing about, attempting to pull loose from the soldiers holding his arms. The thought of the sharp blade near his private parts was one that Gerard was having difficulty coming to grips with. In fact, he absolutely did not want to have to come to grips with it. The soldiers restraining him were having difficulty maintaining a firm grip on his arms.

"Hold still," Blackburn calmly said. Followed by more struggling and cursing from Gerard.

"Damn it, I said hold still!" said a slightly less calm Blackburn. Again followed by more struggling and cursing from Gerard in an attempt to protect his private parts from what he was sure was going to be a painful mutilation.

Finally, "If you don't shut-up and lay still I'm going to knock your ass out!" screamed Blackburn. "Your dick is as black as a ten day old banana and if I don't get this son-of-a-bitch off you ASAP, we might just as well let the lobster keep it because you're never going to be able to use it again!"

The stark reality of what Blackburn had said to him, coupled with the fact that he had been no more than three inches from his face when he had screamed it, caused Gerard to stop resisting and lay still. Giving Blackburn the opportunity to try and slip the blade between the other pincer. Because of the location of the second pincer, Blackburn did not have much leeway to insert the knife without turning Gerard into a woman. In fact, in consultation with Doc Adams, Blackburn elected instead to drill a gap between the pincers with the tip of the blade, large enough so that Adams could get forceps inside it, and with one squeeze on the forceps, Gerard was finally set free.

A thunderous round of applause followed Blackburn's announcement that Gerard could get up and the Somalis danced wildly about in celebration of the entertainment. High fives were exchanged all around, fresh beers were opened and, now forgotten and neglected as a source of their amusement, Gerard slowly slid down from the hood of the Hummvee. He landed in a pile of naked humanity, desperately clutching his manhood in one hand and a cold beer in the other. He would be all right. The soldiers were a little more nonchalant in their evaluation of Gerard's health, offering to take a picture of his genitals while they were still swollen and extended, sending it to his wife along with a note saying how much he was looking forward to their reunion.

Soldiers also gathered around to take pictures of the lobster, which had regained its senses and was as lively as it had ever been, viciously popping its pincers at anyone who so much as threw a glance in its direction. Eventually, following a lengthy photo op, the lobster was taken back to the surf and released for two reasons. One, it had kicked some serious U.S. Army ass and deserved to live as a result, and two, no one wanted to eat it because they knew where the claw had been.

Dash, while the soldiers were returning the lobster to the surf, noticed something shiny lying on the ground in front of the Hummvee and walked over to pick up the forceps, still lying in the sand where they had been dropped in all the excitement. It was then that Dash noticed the lobster had secured such a tight grip on Gerard's genitals that Adams had actually bent the forceps when prying apart the pincer. For the remainder of the time he was in Somalia, Gerard never again got into the waters of the Indian Ocean.

**

Their frequent wanderings around the city also provided certain moments of levity; fun was not just restricted to the beach at Jesira.

"Dash," Major John Whidden called out one day in early September, "you want to get off the compound for awhile and go with some of us down to the port? A ship just arrived and there are supposed to be some field desks from the 351st aboard. Thought we'd go down and check for them. You're welcome to come along if you'd like."

"Yeah," replied Dash, bored with life on the compound. "I'll even drive for you."

Because of the increased security requirements resulting from the JTF's continual harassment of the Somalis, a minimum of four Hummvees were required for any trips off the compound, two of which had to be equipped with an M-60 machinegun. Blackburn went along in one of the machinegun cargo Hummvees with Gerard serving as his driver and Mike Brown standing in the back of the vehicle manning the gun. This vehicle was second in the march order, following the lead HMMWV occupied by Dash and Whidden. Members from the 351st occupied the two other vehicles.

As the convoy turned off 21 October Road and onto Medina Road, entering the busy city, it was evident that the young Somalis were restless as large numbers of them were gathered on every street corner, a common yet disturbing sight in the city. The young men would attempt to steal anything that they could get their hands on as the vehicles drove past, a ritual that had lately become a sport for the Somalis and a contest of will for the soldiers. To avoid being victimized yet again, soldiers would spot a gang of young Somalis standing along the street, obviously up to no good, and attempt to speed past them. The Somalis, like dogs chasing a car, would see this increase in speed as a challenge and dash after it. Sometimes they were even so bold as to dash after it before the vehicle had passed, causing several of them to be run over by anxious soldiers. Usually, however, the Somalis would simply reach inside the vehicle as it sped past and steal whatever they could grab. Many a soldier had lost their sunglasses in this manner. Others lost MRE's, bottles of water, magazines of ammunition, binoculars, sodas, or anything else lying loose in the vehicle, including berets and soft caps. The Somalis never attempted to steal a weapon for had they done so they would have immediately been shot dead, and they knew it. But anything else inside the vehicle was considered to be fair game. The Somalis really didn't have any use for any of the items they stole; it was just the thrill of the chase that excited them. The whole game they were playing didn't really amount to much but the stealing angered the soldiers and made them dislike the Somalis even more than they already did.

The rampant stealing became such a problem that it was SOP to have at least one ax handle in every Hummvee. It was neither acceptable nor legal to shoot one of them for stealing. But if a soldier could catch them in the act, a sharp blow upside the head or across an outstretched arm with an ax handle had a tendency to persuade them to go elsewhere for fun. Known as "Somali-be-good-sticks" the ax handles were often more valuable to carry than an M-16 in warding off the determined efforts of thieves.

The Somali teen-agers knew they would not be shot for stealing a pair of sunglasses off a driver's face, but they quickly learned that the same driver, carrying an ax handle, would beat the dog crap out of them if they got caught. This fact dampened their enthusiasm a little but stealing was so ingrained in the young that the Prophet Mohammed himself, "Peace Be Upon Him," could not have put an end to it.

Dash had once had a Somali no more than ten years old dive into the back seat of his moving Hummvee, perform a complete summersault, and exit out the other side clutching a Motorola Saber radio in his hands. It had been a marvelous feat of acrobatics by the young man and Dash marveled at his athleticism. Blackburn, who was following behind in another Hummvee tried to run him down with his vehicle, not to injure him, but to get the radio back. The young Somali was too quick and escaped by slipping between two buildings that were too narrow to drive the Hummvee between. Blackburn then keyed his own Saber and called the young Somali, offering to pay him for the radio if he would just bring it back. The little Somali had replied, in perfect English, "Fuck you, GI!" and the team remained short one Saber radio until newly arriving reservists brought a replacement with them.

For two days following the theft, until the battery went dead on the Somali's radio, Dash would listen as he and Blackburn cursed at one another over the airwaves. It was better entertainment than anything Oprah Winfrey had ever produced, and with a lot more drama as Blackburn would often get fighting mad, calling the young Somali all sorts of names, only to have the Somali repeat all of them back to him with perfect diction. Blackburn seemed relieved and more at peace with himself when he could no longer raise the kid on the radio to start an argument with him, being content instead in arguing with everyone else at every available opportunity.

In an effort to prevent this sort of pilfering, in addition to carrying the "Somali-be-good-sticks," the Hummvees traveled very close together while moving through congested areas, often virtually bumper to bumper. It was a technique that helped a little, but the Somalis were constantly reaching into vehicles as they passed by anyway.

During this particular trip, as they drove down Medina Road, it was apparent to Dash that Whidden had not been off the compound very often. The sight of the Somali gangs would cause him to sit erect and reach for his can of pepper spray, which he would then spray at the Somalis as the vehicle drove past. On one such occasion Whidden stuck both his head and the pepper spray outside the vehicle and gassed himself. With the vehicles moving in excess of thirty miles per hour, the wind had simply blown the spray back into his face.

"Gawww, shit!" screamed Whidden, with a large stream of snot hanging from his nose, "stop the truck, I can't breath!"

"Bullshit," countered Dash, "if we stop the truck the Skinnies will be all over us. Suck it up until we get to the airport and you can wash it out of your eyes. We're almost there." For the remainder of the trip Whidden continued to spray the gas even though he couldn't see a damn thing. Hoping against hope that his efforts would keep the wolves at bay long enough for them to reach the safety of the airport.

Increasing speed the four Hummvees moved as one through the busy Mogadishu street, finally pulling through the airport gate when Blackburn's vehicle shot ahead of Dash's, immediately turned sideways and braked to a halt, forcing Dash to brake to a quick stop as well. From out of the vehicle emerged a highly perturbed First Sergeant Blackburn. Strolling up to Whidden with a look on his face that only a mother could have loved, he yanked the pepper spray out of his hand and shouted at him, "Major, if you keep spraying this shit I'm going to shove it up your ass!"

It was then that Dash noticed it wasn't only Whidden that had snot hanging to his knees, so did Blackburn, Gerard, and Brown. All the while they had been traveling Medina Road Whidden's constant use of the pepper spray had gassed the vehicles traveling behind.

***

On another occasion, while visiting a local Khat market, one of the Somali teen-agers, stoned out of his head, challenged Dash to a fight. In his pigeon English, the young man simply walked up to Dash and announced that he was going to kick his ass, a threat that Dash initially ignored. As the Somali became more aggressive and began flicking jabs near his head, Dash told him to go away, thumping him in the chest with his ax handle as a point of emphasis. The Somali was every bit as large as Dash and since the soldiers were outside their vehicles and surrounded by Somalis, getting baited into a fight didn't seem like a very good idea. Then, like all stone-freaks and alcoholics, the Somali did something completely unexpected and incredibly stupid. He lifted his foot off the ground and in an impressive display of flexibility placed it behind his head, leaving him standing on one leg while still challenging Dash to a fight. It was an apparent act of intimidation by the Somali that he clearly did not understand the consequences of doing.

Neither Dash nor Blackburn could resist the sudden impulse. Dash swept the Somali's leg off the ground with a quick kick the same instant that Blackburn struck him across the bridge of the nose with an ax handle, sending him flying backwards into the crowd and landing in a rumpled, bleeding heap with a broken nose. As his friends rushed forward to avenge their leader's ignominious defeat, the sounds of knuckles, boots and kiln-hardened oak ax handles smacking against bare flesh could be heard a block away. It was a great fight and a real bonding experience for the soldiers who participated. It was also a fight where not a single shot was fired and other than a few broken bones, no one got seriously hurt. But it sent a clear message to the young Somali males. In fact, after that day the soldiers and Somalis seemed to have come to an understanding. "You don't mess with me and I won't mess with you," seemed to be a message now understood by all the young men hanging around the Khat market.

The soldier's time in Jesira was not just about fun and games, though admittedly most of it had been exactly that. But there was a serious side to it as well. It allowed them the time to cultivate a personal relationship with Moe-Moe and the other Somali men. The benefits of which were that these men would then keep the team informed as to the wanderings of Aideed, apprised of the growing anti-American sentiments inside the city and areas that were still considered to be safe. But, most importantly, Jesira provided the team with a secure place other than the UN compounds if they ever got trapped inside the city. The streets on the south side of Mogadishu would be relatively smooth sailing for a convoy faced with having to escape danger. With Jesira a convenient and well-known rally point the SOF soldiers knew that if all else failed to go to Jesira. Someone would eventually come there to find them. It was an ace in the hole that none of them wanted to have to use but it was comforting to know that it was there if ever needed.

As a result of Moe-Moe's frequent updates, the CA soldiers seemed to know much more about the Mogadishu political environment than the UNOSOM personnel being kept locked inside their UN compounds. So much so that during CMOC or UNLSC staff meetings they often volunteered information that no one else, including the intelligence analysts, had any knowledge of. This knowledge was a double-edged sword because CA personnel were then both sought by the JTF analysts trying to catch Aideed while simultaneously being despised by these same people for having unrestricted freedom of movement around the city. It often seemed to the SOF soldiers as if all other UNOSOM personnel, military and civilian, remained voluntarily or involuntarily locked down on their compounds. Certainly the American military commanders' obsession with not getting any more of their soldiers killed, keeping them restricted to compounds and secure neighborhoods, was negatively impacting on the ability to collect intelligence, the single most critical factor in an Operations Other Than War (OOTW) environment. With the exception of the SOF, soldiers confined to their compounds in Mogadishu were bored and their commanders were absolutely clueless regarding the environment outside their own compound gate.

One of the most common mistakes resulting from this "bunker mentality" was that it was too dangerous for anyone to venture into Aideed's "Indian country," the Black Sea neighborhood of central Mogadishu. SOF troops, NGO aid organizations, Pakis, reporters, and various and sundry relief workers often went into the center of the city. It was dangerous; but for an occupying force trying to stabilize an area, it is even more dangerous for soldiers to remain hidden within their barbed-wire compounds and not know what was going on out of their sight. Had the American commanders continued to operate inside the city after Aideed's killing of the

Pakistani soldiers as they had been before the killings, they would have been able to capture or kill Aideed without having had to resort to the Keystone Kops antics of the JTF.

But they hadn't, and as a result, now that timely, accurate intelligence was more crucial than ever, the JTF was in a poor position to collect it. They were now forced to rely on information collected from a motley assortment of clan spies, alcoholics, drug addicts, and near-do-wells of every stripe and nationality, completely forgetting that they had at their fingertips the greatest collection source any military commander could ever ask for; boots on the ground. With the exception of SOF, they never asked to use any of them.

As a result of their frequent trips throughout Mogadishu, Dash's team was being asked to deliver certain items, like medical supplies, to key Aideed areas in the city, such as the Volunteer Hospital and Digfer Hospital. The pretense for such trips was medical resupply missions for Doctors without Borders, but the real purpose was to cultivate intelligence sources in the hopes of assisting the JTF with their attempts to capture Aideed. On one such trip into the city they were shocked to encounter an old friend working for an Islamic charity group headquartered in the Volunteer Hospital on Hawlwadig Road, not far from the Bakara Market.

***

Blackburn was the first to notice him.

"Moe, is that you?" inquired an incredulous Blackburn of a tall, robed, long bearded figure standing in the foyer of the hospital.

At first glance Dash had paid no attention to the bearded male figure standing in the middle of the foyer busily directing the placement of the cots and medicines the CA troops had brought with them. Such people were common to all of the Islamic groups operating in the city. But upon Blackburn's inquiry, followed by the gleaming white smile, Dash immediately recognized the lone figure as being their old Saudi friend, Mohammed Al-Assiri. Approaching both Dash and Blackburn, Assiri extended his hand in friendship but, tellingly, did not greet either of them with the customary cheek kisses they were so accustomed to receiving from him.

"What a surprise to see the two of you here," said Assiri.

"And the same with seeing you here," countered Dash. "How long have you been in Mogadishu?"

"I guess a couple of months now. How about you two?"

"Too damn long," answered Blackburn. "I've been here since December, almost a year now. The Major got here in May. We're not scheduled to leave until after Christmas."

The past few days Dash had noticed a subtle change in Blackburn's attitude. A surlier, caustic one had recently replaced his usual jovial demeanor. It was not unusual for soldiers to undergo such changes in attitude on extended deployments, and Blackburn was showing all the signs that he was getting fed up with the meaningless efforts to save Somalia. His bad attitude was nothing serious, just a common and constant malady suffered by soldiers approaching the burnout phase of life in the field. Dash was contemplating sending him for an incountry R&R to Mombassa, Kenya, to recharge his batteries. Such short breaks often worked wonders on a man's attitude, making them feel like a new man when they returned to duty.

"What about you?" asked Dash. "What have you been doing since we last saw you? The Saudi authorities were in a tizzy when you disappeared after the Gulf War."

"Yeah, well, I wasn't too happy with them either," said Assiri. "When they failed to hold the international community accountable for what Saddam did to the Marsh Arabs I kind of lost my stomach for the Royals' cause."

The Americans knew that Assiri had been highly upset with the way post-war Iraq had been allowed to deal with its insurgency problem. The coalition had seemingly turned a blind eye to Saddam's vengeance at a time when it could have exerted tremendous influence throughout the region. Instead the coalition had granted Republican Guard forces the authority to fly helicopters and send Saddam loyalists back into Southern Iraq to cap the insurgency, resulting in many unnecessary deaths. Still, as a realist himself, Assiri must have known that this was a possibility. The idea that the coalition would refuse to support something not considered to be in its own interest had to have occurred to him prior to the end of the ground campaign. Assiri had seen enough of war in his life to know that both war and politics are a dirty, nasty business.

The source of Assiri's anger was something Dash and Blackburn had often discussed and, if ever presented with the opportunity, had vowed to ask him. That opportunity had just arrived, but Dash felt that it would be wise to be circuitous in speaking with Assiri, who seemed distant and apparently wanted to remain that way. After some small talk regarding careers and family Dash broke the ice in an attempt to focus the conversation on his regional contacts.

"So, where did you go to clear your head after the war?" asked Dash.

"To the Sudan to visit with my uncle Osama. I'm sure you knew that he had been exiled from Saudi Arabia."

"Yeah, I knew that," replied Dash. "And what guidance did Osama offer that finds you now, two years later, working with an Islamic charity group in Mogadishu, Somalia? Seems like a quantum leap backwards from your life as a Saudi military officer."

"Yes, it would seem so," said Assiri, lightly stroking his beard as he spoke. "But it is actually a better life that I have now, helping the Muslim people. Throughout the region, in the Sudan, Ethiopia, Djibouti, Eritrea, and now Somalia, there seems to be a western vendetta against the Muslim people. A desire to punish rather than help them." Then, with a large sweeping motion of his arms he announced, "Unlike others, whatever assistance I can provide these people I am glad to provide, asking nothing from them in return except for their love of Islam. Muslims across the globe must learn to take care of one another and confront their common enemy, western governments who consider themselves to be more powerful than God, using money as their prophet."

Both Dash and Blackburn felt the impulse to point out to Assiri that this "vendetta" he was describing was usually as a result of some terrorist activity perpetrated by a group of Muslims on unsuspecting infidels, such as Jews in Israel and American soldiers and embassies throughout the world. But by the way he was stroking his beard, they could tell that their old friend was not in any mood for a discussion regarding the merits or demerits of Islam; he was in a teaching and preaching mode, not a learning mode. Assiri was now exhibiting those same characteristics of intolerance and self-righteous arrogance worn by all religious fundamentalists from California to Calcutta, professing to know God's grand plan and being quite willingly to share their knowledge with those around them, whether their audience cared to hear about it or not.

Instead of confronting Assiri in an argumentative manner, which is what he wanted to do, Dash elected instead to see if Assiri would be willing to share information with the Americans regarding their efforts to catch Aideed. To do this he knew that he had be indirect, non-confrontational and attentive, allowing Assiri to talk at length while he tried to pick out the nuggets of intelligence his Arab friend carried inside his head.

"With all that is happening in the world today, I can see how you might feel this way," said Dash, hoping to strike a sympathetic chord with his old friend. "But here in Somalia, it has very much been Muslim on Muslim violence and the United States has no motive beyond stopping the violence and feeding the people."

"That may have been true initially," replied Assiri, "but since the counterattack by Aideed against the UN forces, the West has lost the legitimacy of having intervened in a civil war for humanitarian purposes. It has declared war on the rightful leader of a Muslim country."

"Counterattack!" sputtered a disbelieving Blackburn. "What damn counterattack? The killing of the Pakis was plain and simple murder. When had they previously attacked Aideed's forces?"

"So much for subterfuge," thought Dash. *"I'm really going to have to give my First Sergeant some time off."*

"The Pakistanis were attempting to steal Khat from Aideed in an attempt to weaken his image in the eyes of his fellow clansmen. They were doing it because Boutrous-Ghali and his hired American killers ordered them to," Assiri emphatically stated.

This was not the first time that Dash had heard from a Somali or, in this case a fellow Muslim, that the Pakis, themselves Muslims, had been attacked because they were trying to cut in on the lucrative Habr Gidr drug trade. Unfortunately he had never been able to confirm this allegation through either UN or American intelligence channels, but it was a widely held belief among the Somali people. It was such an unquestioned fact in Jesira for instance that Moe-Moe had once matter-of-factly told him, "Everyone knows that!" as if Dash had just fallen off the turnip truck.

"You're out of your goddamn mind!" roared Blackburn.

"The First Sergeant and I aren't really doing a good job of communicating our intentions," Dash thought as he watched Blackburn rise up in anger to the absurdity of Assiri's remarks.

"What in your pea brain would leave you to conclude that America considers Aideed to be such a threat to its efforts in Somalia that he should be killed?" Blackburn asked.

"I don't know why America feels this way," responded Assiri. "I just know that it does. You tell me then, First Sergeant, why are your Rangers so obsessed with finding him? It wasn't American troops that he ordered killed."

"No, it wasn't American troops he killed. But America is the only nation with balls enough to enforce the belief that it is unacceptable for some tin horn warlord in a backwater African country to essentially declare war on the world by killing soldiers who are protecting all of the people and not just some of them."

"Maybe that is the source of their anger," Assiri said with a slight smirk on his face. "Maybe all of the people aren't being helped, just those who are willing to bend to the dictates of a non-Islamic nation like America."

"Neither the UN or America declared war on Somalia," Blackburn fumed, angry with himself for getting drawn into an argument with a man who had obviously become a religious fundamentalist himself.

Like most mature adults, Blackburn had learned long ago to never mud wrestle with a pig. It would only accomplish something if you enjoyed getting dirty, sweaty and smelly while achieving absolutely nothing. Since you placed yourself in his element, the pig would just love it. Besides, Blackburn really couldn't explain what America was trying to accomplish by chasing Aideed all over Mogadishu. As a professional soldier he was embarrassed to admit to Assiri that he felt the same way about the futility of blaming all of Somalia's problems on one man or on one clan. He knew that it took a concerted effort by everyone involved to make Somalia as screwed up a country as it was. Catching or killing Aideed would do little to change that.

"That would depend upon whether you want to listen to the truth or if you're stupid enough to accept UN propaganda," Assiri calmly responded.

Despite knowing better Blackburn responded.

"I'm getting a little tired of an educated person such as yourself blaming every Muslim problem on outsiders," he fired back. "Just when and the hell are Muslims going to start accepting personal responsibility for their own failings to go along with their highly exaggerated sense of pride for Islamic accomplishments? Which, by the way, there hasn't been a whole hell of a lot of since the European Dark Ages."

"Just as soon as you people leave us alone!" came the acid answer.

Dash could see that things were getting out of hand and quickly attempted to steer the conversation away from politics and bring it back to people, places, and contacts known to Assiri that might be helpful to the UN cause. But following the heated exchange between he and Blackburn, Dash might as well have beaten his head against the wall. Assiri had changed and not for the better. They had not been able to determine exactly who funded his organization, nor who they owed their allegiance to, nor what their real purpose was in Somalia. But Dash and Blackburn knew that it had been motivated by a desire to do more than just feed the hungry. They strongly suspected that the Islamic charity group was a front for Al-Qaida and its benefactor, Osama Bin-Laden. What their ultimate objective was only time would tell.

They would later be told by Moe-Moe that Assiri had been sent to Somalia along with several other fundamentalist Islamic soldiers by Bin-Laden to teach the Somalis how to shoot down American helicopters, just as the Mujahadeen had shot down Russian helicopters in Afghanistan. Except here, without America's help, they would not be able to use the much more effective Stinger Missiles; they would have to use the Rocket Propelled Grenade instead.

RPG's are Russian made anti-tank weapons. They were not designed to be used as anti-aircraft weapons and it is extremely dangerous to use them in this manner. The backblast will literally blow the legs off of the shooter when fired upwards, pointed towards the sky. Because this weakness is well known to American battle planners, they never feared RPG's being used to shoot down helicopters. But the American helicopter pilots feared them. Then again, pilots seemed to fear everything fired from the ground since they would die if the planners were wrong while the planners could simply dismiss their death with, "damn, who'd of thunk it!" The planners were wrong. In fact the Somalis had already shot down one Black Hawk helicopter with an RPG on September 25th before using them against the JTF in Mogadishu. This was known by the planners and they should have gone back to the drawing board. Instead, as a telling indicator of how impervious the planners felt the Black Hawks to be, and how impotent they felt the Somalis to be in the face of 21st century high technology, they wrote it off as having been a lucky shot by the Skinnies.

The Somalis recent success had not been an accident. Assiri and others like him were working hard, training them to use the RPG's against the helicopters. To compensate for the known shortfalls of the RPG, the fundamentalists taught the Skinnies to dig holes immediately behind the weapon and fire the backblast into it while lying supine in the street. They taught them to place a metal funnel on the rear of the weapon to disperse the backblast skyward, allowing them to fire into the air while kneeling in the street. They taught them tactics, such as staying off of rooftops, ambushing the helicopters from the rear as they passed overhead, aiming at the vulnerable tail rotor. They also taught them to modify the missile itself from point detonation designed to penetrate armor to one with a timing device to make the missile explode in the air, like a hand grenade, eliminating the effects of the missile returning to the ground, exploding and killing their own people.

But, even more important than the weapon itself, the fundamentalists taught the Somalis that by firing the RPG at the helicopter that they could knock one out of the sky. Something the fundamentalists desperately wanted the Somalis to do because it would force the Americans to stand and fight, man to man, in the dusty, dirty streets of Mogadishu. Presenting the Somalis with an opportunity to attack America's most vulnerable spot, an unwillingness to see any of its soldiers die. Something the Somalis themselves found incomprehensible. For them, dying for the clan was considered an honor. For them, war was much more than a temporary game, it was a way of life that most of them had been born into. They would be happy to show the Americans flying around above them, feeling invulnerable to ground fire, what war was really all about. Regrettably, America was about to give them the opportunity to demonstrate this desire.

Following their unfortunate exchange, the three former friends mumbled a few misgivings for not having stayed in touch and promised to do so in the future. They cordially shook hands and seemingly departed as friends. But, despite the fact that the soldiers returned to the hospital several times after that day, they never again saw Assiri there. He had disappeared once again, making the brief reunion just another weird occurrence in an otherwise weird place.

And so it went for the CA troops as they tried to both amuse themselves and accomplish something meaningful with their time. As they continued to drive through the city, they could feel the tension rising within it and then, on 3 October, Mogadishu exploded.

CHAPTER 20

" **H**ere they come again," shouted Blackburn through his radio when the UH-60 Black Hawks, MH-6, and AH-6 Little Bird helicopters roared by overhead, streaking north after having made a U-turn over the Indian Ocean. They were so close that their vehicles shook as the aircraft sped past.

"I wish they'd hurry up and catch Aideed!" transmitted Dash in return, barely hearing his own voice over the din of the low flying aircraft.

The CA troops were just entering the K-4 roundabout following a Feed the Children food convoy that Blackburn was leading. The K-4 intersection was a well-known traffic landmark inside the city the CA troops often used as a linkup point for convoys. It wasn't far from the security of the American controlled airport and offered rapid avenues of escape in virtually all directions. Today they had been requested to accompany a food convoy to a distribution center near the Bakara Market about a mile northwest of their current location. The helicopters had passed overhead, streaking north for another raid inside the city, or possibly just another false insertion replicating a raid, just to keep the Skinnies on their toes. The JTF had been doing a lot of both recently and every time they had soldiers on the ground would follow them with their eyes waiting for the inevitable, one of them crashing into the city.

Increasing the possibility of that happening today, this mission appeared to be different from those that had preceded it, being conducted during the middle of a bright, sunny, Africa-hot, 3 October Sunday afternoon. It seemed to be an unusual change in tactics as most of the other raids and false insertions had been conducted in the dark, a much calmer time to be doing such things inside a city waiting for an opportunity to explode in anger. The middle of the afternoon, fifteen hundred hours local to be exact, was a time when the Somalis would be high on Khat and gathered together in clan assemblages discussing whatever it was that Somalis discussed during such times. Conducting a raid inside Mogadishu at this time of the day would be similar to inserting a stick into a hornet's nest to see if it was occupied. Once it is discovered that the hornets are home, it is too late to run away.

The noise made by the aircraft had been deafening as more than a dozen helicopters passed by close enough for the soldiers on the ground to clearly see their comrade's legs dangling outside, riding loosely inside as if they were on a roller coaster ride at Disney World. Some of the Rangers inside the Black Hawks, noticing the troops on the ground, pumped their arms up and down in excitement, signifying that they were on their way to a kill, waving to them as if they were stars in a Hollywood movie.

For many of these Rangers their frequent raids into the city had been as if they were characters in a Hollywood movie. The average age of the Ranger Task Force was nineteen and most of them had never experienced combat before. The Delta Force, or D-Boys, scattered throughout the helicopters were older and more experienced than the Rangers. These men had seen war several times during their military careers in places such as Grenada, Panama, Desert Storm and countless other little "skirmishes" the general public would never hear about. Consequently, they flew by in unanimated silence, knowing that this was neither a movie nor a game. These combat veterans knew that no matter how many times they had done it before violent death was always waiting for them around the next corner. They were intimately familiar with the fact that while experience and training would certainly help, these were never a guarantee that a soldier would walk away from a fight simply because they were better trained and equipped than their opponent. Something the young Rangers, the Crème Della Crème of American youth, were about to find out for themselves.

From his position at the rear of the convoy, Dash watched the helicopters disappear behind the taller buildings of the Black Sea neighborhood near the Bakara Market, heading north over the city. Then, although he could no longer see them, he heard them screaming back over the city, low and fast, heading south, finally coming to a noisy hover over the market and the Olympic Hotel. Almost immediately he could hear the shooting.

The CA soldiers had received no warning of a pending raid when they agreed to escort the food convoy into the city, nor had there been any requirement for anyone to tell them of such plans. Although on paper there was but one chain of command in UNOSOM, the practical realities on the ground were quite different. The UNLSC, a multi-national organization for which Dash worked, was under an entirely different chain of command than the purely American Joint Task Force. As a result there was seldom any joint planning that took place between the organizations. The Task Force didn't trust UNLSC, and the UNLSC didn't trust the Task Force. Neither ever knew what the other one was doing, at least not as far down the chain as the operator level. Which was unfortunate because the UNLSC with their frequent humanitarian trips into the city in support of some Non Governmental Organizations (NGO) effort to feed the Somalis had always been in a better position to capture Aideed than the Task Force. It may have been less dramatic to simply drive up to an Aideed meeting houses with a truckload of Care foodstuffs concealing a group of D-Boys than arriving with an armada of helicopters, but it would have been just as successful with far less risk.

The problem with such a scenario was that the UN agencies would never allow themselves to be used by the American military to conduct such a mission. A group of D-Boys could have never been hidden in trucks marked with a Care logo because it would have violated Care's cherished principle of neutrality. A principle that despite the killing of twenty-four Pakistani soldiers and an untold number of civilian relief workers, the theft of thousands of tons of supplies, and a declaration of war against the UN and any agency working with it, they still seemed to hold near and dear. Falsely believing that they were above the fray simply because they were filled with good intentions.

If both the UN and the NGO's had ever accepted the fact that they were actively involved as participants in a war their intelligence collection capabilities, coupled with a country like America's military might would have made an unbeatable opponent. People like Aideed would not have had a chance because despite America's willingness to provide the muscle for combat operations it was unable by itself to collect solid, reliable, current intelligence. The type of intelligence that NGO's routinely dealt with and the type of intelligence that provides the most critical factor in efforts to catch a single individual. As it was, the various NGO's kept to themselves and shared little information with analysts, leaving America to essentially go it alone, which was precisely what it was doing in Mogadishu blindly flitting about the city in its efforts to catch Aideed.

***

"Damn," said Blackburn, listening to the escalating gunfire, "sounds like they found someone home this time."

"Yeah," replied Dash, "I just hope that someone wasn't expecting company."

The initial sounds of gunfire consisted mostly of M-16 and the helicopter mini-guns. But as the battle progressed there was a growing chorus of AK-47 fire added, so loud in fact that it often drowned out the sounds of the M-16's and mini-guns.

From where they were sitting the soldiers could occasionally glimpse a Black Hawk or one of the Little Birds dashing out of the fray, banking above the skyline, then darting back in with guns blazing. Whatever the soldiers on the ground had gone in after, they had found; or maybe it had found them. Either way, Dash knew from the sound of things that one hell of a battle was beginning to take shape not far from where they were standing.

As Dash was lost in thought wondering if the Rangers were still as excited about the prospect of a gunfight as they had been when they recently flew overhead, the Feed the Children food convoy slowly rounded the intersection. Then, with rush hour horns blaring, they stopped, blocking afternoon traffic as the drivers looked anxiously into the distance towards the sound of the escalating gunfire. Blackburn, at the front of the convoy, had stopped in the middle of the intersection to approach the convoy commander; a young Frenchman seemingly enamored with himself, wearing a bright yellow scarf around his neck and a pair of Gucci sunglasses beneath his Armani baseball cap. Walking from his Hummvee to the commander's truck, Dash saw him stop to watch as several more helicopters streaked into the fray. Blackburn simply wanted to confirm the obvious with the convoy commander; there would be no humanitarian food deliveries into the city today. No one in their right mind would even want to go near the city today.

While Blackburn was crossing the intersection to tell the convoy to turn around and go home, Dash switched the radio frequency to the Task Force Command push and immediately heard the sobering news that a Black Hawk helicopter had been shot down near the Olympic Hotel. He knew then that this was going to be a long afternoon for the Task Force. But they were trained for just this sort of contingency, rehearsing their actions over and over until the soldiers knew their roles and responsibilities by heart. He also knew that they had a Combat Search And Rescue (CSAR) package available to secure the crash site. Still, he paused and said a silent prayer for those who had already lost their lives, as well as for all of those who were about to. At the time he had no idea that he should have included himself and his people in his prayers.

As he continued to listen to the frantic calls over the radio, calls often drowned out by the sound of gunfire, Dash looked back across the intersection and noticed that the convoy was still not moving. From a distance it appeared that Blackburn was having difficulty communicating with the convoy commander. As Dash watched, he could see Blackburn occasionally point towards the sound of gunfire and wave his arms as if to emphasize the dangers.

Blackburn, who spoke no French was indeed having trouble communicating with the Feed the Children convoy commander and called Gerard over to assist him. Gerard explained to the commander that it was too dangerous to venture into the city with the fighting raging in the area of the Bakara Market, an obvious observation for someone grounded in reality. However, the young and idealistic convoy commander was anything but grounded in reality. He was adamant that his convoy was not involved with any of the people fighting and that he would simply drive to the distribution point and unload his supplies. "Surely those fighting can tell that this convoy is a nonbelligerent," he sniffed with aplomb. "Besides, your little fights with the Somali's never last for very long; it will be over before we reach the drop sight." Up until today Blackburn would have agreed with his assessment, but the volume of gunfire coming from the city told him that today might be a different fight, today it might be the JTF that got caught and not the Somali's.

Gerard even argued with the convoy commander, telling him in no uncertain terms that he would probably be killed if he delivered the supplies today. The commander, with typical French arrogance, told Gerard that "You Americans are so full of shit!" Gerard, running out of patience and growing increasingly nervous standing in the open near a gunfight, translated the response verbatim to Blackburn, who had long ago run out of patience for idiots himself, in or out of uniform.

Blackburn, still in a sour mood and in need of some serious R&R, simply smiled at the young Frenchman. He told Gerard to tell him that since the soldiers were dressed in military uniforms, it would be too dangerous for them to accompany the convoy any further and simply bid them adieu. Both soldiers returned to their vehicles and pulled them off the road so the convoy could pass.

Thinking that it was a fait accompli, as the convoy rounded the circular intersection, Dash assumed that it would make a complete circle and return from where it had recently departed, heading southeast on a return route to get there. When they turned northwest instead on Via Lenin Road, turning directly toward the sound of the fighting, Dash drove to Blackburn's location and asked what was happening. Blackburn shrugged and said, "The commander insisted that no one would engage his convoy because it obviously belonged to people who were here to help the Somalis, not to people who were here to kill them."

"Does he realize what is ahead of them?" asked a disbelieving Dash.

"No, Sir," Blackburn confidently stated, "if he did, he wouldn't be going there."

"Shouldn't we stop them?" asked Dash.

"We don't have any authority over these people," answered Blackburn. "And I for one do not want to stand out here in the open and argue with them. Who knows, they might even make it to the supply warehouse before the Somali's see them coming. From the sounds of things they've already got their hands full with the JTF."

"Top, come on," Dash said almost apologetically. "It isn't right to watch them drive into a firefight, no matter what their intentions are. I'm afraid that the fight might spill over to where they are going. Remember, we were sent here to protect them."

"Yes, Sir. I suppose your right," he said. Then, reluctantly admitting that he may have made a mistake, immediately atoned for it by offering, "Maybe we should follow along behind them just in case someone out there doesn't share the commander's conviction that noncombatants are not to be engaged."

"Probably wouldn't hurt," answered Dash. "Besides, I would guess that bandits will attempt to steal the load before they get to the drop point anyway. If they do, we'll escort them back then, by gunpoint if necessary and Colonel Degan can deal with the fallout from the NGO's complaining about us interfering with their ability to conduct business."

As the six Hummvees pulled into line behind the last truck in the convoy, it was obvious that the Malaysian drivers did not share in their commander's conviction that the Somalis would not shoot at them. Three of them turned off at the first available road heading southeast, three blocks after leaving the K-4 intersection. Then, two blocks later, two more trucks turned off Via Lenin heading southeast. The drivers wanted no part of what lay before them. With the crew abandoning ship at a rapid rate there were now only two trucks remaining in the convoy. The commander's, who failed to notice that the once robust convoy to his rear had dissolved like a snowflake in hell, and one other immediately behind his truck that was apparently being driven by one of the dumbest men still alive in Mogadishu. Behind these two wandering sheep followed the CA vehicles as if they were watching the beginnings of a disaster — uncomfortable with watching, but too curious to turn away.

Even while following behind the loud 2-½ ton trucks, the noise of gunfire could clearly be heard; yet the French convoy commander blissfully continued to drive towards it. It had to have been a curious sight for anyone watching. Several of the helicopters firing in support of the trapped Rangers flew low and slow over the trucks as they approached the city. The pilots were trying to sort out in their own minds if the trucks were part of the JTF team sent to snatch the prisoners or simply NGO trucks lost in the city. They certainly didn't consider the fact that someone would be foolish enough to intentionally drive unarmed vehicles into the middle of a raging firefight.

Then the inevitable happened. As the small convoy approached the intersection of Via Lenin and National Street, two Somalis armed with an RPG and a bad attitude failed to recognize the trucks as belonging to noncombatants and fired at them. It was a moment of curiosity to the soldiers following behind since they hadn't expected to get this far before someone ambushed them.

Dash was the first to see the telltale smoke of the missile as it streaked toward the trailing truck. The round struck the truck mid-center, just behind the cab, fortunately missing the driver but blowing the trucks contents high into the air, covering Dash's Hummvee with a blizzard of white rice that left him temporarily blinded. As Dash fought to see through the descending cloud of rice, he focused on the location where the missile had first emerged and saw two Somalis, one with a now empty launch tube and one with an AK-47 standing in a narrow alley sandwiched between two sandstone buildings.

"Target right!" Dash yelled into the radio as he fired a quick burst from his M-16 in the direction of the two gunmen, missing both in his excitement. The Somalis simply disappeared, darting around the corner of the building like field mice looking for a hole.

As Dash continued to observe the spot where he had last seen the gunmen, Blackburn spurted passed his Hummvee to attend to the wounded driver. Although not hit, the driver had been stunned by the explosion and was crawling through the sand in an effort to get as far away from his vehicle as he possibly could. Startled by the loud explosion behind him, the Frenchman, belatedly but certainly, realized that he was not going to be welcomed as a noncombatant and ordered his driver to make a U-turn. While this was certainly the appropriate decision, it was the wrong place to make it. As soon as the driver left the asphalt his truck got stuck in the soft sand and he panicked. Racing the engine and spinning the wheels, the driver threw sand high into the air in a futile attempt to free the truck from the deep sand and buried it up to the axles. All the while the commander dangled out of the passenger window franticly waving for the Hummvees to come forward and help.

To his surprise, Blackburn found the driver of the second truck unhurt but with eyes larger than the headlights on his now burning truck, which had been carrying cooking oil in addition to the rice. Ignited by the RPG missile, the oil caused the truck to burn as if it were an emergency roadside flare.

The three cargo Hummvees armed with M-60 machineguns pulled off the road in a classic herringbone formation and prepared to provide covering fire for the extraction of the convoy personnel. Brown, who had seen the same two Somalis Dash had shot at, waited for them to reappear in the narrow alleyway. When they did, armed with a new missile and several of their friends, Brown dropped two of them with a quick burst from his gun, the 7.62 rounds slamming them against the building wall before depositing them in a heap in the garbage strewn alley. Those who were left standing disappeared once again around the corner of the building and began shooting at the soldiers, precipitating a brief firefight as the M-60's returned their fire with a vengeance.

Now under fire, Blackburn loaded the dazed and frightened driver into his vehicle while Dash drove up to the Frenchman's truck and he and his driver quickly jumped into the backseat of the Hummvee. Everyone knew that there would be more Somali gunmen any instant and they had no desire to stay there to greet them. Not surprisingly, the convoy commander now shared in their desire to leave the area. He no longer seem to care about his precious cargo and had literally knocked his driver out of the way while scrambling into the relative safety of Dash's vehicle. He also no longer seemed concerned that he appeared to be violating the sacred ground of neutrality by riding in a military vehicle, complete with guns and people who knew how to use them. In fact had used them, recently killing the two men who had tried to kill him.

Under the circumstances, with a vicious battle raging inside the city, the ride back to the airfield was relatively uneventful as most Somali gunmen raced towards the battle and away from them. A few Somalis did shoot at them as they sped by but their efforts were of little consequence. The soldiers had already learned that with the exception of a few dedicated regulars, most of the Somalis couldn't shoot worth a damn, especially at a rapidly moving vehicle. Still, it is difficult to find solace in knowing that people shooting at you are poor marksmen. It would have been much more comforting if they stopped shooting all together. However, the French commander was unaware of the Somali's reputation of being poor marksmen and with each shot fired he would flatten on the floorboard of the vehicle. Temporarily forgotten was his dream of a safe and caring world where people held hands and lit candles in peaceful protest to the harder side of life. His dream of living in such a blissful world had been destroyed by one RPG that hadn't even hit his vehicle or killed any of his friends, events that soldiers routinely experience in every war zone in every part of the world.

With the exception of the minor gunfire, the ride back through the city was uneventful until they arrived at the airfield. As a result of their own difficulties, none of the soldiers had been monitoring the JTF radio frequencies and had not heard the latest information. It seemed that not one, but two helicopters had been shot down, crashing into a sea of pent-up hostilities in Aideed's Mogadishu. The fight that everyone with combat experience had been dreading was now occurring and both the United States military and the Somalis were busily preparing for it. Aideed's militia was now barricading the road the soldiers had just taken to get out of the city. To return to a location so recently abandoned would now require a bloody fight and the soldiers would have to go several blocks beyond the abandoned truck to reach the downed helicopters. The stage had been set for a fight that no one in UNOSOM or Washington had envisioned; yet the soldiers who had been working the city streets had vehemently been warning everyone against. It would be a fight that could not possibly produce a winner, no matter the outcome.

***

The airfield was a blur of bloody activity. Three or four Hummvees driven by an element from the trapped Rangers had fought their way out of the city, bringing several wounded and dead out with them. A medical triage had been set up where the wounded were being separated from the dead and the soon to be dead, while at the same time a rescue mission was being mounted to move to and secure the second crash sight.

Taking stock of the situation and listening to the many conversations swirling around him, Dash overheard a conversation by one of the Rangers explaining the second Black Hawk had crashed in the Wadigley neighborhood. It had gone down near the intersection of Hawlwadig Road and National Street, an area the CA soldiers were intimately familiar with. In fact, unbeknownst at the time, they had been less than one mile from the site when they had rescued the Frenchman.

As Dash observed the scene it became apparent that the Task Force lacked the assets to react to a situation with two helicopters being shot down. The organic CSAR package designed for this purpose had moved to the first crash site and when the second bird went down, the Task Force Commander, Major General William F. Garrison, had been caught in the worst possible circumstances. Troops under his command were dying and he was not able to rapidly react to help them.

Of real concern for all those participating in the events to follow was the hurried manner such an operation requires. A rescue mission under fire is not an ad-hoc activity that can be effectively pieced together on the fly. It is much more complicated than just jumping into vehicles and following someone to a crash site. There are numerous coordination issues that should be resolved first. Life and death issues like radio frequencies, call signs, routes, actions on contact, fire control measures, treatment of wounded and dead, medevac procedures, etc., etc. A never-ending litany of critical issues must be planned for before, not after the first man goes down with a bullet in his chest. None of these things were happening. The only mission guidance ever transmitted was to "get back to those pinned down as quickly as possible and get them out of there." A simple solution to a not so simple problem, but action, not talk, was what was now required from everyone involved.

Turning to Blackburn, Dash was all business, as was the seasoned First Sergeant. "Top, take the vehicles over to the Ammunition Supply Point and triple every man's basic load. Pick up some LAWS if they've got them. I'm going to find out from someone how this thing is going to be Command and Controlled (C2)."

"Roger, Sir!" answered Blackburn. Then, almost as an afterthought, he asked, "What about our passengers?"

"Tell Gerard to explain to the Frenchman what is happening and that if he wants another once in a lifetime adventure today, then we will arm and equip him as well, same with his driver. Otherwise this is as far as we're taking them." Later, when the convoy was ready to depart Dash looked for the Frenchman only to discover that he was long gone, having caught a ride back to his compound with another agency truck.

Dash sought a Ranger lieutenant and received call signs and frequencies from him; there were no other coordination procedures discussed. The plan was simply for them to be vectored to the crash sight by aircraft flying high overhead. Beyond this, "flying by the seat of your pants, making up shit as you went" would handle everything else that was likely to occur. A mindset that Dash fought hard to overcome yet every question he asked was met with wishful thinking, not serious thought. It was as if every effort was being made to avoid having to deal with the obvious like, "who backhauls casualties?" Or, "who rescues the rescuers if we get cut off?" It seemed as if the method for dealing with such issues was to avoid talking about them, pretending that the cover fire from the helicopters flying overhead would keep anything bad from happening. Dash now understood what he had been observing while watching the Rangers flit about in Mogadishu with their macho attitude of invincibility; they had been playing at war, hoping to survive on sheer intimidation, an accident waiting to happen. Now it finally had. But this was no time to complain about the woulda', coulda', shoulda,' of the mission. There were young men dying out in the city and he and every swinging dick on the airfield were going to do their best to put a stop to it.

***

The vehicle march order for the rescue convoy was for the CA vehicles to bring up the rear, following four Ranger Hummvees in front and three five-ton trucks sandwiched in the middle. Success was contingent upon speed and overwhelming firepower. If they got bogged down the trailing CA vehicles and soldiers were to be used as a maneuver force. They were to move, dismounted or mounted, in order to provide covering fire for the lead vehicles, helping them break contact should they become immobilized by fire. If the fire were light enough, the lead vehicles as well as all the trailing vehicles would simply push through it, saving time and hopefully saving lives. All of the vehicles were to move in close interval, virtually bumper to bumper to prevent one of them from making a wrong turn, resulting in isolation and destruction by a hostile mob of Somalis. An ad hoc plan for an ad hoc mission. But there weren't a hell of a lot of other options available to them and all of the soldiers had been taught that a bad plan vigorously executed was better than a good plan that is too complicated to be understood or implemented. As a firm believer in such logic himself, upon hearing the final concept of operations Dash thought that if simplicity was the key to success then they were well on the road to a major accomplishment because he had never witnessed a simpler plan.

As the convoy departed the east gate of the airfield, Dash listened to the C2 Black Hawk providing directions to the crash site from high overhead. The Ranger lieutenant leading them was to take an immediate left on Tanzania Street, followed by another left at the next intersection. "Just follow my instructions," the pilot relayed through the radio, as if directions would be the most difficult problem they would encounter. In keeping with the theme of "Keep It Simple Stupid," or "KISS," the pilot could have abbreviated all of his radio transmissions with the following guidance: "As long as you're being shot at, you're going in the right direction."

As the convoy began rolling off the airfield, the gunfire inside the city turned into a dull roar that served to magnify the rescuers' feelings of apprehension as well as their sense of urgency. The many tracer rounds flying through the air made the city look like a fourth of July fireworks show in broad daylight.

Like most instances when clock watching becomes an obsession, the seconds quickly seemed to turn into minutes and the minutes into hours as the convoy crept along. "Hurry up, damn it! Let's get going!" Blackburn yelled out to no one in particular. It seemed to him as if everything was moving in slow motion.

The CA vehicles sat parked inside the airfield fence, waiting with anxious anticipation to fall in behind the last truck to begin their own movement across the street and into the city. Then, as anyone who has ever been in combat can attest, after the first thirty seconds when everything had gone exactly as planned, everything turned to shit when gunfire erupted from all around the lead vehicle. The CA vehicles hadn't even left the airfield yet; an omen of things to come that immediately told Dash that if this was what awaited them inside the city then there was no way in hell they were ever going to be successful. No matter how simple the plan or how much cheerleading they were receiving from the C2 birds flying high overhead encouraging the Rangers to "just keep plowing straight ahead."

For the first time in his military career Dash now understood how General Custer must have felt when he looked up and saw all of those Indians he had been chasing do an about face and come after him. He felt like throwing up.

Dash had split his six vehicles into two fire teams of three vehicles each, one led by him, the other by Major Whidden, and when the shooting started he immediately ordered his team to dismount and move forward to provide covering fire for the lead vehicle. As Dash, Blackburn, Brown and Gerard made their way to the front of the convoy the lead vehicle driver threw his Hummvee into reverse and backed into the vehicle following it. As did the second vehicle, followed by the third, etc. The action had been an understandable impulse but it left them more vulnerable than if they had simply blasted their way through the initial volley of gunfire. It left them in the kill zone longer than they otherwise would have been, and when people are trying to drive or direct the actions of a driver, they are not firing their weapons. Always a bad thing to not do during a gunfight.

Fortunately, the CA soldiers were able to move into position to fill this gap in firepower. They killed several Somalis firing from windows, and the helicopters flying overhead made several gun runs to clean off the rooftops. This allowed the trapped vehicles to get out of the kill zone with no serious casualties but it took several minutes to turn the three large five-ton trucks around and they certainly weren't getting any closer to the crash site.

The convoy was then directed by the C2 aircraft to return to the airport gate and take a right, which it did but was again confronted by a large obstacle. A big roadblock that the C2 helicopter evidently couldn't see. The construction of the roadblock indicated that it was not a spontaneous barrier as it consisted of dirt, junk, furniture, vehicle hulks, chunks of concrete, wire, dead animals, and anything else that had been handy, including several burning tires. All were actions clearly indicating that the Somalis were going to make a stand to keep the rescuers from reaching the trapped Rangers. It would have taken an engineer platoon several minutes to clear a path through the mound of debris and time was something they did not have; nor did they have a tank or bulldozer to simply push through, something they desperately needed to be able to do.

***

Ironically, when hostilities had escalated inside Mogadishu and the decision to send the Ranger Task Force had been made, requests for Tanks, Bradley Fighting Vehicles, and heavy engineer equipment to accompany them had been disapproved by then Secretary of Defense Les Aspin. Following the recommendation of then Chairman of the Joint Chiefs of Staff, General Colin Powell, Aspin felt such a request to be a precursor to "mission creep," something he and Powell desperately wanted to avoid. Because they were ill equipped to fight in an urban environment soldiers were now being killed in the dirty alleys of an African city that most of the world couldn't find on a map. Preventable deaths that Powell and Aspin should have feared more than mission creep. In fact, with the advantage of twenty-twenty hindsight, such equipment should have been part of the original deployment package, then mission creep would never have become a political issue in the first place. In the years following Mogadishu, Dash often wondered how it was that experienced people like Aspin and Powell could fall victim to the same wishful thinking that plagues many of the UN agencies, believing themselves to be immune to the forces of evil that exists in backward countries like Somalia. Little did he know that he would see this same impulse to "get by on the cheap" again when American forces invaded Iraq several years later. It is as if we never learn from our mistakes.

***

After turning around yet again, the convoy was instructed to take a long winding road all the way around the city and approach the crash site "through the back door," as if the Somali militia fighters, the Mooryan, wouldn't notice them coming. Listening to all this inane chatter over the radio Dash had finally had enough. Keying his own radio he shouted through the microphone, "We need to return to the New Port and get some tanks from the Pakis so we can force our way through!" he shouted to the C2 bird overhead. "If we keep dicking around like this there won't be any need to go to the crash site; everyone and everything will already be gone! It isn't going to do anybody any good if we get bogged down in the city! Someone will just have to come rescue us."

"Roger," responded the C2 bird, "command is already working the issue requesting the Paki tanks."

"Roger, understand," replied Dash, "I'm going to take this convoy to the port to see if I can speed up that request."

With Dash now taking the lead, the convoy sped to the port and began lengthy, fruitless negotiations with their Pakistani comrades in an attempt to get them to join in the fight with their tanks. Or, barring their active participation, at least allow the American soldiers to borrow a couple of them. Both Dash and Blackburn had driven tanks before, though not the M-48 Pattons that the Pakis were equipped with. But, they reasoned, how damn hard could it be. Both men secretly relished the idea of firing the tank's main gun at a Somali sniper hanging out a window. After surviving a withering crossfire at the first ambush site, they were definitely in a foul mood. For them, watching a Somali sniper's ass sail through the air after having been hit by the big 105mm main gun would be akin to having an orgasm. Unfortunately, it was a sight that would have to wait. Despite the fact that it had been Pakistani soldiers who Aideed had ordered killed that started this whole sordid affair, the Pakistani commander was not jumping at the chance to avenge his countrymen's deaths, a hands-off attitude that is prevalent among UN nations.

Most UN nations seem to be willing to accept a slap across the face, turning the other cheek as it were, in response. This is a completely different response that one can expect to receive from third world people like the Somalis. Unlike the UN member states, in the clan environment of Somalia, if any of their people are killed, like an elephant, they will never forget nor will they ever forgive the people responsible. The Somalis always wanted immediate revenge. In a world where a willingness to die for a cause was an overriding factor, Dash felt that the simple rules of the clan were far superior to the theoretical rules of a nation. Clansmen never have to wade through several feet of bureaucratic reluctance before taking action, nor do they care that other people disagree with them. They think with their hearts and avoid making things any more complicated than they really are by refusing to turn the problem over to an impartial third party who will do little more than analyze it to death.

It wasn't that the Pakistani commander did not want to help, he told Dash. It was just that he had already committed his tanks to be a part of a Quick Reaction Force, or QRF, rescue attempt spearheaded by the American 10th Mountain Division. The QRF was currently being assembled at the university compound on the other side of town. The plan was to augment it with some of his tanks along with condors from the Malaysians. "Together we will all kill Aideed's men tonight!" he proudly boasted. The idea that it would be several more hours before the QRF could make its way to his location seemed an irrelevant point to the Pakistani commander who seemed quite content with the Muslim attitude of *"Ensha Allah,"* God willing. Time was of no concern to him.

Despite Dash's repeated attempts to get the Paki commander to release two of his tanks for immediate use, he would not budge, maintaining that he worked for the United Nations, not the United States. Frustrated and angry, knowing men were probably dying as a result of these delays, Dash led the convoy back to the airfield to await the arrival of the QRF. Led by Lieutenant Colonel Bill David, QRF Commander, and consisting of soldiers from the 2nd Battalion, 14th Infantry, 10th Mountain Division, the QRF, through no fault of its own, had been no better prepared to launch a rescue mission under fire than the JTF had been.

Dash arrived at the airfield at 1800 hours, but they did not depart with the QRF until after 2130, then only going to the port to link-up with the Paki tanks and the Malaysian condors. This "gagglefuck" of vehicles, as Lieutenant Colonel David called it, did not depart the port until almost midnight.

***

Had proper coordination been enforced between Garrison's Task Force and the other UN units, especially the QRF, becoming Standard Operating Procedure, this time would have been reduced to less than one hour, quite possibly reducing the number of men killed that night. Their deaths were as much a result of faulty egos as they were of faulty intelligence, and it did not have to be that way. As Abraham Lincoln explained in his constant fights with Union General George McClellan: "War, or more correctly, the outcome of war, is just too important to be left to the Generals."

American reluctance to demand that the UN become a problem-solver rather than a problem-enabler, coupled with its own insane desire to "go it alone" anytime that a consensus can't be achieved, is a combination made in hell. It will never work. Either one or the other, or both, have to change their attitudes and their abilities if they expect to achieve any credibility with violent nations.

UN officials must stop signing up for missions to fix the unfixable until the people living in a broken country agree among themselves what they want for an outcome. Without this agreement the UN will be viewed as an intruder in a nations sovereign affairs, as it was viewed in Somalia, rather than an impartial arbitrator. For its part, the United States must stop believing that violence will always trump diplomacy. The American military cannot be a "meals on wheels" with guns, nor should it be expected to. If peacemaking is the mission, then bring the guns. If peacekeeping is the mission, then bring the meals. Stop confusing the two. The Somalis themselves saw the irony in this. Their stated belief, often said with tongue in cheek but with a sincerity to match, was that America was simply fattening them up for the slaughter. For the Americans who served in Somalia the Somalis were right; other than the slaughtering of them little else was achieved by America being there.

***

The route this enormous convoy was to follow was basically the same as that attempted earlier by the Ranger lieutenant but this time, with the tanks and condors, they could overcome the roadblocks. Another slight change was that upon reaching Hawlwadig Road, the convoy would split into two separate elements; one element going to the first crash site and the other element moving to the second crash site. Once there they were to evacuate the living, retrieve the remains of the dead, and destroy any items of value still aboard the helicopters. After which they were to join forces once again and move to a holding area, an old soccer stadium occupied by the Pakistanis, to regroup before finally returning to their respective compounds.

Because of their familiarity with the city, the CA vehicles were to follow behind the Paki tanks from the airfield to K-4, after which the tanks would drop back in the convoy and the CA soldiers would pick up the lead. This was necessary because after K-4 the streets became narrow, limiting the maneuverability of the tanks and leaving them vulnerable to RPG's. They would remain close to the front of the convoy, however, as would the condors, large white armored vehicles marked with the UN logo. The soldiers called them "whales" or coffins on wheels because they were lightly armored and in their bright white paint scheme, hardly inconspicuous. The armored vehicles were to be used to push through the many roadblocks the Somalis had established, all of which had mounds of burning tires surrounding them. According to American intelligence analysts the Somalis used the fires as signals. And they may well have been. But their real value was that they negated the American's Night Observation Devices (NOD's) and thermal sights, a fact well known to the Mooryan because it had been taught to them by bin Laden's Arab Mujahadeen sent there to train them. It was also a fact easily dismissed as being irrelevant by US battle planners since it was daylight when the battle had first erupted and they considered the Somalis too inept to fight with any measure of sophistication. The planners failed to realize that this was a trap that the Somalis had rehearsed many times before with their Mujahadeen cadre. Those who simply believed the fires to be highly visible reference points for the Somali gunmen never could explain to those who knew better why the Somalis didn't know their way around inside their own city, having to be guided by the bright light and smoke from the fires.

✳✳✳

Once again, just as happened with the previous attempt, when the first tank rolled across the road it was met with an RPG that skidded across its hull, exploding with a thunderous roar against the wall of a building across the street. The explosion left a large hole in the building and rained cement on the tank. The second tank, traveling in overwatch, immediately fired a main gun round at the RPG gunner and more cement, dirt, asphalt and various and sundry Somali body parts exploded into the air. If nothing else it showed the mostly nonsuicidal RPG gunners that a new tactic would be required when dealing with armor.

As a result of the additional firepower of the tanks, with the exception of the first RPG, the only real resistance the convoy encountered during the short run to K-4 was from small arms fire, most of which was harmlessly directed towards the tanks. For some inexplicable reason the Somalis did not seem to understand that their ambushes would have been far more effective had they let the lead vehicles pass, opening fire on the soft skinned vehicles following behind the tanks. Even after the convoy cleared the K-4 circle and the tanks were no longer in the lead, the Somalis continued to fire at them as if they were a prized trophy animal surrounded by lesser, punier herd animals. Evidently, even the experienced Mujahadeen fighters had not been able to overcome the impulses of the rapid Somali gunners.

After pushing their way through the K-4 roadblock, the tanks reverted to trail formation behind the CA vehicles that now took the lead. The tanks followed close enough to provide covering fire and to be used to bulldoze through obstacles, but not out front where they could be trapped by RPG crossfire from the buildings; but the CA vehicles could.

No sooner had Dash moved to the front of the column than a withering cross fire blew the windshield out of his Hummvee. An instant later an RPG sliced through the fender of the vehicle as if it were made of paper, luckily not exploding until it had exited through the driver's door and impacted on a vehicle hulk along the side of the road. The missile had come near enough that either the fins or a piece of Kevlar off the vehicle sliced a gash in the driver's leg. As a result of this near miss, a conscious decision to advance under fire was made and nobody wearing an American military uniform gave a tinker's damn who or what might have been in the line of that fire.

The south side of Via Lenin road was mostly shacks and empty desert, posing little threat of an ambush. It was the north side of the road, marking the beginnings of central Mogadishu that was of real concern. Accordingly, reconnaissance by fire was focused in that direction. The M-60 machineguns on the cargo Hummvees kept up a steady volume of fire on the buildings and alleys along the road, making it very difficult for an RPG gunner to take an effective aim on the vehicles. As expected, when faced with a high volume of fire, the majority of the Somali fighters became a little nervous. Most had shown up to kill Americans, they had no burning desire to be injured or killed themselves. And although they continued to fire at the convoy, because of the volume of fire ripping the city apart around them, none of them did it with any degree of accuracy.

When the machineguns needed a fresh supply of ammunition, a Hummvee would be sent scurrying back to an ammunition truck imbedded in the convoy and return with several cases of 7.62 linked ammunition. Soldiers even had to swap out gun barrels on several occasions because they became so hot from the constant firing that they had run away, spraying bullets everywhere, causing the gunner to have to break the links to keep the barrel from melting. During such lulls helicopters would sweep the area along the route with their mini-guns and rockets or the tanks would rake the area with their .50 caliber heavy machineguns.

There was never a moment during the entire march that guns were not being fired at anything that even remotely resembled a target inside the city, even after turning north on National Street and entering the heart of the city itself. A tremendous amount of firepower went into the streets, alleyways, highways, buildings and homes of Somalis that night. Unfortunately, many innocent lives were lost as a result. However, there were many Mooryan killed as well because there were a hell of a lot of them firing AK's and RPG's at the convoy from surrounding buildings. And when they did, the convoy's enormous firepower would then very quickly reduce those buildings to a heap of rubble.

The fight through Mogadishu was a time for the release of unbridled passion for the American soldiers, especially the passion of unrequited anger. By the time of the fight American soldiers had become greatly disillusioned with the entire belief that Somalia or the Somalis themselves were worth saving. For the soldiers, the obvious solution to the tribal warfare of Somalia had always been to single out which tribe America didn't want to survive, and turn them loose on it. Instead, they had been expected to be referees. Now, for the first time since the soldiers had been in Somalia, war had been officially declared and they were being turned loose on somebody. On whom war had been declared they didn't know, nor did they care. All they knew was that the war would only be a temporary respite from all of the insanity they had witnessed in Somalia. They were also acutely aware that when it was over they would once again be forced back under lock and key inside their compounds. Which, for many of the soldiers, left them with little time to "bag their limit."

Enhancing their ability to "bag their limit" was the disappearance of the restrictive rules of engagement. They were no longer being limited to self-defense. Tonight, on a continent and in a city completely foreign to most of the soldiers, the world of unrestricted combat had opened up. The only rule that now applied was a very simple one that soldiers have always understood; if it moved it died. Often interpreted to mean that if it might move, it had to die. Throughout the convoy soldiers were constantly firing their weapons at real and imaginary targets. The only fire discipline imposed was when a weapon became too hot to hold on to. As a result, the din of gunfire was so loud that most of the soldiers suffered a partial hearing loss for several days.

Despite the overwhelming fire superiority enjoyed by the convoy, because of the constant obstacles placed in its path, progress was often slow and tedious. On several occasions' obstacles had to be removed by hand for fear of mines having been placed in them. With each stop soldiers would dismount from vehicles and fire into the city, often moving close enough to buildings to throw a hand grenade through an opening, adding to the considerable carnage already being wrought by the helicopter rockets and min-guns.

Over the course of the march through the city Dash and Blackburn continued to shoot at Mooryhan fighters. Each had started the night with a basic load of fifteen hundred rounds and they had expended twice that much already. All of the other CA soldiers were in the same position. They had fired so many rounds that it was a waste of time to talk to any of them over the radio because none of them could hear well enough to understand what was being said over the roar of the constant gunfire. Finally, still belching smoke and fire as it shot up the surrounding city, they reached the release point at Hawlwadig Road where the convoy separated, half moving to rescue the Rangers pinned down near the first crash site and half moving to the second crash site. The CA vehicles moved to locate the second site.

Since this crash site was relatively close to the intersection of Hawlwadig Road and National Street it was decided that all but eight Hummvees, the six CA vehicles and two belonging to Delta, would remain on National Street. If the entire convoy moved to the crash site there would likely be another "gagglefuck," as it would be required to spend more time on the shooting gallery streets of Mogadishu.

Being a party to such an enormous convoy moving while under fire had been an exercise in frustration that none of the veterans had ever experienced, nor did they ever want to experience it again. It had been nothing short of chaos and fit right in with everything else they had seen in Somalia. Blackburn would later remark that trying to control the entire mob from the front when he had no inkling where everyone was had been like "trying to herd two hundred cats into one damn gunny sack." He was not alone in feeling this way. At no time during the march into the city did anyone on the ground have a clue where everyone else was. It is doubtful that even the C2 helicopter flying high overhead knew the answer. Yet he kept transmitting helpful guidance such as "turn left at the next intersection," a difficult task to perform in a city where the alleys and the streets were unmarked and in the dark looked alike as all of them consisted of windblown sand and garbage. On those rare occasions when Dash could hear the C2 bird, he would look skyward and wonder just who the hell this guy was talking to as everyone in the convoy was located at a different intersection. Miraculously, they made it anyway.

Now, split apart from the main convoy the Hummvees drove east towards the ocean, cautiously approaching the crash site the soldiers put on their NOD's. Now that they had moved away from the large fires caused by the burning tires, the Night Observation Devices were effective once again. They also took solace in noticing that the gunfire being directed at them had decreased considerably since leaving the convoy, which seemed to act as a bullet magnet for every Somali with a rifle.

The helicopter had crashed behind some shacks and could not be seen from the road so the decision was made to move to the site on foot. Along with the D-Boys Dash and Blackburn dismounted, worming their way through a maze of footpaths until they reached the site where Dash and Blackburn provided security for the D-Boys to conduct a search of the area. No one was there, no dead Americans and no dead Somalis. Just a kaleidoscopic array of bloody trails made by bodies being hurriedly dragged through the sand. Dash and Blackburn continued to provide security as a D-Boy placed several thermite grenades on the aircraft and set it afire, destroying anything of military value that might have been left inside the helicopter. A wasted effort because even in the dark they could tell that the Somali mob had already swarmed the aircraft carcass like starving jackals, stripping it bare of anything not securely welded to the frame.

After destroying the aircraft and confirming that no American bodies had been left nearby, they returned to the convoy and began leading it out of the city towards the Pakistani stadium. By the time they started moving the sun was just beginning to break over the horizon and the soldiers removed their NOD's for the trip out of the city.

***

In the dim morning light the soldiers continued to fire at targets as they moved towards the Pakistani Stadium, but they consciously took a more deliberate aim than they had in the dark when they had been more apt to "spray and pray" than "hold and squeeze" their shots. That is the more experienced soldiers were taking aim; the majority of the convoy following behind them, however, was still very much in the "rock and roll" mode of automatic fire.

This precision shooting meant the SOF soldiers were firing less ammunition, but more accurately. Such precision should have resulted in more one shot kills. But to his dismay Dash noticed that this increased accuracy was not translating into more kills, much less one shot kills, seeing many Somalis absorb several hits before finally scampering away. Many of the gunmen never even fell to the ground after they were hit, often returning the soldiers' fire with fire of their own after a solid chest hit that should have stopped them in their tracks.

What Dash was observing was what a friend of his serving in Delta had warned them about; the new green tipped 5.56 ball ammunition was not worth a damn when it came to killing a thin skinned human being. If a bone or vital organ was not hit, the hardened bullet simply passed through them, leaving a hole no larger than if they had been stabbed with an ice pick.

These observations confirmed for Dash the reputation that the new bullet was not a round to bet your life on. For this reason Dash, Blackburn, the D-Boys, and other experienced soldiers always brought along some hollow point hunting bullets, despite their presence on the modern battlefield being strictly verboten under the laws of land warfare. Critics of lead bullets decry the extensive wound channel they leave in a body, a fact that seems to miss the point of having shot someone in the first place. Soldiers are not people who spend a lot of time worrying about killing someone *"to dead."* They would rather explode their target than leave him with the ability to return fire. If lead bullets work best to accomplish this, then that is what soldiers will choose to use, especially during a close encounter where return fire is less likely to miss them. But Dash had long since shot up all of his hunting bullets, leaving him dependent upon the new bullets, designed to puncture metal and cement, to knock a man off his feet with one shot. So far, at least based upon what he was observing, the new round was proving itself to be a miserable failure.

On several occasions Dash had aimed dead center at almost point blank range and fired at a gunman, seeing his shirt jump as the rounds hit his body; yet the gunman remained standing, leaving him dangerous and requiring several more rapid shots before finally knocking him to the ground. As a result the soldiers were firing their M-16's in three round bursts to compensate for this lack of killing power, expending just as much ammunition as if it were still dark.

Observing the ineffectiveness of the new round, Dash had taken to shooting at the head because a hit there was certain to drop the gunman. However, in the heat of battle it is not easy to hit a man in the head, no matter how deliberate the aim. Dash and all the others would complain loudly and long to the powers that be regarding the ineffectiveness of the new ammunition. But when he retired from the Army the same green tipped bullets were still being used and the men who routinely killed for a living, like the D-boys, were still complaining about them.

***

The scene at the Pakistani stadium could only be described as shocking. Bodies and parts of bodies were scattered about on the soccer field. Doctors and nurses were scurrying about in frantic attempts to triage the casualties. The screams of the wounded and the shouts of the doctors were almost as loud as the gunfire had been. Amidst all this chaos was a Pakistani waiter with a white towel draped over his arm carrying a gleaming silver tray covered with drinking glasses. The waiter wandered amidst the pandemonium offering anyone who would pause long enough to listen to him a cooling drink of water, an act of civility in an otherwise hellish place that Dash found totally disconcerting and fantastically ironic. At the moment, with their adrenaline still at fever pitch, none of the soldiers felt like being civil with anybody. There were still people unaccounted for, presumably still being held inside the city. Whether they were dead or alive did not really matter to the surly troops, they just wanted the missing soldiers returned. Either that or they were going to go back into the city and get them, a natural thought for soldiers to have and several of the D-Boys had already acted on as they reloaded magazines and headed back into the city to find their missing comrades. But it was an impulse that was to lead to one of the biggest disappointments in Dash's military career.

The idea that they were not going to be allowed to go back into the city to find their comrades had not even been considered. Words like diplomacy and negotiations are not often considered when soldiers are staring directly into the eyes of an enemy who may be killing their friends. In the soldier's world, a world where taking care of one another is all that matters, it is an unwritten code that soldiers do not leave their comrades at the mercy of their enemies. Not if they can help it. In their world, no one gets left behind because unlike any other profession, if soldiers are unwilling to sacrifice for each other there can be no such thing as an army. When individuals believe that their own selfish wants and needs are more important than the wants and needs of others, a group of young people with guns is simply an undisciplined, self-serving mob. A gang in uniform. Something the United States should never expect nor be willing to accept.

Neither is a soldier's bond with his comrades something to be lightly dismissed or discouraged by politicians with a more complete view of the "big picture." Denying soldiers the opportunity to do everything in their power to protect one another establishes a precedent that not only emboldens future enemies, it also breaks the spirit of the troops, dampening their morale. A combination that has led to the demise of previous great powers, like the Holy Roman Empire, when the Romans succumbed to the temptations of imperial overstretch then lost the desire to wield the sword to control it. Historically, an unwillingness to put it all on the line has allowed countries and peoples with far less political and military power, but a willingness to put its armies in the field to win a war, not just maintain a tentative peace, to destroy great powers.

CHAPTER 21

"Top," ordered Dash as soon as they pulled through the university compound gate, "take the vehicles over to the ASP and draw some more ammo. Then meet me at the QRF TOC. I want to find out when the operations order will be issued and what the concept will be when we go back out."

Thus began one of the most disheartening days in Somalia for the American soldiers, even more discouraging than the past several hours had been when eighteen Americans had been killed and dozens more had been severely injured. For the soldiers the recent battle had been a beginning, not an end, as the aircrew involved in the second crash was still unaccounted for. Until they were accounted for, it was standard procedure to assume that they were still alive and being held prisoner inside the city. As part of their training, they knew that if a rescue mission was being planned that it would occur sooner rather than later, before the prisoners were moved to a more distant location.

Going back out into the city was not something that any of the men wanted to do; yet they were filled with a strange mixture of fear and grim determination. Fear at the thought of running the deadly gauntlet of gunfire again, grim determination because they were not yet through. There were still people missing and unaccounted for. The missing were more than likely already dead, but since no one yet knew for sure, there existed a sliver of hope that one might still be alive, waiting for his buddies to come find him, kick down the door and bring him home. This was what soldiers are expected to do for one another, and everyone wearing a uniform knew it. Their personal anxieties would have to wait until they finished what they had started, even if that meant killing everyone in Mogadishu.

As Blackburn took all the vehicles and crewmembers to the ASP, Dash began the walk from the compound gate to the Tactical Operations Center of the QRF, a distance of maybe three blocks. As he walked he noted the lack of frenetic activity he would have expected to see when rearming and equipping a large group of soldiers for a continuation of combat operations. He didn't see any excited yelling, cursing, or running around in the helter-skelter manner that usually accompanies such an endeavor as people try to maintain their edge while making sure nothing is forgotten. All he saw were soldiers standing in line at the mess hall waiting for breakfast to be served. Instead of exhibiting an air of excitement, the university compound seemed to be as quiet and routine as if today was going to be just another boring day in Somalia. Approaching a small group of 10th Mountain soldiers standing near the mess hall, smoking and telling each other war stories, Dash asked them if they were ready to continue the fight.

"Yes, Sir," one of them replied, "but no one has said anything about going back out. We were told to grab some chow and then go back to the company area to clean weapons."

"That's odd," Dash thought. After some small talk with the soldiers he simply told them to "stay tight and wait. With the tanks and condors still available I am certain that something is being planned to force the hand of Aideed."

"Roger that, Sir," replied one of the soldiers. "If we do go back out, make sure we get to be up front this time. You SOF guys did most of the shooting last night and we would like to kick some ass ourselves."

"I'll keep that in mind," replied Dash, hoping that the UN staff and embassy personnel had the same fire in their bellies that these soldiers had. At the same time he also knew that whatever decision was being made would have more of a political component to it than a military one. That realization made him nervous. There were too many weak-kneed people in the political and diplomatic communities who had been placed in positions of responsibility around the world and several of them were now in Somalia.

Based upon what the soldiers had said Dash noted that the war stories were already getting a little out of whack. From what he could recall of the enormous volume of fire coming from all locations in the convoy, he found it hard to believe that any soldier returned to base with his magazines still full. There had been much more shooting than just what the SOF soldiers had done. The 10th Mountain Division had suffered several casualties during the fight. None killed, thank God, but several had been wounded. Dash did not know where the soldiers he had spoken with had been in the convoy but many of the 10th Mountain soldiers had given a good account of themselves and had been bloodied in the process.

During one instance at a Somali obstacle that had been placed at the intersection of Via Lenin and National Street, two QRF soldiers had gone forward with Dash and Blackburn to assist in checking it for mines when both had been hit by a burst of gunfire. The two soldiers had been standing in the middle of the street, one on each side of Dash when the gunman fired from a rooftop. One of the soldiers was struck in the hip, the other in the neck, creating a brief panic as the medical personnel rushed forward to treat the wounded and both Dash and Blackburn rushed rearward dragging the wounded with them. Both parties missed one another in the noise and confusion, milling around in the intersection yelling, shooting, and being shot at. Eventually they gathered near a condor, using it as an ambulance to evacuate the wounded soldiers.

Others had been hit that night as well, making it a long, hard fight for many of the 10th Mountain soldiers. Lady Luck had been with the CA troops for none of them suffered any gunshot wounds even though they were in the thick of the fighting all the way through the city. The only injury any of them had sustained was when Gerard had tripped over Dash and broke his pinky finger.

The accident occurred when the team had dismounted and moved to clear a building from RPG gunners before the condors drove past. Having raced through the building and killing several Somalis they were leaving, running down an outside stairwell when Dash dropped to a knee to shoot through a shellhole in the wall at a gunman he saw running down the street. Gerard was running down the stairs behind Dash and did not see him stop and drop to his knee, performing a complete summersault when he tripped over him. Gerard rolled and bounced all the way to the bottom of the stairwell in a rattling cacophony of equipment and cursing, breaking his finger in the process. At first the other team members thought he had been hit and in his normal hypochondriac voice Gerard reinforced this belief when he cried out, " I think I'm done for!" as he held up his hand with his little finger sticking out ninety degrees.

"Shit!" yelled Blackburn, patting him down, franticly feeling for wet spots and not finding any. "You ain't hurt! Get your fat ass up and let's get the hell out of here." He then produced a roll of duct tape they all carried for binding prisoners and taped the broken appendage to Gerard's other fingers. This field expedient left Gerard not much worse for the wear since he continued fighting throughout the night, all the while bitching about the pain he was in to anyone who would listen to him. He finally had a doctor splint his finger when they reached the Pakistani stadium.

***

When Dash entered the QRF TOC there was only one captain and one sergeant on duty. He had never met either of them before and after being told that there would be no rescue attempt he doubted that either one of them wanted to ever see him again.

"What the hell do you mean you have been ordered to stand down?" Dash yelled at the young 10th Mountain Division captain. "Are you all a bunch of pussies?" Wisely neither the captain nor the sergeant responded to his outburst, both simply stared at their boots as Dash vented.

"Where are your S-3 and commander? I want to talk to them. There are still people inside that city and I know for a fact that some of the D-Boys have already gone back in after them. We can't just walk away and leave everyone out there!" Dash fumed as he pointed in the general direction of Mogadishu.

"Sir, the commander and S-3 are both over at the embassy speaking with Admiral Howe. I'm sorry," the young Captain apologized. He was just as angry about the order as Dash was. And seeing the telltale moisture welling in his eyes,

Dash stopped short. He could tell that this young man was filled with the same emotions he was.

As Dash reached for the door to leave he said the only thing he could think of saying at the moment. "No, Captain. I'm sorry. I'm sorry for all of us. If Aideed comes out of this thing looking like he won soldiers around the globe might as well pack up and go home because any thug with a gun will believe that he can intimidate us. We will have no credibility whatsoever!"

***

Dash took his time before returning to the G-5 section where Blackburn had assembled the vehicles and was busily conducting pre-combat checks. When Dash told him to stand down, that there was no immediate plan to launch another mission to recover the missing, he was flabbergasted. It went against the grain of his very soul, causing his already short fuse to burn even brighter. But, professional that he was, he accepted his orders and went about his business taking care of the men and their equipment. It was quite evident, however, to any watching, that he was not a happy soldier.

The remainder of the day was spent visiting wounded soldiers in the hospital and cleaning equipment. They kept the ammunition they had drawn in the hopes that someone with enough horsepower and common sense would see the error in their decision to not put Aideed in his place and demand the immediate return of all remains or prisoners — or else.

"The longer we wait the harder it will be to find them." Blackburn said later that evening, reiterating Dash's very thought. Then, on the television inside the G5 office where they were assembled cleaning weapons, CNN began rolling film footage of a body being dragged through the streets of Mogadishu. An American body.

Except for the excited chatter coming from the television, a pin could have been heard dropping as the soldiers sat mesmerized by the horrible images they were seeing on the screen. As they stared at the television, the image of a fallen soldier stripped naked of everything but his underwear, hands bound above his head, was being dragged through a throng of laughing Somalis who would periodically kick the body and hit it with sticks. It was as despicable a sight as any ever shown. The film footage played over, and over, and over.

"This is too damn much," Blackburn finally said, breaking five minutes of absolute silence. "If they've killed everyone and are now mutilating the bodies, I say we fuck-up the whole lot of 'em. Kill every bastard in this city. Men, women, kids, chickens, goats, ducks, I don't care. If these people want to behave like animals then so by God will we." Then, as quickly as he had exploded, the biggest, baddest soldier in Mogadishu silently sat down, slowly put his head in his hands, and started crying, an unexpected sight that shocked everyone in the room.

"It's not supposed to be like this," Blackburn said between sobs. "American soldiers are not supposed to be dishonored this way, just so some fat-ass civilian back in the States can be entertained over dinner and drinks. Has the whole damn world gone insane? What the hell has happened here? How did we go from a policy of feeding people one day to a policy of war the next? How the hell did that happen?"

Except for the continual droning of the CNN talking head Blackburn's retort was met with nothing but silence. Dash and all the others continued to sit still, uncomfortably watching in wonder as they listened to the first sergeant vent his frustrations with what was taking place not a mile from where they were now sitting. They had no answers to his questions, which were rhetorical anyway. Blackburn was simply releasing his pent up emotions before they consumed him, his venting acting a cathartic release for all of them.

Yet at the same time Dash felt that watching Blackburn in such despair would have a negative effect on the other soldiers in the room. Something he did not want to see happen in the event they were called upon to reenter the city. So even though Dash knew that Blackburn did not expect an answer to his questions, he felt the need to speak in response to them, if for no other reason than to keep himself from breaking down as well. Combined with Blackburn's emotional response, Dash's breaking down would be a sight certain to break the spirit of everyone in the room.

"Top," he began, collecting his thoughts as he spoke, "what we have become is a victim of blind ambition. And we are all in this together, the UN, the politicians, the generals, and the soldiers. We have become so impressed with Americas military might following the successes of recent wars that we assume other people and nations, logical people and nations, will be equally impressed as well. Like God, America now believes it can fix the unfixable. We believe that if the American military shows up on foreign shores that people living there will now do as we say if for no other reason than they should logically fear us. What we confirmed last night is something that soldiers have known for a long time, the world is not a rational place. It is a world of haves and have-nots largely because the have-nots are not logical, rational people. Certainly not in the sense that the western world defines it: that all people should have the opportunity to live a successful, secure life no matter what their background or personal beliefs. But this belief is based upon the assumption that all people are willing to leave the historical baggage behind in order to begin anew. What we have seen in Somalia is that not all people are willing to leave that baggage behind." Glancing around the room as he spoke, Dash noticed that all eyes seemed to be on him and off Blackburn, exactly as he had hoped.

"Ask a Habr Gidr woman walking right now on Hawaldig Road if she wants peace and she will answer yes," he continued. "And so will her children. Ask her if peace means having to share power with the Abgal tribe and she will reply, 'With those animals. I would rather die first.' And so will her children because Mama teaches it to them. They grow up hating and give no thought as to whether they are right or wrong. Hate is as natural for some people as breathing. Unfortunately, idealists stop after asking the first question, leaving people like us to deal with the ramifications of the following answers."

Now even Blackburn was paying attention to his lecture, attentively listening to him as if he were another long-winded visiting college professor pretending to know what he is talking about. In fact Dash was pulling ideas out of his butt hoping to break the tension. And, since it appeared to be working, he continued.

"Had the idealists taken the time to conduct non-agenda driven interviews with the Somalis and honestly reported the results to the world before the decision was made to save them from themselves, I seriously doubt that we would be here today. But they didn't. Instead, some bureaucrat applied western logic to a non-western problem and decided that we could force them to see the light. What we discovered instead is that people who live with the certainty of death every day do not fear America simply because she has bigger and better guns than they do. This fact might impress them but it sure as hell doesn't scare them, certainly not enough to get them to change their ways. Many of the world's failing people simply have no desire to change, and no one can force them to."

"This is simply incomprehensible to an American," he continued. Noticing that CNN had already moved on to other important news describing a Hollywood celebrity's pending divorce. "We simply cannot believe, even refuse to believe, that any human being would voluntarily choose to live the way the Somalis are living and that it is not being forced on them by anyone other than themselves. Yet, try as we might, change never seems to happen, certainly not over night and America, in particular, does not have the patience for the centuries of effort such change will require, if it is required at all."

Looking around the silent and attentive room Dash made an attempt to end his thoughts on a positive note. "If anything good comes from last night's debacle, it might be that America will finally come to grips with the realization that not everyone in this world shares the same vision of what peace and harmony mean and we will stay the hell out of their business."

"But I doubt it," responded Blackburn, slowly coming out of his emotional low. "There are too many wishful thinkers in this world and not enough hard core realists."

"Top," Dash quickly asked now that his first sergeant was listening and not just commiserating, "what do you say you and I take a little walk. I'd like to discuss something with you in private."

***

As they slowly walked the corridors of the empty university Dash began speaking. "When I called Fort Bragg earlier this morning to let them know that none of our people had been killed or wounded I was told sources inside the city have confirmed there is an American still alive. Aideed's militia is holding him hostage somewhere inside the city. The only reason I didn't mention it to you earlier is because I am waiting for confirmation from a second source. I suspect that CNN will pick up on this story shortly and begin broadcasting it to the public. When that happens, I am going to assume that it is true and I am going to go after him."

Dash then asked a question he already knew the answer to. It was reminiscent of a question Blackburn had asked him in the embassy cafeteria in Riyadh two years earlier when they had made the DCM an official stepfather. "What I want to know from you, First Sergeant, is are you in or are you out?"

As Dash's words began to sink through the remorse and self-pity that Blackburn had earlier expressed, it was as though a total transformation had taken place. His spine straightened and he pulled his shoulders back, erecting himself to his full height. He stopped, grabbed Dash by both shoulders, turned him face to face, looked him straight in the eyes, and in a voice still cracking with emotion answered, "Hell yes, I'm in!"

Dash would later remember this moment as being one with strangely mixed emotions. He was energized knowing that he was going to be a part of something larger than himself, attempting to find and rescue a fellow soldier, but at the same time, he was fearful that going back out into the city would get them both killed. But when he looked into Blackburn's tear filled eyes, the emotion of the moment seemed to erase the fear of death, replacing it with a conviction that no matter what would happen, it could not be any worse than the torture they were experiencing by doing nothing.

"By the way, First Sergeant," Dash concluded, "that two day growth of beard you have is starting to look good, don't shave it off."

"You either, Major." Blackburn responded with a smile.

***

Back in the G5 office Dash explained to his commander, Colonel Degan, that he and Blackburn had some unfinished business to attend to down at the Port. He asked that a convoy be put together to accompany he and Blackburn for their trip there in the morning. He also stated that neither he nor Blackburn would be returning with that convoy, electing instead to spend the next several days at the Port tying together some "loose ends."

The wise old colonel never once asked for an explanation of what they would be doing at the port. He knew better. Prior knowledge of what was being planned would make him a willing participant, making him eligible for a court martial if the rescue attempt failed. Instead, the next morning, Colonel Degan was present when the convoy departed and he saluted both soldiers, wishing them the very best in their attempt to tie together those "loose ends." Degan was an American soldier too.

***

On the way to the port the convoy made a stop in Jesira where Dash had a conversation with Moe-Moe, requesting that he deliver a message to an Arab friend of his working for an Islamic charity group at the Digfer Hospital. Then they drove to the port and began waiting, their escort convoy returning to the university compound. All that day they waited when, just before dark, the driver of a truck that had been emptying Porta-potties near the port terminal approached Dash's Hummvee. The two were killing time playing a spirited game of Spades when the man approached and asked in pure Saudi Arabic dialect which one of them was Major Tom Dash.

"I am," said Dash, also speaking in Arabic. Startled that the man was so bold and direct.

"I have a message for you from Mohammed," the driver carefully said, eyeing both Dash and Blackburn suspiciously. He was wearing a pair of blue coveralls, on the back of which was written "Tammimi Global," a Saudi subsidiary of Brown & Root, which is itself a subsidiary of the immense Haliburton Industries, at that time being chaired by the former Secretary of Defense, Dick Cheney. "He will meet with you in the morning at the petrol station at the market on Medina Street. You know of this place?"

"Yes, I know of this place. What time will he be there?"

"In the morning, before twelve. Be there."

Then the Arab employee turned on his heels, got back in his "shit sucking" truck and left, reminding Dash with his last answer that he despised the American obsession with time. In his world things happened for a reason, not simply because they had been put on a schedule. Morning meant morning. If it didn't happen then it would happen the next day or the day after that, *"Ensha Allah,"* God Willing, an annoying habit most Saudis have that Dash had forgotten about. The driver hadn't minded in the least reminding him of it. As he watched the truck drive away Dash made a mental note to have the contracting officers do a better job of vetting the people they hired before allowing them the freedom to roam all over what was supposed to be a secure area.

***

"It's been two hours," Blackburn complained, "do you think he will show?"

"He'll show," Dash answered. "We've got to be patient. We need his help."

It was only six o'clock in the morning. They had arrived in the Market before daylight because they did not know when to expect Assiri, knowing that if they missed him they would lose their best chance to get the pilot released.

During their time at the port they had learned that the name of the pilot was Michael Durant, a member of the Night Stalkers of the 160th SOAR from Fort Campbell, Kentucky. They had wanted to go to the airfield and talk to some of their Delta friends, as well as to the Rangers, to see if they had any information that would help narrow their search. But they couldn't leave the port, expecting a message from Assiri at any possible moment. When it had finally arrived, they hadn't had time to speak with anyone before having to meet with him.

Assiri would be the first person with any hope of having inside information that they might be able to exploit. It was essential that he help them. They certainly could not pull this off in the blind, rushing about Mogadishu shooting people. Such foolish antics were what had led to this predicament to begin with. Instead, they desperately needed a way of obtaining good, solid, timely intelligence and they needed it now. Either that or they needed the entire might of UNOSOM, every man, every vehicle, every gun and every helicopter lined up on Hawlwadig Road, pointed straight at the heart of Aideed while announcing, "This is how bad we want the pilot back. How bad do you want to keep him?" A move that in his wildest dreams Dash could not envision the United Nations as having the balls to do. Yet at the same time a sight that he knew Aideed would understand and would give in to. Aideed had already lost too many men and expended too much ordinance to be in a position to continue a fight with anyone more powerful than the Boy Scouts. He certainly was in no position to continue a fight with a formidable military force like UNOSOM's. The threat of another attack would work if tried because at the heart of the matter Aideed was a bully and a bully is a coward in hiding. Problem was, the UN fit that same mold and it had been Aideed who had called their bluff, not the other way around, and as proof of the theory that confronting a bully would reveal a coward, Aideed was now winning. As always, who had been right and who had been wrong had nothing to do with the outcome.

Parked outside the market, sitting in their Hummvee, the two American soldiers felt conspicuous and vulnerable after the recent fight in the city. Many of the Somalis now eyed them warily, circling their vehicle at a distance like a predatory pack of wolves looking for a weakness. Which was not entirely uncommon behavior in this part of the city but, still, an even greater air of hostility could be sensed this morning, leaving Dash and Blackburn fingering their weapons while sitting inside the vehicle. The Somalis living around the market, mostly Abgal tribesmen had never warmly received them but they had never felt the fear of being attacked there before either. As they sat waiting for Assiri, they could only hope that their luck held for another day.

As daylight broke across the city a group of children could be seen playing in the street while their mothers shopped the market for the latest in fresh fruits and vegetables. Some of the women had been accompanied by their husband or teen-age sons, most of whom seemed more intent on scavenging remnants from last nights khat sale than on handling the abundance of food scattered across the bins and tabletops of the market. Others obediently followed behind their wives like an American male follows his wife or mother around a shopping mall, walking three steps behind, head bowed, as if being forced to do something against their will, like a small dog being taught to heel. The abundance of food in the market caused Dash to recall the stupidity of declaring a famine as the principle reason for America having intervened in Somalia's civil war.

Watching the children play, Dash could detect that one of them, a little girl who could not have been more than six or seven seemed to be paying an undue amount of attention to the Hummvee. She appeared to want to approach the vehicle but was too shy and uncertain to do so. Taking a stick of gum from his pocket, Dash held it up so the little girl could see it, hoping to entice her closer so he could speak with her. Most American soldiers love children and neither Dash nor Blackburn was any exception. They played with the Somali children any time they got a chance because a child's innocence and energy offers a brief escape from the tedium and insanity of a place at war with itself. Such times of play caused Dash to reflect upon his belief that if the adults were more like the children who had not yet learned to hate there wouldn't be any wars and there wouldn't be any soldiers.

When the little girl caught the glint of the tin foil wrapper, she was emboldened enough to approach the vehicle, though warily. Offering encouragement Dash held the stick of gum at arm length and asked, "Would you like some gum?"

"Yes," the little girl replied in broken English, "and this is for you." Reaching inside her blouse she withdrew a slip of paper and handed it to Dash with her tiny hand, grabbing the stick of gum with her other hand, then turned and fled, awkwardly trying to unwrap the stick of gum while running away.

The note was from Assiri. He was in an abandoned police station behind the market, waiting for the two Americans.

CHAPTER 22

"I apologize for the delay before responding to your request to meet," began Assiri. "Being seen together isn't the safest thing for either one of us right now and I'm still not sure that helping you is the proper thing to do. But since you asked, I can't very well turn my back on friends." He motioned for them to sit in a couple of comfortable chairs that had been left in the police station along with a matching sofa, the furniture evidently having escaped the Somali scavengers who had stolen everything not already cemented to the floor in every building in the city. By all appearances they had stolen everything in this police station too, as the electrical wiring was gone. The slits left from pulling the wire through the stucco wall made the room appear as if a mad man with a chain saw had gone on a rampage. Exactly how the furniture had ended up here was anybody's guess, and the least of their worries, but its presence was a mild curiosity.

"I also apologize for having had you disarmed before meeting with you. I trust you not to attempt any stupid acts of bravery but the others don't," he said with a broad sweep of his arm, reminding them that they were not alone. "In fact, there are people here who would rather that I left you armed in the hopes that you would try something stupid, if you get my meaning."

"We get your meaning," Dash responded. "We didn't ask to meet with you in order to pick a fight."

"Good," replied Assiri, extending his arms in a welcoming gesture, "in that case, 'Ahlan wa sahlan', welcome."

It was obvious that Assiri or members of his group were using the abandoned police station as a headquarters and had been for quite sometime. In comparison to the surrounding buildings, it was well maintained. In addition to the furniture, sleeping mats were scattered about the floor and water jugs were neatly stacked in the corner of the room. At least one TACSAT radio sat on a table at the far end of the adjoining room. Who would respond if the radio were to be keyed, the Americans would never know, but they were absolutely certain that it had not been put there as a prop just to impress them. Assiri was either wired into someone else's headquarters or he was that headquarters.

In addition to the equipment and material inside the room four Arab guards stood rigidly against the wall, angrily staring at the American soldiers as if they wanted to kill them. Neither Dash nor Blackburn had any doubt that without weapons in their hands or Assiri's presence in the room they would do exactly that. As he glanced around the room, making fleeting eye contact with the guards, Dash wondered how many of these same men he and Blackburn had fired at during the fight in the center of the city. He also wondered how many of these guards had shot back at them that same night.

"I assume that you're here because of the captured pilot, what is his name, Michael Durant?" Assiri continued. "When I first heard of the pilot's capture and the lack of political will to do anything to free him except lodge a diplomatic protest, I expected the two of you to come looking for him. I did not expect to be involved with it myself, but since you have asked for assistance then I feel compelled to explain my reluctance to provide it."

"Holy Christ!" Dash felt like saying to Blackburn. *"Of all times for Assiri to want to preach to us."* But he remained silent and braced himself for what he knew was going to be a major league ass chewing. Like most Arabs, Assiri held dearly to the cultural precepts of talk as being synonymous with action. He could have cared less whether his audience felt that they had the time to sit still and listen to it.

"Keep in mind that this pilot is a captive because of American aggression against the Somalis, not the other way around. This whole mess of open warfare is of America's own making. The absurdity of attempting to arrest a Somali clan leader was begun by you!" he lectured them.

Pointing his finger directly at the two soldiers he scolded, "Because of your efforts to catch Aideed you are now considered to be an unwelcome and unwanted invader of a Muslim nation. As such, my uncle is insistent that I not offer my personal assistance in any negotiations between you and Aideed. Such an act on my part would appear divisive to my fellow Muslims. All of Islam now believes that America was wrong to declare war on a Somali warlord, and we believe that you did so only because Aideed and his people are poor Muslims. During all of America's years in Vietnam no one ever tried to arrest Ho Chi Minh," he seemingly offered as proof of this theory.

"Also," he abruptly announced in the event that someone should ask, "I cannot tell you where this pilot is being kept because I simply do not know."

It was apparent to both Dash and Blackburn that Assiri was taking a big risk meeting with them like this, trying to provide assistance without seeming to be anxious to help America or the UN in its fight with Aideed. The soldiers were also quick to realize that his desire to lecture them was being offered more for the consumption of others in the room than for either Dash or Blackburn. They already knew that the only reason he was helping them was because he knew the two of them to be men of honor, as he considered himself to be, and they had all been, at one time, friends. Theirs was more of a military brotherhood than a simple relationship.

As Americans with a well-developed sense of history, however, both men knew that even brothers could be separated by ideologies, a belief that the group culture of one is superior to that of the other. American families had often been split apart by ideology during America's Civil War, a time when families took their disagreements to the battlefield to be resolved with bullets rather than into the parlor where they could be resolved with words. Like those who fought for either the blue or the gray, Assiri had as great a belief in the righteousness of his cause as did American Civil War soldiers in theirs. A fact misunderstood by most Americans when they argue that anyone who would resist equalitarian principles, unity, and greater wealth had to be crazy. Assiri was no "crazier" than Robert E. Lee was or Jefferson Davis had been when seeking a different way of life for the South. They and their many followers simply chose a different way of life for themselves; and were willing to die for their cause. Which was why Assiri often felt compelled to frame his argument against UN involvement in foreign affairs as a contest of will between America and Islam. Assiri knew better than to limit his criticism to the United Nations. As a political body everyone in the room felt that the UN was of little consequence without America's support. Like an October leaf blowing in the autumn wind, its political will was as tenuous as if it were held together by a dry stem. It is incredibly easy to sever UN resolve.

As for the actual politics of what had happened in the small African country, Assiri personally could have cared less regarding UN or American efforts to save the Somalis from themselves. Like most of the American soldiers serving there he too considered Somalia to be a lost cause. But unlike the American soldiers, he never felt that saving the Somalis was the real reason America had sent them there.

Assiri believed that the creation of UNOSOM had simply been another blatant attempt by the West to force a secular belief system on a Muslim nation in order to weaken Islam's grip. He knew that none of the reigning Somali warlords had requested outside assistance. Other people, mostly westerners, had unilaterally decided to help the Somali people by imposing their own sense of justice on them, forcing the people to adopt a life of western influence, subjugation and exploitation just as they had the people of the Middle East. Many of these same westerners also believed that their ways were so superior to that of nonwestern nations that any human being who believed differently had to be doing so out of force. These idealists always seemed to mistakenly believe that when shown the many advantages of democratic rule and equality, the rest of mankind would embrace western ideas with open arms.

Had the true believers in this theory taken the time to speak with any of the Arab Mujahadeen guards in the room instead of just to their like-minded elitist foreign friends, they would have learned that these young men had a different opinion regarding the merits of westernization. But idealists never bother to speak to those who disagree with them, choosing instead to speak only with foreigners most like themselves, essentially reinforcing their own arguments. Leaving them to mistakenly believe that since Western governments speak for their constituents, so too must all others. Nothing could be further from the truth. In most of the world, and especially in the Middle East, a man like bin Laden speaks for more people than do the Saudi Royals, a fact that makes democratic idealists extremely uncomfortable. So uncomfortable, in fact, that they continuously choose to ignore it while constantly expressing surprise that every nonwestern nation seems to always have a "small and vocal" minority opposing their efforts to "help" them.

This is a monumental mistake for academicians and politicians to make. It is also hard to understand that it continues to be made given historical fact. To use but two recent examples, neither politicians nor academicians felt that Adolph Hitler or Saddam Hussein were considered to be worth speaking to until after they acquired so much power that they could no longer be ignored. Largely because these individuals — a Bavarian corporal and a contract killer who both spent time in prison — were so far removed from the elitist's world that they were disregarded as being insignificant by those used to dealing with a "smarter and prettier" clientele.

But there are those who do routinely speak with people who disagree with them *and* they usually come from the lower rungs of the social ladder themselves — soldiers. Soldiers know from firsthand experience that the world is full of people who are so resistant to the spreading of western ideals inside their country that they will line up to kill those doing it. They know this because they are the ones killed. They also know that with the exception of other soldiers, no one ever seeks the opinion of these people. Something soldiers find to be incomprehensible because they know that if someone wants to find out what is *really* going on in a military unit, you ask the privates, not the generals.

The Mujahadeen simply felt that Somalia was as good a place as any other to continue their Jihad, or Holy War, in order to thwart western ambitions. If America came into their backyard to spread false beliefs, especially if invited by a UN they were at war against, then the Mujahadeen would fight them there. This was the only reason any of them had come to Somalia. Now, offering the Mujahadeen soldiers encouragement that their efforts were achieving a certain measure of success, the Americans were here today asking Assiri for help, a clear indication that they were on the right track.

Although he had been speaking to them in English, Assiri was being watched attentively by the guards. All of them had traveled from the Sudan on bin Laden's purse strings as Al-Qaida soldiers offering their support to anyone or any group that had as its primary objective the killing of Americans. It was pure irony that they now found themselves in a room with two of them and were being prohibited from exacting their vengeance. It had to have been grating on both their nerves as well as their trigger fingers, which, Dash noticed, were in perpetual motion stroking the trigger of the AK-47 rifle that each carried at port arms high across his chest.

"But I can be of some assistance," Assiri graciously continued, offering them hope when they realized that he hadn't summoned them here just to administer a seminar. "I have taken the liberty of producing press credentials for both of you," he smiled. "These credentials identify you as being reporters working for the Al-Jazeera news agency. These credentials and your ability to speak Arabic should gain you access to the Black Sea neighborhood of Aideed and, hopefully, access to the American pilot. I would suggest, however, that you begin your quest with the pretense of wanting to describe the battle in Mogadishu by telling the Somali side of the story, despite the fact that some reporters seem to be doing that already."

Assiri had always felt ambivalence when reading or watching the American media's reaction to national and international news events. He appreciated the freedom of the American press to report contradictory political opinions, something that was rarely found in the Middle Eastern media outlets and virtually nonexistent in the state controlled Saudi media. Yet despite his admiration of a free press he could not help but despise the way the American media often attacked political decision-makers with prophecies of doom and gloom. It seemed to him as if the media was a caricature for the worst type of back seat driver, always offering criticism after the fact, but never offering suitable alternatives. To Assiri and other like-minded Arabs it seemed illogical that the media could be so astute that it could intricately describe all that was wrong with a political decision, but never describe what was right with it. It was a characteristic of American culture that he found unsettling for he knew that American society was nowhere near as disjointed in its thinking processes as the media portrayed it to be. Yet he himself often used stories filed by American and British reporters as classroom aids to instruct his Mujahadeen soldiers on why they should resist westernization. Both he and Osama had found it easier to simply read the Mujahadeen soldiers critical western newspapers and have them watch critical western televised news than attempt to make up their own reasons why the west was so decadent.

To an uneducated person with no other frame of reference, the Mujahadeen soldiers were a prime audience for such stories. Coming from a culture where political violence, not compromise, was the key to remaining in power, the constant media attack made the American government appear to be weak. No strong Arab leader would be so openly criticized more than once before both the reporter and his editor simply disappeared. American media portrayals of controversial events often made it appear to people ignorant of democratic ways that the American government was at war with its own people, that they were being held prisoner, patiently waiting to be rescued. After several hours of indoctrination from such negative reporting it was even believable that the average American would thank the Mujahadeen for freeing them from such a tyrannical government. Assiri could not help but smile at his good fortune; for at times he almost felt that he should be paying the major American media outlets for the free propaganda they were providing him. He could have never concocted such believable and illustrative stories of decadence and deceit himself because neither he nor Osama had been blessed with that active an imagination.

"Have either one of you ever worked as a reporter?" Assiri asked with concern in his voice.

"No," answered Dash.

"Me either," said Blackburn, but optimistically added, "but how damn hard could it be? You ask questions and pretend to care about the answer."

"You should be alright," Assiri cautioned, ignoring Blackburn's caustic remark. "Just avoid interviewing people who have had experience with real reporters. As you know, the media left after four reporters were killed attempting to cover the attack last July on the Abdi house, the first mistake of many that you have made here," he chastised them, taking the opportunity for a little dig at the American's plight.

"But," he continued, "with the recent fight in Mogadishu, they are streaming back into the country like sharks to the smell of blood. The Somalis, like people everywhere, enjoy seeing their faces on television or their names in print. It won't be difficult to get people to talk to you; the trick will be in finding someone who has something important enough to say that they are worth taking the time to listen to. Most of them will simply be seeking their fifteen minutes of fame."

"Yeah, I understand," Dash replied as he fingered the press credentials that had been handed he and Blackburn by the guard nearest the door. It was obvious that the guard spoke English as Assiri had made no reference to what he was saying in any other language but English; yet he had clearly understood the statement, passing them the credentials without any further prompting from Assiri.

"I also procured a hardened, bulletproof Toyota Land Cruiser for your use. Since you are representing Al-Jazeera you might as well look the part."

Assiri pushed back in his chair, briefly stopping the flow of information so the Americans could absorb the significance of what he was telling them. Driving a hardened car was something most reporters had not yet learned to do, but even Assiri felt vulnerable on the streets of Mogadishu if not wrapped inside a cocoon of protection. The city streets were teeming with well armed, cocky young men who were not at all particular about who they killed.

"I have also asked some of my more influential contacts to prevent any real Al-Jazeera reporters from coming into Somalia for the next three days, which gives you until 9 October to complete your business."

This announcement was even more startling to Dash than the fact that Assiri had been able to get an armored car. Neither the White House nor the Pentagon had the power to stop an ambitious reporter's trip to a war zone. Yet Assiri had given them three days during which they would be the only Arab media representatives in the city, a remarkable feat of control that was a clear indication that Osama bin Laden's Al-Qaida organization had a span of control far beyond any other known terrorist group.

"I will keep your weapons and your vehicle here with me," Assiri continued, unaware that his last announcement had been far more telling of his powers than the acquisition of an armored car. "Reporters do not drive Hummvees or carry weapons. If you do not return for them I will make sure that the vehicle and any personal effects you have are left in a conspicuous location at the port. In the unlikely event that you survive this charade, then arrangements will be made for you to retrieve these items at a location yet to be determined. We will not speak together again following this meeting. It has become too dangerous for all of us. Do you understand?"

"Roger," both men said simultaneously. Then Dash continued with a question of his own, "Why are you bothering to help us now?"

"Several reasons," began Assiri. "First, I have no desire for Aideed to be successful. He is a loose cannon that will bring nothing but despair to Somalia, as he is doing now. The political problem for Somalia is that there isn't anybody else here that can do the job any better than Aideed. He has the guns and now, since defeating American troops, he has the reputation to unite the country. The battle in Mogadishu made this man a local legend. It gave him power; it didn't take it away.

I know that American soldiers will measure their success in the recent battle by the body count, which is an irrelevant measure because it is obvious that many more Somalis were killed than Americans. Unfortunately, for people who follow war as if it were a game scoreboard, third world countries like Somalia do not measure success or failure by the number killed, they measure it by who owns the street once the smoke of battle clears. And ownership of those streets goes to the Somalis, a fact that the world cannot deny no matter how America's fixation with the body count tries to twist this truth to its own favor. It is why Aideed allowed the body to be dragged through the streets, to demonstrate that he still owns them," he cautioned by waving his finger back and forth. Seemingly always mindful of the American mistake in Vietnam when politicians and generals who should have known better tried to equate success with the number of dead. Assiri rightly believed that wars are about changing people's attitudes; more about changing minds than creating dead bodies, and American politicians did nothing to make the Vietnamese change their minds regarding the future they had chosen for themselves. Neither were they in Somalia and Assiri relished the opportunity he had to make comparisons.

"Fortunately for all of us," he continued, "the bloody fight in Mogadishu may be a lesson for the world to learn from because all those believing that they know best will now have to adopt a wait and see attitude regarding who ultimately grabs the reins of power in Somalia. The United Nations won't dare risk any more lives trying to protect dying Somalis, not after Mogadishu. Nor will America go after Aideed with guns blazing again, fighting in the streets as if Mogadishu was Berlin and Aideed was Hitler," he said, continuing to wave his finger in the air as if he were scolding a small child.

"The world needs to simply stand back and let peace happen, quit trying to make a silk purse out of a sow's ear," he lectured. "Somalia will never look like a country modeled after an American style of democracy. The damn lies that Jeffersonian democracy will erupt in Somalia or anywhere else in the world with the death of one warlord like Aideed is just that, a damn lie. Unless you plan to take over the country yourself, someone equally as bad will simply move in to the power vacuum and take his place. In fact, if America is serious about having a democracy in Africa, let President Clinton call for a popular vote in Somalia today. Run Aideed against Boutrous-Ghali or anyone else and see who gets the most votes. Disregarding your Electoral College, isn't America's concept of democracy still majority rule, what the most people want?" he smiled, satisfied that he already knew the answer. "Americans only want a democracy when the people living there already agree with them. Otherwise they will continue to support dictators who can club the people into submission long enough for America to make a profit. Crony capitalism is your version of democracy, not majority rule!"

Dash had always been amazed at Assiri's grasp of American colloquiums. It made him sound more American than most Americans, and they were always thought provoking. However, this time, he was wasting both his criticism and his witticism because he was preaching to the choir. They had engaged in this same conversation many times when trying to determine what America believed would actually be accomplished by forcing a peace in Somalia before there was a clear winner in the ongoing civil war. Both knew that a Somalia peace accord might play well on the Washington cocktail circuit but they also knew that such a peace would be of short duration as the Somalis went back to fighting amongst themselves as soon as the world lost interest in their struggles. The UN, dependent upon American guns and money, yet shackled tightly to America's notoriously short attention span, would also quickly lose interest in the future of Somalia.

As soldiers, they also knew that the requirement to maintain a tentative peace in Somalia would be hung around the American military's neck like a dead fish, ripening with age as they were forced to deal with all of the underlying problems as a peacekeeping force. Problems of a social, cultural, religious, and economic nature that politicians are quick to distance themselves from because outside forces, be they military or political, cannot fix them. Making the prospect of undertaking long term nation building an Albatross for any ambitious American politician to put in his or her platform.

But there is an underlying problem with nation building that surpasses internal political differences. When peacemakers arrive they assume the responsibility for everything that does or does not happen from that point forward. The people living there continue to do what they have always done to solve the underlying problems — nothing! As a result, the peacekeepers never get to leave. The assumption that angry people welcome peacekeepers as arbitrators to help achieve a compromise that everyone can live with so they can get on with their own lives is diplomatic hogwash. Peacekeeping simply provides the UN an excuse to ask for more money.

In all their conversations together neither Dash nor Blackburn had ever come up with so much as one good reason why the world was so intent on spending time, money and effort in Somalia until the Somalis themselves were willing to make a change. It simply made no sense to them that resources were being wasted on such a thankless effort. The fact that educated, experienced, worldly politicians did not recognize this as well made even less sense to them.

"Second, I have no personal animosity towards the two of you," Assiri said. "If I can help you save another soldier's life, why wouldn't I? My complaint is with your government and its policies of globalization, not with its soldiers. Your country always seem to gain admittance to countries by waving money in the face of the local rulers, enticing them to forget their tribal roots for something as superficial as financial wealth. Why doesn't your country just let the world come to America?" he asked rhetorically. "Quit reaching out for them, dragging them into your orbit, jamming your cultural and social mores down everyone's throat as a prerequisite for your acceptance?"

"I don't agree that America is trying to bring Somalia into our economic sphere," countered Dash, reluctantly being dragged into the argument. "I believe that we came here in order to stop the violence. That may have been naive but I don't suspect any other ulterior motives."

"No," responded Assiri. "I will grant you this argument. Despite America's imperialistic ambitions, even I have a hard time believing that she would attempt to spread her economic wings in Somalia. But there are many other ways that she seeks to insidiously impose her will on others. For example, you know that one of my children, a son, was born in America while I was serving at Fort Lewis, Washington. My son is automatically granted United States citizenship under *jus soli,* law of the soil, and as an American citizen he can sponsor my family should we decide to live in America. Yet as a Muslim I have four wives, my religion allows it, but American law requires that I bring only this son's mother to America as my wife, forcing me to divorce myself from the other three before I can be legally admitted. By what authority can I be made to comply with such a thing? By man's law? I am already behaving in accordance with God's law as clearly written in the Koran. Is not God's law more powerful than that of man? How could compliance to man's law instead of that of God be beneficial for any Muslim man or woman? Such a requirement is an attack on Islam, and it is wrong. Muslims are not Mormons. We will not sell our belief that polygamy is God's way for man simply because a few promised federal dollars are waved in our face."

Assiri had that old familiar gleam back in his eyes as he spoke the Muslim equivalent of fire and brimstone.

"Such blatant boldness is a tragedy," he fumed, "because I have nothing but respect for the American military and take no pleasure in having to fight it. But fight it we will even though it is not the military's fault that it is being forced into a confrontation with Islam. Your military is still an extension of your political arm." Then, looking around the room to ensure that the Mujahadeen guards were listening to every word he was saying, added, "I intend to eventually cut that arm off."

"Third," he said, with a devilish smile brought on by the pleasant thought of stopping the vaunted American military machine, "I am helping you because I think it will be best for the Somali people. If Aideed is foolish enough to try to trade, negotiate, or sell the pilot back to America, he will be making a big mistake. A mistake for which the Somali people will ultimately pay the price. I have lived long enough inside your country to know that American citizens will not stand for political blackmail. They would rather destroy Somalia and everyone in it before giving in to a man like Aideed. Even now there is a huge armada of ships, planes, and additional troops being manifested for Somalia in anticipation of a future fight with the Habr Gidr in order to get the pilot back. Something that could be done today with a show of force by UNOSOM if it weren't so cowardly."

"Additionally," he concluded. "Ambassador Oakley, the last American Ambassador to Somalia, is scheduled to return on 8 October, two days from now, to meet with Aideed, hopefully to arrange for the release of the pilot. Oakley feels the same as I do. If Aideed attempts to use the pilot to blackmail America, the city of Mogadishu will be recorded in future history books as the city that was, because it will be no more. Like a modern day Atlantis, American bombs will sink it beneath the ocean. As a man of compassion and a fellow Muslim, I do not wish for this to happen, even to a perennial hard case like Somalia."

"Those are all good reasons," admitted Dash, getting caught up in Assiri's argument, "but you are aware that the United Nations, with America's assistance, came to Somalia for egalitarian reasons, not for war. UNOSOM was a mission to feed people, Muslim people, who were dying of starvation, being killed by other Muslims I might add. It was a mission that had great success until war was declared on the UN. It was Aideed's attack on the Pakistani soldiers that led us to where we are today and it has to be Aideed's atonement that will allow the UN to continue in its efforts to bring peace to Somalia."

"Nice try Dash, but peace will come to Somalia when pigs can fly," laughed Assiri. "Or when the biggest, baddest, nastiest warlord in Somalia kills off all of his political opponents. Something that America's presence here is simply delaying, yet it is always the natural course of events. People armed with the latest in weaponry simply don't surrender their cause because someone wants to sit at the table and talk to them. People have to die first; it really is no more complicated than that. If the world cannot stomach the pain of watching the fighting and dying, then it has the option of changing channels. But one simple rule will always hold forth no matter how your heart feels about it. Power and violence may on occasion earn respect, but always, always, they garner attention. It is simply the way of the world."

"I too am a soldier Moe," argued Dash. "I understand the need to kill but is it wrong to try other alternatives, like peaceful negotiations, before resorting to violence?"

"No," Assiri responded, "that wouldn't be wrong. But that is not what happened in Somalia. The UN was supposed to act as a facilitator for negotiations. Instead, primarily at American insistence, it assumed the role as the biggest warlord in the country. Imposing its will on all the other warlords, assuming them to all be of equal strength and anxious for peace, which they certainly were not. Aideed's Habr Gidr clan was winning the war until the UN 'do-gooders' showed up. The only option presented to Aideed since then has been for him to sit at the same table with lesser warlords and treat them as his equal. No man will do such a thing! I ask you, why would a person who has a chance to take it all be willing to negotiate for less? It simply doesn't make sense; yet it is exactly what the UN tried to get Aideed to do, so he fought back the only way he knew how with bullets and blood."

"Neither the United States nor the United Nations wants to rule Somalia," Blackburn chimed in, getting bored with simply listening when he had an opinion to share. "It would be like trying to manage a street gang in heat. Besides, what the hell would they want with it?"

"No, you're right, Top," countered Assiri. "Neither the UN nor America wants to rule Somalia, but neither do they want it ruled by Aideed because that would be an admission that violence is still the way to political power. The West would rather a 'kinder and gentler' approach to acquiring power be rewarded, totally dismissing the fact that Somalia is no more ready for democratic elections to mirror the American experience than Saudi Arabia is. Quite frankly, who rules Somalia and how they come to power is really no one's business but the Somalis. Everybody else simply needs to sit this one out until one person or one group has enough control inside these borders that Somalia can even remotely once again be called a country."

"As for what they would want with it, First Sergeant," Assiri responded to the second half of Blackburn's question, "how does the beginning of a 'New World Order' sound to you. President Bush used those exact words in describing the world following the collapse of the Soviet Union and again following the defeat of Saddam during Desert Storm, never pausing for even one instant to appreciate how such a declaration would sound to non-American ears. But I suppose such arrogance is to be expected. After all, what exactly are the responsibilities of a lone superpower if not ending civil wars while simultaneously creating a market for American goods?"

"By the way, First Sergeant," Assiri continued with what appeared to be a response he himself had listened to many times before. "What exactly is a 'New World Order' anyway? Will we recognize it when we see it? The only thing I can visualize is that it will be shaped like a pyramid and America will be at the apex with all of the other countries jockeying for positions near the bottom. Sorry, but I just can't play along with a 'New World Order' that has America dictating its desires to others and making slave laborers out of third world people."

"You know what Moe?" Blackburn retorted, finally having heard enough and losing control of his already short temper. "You take great pleasure in reminding Americans of their simplistic views regarding a complex world but I'm getting a little fed up with your simplistic views of a very complex world as well. What you, your uncle Osama, and every Arab male in this room are really advocating is a return to tribal government. In case you haven't noticed, while the Muslim world has been in a deep sleep dreaming of days long past, nation-states replaced the tribe as a governing unit. It's time that you woke up and admitted to this fact. Your desire to dismantle the modern world and govern it with tribal law is as backward an idea as doing away with the automobile and returning to the horse and buggy. It simply won't fly in the face of reality. Such a belief is even more ludicrous than the United Nation's belief that the world is ready for a non-government government with itself at the helm!"

As soon as Blackburn opened his mouth Dash knew that he was about to witness another spirited discussion between he and Assiri. It seemed an odd and inopportune time for such a discussion but he knew that it would take place anyway. Even though they were running short on time and would probably be dead by morning why should today be any different?

"The 'fassel'," continued Blackburn, "or tribal court you're advocating the world return to served Islam well in the past, but it is no substitute for a world that revolves around international business and commerce. It is too slow, too cumbersome, and too damn parochial to be effective. Modern courts must consider all points of view, from all nationalities and religions, and the communality of the tribe is much too narrowly focused to be capable of doing this. In a fassel, seniority is based more on age than on education or experience, a fact that guarantees social, political, and economic stagnation," he warned by waving his own finger back at Assiri. "The success of America stands in stark contrast to this rule of seniority. As an upstart country without long established roots of its own, America kicks ass and for a people like the Arabs, people who believe that success can only be built upon a solid foundation of the past, she repudiates all that you hold sacred. After all, not too many old people in any society embrace change. And Arab culture is old, Moe. Like everyone else, Arabs would rather stay in their comfort zone and do things the way they have always done it. Not a very good idea in a rapidly changing world, a world where individualism and personal accomplishment are considered to be of greater value than a person's family name, tribe, religion, or nationality. All things that the fassel completely ignores."

"I dis…" began Assiri.

"In fact," emphasized Blackburn, pointing his finger straight into the air and interrupting Assiri's rebuttal, "the fassel negates individual responsibility and thought, believing that a person does right or wrong because of what he is rather than who he is. Making the fassel incapable of rendering an objective opinion on what is best for everyone and not just the chosen few. The fassel also places the rights of women and nontribal members right up there with farm animals —they have none. Prejudice is what drives fassel opinion and Islam, not secular law, forms the basis for all decisions."

Assiri thought about saying something in response then thought better of it. He could tell that Blackburn was not yet finished with his own diatribe.

"Hell," Blackburn raged, "even Hammurabi saw the fallacy of tribal law, which led to his codification of laws for everyone, taking power away from the regional tribes and making the application of law more universal and egalitarian. Equal justice for everyone, at least in theory, was promoted in order to put an end to all the petty bickering that goes with the fassel."

"So," he said with a little less fervor in his voice, "if your uncle gets his way, Moe, there will be more wars, not fewer. Because the world will revert to a time when clusters of people, call them tribes, religions, cults, whatever, had more power than the state, a time when there was perpetual war. Like you said, as a compassionate man and a soldier I don't want to see this happen."

Finally calming down Blackburn drew a deep breath, looked Assiri squarely in the eyes and concluded, "So why don't you quit trying to blow smoke up my ass about what a wonderful world this would be if we only returned to the past. It's bullshit and you know it. What Osama really wants is control, just like any other megalomaniac. He could give a shit if people were freer or happier as a result."

"That's quite a rendition of history, First Sergeant," Assiri calmly stated, refusing to succumb to what he saw as taunts from Blackburn. "Unfortunately it is revisionist regarding the facts. Many of the nation-states that you seem so fond of were created by the western powers to serve their own economic ambitions. The entire continent of Africa and most of the Middle East would fit this description. The people living inside those nation-states have very little in common with one another other than that they coexisted within a geographical boundary drawn on a map by colonial powers. All of these boundaries were centered on the resources of the area with no consideration given to the many tribes living there or their historical relationships with one another. As a consequence, many of those tribes are now required to consult with ancient enemies if they wish to live peacefully beside them like natural neighbors. Something I can assure you they most certainly do not want. So your belief that these tribes will put aside their long-standing animosities toward one another simply for the benefit of a faceless state bureaucracy is worse than wishful thinking, it is stupid. Which is why you now find yourself up to your collective asses with problems in a place like Somalia," he emphasized by shaking his own finger back at Blackburn.

"Another area in which you are mistaken regards my uncle, Osama bin Laden, as being a megalomaniac," Assiri cautioned. "He may be a lot of things, wealthy, charismatic, charming and intelligent, but he is most certainly not a megalomaniac. He shuns the spotlight and is quite willing to sacrifice both his wealth as well as his life for his beliefs. These are two things that a person who believes himself to be omnipotent usually isn't known for. Then again your interpretation fits into the simplistic analysis of most Americans. For you it is either all good or all bad, all right or all wrong, black or white, positive or negative. As linear thinkers you refuse see the many shades of gray or combinations of good and bad that are in all things." With a final wave of his hand Assiri signaled that the time for conversation was over. With typical Arab abruptness he wrapped things up.

"We could talk for days of such matters and I truly wish that we had that kind of time because I enjoy the challenge of our discussions together. But your chariot awaits you, gentlemen, and I can assure you that time is the one thing you do not have a lot of. So, this conversation is over."

With that said Assiri rose from his seat and motioned towards the door, guarded by two large guards with flowing beards and coal black eyes. Eyes firmly riveted on the two Americans, wishing for them to say or do something foolish so that they would be justified in gunning them down, despite the fact that they were invited guests. To their disappointment neither Dash nor Blackburn were foolish enough to grant them their wish. Sensing the danger, both simply stood up and walked out the door without saying another word.

Entering the courtyard of the once abandoned former police station, the two men approached their Hummvee, opened their rucksacks and withdrew from them some civilian clothes that would make them appear to be more like reporters than their desert camouflage uniforms did. Besides, their beards had grown long enough to make them appear to be out of place while wearing a uniform, drawing stares and eliciting questions from other soldiers.

As they were going through their rucksacks retrieving their "civvies," changing clothes as they did so, they were kept under the watchful eye of one of the guards who had been inside the room with Assiri. Even so, both Dash and Blackburn found the opportunity to take small pistols out of their rucksacks and slip them inside the waistbands of their blue jeans. Both men carried the small handguns for occasions such as this, when a hide-gun would be their only option. Dash concealed a SIG Sauer P-230, .380 pistol inside his pants and Blackburn concealed a small rimfire Smith and Wesson .22 caliber Kit Gun revolver inside his. Though they would no longer be loaded for bear as reporters, they certainly were not going back out into the mean streets of Aideed's Mogadishu with no protection at all.

**

"This is quite the truck!" commented Blackburn as he admired the plush interior of the hardened Toyota Land Cruiser. The little Japanese vehicle had every available option imaginable: power windows, power seats, Alpine stereo and an On Star navigational system that apparently received its feed from a military satellite orbiting high overhead. At least Dash was unaware of any commercial satellites offering such a service to cover the vast wasteland of Somalia. Yet this system was programmed with a map of Mogadishu that told them their ten-digit location with unerring accuracy. It had to have been tied in to a sophisticated system somewhere, as was the cell phone mounted on the console.

"Yeah," replied Dash, agreeing with Blackburn's assessment of the vehicle. "Theoretically the Kevlar body plating and Mylar coating on the windows are supposed to be able to stop a 7.62mm round. A theory that I hope we don't have to validate."

"No," laughed Blackburn, "it wouldn't do well for Toyota's marketing plan if CNN showed film footage of our bullet riddled bodies slumped over in the seats. Play hell with their sales pitch, wouldn't it?"

Blackburn was back in his element now. Having vented some of his frustrations with Assiri, he was now acting as happy as a Lark, seemingly oblivious to the danger they faced.

"Major," Blackburn continued with a twinkle in his eye, "how would you like to be the officer tasked with briefing the press on what two dead American soldiers were doing in Aideed's Mogadishu carrying press credentials and hidden hand guns? That would be Saturday Night Live material, wouldn't it? A person wouldn't know whether to grab for his ass or his career before attempting to answer all the reporters' unanswerable questions," he laughed.

Blackburn seemed to possess a sense of humor unlike any other Dash had ever witnessed. The more dire the conditions the greater his humor. The prospect of danger always seemed to bring out his devilish side. Whether it was his way of dealing with stress or simply an attempt to fortify the courage of those around him Dash never knew, but his sense of timing always seemed to be out of place. When others were ready to give up, Blackburn was always at his contagious best.

"Certainly wouldn't be much fun," Dash answered, visualizing Colonel Degan having to field such questions and at the same time wondering about Blackburn's fixation with the macabre vision of their own death.

"Tell you what I'd say though," Blackburn continued, his voice suddenly serious and rising with emotion. "I'd tell the bastards that at least two of us died doing the right thing instead of hiding behind barbed wire pulling our puds. Press might not understand that answer but the soldiers who heard it damn sure would. There are some unhappy young men wearing uniforms right now who are pissed off with the lack of UN response regarding Durant. Wouldn't take much to get them to fix bayonets and go back into the city looking for him."

"I know," said Dash, "but this is the way to do it, the way we are trying to do it now, low level, without a lot of trigger-happy people involved. There's not much point in killing several hundred more Somalis when all the other options haven't been exhausted."

"No," Blackburn responded with regret. "I suppose that blowing up Mogadishu wouldn't be the right answer, but neither is doing nothing. If America withdraws from Somalia after a gunfight and a few casualties, all of the global idiots out there will believe that we don't have the will to fight. Every tinhorn gunman and dictator watching will be willing to test U.S. resolve in the future, ultimately resulting in an attack on America herself. Unfortunately no one in America seems to see it coming, pretending that if we leave them alone they will leave us alone, forgetting that for every McDonalds built in a foreign country there is an ancient power base that is being challenged. And it isn't the building of the McDonalds that is wrong, it's the reluctance to see the dangers associated with building it in a country other than America. It is too obvious a danger to constantly dismiss. I'm telling you, Sir, one day one of these extremist bastards is going to get their hands on a WMD and the world is not going to be pleased with the results."

The two drove in silence for maybe one minute as they both thought about the ramifications Somalia would have on U.S. foreign policy when, bored with the silence, Blackburn finally said, "But first we have to deal with the moment. Where to, boss?"

"Let's start at the Olympic Hotel and see where it takes us."

CHAPTER 23

Driving past the airfield both Dash and Blackburn cast wistful glances at the security the gate guards and concertina wire promised, a pleasant thought that was difficult to resist as both men fought hard to control their growing apprehensions. Returning to the streets of Mogadishu without a large contingent of well-armed men was not something that either one of them wanted to do; it was something that they had to do. Their sense of honor demanded it.

Avoiding the temptation to drive onto the airfield they continued north, approaching the K-4 traffic circle which, in the noonday heat, appeared to be relatively normal. At least they weren't noticing the usual hate-filled glances they always received in this part of town, failing to remember that they were no longer soldiers riding in a Hummvee bristling with guns. Instead they were now civilian reporters riding in a decked-out Toyota Land Cruiser that had *"Al-Jazeera News"* stenciled on its sides, a disguise that clearly placed them in a different light amongst the normally hostile Somalis.

Rounding the K-4 circle, Blackburn sped the Toyota northwest on Via Lenin Road, past the many obstacles they had fought their way through in the dark three nights ago and past the two vehicles remaining from the French commander's Feed The Children food convoy. The trucks were now just two more rusting hulks of metal as they had already been stripped bare, adding to the ambiance of despair in the hopeless city. Except for the still smoldering debris scattered along the roadside, there was no evidence that the scene had recently been a battlefield where the enormous convoy of tanks, condors, and 10th Mountain vehicles fought their way into the heart of the city. The road had been picked clean of anything of value. Some enterprising entrepreneurs had even salvaged the thousands of spent shell casings once scattered along the road.

However, after they turned northeast on National Street and approached Hawlwadig Road the scene changed, taking on a definite look of having recently been a battlefield. Many of the buildings where the Somali gunmen had fired from were now piles of rubble, looking as if a huge storm or earthquake had leveled the area. Children could be seen picking through the debris scavenging whatever brass they could find or whatever copper wire still remained inside the now demolished walls. They would later take their findings to the Bakarra Market where it would be sold by the pound to traders who would melt it down and sell the copper and brass on the open market.

At this time of day the large crowds were not yet out, giving the many streets and alleys the ghostly look of an abandoned city. Dogs could be seen roaming around the neighborhoods, carrying bones and pieces of meat that neither Dash nor Blackburn wanted to know the origins of. People could also be seen wearing bandages, covering recent wounds received as a result of the ferocious fighting that had consumed this part of the city. Many of the wounded had simply been trying to flee the area and had been caught in a withering fire from the helicopters flying high overhead. Most had not been fighters, but hapless people caught in a war raging around their homes, suffering the unfortunate consequences of having been in the right place, but at the wrong time.

As bad as the buildings looked on National Street, when they turned on Hawlwadig Road and drove the four blocks to the Olympic Hotel it was if they had entered a graveyard. The area around the hotel didn't look like ground zero, it looked lower than zero. A person could not have placed a hand on any of the buildings along Hawlwadig Road, near the Olympic Hotel, and not covered at least two bullet holes with their palm. It was the most devastated city that either Dash or Blackburn had ever seen, reminiscent of the many pictures depicting the aftermath of the fighting in Berlin or Moscow during World War II. Even in broad daylight the scene was almost frightening. For the men who had been trapped here for one long night, it had to have been pure hell.

Even though the streets were relatively empty, when Blackburn pulled up in front of the hotel and they stepped out of the vehicle, their press credentials plainly visibly on their shirts, they were immediately swarmed by a mob of Somali men that materialized from out of nowhere. One moment they had been alone, the next moment they found themselves surrounded by a howling mob of well-armed militia fighters.

Shouting and yelling in Arabic, a language that had once been taught in the Somali school system, the fighters began pushing and shoving one another to be first in line. All wanted to be interviewed by these two Al-Jazeera reporters, each claiming to have some unique story to share. The more aggressive screamed out that they had killed many American soldiers, or had rescued many Somali wounded, or had been extremely brave under the withering helicopter fire. Like people everywhere they just basically wanted to take advantage of the available opportunity to bullshit their way into print.

At first the two Americans were overwhelmed by the boisterous crowd, trying to ask what they felt to be intelligent questions but shocked by the volume of the responses and the aggressive mannerisms of many of the Somalis, already high on khat and whiskey. The combination of which was something that had been occurring with increasing frequency since the relief agency personnel arrived in Somalia with their western drug of choice, alcohol.

Dash asked a man nearest him how many Somalis had been killed in the fighting and the man answered five thousand. Blackburn then asked the same man how many Americans had been killed and the man again answered five thousand. Dash then asked him how he knew that five thousand Americans had been killed and he screamed, shaking his rifle above his head, "Because I killed all of them!" Following which Blackburn looked at Dash and said, "This isn't going to be nearly as easy as I thought it would be."

And so it went for several hours as the two of them dealt with an entourage of charlatans that would have made a dildo salesman blush. Each man boasting why his story was worth listening to, as opposed to that of his friend, who just happened to be standing next to him shouting out his own version of the truth. When Blackburn asked one of them why his story was more important than that of his friend, he raucously answered, "because my friend hid behind me the entire time, shooting at the Americans from beneath my armpits!" Then he laughed hysterically at the mental picture he had painted for himself.

Without exception, the drugs and alcohol coursing through their veins heavily influenced each storyteller's recollection of events. Having to sort through their many and barely lucid tales left both Dash and Blackburn wondering why the hell anyone would ever want to be a reporter.

Then, just when they thought that their afternoon had been a colossal waste of time, a young boy appeared in the crowd and showed them a CVC helmet that he had taken from one of the helicopters. "The one down the road," he told them, pointing in the direction of the crash site Dash and Blackburn had gone to that fateful morning. He also claimed to have seen a pilot being taken away, carried high above the crowd, bleeding but still alive. "The helmet," he said, "belonged to that pilot."

Intrigued by his recounting of events, Dash asked to see the helmet, but first he had to give the kid five dollars in case he wouldn't give the helmet back. Trust was a commodity in short supply in Mogadishu. While digging into his pocket for the money, the young man casually rotated the helmet so Dash could read the name on the back; it read "CWO Durant, Night Stalkers." Dash almost ripped his pants apart trying to fish out the five dollars. Knowing that they now had something worth pursuing, they separated themselves from the mob of boisterous Somali men by coaxing the boy into the back seat of the Land Cruiser. They then drove him to the spot where he had found the helmet. As they suspected, it was the crash site of the Black Hawk Super Six Four, the helicopter that had been piloted by Michael Durant. They now had their first actionable lead.

Leaving the vehicle parked in the street, Dash and Blackburn accompanied the boy through the maze of shacks and alleys of wind drifted sand to where the remains of the aircraft could clearly be seen. The boy explained that he had been standing in the street listening to the sound of gunfire when the helicopter had come crashing down. Already frightened, he told them that when the helicopter crashed he had taken refuge beneath the hulk of an abandoned automobile, pointing at a rusting pile of metal directly across the road from the aircraft. He had been hiding under the car when the mob stormed the crash site. From beneath it he watched the entire chain of events.

He told of the bravery of two soldiers who had fast roped onto the site to protect the pilot from the swarming mob. He described for them the hysterical anger that possessed the swirling mob as they fought with the two soldiers. Many Somalis had been killed but eventually they had flowed over the crash sight like molten lava, killing all except for the pilot, whom they carried away.

Because the fight had been filmed by an observation helicopter flying high above the crash site, the two soldiers, Randy Shugart and Gary Gordon, would both be posthumously awarded the Congressional Medal of Honor for fending off the rampaging mob for as long as they did. By all accounts, it had been an act of extreme bravery by two very brave men who had purposely placed themselves in harm's way trying to protect the defenseless pilot until help arrived. Unfortunately, help did not arrive until long after both men had been killed and Mike Durant had been taken prisoner.

Everything the boy told them seemed to match what they knew to be the facts. So they told him that if he really wanted to be on television he should take them to where they had taken the pilot so they could interview all of them together and take their picture. The boy was very much in favor of doing this but he truthfully acknowledged that he didn't know where the mob had taken the pilot because he had remained hidden until they began carrying him away. It was then, while they were distracted with their prisoner, that he had been able to pick up the helmet, making his own escape in the opposite direction. Finally, he confessed to them that he hadn't seen the pilot since that afternoon.

Dash asked him if he thought he could discover where the pilot had been taken and would he be willing to take them there.

"Sure," said the boy, "but it will cost you, umm, one hundred American dollars."

"Sold," Blackburn quickly responded, "but not until we actually see the pilot. Now go find him and meet us back in front of the hotel as soon as you can."

Returning to their vehicle, they watched as the young boy streaked down the road, apparently with a destination in mind. They didn't care where he went, just as long as he produced results. Climbing back into the Land Cruiser, Blackburn turned the ignition key to start the truck and nothing happened. Switching the ignition to the off position he once again tried to start the truck and again, nothing happened.

"Now what the hell is wrong?" he said as he pulled the hood release. "Just what we need now is car trouble." Getting back out of the vehicle he walked to the front, raised the hood and exclaimed in a surprised voice, "I'll be damned, some enterprising Somali stole our battery!" They had left the vehicle unattended for less than five minutes. "And they did it without lifting the hood!" said a smiling but genuinely baffled Blackburn. In Somalia nothing was ever safe.

CHAPTER 24

After Blackburn stole a battery out of a Toyota pickup to replace the one in the Land Cruiser — turn about being fair play in Mogadishu — the two of them drove back to the hotel and began waiting for the boy to return.

By now it was late afternoon and both the hotel and the nearby Bakara Market were teeming with people. Blackburn found a place to park the Toyota on the east side of the Olympic Hotel and as the sun began its descent, seeming to disappear into the distant shimmer of the Indian Ocean, the four story building provided shade for them.

They remained with the vehicle, reclining the bucket seats inside it, catching what little sleep they could. If they left it unattended anywhere but on a secure compound, the roving street gangs would steal everything but the paint.

As they observed the comings and going of the neighborhood, they constantly had to fend off would be media legends that, noticing the Al-Jazeera News logo on the vehicle, insisted on telling them their stories. All of which were told with such embellishments that one-hundred men could not have performed the feats of bravery each of them alleged to have performed single handedly. Sitting in the Toyota watching the people slowly mill about Dash and Blackburn noticed that even though the fighting in this neighborhood had exceeded anything either one of them had experienced in Vietnam, it had been just another day in Mogadishu for the Somalis. Now that it was over they were content to chew their khat, drink their whiskey, and tell lies to anyone willing to listen to their stories. In somewhat of a pathological way, the Somalis seemed to be rather content with their pitiful lives, like an alcoholic who refuses to admit that he has a problem, blaming his faults on everybody but himself, resisting any efforts to help him.

***

As they sat in the Land Cruiser killing time, Blackburn revealed to Dash what it was that had so obviously changed his demeanor from one of being a buoyant, can-do type of man to being a crotchety old curmudgeon difficult to get along with; he had decided to retire.

"Just to keep you informed, Sir," Blackburn said out of the blue. "When I return to Bragg, I'm going to drop my retirement paperwork."

"Why now, Top?" Dash asked in genuine surprise to the unexpected announcement. "I thought you were going for thirty?"

"Yeah, that was the original plan. But I talked it over with the wife and we've come to grips with the reality that the Army is going to get sucked into more and more missions like Somalia. I did not become a soldier to be a social worker or a cop. Nothing wrong with being either, but if that is what I wanted to do, I wouldn't be in the military, I would be a social worker or a cop. This nonsense of traveling around the globe pissing on dysfunctional people's fires is beginning to wear on me. You do know that when we are finished in Somalia, whatever the hell that might entail, both Haiti and Bosnia are looming on the horizon?"

"Yeah, I know," said Dash, "but that doesn't necessarily mean that you will be a part of it."

"Major," Blackburn said in an exasperated voice, "the military is being drawn down to the size of a gnat's ass while the requirements to deploy are growing. Just who in the hell do you think will be deployed if not people like us? I've already got over twenty years in and you're getting close to it yourself. Guys like us have no leverage when picking and choosing our assignments. Those pricks at Army Personnel Command never go anywhere themselves but they don't even think twice about sending us on back to back unaccompanied assignments. I'm just getting fed up with being gone all of the time and never really accomplishing anything while doing it. I mean, who really gives a damn about Somalia for Christ's sake? What in the hell do missions like this have to do with defending America?"

What Blackburn was expressing were feelings that many soldiers were experiencing. The growing belief in Washington that it was now fashionable to place a soldier on every third world street corner to demonstrate to the world how compassionate and caring America had become was not a vision shared by many of those actually having to do it. In the six months he had been in Somalia, Dash had killed several people and watched in disbelief as the American casualties grew in numbers of dead and wounded. He had also been shot at, spit on by people known to have tuberculosis, been hit with bricks and boards on numerous occasions and been involved in at least half a dozen fistfights with Somalis. And not one damn thing had been accomplished by any of it. Somalia was as bad now as it had been the day America first arrived, maybe even worse. Such awareness caused those who were old enough to have experienced Vietnam to make comparisons between the two and it scared the hell out of them. Defending America was one thing, they had all signed up to do that, but defending a world that you do not own from itself is something entirely different. No one but God or someone who thought that they were God would voluntarily sign up to do something like that.

"To be perfectly honest, Top," Dash responded, "I have no intentions of staying beyond twenty years myself. If I could, I'd drop my paperwork with you because I smell another Vietnam out there. There are too many people coming to power in America with short memories and I fear that one of them will eventually get us into a war to rid the world of evil, not just communism. I know that sounds bizarre and is difficult to get your mind around in this day and age, sounding like something from out of the Crusades, but it could happen if the climate were right. Hell, in the right political climate anything is possible. I realize that a leader would have to suffer a God complex to start a war to eliminate evil. I mean ultimately, destroying evil means killing the antichrist. You know, slaying the devil. A pretty damn presumptuous mission for a mere mortal to give to other mere mortals. But if the political and religious stars were all in alignment with one another, it could happen. Before it does I want to be long gone. As a young man I went on a witch-hunt looking for communists in Vietnam and we all know how that one turned out. I can't imagine what a witch-hunt looking for evil people might look like. Hell, the world can't even agree on a definition of evil much less put an end to all of it. After all, fighting against evil is what bin Laden claims he is doing, and I believe him to be a complete mad man!"

***

It was well after midnight when the young boy returned, and this time he was not alone. Three hardened Somali gunmen, undoubtedly members of Aideed's Habr Gidr clan, were escorting him.

Dash was on watch with Blackburn resting in the passenger seat beside him when he first noticed the trio of gunmen, two of whom carried AK-47's like firewood atop their shoulders. They turned the corner of the hotel and walked purposely in their direction. At first he failed to notice the boy, following along behind them like a truant child being led into the principal's office.

Tapping Blackburn's shoulder Dash said, "Better wake up, I think we have company."

"Yeah, I see them," Blackburn answered, sitting up straight and rubbing his five-day growth of beard. "This ought to be interesting." Both men felt for the comforting bulge of the pistol that each had hidden in his waistband, seeking the security of knowing it was still there if they needed protection.

"Remember, Top," Dash cautioned, "we're reporters. Don't overreact to anything they say or do."

"Roger that, Sir. I'll follow your lead," he replied.

Two of the three gunmen were dressed in the typical skirt, the ma-awis, worn by most of the Somali men. The third, walking in the center of the trio, was dressed in western attire, wearing a pair of black slacks, a white T-shirt, and an unbuttoned long sleeve shirt that flapped loosely about him. In the dim light afforded by the numerous cooking fires still burning along the street, Dash could see that the man walking in the middle also wore a pair of New Balance tennis shoes. The trademark "N" on the sides seemed to blink on and off as it reflected the light from the many fires he walked past. This man was apparently unarmed and walked with the body posture of one on a mission.

With the windows already rolled down, Dash stuck his head outside the vehicle and yelled for the boy to come to him, acting as if he had not noticed the gunmen he was walking closely behind. Instead of approaching closer the boy stopped where he was, looking nervously about, and the three Somali men approached. Never a good sign.

"Watch yourself!" whispered Blackburn.

"So you are the reporters who wish to speak with the American pilot," said the man in the middle. "Why would you wish to do such a thing?"

"Because we are reporters," answered Dash. "The pilot is a big story for Al-Jazeera. They sent us here to get an interview with him."

Dash was hopeful that the man he was speaking to would be as anxious to get his face on television as the other Somalis he had spoken with had been. But noticing the distrust in his voice, Dash immediately recognized this to be a false hope. This man had an interest in something much larger than achieving his fifteen minutes of fame.

"You do not look like reporters," said the Somali, eyeing Dash warily. "You look like CIA!"

Despite the threatening tone with which it had been delivered, such a pronouncement by a Somali was not unusual. Even when they had been wearing their uniforms while escorting humanitarian deliveries in the Black Sea neighborhood of central Mogadishu, they had often been accused of being CIA spies. They had a canned response to such an accusation and when delivered it usually elicited laughter from the Somali accuser. Either because he failed to detect the look in this Somali's eyes or he simply misread the signs, Blackburn used it again.

"And just what and the hell is a CIA?" he said. Phonetically pronouncing CIA as "See Ya."

"Get out of your vehicle!" the Somali hissed. "If you think this is some kind of a joke," he spit, "I will kill you, skin you, cook you and then eat your heart for my breakfast!"

The encounter was one of those bittersweet moments in life. Bitter because they had found a Somali who wasn't playing a game with them and sweet for the very same reason. They now knew that they were speaking to someone who was not simply blowing smoke up their ass.

Reluctantly they stepped outside the truck, one on each side. The two Somalis with rifles moved to each side so they could better cover the reporters and protect the man in the middle. It was obvious that they were bodyguards, but not experienced bodyguards because both kept their rifles atop their shoulder, a position that would require several critical seconds before it could be brought down into a firing position. Then again, they probably reasoned, what trouble could be expected from two unarmed reporters?

"We are not here to cause any trouble," Dash began apologizing as soon as his feet touched the hot asphalt. "We are sorry if we offended you."

"Yes, Sir," reaffirmed Blackburn, "no harm intended."

The Somali never said a word in response but glared at them instead for several seconds, making both men nervous as they glanced from Somali to Somali in anticipation of which man each would shoot first if things got out of control. The Somali leader, misreading their anxious glances to be caused by fear rather than anticipation, finally felt that he had them properly intimidated and reached out with his hands to check the press credentials pinned to the front of Dash's shirt.

"Why would the Arab world be interested in hearing from an American prisoner instead of from the Somali fighters who captured him?" he casually asked while reading the credentials.

"The interview is not intended for the Arab world," Dash quickly answered. "Al-Jazeera intends to sell the interview to the American media for a tidy sum. We have already spoken to many of the Somali fighters; we know that the Arab world is interested in hearing from them."

"Now you're speaking my language," the Somali smiled. "How much will Al-Jazeera pay me for taking you to the American for the interview?" he asked, explaining his real reason for being here tonight.

"I can't answer that," Dash replied, "but I am sure they will make it worth your trouble."

"My name is Ali Hassan," the man said, smiling and extending his hand in false friendship, "maybe we can do some business."

Ali Hassan explained to Dash and Blackburn that in order for him to help them arrange for an interview that he had to have $10,000 in U.S. dollars, up front. A typical sum that many of the Somalis had asked for in the past whenever they had been asked for assistance, even if that assistance was something as simple as emptying a trash can. Blackburn maintained that the Somalis had arrived at this figure because of the once popular American television show that used to play on Mogadishu television, *The $10,000 Pyramid.* Having no other explanation for such a common occurrence themselves, everyone else simply accepted Blackburn's logic.

Because of their past experiences with the Somalis, Ali's offer hadn't come as a surprise to the Americans, but neither were they in any position to do anything about it. They certainly didn't have that kind of money with them, nor did they have access to any CIA operatives that could get it for them. Instead, they did the next best thing by taking a page from the CIA playbook; they lied to him.

"I can get you five times that amount," bragged Blackburn, causing all three Somalis eyes to light up like streetlights. "But first you will have to offer proof to our bosses in Qatar that you have knowledge of where the pilot is and that you have the ability to arrange for an interview. They will not pay without this verification."

"I understand," said Ali, "they are businessmen, just like me. What would it take to convince them that I am telling the truth?"

"Well," answered Dash, "you can take us to where he is at, show us that he is still alive, and we can vouch for you."

"No," responded Ali, shaking his head as if to emphasize his point, "that wouldn't be a good idea."

"Why not?" asked Blackburn. "It would give us proof to take to our boss for you."

"I know," replied Ali, "but there are other people I must consult with first."

"Take us to these people, we will help you convince them," Dash added.

"No!" answered Ali, again shaking his head. "These are things I must do for myself." He had apparently already decided that he did not want to split the money more than three ways. Then, attempting another approach, he asked, "What if I bring you a picture of the pilot, would that be proof?"

"It would be better than nothing," responded Dash, "but it would be better if one of us actually saw him before having our boss send the money. You know, $50,000 is a lot of money." He hoped that the thought of the money would entice him to take risks that he was so far reluctant to take.

It was obvious that the thought of that much money was having an effect on Ali, as it was on the two gunmen with him. All three were practically salivating at the thought of what they could do with $50,000. But, alas, Ali wouldn't budge, no matter how much he was prodded by the two Americans, insisting that the best he could do on such short notice was to bring them a picture of Durant, still alive and being cared for, in exchange for the money. Once he had the money, he told them, he would arrange for the interview.

"You must go back to the reporters' pool at the airport and make arrangements for the money," instructed Ali. "I will personally take a picture of the pilot and meet with you tonight, around six O'clock, at the cigarette factory on 21 October Road. Do you know where that is?"

"Yes," Dash answered. "We'll be there."

Once the three Somalis departed, Dash asked the young boy, who had remained silently standing in the background until the three Somali men left, to follow them and come back to him with information on where they went, offering him $100 for his troubles. Then, noticing that he no longer had the CVC helmet, Dash asked him where he had left it.

"Ali," the young man said pointing over his shoulder, "he took it from me. He intends to sell it to another reporter. One from America." Then he turned and ran away, anxious to earn the hundred dollars Dash had promised him.

"As if we need a real reporter screwing this up," Dash said to Blackburn after the boy was gone.

"You know of course," Blackburn said, watching the young boy disappear into the darkness, "we're more than likely being set up for a hit."

"I know," replied Dash, "but it is all that we've got and we're going to have to accept the risk."

***

The sun was just peeking over the horizon when the boy returned to the vehicle. He collected his $100 from Dash while desperately trying to raise the ante. He knew where the men had gone and he knew that they desperately wanted this information. But, try as he might, he could not get Dash or Blackburn to come up with any more money. They couldn't. With the hundred he had already given to the boy, Dash had only one hundred-dollar bill remaining and in Somalia a reporter who had no money got no information at all. They needed to keep something in reserve.

Reluctantly the boy told the reporters that he had followed the three men to a location not far from the cigarette factory. "To a house that was heavily guarded," he said, "with snipers on the surrounding rooftops." He also told them that he had seen something unusual after the three men entered the house. There had been a flash of light that had come from a window in back of the house, "as if someone had just taken a picture using a flashbulb," he said.

In an instant the two men were out of the truck asking the boy if he could take them to where he had seen this flash of light. Being a typical Somali, he said yes, but noting their obvious excitement, he demanded that they pay him $500 first. A sum that couldn't be produced between the two of them.

The money quickly became a nonissue anyway. As they were standing in the street haggling over an amount they had with them, slightly over two hundred dollars, one of the gunmen who had accompanied Ali approached, kicked the boy in the butt, and shooed him away. Blackburn, objecting to losing the services of the boy, reached out to grab him before he fled and was met with an AK-47 barrel being thrust into his chest, stopping him short, standing him straight up, putting a bruise the size of a silver dollar on his sternum. The gunman then stepped back, threatening to smash Blackburn's face with the butt of his rifle.

"Whoa! Hold it!" Dash quickly intervened, stepping between the two of them. "That is not necessary."

"Go get the money, now!" hissed the guard, pointing his rifle at Dash's head.

"Yes Sir, we're going," Dash said, holding his hands up in front of his face, backpedaling towards the door of the vehicle.

Blackburn, rubbing his bruised chest, did likewise and within seconds they had the Toyota turned and heading towards the airfield.

With the truck now speeding down Hawlwadig Road, and the threat of being shot receding into the distance, Blackburn broke the silence. "Before the sun comes up tomorrow," Blackburn threatened, still rubbing his bruised chest, "that bastard's balls are going to be hanging on our rear view mirror."

Dash didn't laugh, and not just because his heart was still in his throat, he knew by the sound of Blackburn's voice that this was not a threat, it was a promise.

***

Rounding the K-4 circle the soldiers began to have second thoughts about going onto the airfield. They weren't sure but what they might be arrested, the word possibly haven gotten out concerning what they were attempting to accomplish. The idea that two American soldiers, dressed as civilians and carrying guns, were attempting to rescue Durant by force would have caused everyone in their chain of command, all the way to the White House, to have cardiac arrest. Besides, it wasn't as if they were really going to go to the reporters' pool and call Qatar requesting money. But after parking across from the airfield and debating it, weighing all of the possibilities between going onto the field and not going, they decided to risk going because if the Somalis had anything that was good, it was their spy network. It would be just their luck, Blackburn theorized, that one of the gate guards would report back to Ali that he had never seen the reporter's vehicle return to the airfield.

Driving onto the airfield in civilian clothes was far different than it had been when in uniform. The guards ordered them out of their vehicle, passing a mirror beneath it and checking the interior for explosives while simultaneously checking their press credentials as if they were looking for diamonds, delaying them for an inordinate amount of time. Thinking that it would speed up the process, Blackburn produced his military identification card and handed it to the guard watch commander. Instead, it had just the opposite effect. The sight of the military ID caused the Italian watch commander to ask Blackburn all sorts of questions regarding his dress and facial hair, knowing that the American soldiers he had been working with did not look this way.

Uncomfortable with letting them enter the airfield the watch commander called his boss, an Italian army lieutenant with a better command of English for guidance. The lieutenant came to the gate and began asking Blackburn the same questions that the watch commander had already asked him. Causing Blackburn to argue vociferously with both of them, alternately speaking in English, German, and Arabic in order to get his points across, which only aroused greater suspicion from the lieutenant.

Patiently watching this circus from the background Dash finally approached the squabbling mob and essentially pulled rank, but with a Chicago flair attached to it. He withdrew his own military ID card, handed it to the Italian lieutenant along with a twenty-dollar bill and said, "I am Major Tom Dash, United States Army Special Operation Command, and this man is my first sergeant. We are conducting a top-secret mission for President Clinton and we are not authorized to divulge any of the details to people without a Top Secret, need-to-know security clearance. If you don't give this man back his ID card and lift the barrier arm so we can drive onto the airfield, I will make a phone call and get you fired. Now, what do you want to do?" he threatened.

Taking three steps back while pocketing the twenty dollar bill, the Italian lieutenant snapped a smart salute, followed by a resounding "Yes, Sir!" He then performed a spectacular about face and raised the barrier arm. With a sweeping motion of his arm he bowed at the waist, smiling at them as they drove past, welcoming them onto his airfield. Dash could only hope that if Ali did have someone watching this comedy, they missed the Italian's salute.

As they drove through the gate Blackburn couldn't restrain himself. He looked out the window at the lieutenant and said, "Fucking idiots!" To which the lieutenant smiled an even bigger smile and waved back. Dash simply reflected on how well hollow threats, bullshit and money worked to trump logic. Then, recalling that he was still in Somalia, wondered why that should surprise him. Since he had been in Somalia he hadn't seen anything but threats, bullshit and bribes work to get anything done. Logic was something in short supply for both the Somalis and the people who had regrettably decided to save them.

***

Now that they were on the airfield they figured they might as well continue with their ruse and parked the Toyota in front of the tent housing the press pool. That way, if someone were to look, it would appear that they were following through on their promise to Ali to wire Qatar for the money.

With the vehicle conspicuously parked where it could be seen, the two of them walked across the airfield to the hangar housing the U.S. Army Headquarters, the Ranger Task Force, and the D-boys. Walking into the hangar, Blackburn saw one of the operators sitting on his cot reading a Louie Lamour book. Recognizing him as a soldier he had served with before, he approached and said, "Sergeant Paul, it's good to see you still have all of your body parts attached."

Startled by Blackburn's voice Paul jumped to his feet and then, aware that he knew the voice even if he couldn't recognize the face said, "Top, is that you?"

"It's me, dickhead. How have you been?" Blackburn continued, offering his hand to Paul, who took it and vigorously shook it.

"I didn't recognize you with the beard and civvies," Paul said. "What the hell are you up to?"

"I can't really talk about it, it's an ongoing investigation," said Blackburn, trying to make it sound as official as he possibly could.

"I understand," replied Paul, even though he really didn't. "Need any help?"

"Yes," answered Blackburn, "but I don't want to get any more people involved than there already are. By the way, this is Major Tom Dash, Commander of Charlie Company, 96th Civil Affairs Battalion. Major, Sergeant Dave Paul, D-boy extraordinaire."

"Pleasure, Sir."

"Likewise, Sergeant."

"I need a favor Sergeant Paul," continued Blackburn.

"Name it, Top."

"I need two weapons and a couple hundred rounds of ammunition."

"Would that be long guns or short guns, First Sergeant?" Paul smiled.

"Rifles," answered Blackburn, patting his stomach. "I've already got a handgun."

Taking a key ring off his belt Paul walked to the back of the hangar and opened a large wall locker chained to the hangar frame. Inside were several M-16's and 9mm pistols. "Take your pick," said Howe. "All of these weapons were written off as a combat loss following Desert Storm. You don't even have to return them. Anything else you need?"

"One large gym bag," Blackburn said with authority.

"Take mine," said Paul, dumping the contents of his bag on the hangar floor. "I'll get another. Anything else?"

"Yeah," smiled Blackburn, holding up the empty bag. "You wouldn't happen to have fifty-thousand dollars I could fill this with, would you?"

"What?" Paul asked incredulously.

"Never mind," said Blackburn, still smiling.

Now that they had their weapons, and it was not yet 1000 hours, they did what all soldiers do when there is a pause in the action. They went back to the Toyota, crawled inside, turned on the air conditioner and went to sleep.

***

After three hours of sleep both Dash and Blackburn were prepared to plan that night's adventure. They would arrive at the cigarette factory early, well before dark, telling anyone they encountered there that they were to meet with Ali, flashing their press credentials, and avoiding any small talk as best they could. Which would not be easy since the press credentials attracted Somali war stories like camel dung attracts flies. But it was a plan.

Once inside the facility they would identify all the entry and exit points to the building, placing soda cans filled with pebbles near each one. The cans would be tied to a trip wire made out of a roll of string that Blackburn had gotten from the military post office on the compound. These cans, taken from the dumpster near the Ranger hangar, would serve as an early warning device when placed near each window, door, or shellhole big enough for a gunman to crawl through.

The plan was to get Ali to take the bag without inventorying the contents, leading them to where Durant was being hidden. They already knew that it wasn't far from the cigarette factory where they would be meeting. If that failed they hoped to be able to see which building they emerged from before coming to the meeting and, barring that, they hoped to be able to identify the building by the guards and snipers patrolling near it.

Ideally, what they really needed was for Ali to take them to this location, negating the requirement to run the gauntlet of shooters until after they had Durant in their custody. At which time they were prepared to make a mad dash for the Toyota and then drive to the university compound, which was nearer to the cigarette factory than either the port or the airfield.

Their back-up plan, if for some reason they were unable to make it to the university compound, was to continue on to Jesirra where they would wait for daylight before returning to the airfield. Their least favored plan was one where Ali failed to take the bait and inventoried the bag, creating a scene by trying to kill them. If that happened, then they would kill him and anyone else that he brought with him. Then, with the rifles hidden inside the Toyota, they would attempt to rescue Durant by themselves, fighting their way into and out of the building they had him hidden in. They knew from other hostage situations that Durant would not remain at any one location for an extended period of time. If they were fortunate enough to actually interview him, and they reported this location to the JTF, he would be gone before they could react.

At best, any one of these options was fraught with risks that might get them and Durant killed. None of the three were suicidal. But, as a soldier himself, if Durant were given a vote on whether they should try to rescue him or simply abort the mission, they knew that he would vote for it. So would they, their lives being insignificant to the scale of the event at hand. They had long ago made peace with the idea that one man's death is a minor event that says little. Everyone eventually dies. What a man does leading up to his death, however, can speak volumes for those that follow because in the military, especially, the ideal of self-sacrifice is a group benefit. As such, it is an ideal that makes the world a much better place for young people to learn the value of commitment to duty and honor rather than to self. How the three of them had found themselves in this position no longer mattered. What they were doing about it did.

* * *

The cigarette factory smelled of urine and human excrement. It was obvious that it had recently been used by some of the many refugees in Mogadishu as living quarters. Where those people were now was a mystery, but Dash and Blackburn found themselves completely alone in the large, two-story warehouse. There hadn't even been guards posted outside to prevent the refugees from returning, a clear indication that someone with real horsepower had told the refugees to leave, and they had. They would not return until this same someone told them that they could.

Quickly reconnoitering the building they placed the cans and trip wires near all but the main entrance, the one they had just entered, expecting Ali and his entourage to do likewise. Finding a table and chairs that had obviously been recently placed there by Ali, indicating that this was where the interview would be conducted, they arranged them so that they would have their backs to the wall. They positioned the table so they would be facing the door, forcing Ali to sit across from them and giving them a good view of the first floor as well as the catwalk on the second floor. If a shooter entered the building, the catwalk would most likely be his preference as it gave him an unobstructed view of the floor and table below.

Then, satisfied that they had given themselves their best chance for survival Dash went upstairs to the second floor and found where a shooter would most likely position himself, making certain that this spot could also be observed from where they would be sitting at the table below. As Dash walked the catwalk Blackburn moved the table to a location that gave him the clearest view of where a potential shooter would fire from, making certain that he had an unobstructed view of this spot from down below. With final preparations completed they began looking across the rooftops of the surrounding villas, looking for some sign that one of them was being used to house the pilot.

"Mark!" alerted Blackburn, shortly after looking out of a window facing southwest. "I just saw a man with a rifle walk across the rooftop overlooking the shack with the blue piece of tin in the roof. He is on the roof of the cement villa with the high walls," he continued, pointing out across the city. "Come here, you can still see him."

Looking in the direction Blackburn was pointing, Dash clearly saw the sun reflect off a pair of sunglasses a Somali guard was wearing. He could also see that he was holding a rifle in his hands. Then, looking past this man, Dash saw another shooter standing on the roof of a building south of where the first man had been seen. Clearly they were protecting something, but there was no reason to believe that it was Durant. They could have been there protecting any one of the numerous warlords traveling about the city.

Then they saw something unusual, even for this part of the city. A "technical," a pickup truck with a .50 caliber machinegun mounted in the back, pulled up next to the building they were watching and two men got out of the cab. One of them was Ali Hassan because he was wearing the same clothes he had worn the night before, to include the New Balance tennis shoes. Even from two blocks away the "N" shined like a diamond ring on the pinky finger of a Harlem pimp.

Accompanying this technical were two other Toyota pickup trucks, both of which had a canvas tarp covering the bed. Parking near the technical two men got out of each one of these vehicles as well, following Ali into the building with the patchwork blue tin roof.

"That's it," said Blackburn. "That's where they've got him. We need to bust in there and haul his ass out while we've got a chance."

"What chance!" replied an astonished and reluctant Dash. Blackburn's boldness sometimes surprised even him. "It is just now getting dark and there are snipers with a clear field of fire all the way into that building. They would kill us before we got half way there. We need to wait for Ali and go with our original plan."

"I suppose you're right," Blackburn replied disappointedly, "it wouldn't do Durant much good for us to get killed before we reached him. Hard to be this damn close and remain calm about it though," he concluded.

Still looking out the window as Blackburn prowled the room like an anxious racehorse, Dash noticed movement. People were leaving the house where they thought Durant might be hidden.

"Whether we could have made it or not is kind of a moot point now anyway," Dash said. "Here comes Ali and two of his bodyguards, the same two that were with him last night."

Hurrying back to the window, the two watched the trio approach. It was absolutely essential that they knew that only three Somalis were heading their way. An unaccounted for shooter would mean their death. Satisfied that only three were coming, they raced back down the stairs and to the table and chairs they had carefully placed inside the warehouse. As expected, when Ali entered the building he did so with only one gunman accompanying him.

Surprised to see the two reporters already sitting at the table waiting for him, Ali dutifully approached them while the lone gunman positioned himself just inside the entryway, perhaps twenty feet away from Blackburn. It was the same gunman who had struck Blackburn in the chest with the barrel of his rifle.

"I'm surprised to see that you are already here," smiled Ali. "Perhaps you are in a hurry to conduct your interview so you can get out of the city before it is too late, yes?"

"It is not that we are overly anxious to part with your good company," smiled

Blackburn. "It is just that we have other people to interview who have made the same claim that you have made to us. Like you, they too claim to have Durant and will schedule an interview for some money. For a lot less money than we are prepared to pay you, I might add."

The thought that he might lose an opportunity to steal fifty-thousand dollars caused Ali to dispense with all small talk.

"Well," he smiled, getting straight to the point, "it is a good thing that you have come to me first. I can assure you that the others are lying. They cannot have the pilot because I do."

Sitting down in the chair purposely placed there for him, Ali quickly pitched a color Polaroid picture of Michael Durant on top of the table. The picture showed Durant lying in bed, his face battered and swollen, his leg elevated as if in traction for a broken bone, but obviously still alive. Glancing at the photo it was hard to believe that he was still alive. His face was grotesquely swollen and his head looked like a pumpkin with narrow slits cut for the eyes. Even with the poor quality of the Polaroid it was obvious that he was in great pain.

"How do I know that this is a current photo?" Dash asked Ali. "My boss instructed me to not give you the money until we have actually seen the pilot. If I just take your word that the photo is recent, he will not be happy with me."

Before Ali could answer an audible rattling came from upstairs as someone or something had made contact with one of the early warning cans. Noticing that both Dash and Blackburn looked in the direction of the sound Ali quickly exclaimed, "Rats! Damn rats are running all over this warehouse. Sometimes they can scare the hell out of you when you least expect it." Still smiling he looked quickly at the two reporters as he spoke, his eyes peering into theirs with an evil glint that revealed his intentions as clearly as if he had pulled a gun from his pocket. It was a look that told both soldiers it was only going to be a matter of time before he actually did pull a gun.

"Yeah," smiled Blackburn in return, secretively withdrawing the pistol from his waistband and concealing it below the table, "Mogadishu has some of the biggest rats I have ever seen."

"Yes," replied Ali, the smile quickly vanishing from his face. "I can see that you have brought the money with you," he continued, glancing at the large, full gym bag at Dash's side.

Dash had placed the bag where it could be seen, taking their last remaining one hundred-dollar bill and conspicuously leaving one corner of the bill protruding from the bag. A corner that Ali had noticed and was now fixated on, staring intently at the large 100 figure.

"Yes," responded Dash. "We have lived up to our part of the bargain. Now take us to see the pilot, or have him brought here, and you can have the money."

"Well," Ali calmly said, rocking back in his chair. "There is a small problem with doing that at this moment. You see, Mister Aideed does not want anyone talking to the pilot right now. But he did say that we could keep the money for providing you with the photo. Kind of like selling you the picture for $50,000." His smile returned to his otherwise bland face.

At the sound of Ali's declaration, the gunman standing beside Blackburn approached the table and positioned himself not ten feet from the two of them. He stood at modified parade rest, his rifle by his side, butt to the floor, his eyes as glazed as a porcelain cat, clearly reflecting that he had not foregone his daily fix of khat. Blackburn could now see the second gunman standing in the shadows, exactly where they thought he would be, waiting for the signal from Ali to shoot, but holding his rifle by his side as well. It was obvious that none of the three expected any resistance from a couple of Al-Jazeera reporters. Tonight was planned to be just another routine robbery and murder for them. No one would be any the wiser when they found the reporters' bodies in the morning inside their burning Toyota sitting outside the fence near the airfield, all the way across town from the cigarette factory. It would be necessary that they not be suspected, as they hoped to rob and murder many more reporters before finally ransoming the pilot back to the Americans.

"We do not want any trouble," Dash cautioned, kicking the bag closer to Ali. "See for yourself, we have kept our part of the bargain."

As expected, Ali took his eyes off of the reporters for a split second in anticipation of retrieving the bag, ducking his head below the table to get his hands on it, a greedy and foolish move that sealed his and the gunmen's fate.

Before either Ali or the gunmen could react, Dash withdrew the little .380 pistol from his waistband, reached across the table, and when Ali's head reappeared shot him in the face. The force of the 90 grain Hydra-Shok Jacketed Hollow Point bullet knocked both he and the chair he had been sitting in over backwards, spilling him onto the floor and jarring lose the Colt .45 pistol he held in his hand. In a rapidly spreading pool of blood spurting from the gaping hole where his top front teeth used to be, Ali emitted a death rattle that sounded as if he were gargling.

Fired not two feet from Blackburn's ear, the little .380 had sounded as loud as a howitzer, leaving his ears ringing as the shot echoed through the cavernous warehouse. The sight and sound of which had shocked the gunman nearest Blackburn, causing him to make a belated and failed attempt to bring his own rifle into play.

With instincts honed to a fine edge after years of reacting to situations such as this, Blackburn moved with the speed of a cat. Leaping from the chair he slammed a spinning backkick into the man's chest that literally somersaulted him across the floor. The impact of the blow jarred his rifle from him and left him piled in a heap against the wall, sucking for air to fill his now empty lungs like a goldfish out of water. Still crouched low and moving rapidly, Blackburn leveled the little .22 revolver and in one spinning move fired two rapid shots at the gunman upstairs. Who even now, stoned on khat and startled by the gunfire himself, had not yet completed the move to shoulder his weapon, frozen in motion with the rifle halfway between his chest and his shoulder.

Blackburn's first shot ricocheted off the Somali's rifle barrel, striking him in the chest, causing him to cry out in pain as the little Stinger bullet ripped into his lung. Blackburn's second shot hit him in the throat, severing his trachea and lodging against the top of his spine, breaking his neck, abruptly ending his cry of pain. Both he and his rifle toppled from the catwalk, crashing with a dull thud onto the floor below, his still writhing body landing close to the breathless Somali Blackburn had kicked the air out of.

"We've got to move fast, Top!" Let's take these rifles and go get him." Dash yelled while reaching for one of the AK's lying on the floor.

"Roger," Blackburn yelled out in return, "just a minute." Then he quickly dashed over to where the breathless Somali was now stretched out on his stomach, kicking him viciously in the head before placing a foot beneath his prostrated body, flipping him over onto his back. Blackburn then took careful aim with the little revolver and put a bullet through his testicles, leaving him tightly curled into a ball, moaning in pain. Picking up the gunman's rifle, he shoved the little pistol back inside his waistband and ran back to Dash with a breathless exclamation of, "Now, I'm ready to go."

For a brief instant Dash thought that Blackburn was a lot like the Somalis. He never forgave or forgot about an indiscretion either.

With the AK's firmly in hand both men began a sprint across the open ground to where they had seen Ali and the "technicals" earlier. In their haste they failed to notice that the trucks were gone. Had they noticed they would have been more cautious in their approach. As they ran both men kept waiting for the report of gunfire, catching them in a crossfire as they moved across the opening. To their surprise, none was encountered, another telling indicator that should have alerted them to the dangers ahead. Yet their pell-mell race ended in success just outside the door of the blue tin roofed building they had observed from a distance. With Dash providing cover for him Blackburn raced straight to the front of the house and kicked open the door. Rushing inside Dash heard him yell out a few seconds later, "Damn it! They've already moved him!"

***

The 81mm mortar round in the center of the room, taped to the bottom of a chair, had been wired with a three-second-delay fuse that had activated when

Blackburn kicked open the door. The swinging door tightened the wire attached to it and pulled the pin from the nose cone of the round. The delay had given Blackburn just enough time to get inside the room and alert Dash to the fact that the pilot was no longer there. He never saw the round and the blast literally cut him in two.

When Blackburn shouted that the room was empty, Dash took one step towards the door and was met with a shock wave that blew him across the street, leaving him semiconscious and bleeding, covered with blood and tissue that was not his. As he lay there, slowly regaining his senses, he noticed that across his chest rested a leg, separated at the knee and still pulsing blood as he dumbly stared at it. The leg was also not his. It had belonged to Blackburn, whose body had been between Dash and the hot shards of shrapnel when the mortar round had exploded.

Fighting to regain his feet, Dash stumbled back across the street to find his first sergeant, refusing to accept the reality of what he was slowly realizing had just happened. Peering through the door he saw little since the interior of the room was still shrouded in smoke but in the corner of the room nearest the door lay a mangled, unrecognizable pile of flesh. First Sergeant Todd Blackburn was dead.

***

On 8 October, 1993 Ambassador Robert Oakley met with an Aideed spokesman to reiterate that America would not negotiate for the release of Michael Durant. He also emphasized that President Clinton wanted the pilot released, *now!*

One week later, on October 15, Durant was released into the custody of the Red Cross and taken back to the airfield for subsequent MEDEVAC to Landstuhl, Germany where he would be treated for a broken leg, facial fractures, and minor gunshot wounds to his arms and legs. Standing in the corridor of soldiers gathered to see Durant off was Major Tom Dash, who, along with others gathered for the occasion, was holding a small paper cup of whiskey to celebrate the pilot's release and return to the civilized world. To see him off in a proper fashion the men broke into a chorus of *"God Bless America"* as he was carried past them.

Two weeks later, these same men would be at the airfield when Mohammed Farid Aideed would be escorted by United Nations security personnel for a flight to Dar es Salaam, Tanzania, where he would participate in an attempt to bring peace to Somalia. After all of the fighting, all of the deaths, the politicians had brought the events full circle, leaving them exactly as they had found them to be one year earlier. Not one damn thing had changed in Somalia other than the number of graves dotting the countryside, both in Somalia and back home in America. Everyone involved lost.

***

On a beautiful, sunny, Texas October day a military bugler from nearby Fort Hood played a mournful rendition of taps as the coffin was slowly lowered into the ground. The large military crowd in attendance stood rigidly at attention as the drab metal box disappeared from sight.

Blackburn's death had officially been recorded as having been caused by a Somali mortar attack on the airfield. In fact, two days after the battle in Mogadishu one soldier had been killed and another wounded by a Somali mortar attack on the airfield. But most of the soldiers present at the burial knew better. They knew that although Blackburn had been killed while wasting his time in Somalia, he had not been killed for no reason. Each person wearing the uniform understood the impulse that caused Blackburn to place himself in danger when he did not have to. And they knew why he had done it. They only hoped that if ever the opportunity were given to them that they would be allowed to do the same because having to live with the shame of not trying was more of a fear for them than dying would ever be.

In a small cemetery on the outskirts of Killeen, Texas, not far from Fort Hood, a new grave had been dug next to one containing the body of Command Sergeant Major Henry Blackburn. Inside this new grave was placed the body of his son, First Sergeant Todd Blackburn. The epitaph on his gravestone reinforced the thoughts of the many soldiers in attendance. It read:

"OUR STRENGTH IS IN OUR UNITY AND RESOLVE.
SOLDIER ON"

EPILOGUE

Following the debacle in Somalia Tom Dash would remain on active duty for five more years. True to First Sergeant Blackburn's prediction, all five years were spent deployed overseas in Saudi Arabia and Bosnia tracking Islamic terrorists bent on destroying America. The exploits of these five years will be the subject of a future story.

Mohammed Al-Assiri, along with three other alleged terrorists, was executed in May 1995 in "Chop-Chop" square, Riyadh, Saudi Arabia. He had been arrested, tried, and convicted by an Islamic court for his involvement in the bombing of the Office of the Program Manager-Saudi Arabian National Guard Headquarters, a terrorist attack that killed seven Americans and injured dozens more. The elapsed time between his arrest and beheading was less than seventy-two hours. Neither the CIA nor the FBI were granted permission to interview him prior to his execution. Present at his execution was Lieutenant Colonel Tom Dash.

If portions of my story brought a smile to your face, then I have been moderately successful. If portions brought a tear to your eye, then I have also been moderately successful. If my story makes you want to get involved in the political process then it has served its intended purpose because neither the political left nor the political right in this country holds the answers to the future of America. Those answers will have to come from everyday working class Americans because it will be the working class, not the pompous voices seen and heard in the media or studied in the halls of academia that will fight America's current war against terrorism. You, your children, and your children's children will fight it. All those previously mentioned will merely continue to do what they have always done; stand around and chatter about it. But before you decide to ask the penetrating "Why?" "What?" "When?" and "Where?" of your elected officials, I would first like to provide you with some verbal bullets to add to your arsenal. People like Todd Blackburn would demand it of me.

When it comes to debating the reasons for going to war, I can personally attest to the fact that soldiers are not mindless robots devoid of either conscious or opinion. As the immediate recipients of war's fury, soldiers are often the first and most vocal critics of the people and policies endangering their lives. Academicians who give short thrift to the views expressed by the average combat soldier fails to explore their collective intelligence. The individual soldier is much more aware of the nuances of human emotions found in a war zone than any college student, journalist, professor, or diplomat will ever be. Yet an uninformed public continues to accept the opinions of those with "proper credentials" as valid while the opinions of those with firsthand experience are all too often dismissed out of hand. It would seem that the cup of knowledge is upside down! A tragic mistake of reasoning for although they may be suffering and dying because of a political mistake, soldiers are always the first to see the true nature of that mistake.

All Americans must come to grips with the fact that we are at war and were long before the September 11, 2001 attack. Difficult decisions must now be made and the most difficult decision of all centers on the fact that when patriotic young Americans are ordered to war, they go. In so doing some will die. Something America should never be willing to accept unless it is absolutely certain that the cause is just and worth the many sacrifices we ask of our children. But once asked to abandon their cause after the shooting starts simply because the going gets tough or public opinion opposes the effort is simply unacceptable. Neither casualties nor opinions should deter a democracy from its efforts *after* the decision to go to war has been made. And Americans won't be deterred if legitimate reasons for going to war are properly explained *before* the decision to send in the troops has been carefully deliberated. Even then, it must never be forgotten that nobody actually wins in a war. War is a mean, nasty, violent, brutish business. To mix those ingredients together and hope to produce something palatable with it is unrealistic. History clearly shows that war — especially a limited war ending with no declared winner — simply sets the stage for future wars because it never resolves the underlying economic, political, and social problems that provides the catalyst for war.

For that very reason, I am not advocating war as a solution to disagreements between nations; in fact, I would argue just the opposite. But I am suggesting that if the military is to be used as an instrument of foreign policy to demonstrate resolve, then a commitment to wage war has to have already been made before the deployment orders are issued. Not many people in modern America — or Congress as most are not veterans — truly understand the consequences, responsibilities, and commitment that must accompany putting soldiers in harms way as a demonstration of resolve. But there are several million people living outside of America who understand how to test that resolve by attacking those same soldiers. And for the several million who would do this, it will be the results, not the intentions, that count.

As human beings, it is understandable that politicians will occasionally allow passion to get in the way of intellect. But as leaders having life and death decision-making authority over Americas' young men and women, it is inexcusable to send innocent people to a premature death for ambiguous reasons or on the whims of the special-interest elite. The squandering of precious young lives for either reason is criminal, or at least it should be.

Osama got lucky. That fact will do little to alleviate the grief of the many thousands who lost loved ones that horrible day in September. But for the country to believe that terrorists are a bigger threat to America today than a Russian nuclear submarine was during the cold war is a gross exaggeration. Growing up in 1950's America, I can remember when duck-and-cover drills were taught at school as an effort to save yourself in the event of a nuclear attack. I vividly remember the Cuban missile crisis in 1962; an event that caused the world to hold its collective breath as Russia and America threatened one another with nuclear annihilation. To place Osama bin Laden or Saddam Hussein in the same category as a Russian missile attack is sheer lunacy. To invade Iraq because bin Laden attacked America is even worse. Today's belief that all who dislike America are terrorists working in concert with one another parallels the one time belief that communists were all one and the same. A comparable response for the 1960's would have been for the United States military to have invaded China and occupied Beijing because Moscow had missiles pointing at America. No, the threat to America has not grown over the past thirty or forty years, but the testicles of our politicians have gotten smaller. America invaded Iraq largely because of faulty intelligence and an eagerness to believe it, yet Saddam was not removed from power without sufficient justification. In fact, it should have happened more than a decade earlier.

To understand my logic for saying this, one has to begin with facts, not opinions. Whether American troops should or should not be in Iraq are opinions. That American troops are in Iraq is a fact. As a soldier myself, now that we have troops on the ground, this fact overrides any and all opinions, my own included, because I would have to argue that they should not be there. But since they are, I will support every move they make with the following caveat directed toward their political handlers: invading a country to get rid of one man, or a small group of men, was insane. Had America taken her time and applied *effective* international pressure on the Ba'ath party Saddam would have been removed from power just as certainly as he was but with little or no American loss of life. For those who will still continue to argue that it actually made little difference if Saddam stayed or went, I would have to say that you are wrong. It makes a big difference when government officials at any level make hollow threats and then have those same threats jammed back up their butt because they lack the will to enforce them. Such waffling places soldier's lives in danger for no good reason. This lack of will — all bark and no bite — is the source of much of my anger with both a milquetoast United Nations and a toothless American foreign policy. I have no control over the United Nations, but as a voter with the burning desire to influence other voters I will no longer allow my own elected officials to ignore me. As a civilian, until the day I die, I will continue to point out how selectively tone-deaf many of our politicians seem to have become.

I realize that there is nothing easier than being a critic. Especially when one has the luxury of 20/20 hindsight to document their brilliance. But it is an indisputable fact that those of us in uniform and working abroad during the 1980's and especially the 1990's constantly complained to government officials that people around the globe were trying very hard to kill us. With the collapse of the Soviet Union and the rise of militant Islam the world suddenly became a very dangerous place, and no one wearing a uniform tried to keep it a secret. After the Khobar Towers bombing on June 25, 1996 military personnel in Saudi Arabia were under a virtual state of siege, and they reacted accordingly. One month after Khobar I had a bomb dog alert on my car at Eskan Village south of Riyadh and the Air Force guards dismantled the vehicle. They removed the door panels, seats, trunk liner, and spare tire before I could proceed. And this despite the fact that I was a lieutenant colonel in uniform and knew the guards by name! When I went to the Pentagon several months later I discovered that Washington had not increased its security posture one iota. Telling me that our many complaints and warnings were being ignored. It seemed as though those in Washington couldn't or wouldn't stop worrying about making money long enough to listen to us. After all, it appeared, the stock market was booming, why interrupt a good thing. Washington chose instead to continue to ignore a conspicuous, festering crack in international resolve that served as a major precursor to the current landslide of hostilities.

Since the end of the Gulf War in 1991, Saddam Hussein and his cohorts diligently tried to shoot down American and British fighters flying in support of Operation Southern and Northern Watch, enforcement of the no-fly zones over Iraq. The fact that he did this in violation of Desert Storm peace accords and suffered no real consequences for doing so seems to be a fact lost to liberal thought. But this lack of resolve to enforce the written word was not going unnoticed elsewhere in the world; causing people like Osama bin Laden to begin licking their chops. Osama and his many followers later tested this resolve in places like Mogadishu, Riyadh, Al-Khobar, Dar es Salaam, Nairobi, and Aden. As suspected, they discovered the resolve to be weak, all talk and very little action, that the world did not have the stomach for war. In my opinion, today's war against terrorism could have been averted a decade ago. As an immediate consequence of his wanton disregard of international law Saddam's head should have been cut off and put on a stick for CNN and Al-Jazeera cameras to film the first time he violated UN sanctions. Additionally, a copy of this tape should have been mailed directly to bin Laden. So, why wasn't it?

In large part the blame can be laid at the feet of the American media and its obsession with entertainment rather than news. As was admitted in the 9-11 Commission Report, Congress closely tracks trends in what public opinion and the electorate identify as key issues. However, the report failed to mention that both public opinion and the electorate are greatly influenced by what they see and hear on the radio and television and what they read in newspapers. That none of these influential mediums did a good job of connecting the pre-9-11 terrorist dots occurring around the globe would be an understatement as they virtually ignored them because bombs exploding in Africa and Saudi Arabia do not attract dollars or votes in America. This chicken and egg analysis — lack of coverage followed by lack of attention — is why the events of 9-11 seemed so incomprehensible to most Americans and why Congress was allowed to keep terrorism off its radar screen for so long. But, in my opinion, there was an even more sinister reason why the media was not concerned with what was taking place overseas.

Whether America's current crop of war hawks likes to admit it or not, neither Saddam's nor Osama's efforts to kill Americans overseas (especially soldiers) during the past decade was considered by either the electorate or the general public as being sufficient justification for going to war. Presumably because it was *only* military and Foreign Service workers in danger of being killed. Since neither military members nor Foreign Service workers are generally considered to be elitists, their peril could not be sold to the American public as a legitimate reason for removing the powers that be in either Iraq or Afghanistan. The electorate simply did not attempt to sell the belief that we had to begin protecting ourselves at home for one simple reason: they have all become followers rather than leaders and none of them, not one, will touch a contentious issue until after it explodes into a crisis. Our current health care and social security troubles are but two good examples. These issues are ticking time bombs that no politician will seriously discuss because it will make too many people angry and spoil their chance for reelection. Maybe it is just because of my limited imagination, but when a politician says that they are going to *increase* health care coverage for the boomer's retirement *and* cut taxes while *exporting* good paying American jobs overseas it is time to point an accusatory finger. I find it mildly amusing when elitists assume that everyone from Idaho just fell off the turnip truck, but when they start talking to me as if it were true I find it to be offensive. Where in the world is all of this money supposed to come from? Does Washington plan to tax the Chinese and Indian workers now taking *our* paychecks home? Hard decisions — not popular decisions — have to be made and no one seems to be willing to do it.

It was also these same politicians that seemed to conveniently have forgotten that it had not been the soldiers that made the threat to enforce the rules in Iraq following Desert Storm, it had been them. So, when Osama predictably arrived in everyone's living room on 9-11, they had a problem that could no longer be ignored. Rather than admit that they were asleep on their watch, politicians have applied a little subterfuge in order to avoid criticism. Instead of endangered and dying soldiers having been a *cause belli* in their own right, both rich Wall Street and sleeping Main Street were scared into going to war by bin Laden's attack and exaggerated tales of Saddam possessing WMD's that threatened *them* here in America. The fact that Islamic fundamentalists had previously declared war on America and that Saddam had not stopped shooting at American planes for over ten years seemed to matter only to those of us already committed to fighting the war. Consequently, it took an attack by bin Laden and the death of more than three thousand Americans, mostly civilians, to get politicians to finally do their job and help the military protect America. Their reluctance to help simply because it might be unpopular with the voters. In my mind, this is simply unacceptable! Leaders lead, they do not follow behind the flock like so many sheep. Tough love is still love, and I think that the voters in America are mature enough to accept it, regardless of what the pollsters might say.

It is a poor policy to signal to any of America's enemies that it is acceptable to kill her people overseas but not while they are in America. Such a policy confirms for would be attackers that an attack on America is the only way to get her attention. No wonder bin Laden attacked her; he was tired of being ignored! That neither the media nor our elected politicians were trumpeting a clarion call to arms prior to 9-11 is a clear indication that the lives of those who serve are not considered to be on a par with the lives of those who do not serve. And, as further supporting evidence, not only was America unconcerned with Osama racking up American kills overseas, neither we nor the UN seemed to give a damn that Saddam continued to practice air defense live fires on American and British planes following a war that he *supposedly lost*. What would have been the allied response if German or Japanese troops would have continued to resist following VE and VJ day? What has happened to the Truman mentality that brought an end to World War II? When asked by a reporter after dropping the atomic bombs on Japan if he was concerned about killing all those innocent Japanese President Truman responded, "I never gave it a second thought. I was too concerned with *saving* American lives." There are too many "learned" people in America who have no concept of what war really is, feeling that it is a child's game that America only needs to pretend to fight, never having to kill anyone or even make someone angry. Bullshit! War has never been like that and it never will be. War is one nation imposing its will on another by brute force; it has nothing to do with egalitarian ideals or humanity. Death and destruction are the elixirs of war, not justice and compassion.

That America has lost the steel to prosecute a war with the deadly seriousness war requires is evident in our current efforts in Iraq. When Muqtadah Al-Sadr followers barricaded themselves in the Imam Ali Shrine in Najaf, Iraq, the marines chasing them were not allowed under the current rules of engagement to continue their pursuit for fear of damaging the shrine. How do you suppose Al-Sadr's followers learned to do something like that? Could it have been they studied the way we have fought every war since World War II?

Allow me to propose a solution to future problems of this nature. To overcome Washington's reluctance to see war through the eyes of those actually charged with fighting it, the next time American soldiers chase enemy combatants into a religious shrine several phone calls need to be made. These calls need to originate from the senior commander in Iraq and they need to be placed to the parents of those soldiers chasing the enemy combatants. The senior commander must also include in this conference call the President and all of the members of congress representing each soldier's family then, with all of the parents listening to the discussion, serious options must be presented to the elected officials. First, the officials would be reminded that the military had been sent to Iraq with the mission to kill, capture, or arrest people opposing U.S. efforts and, unless there had been a recent change in mission, they were currently prepared to execute it. The senior commander would then carefully explain to the President and members of congress that the people hiding inside the shrine could easily be destroyed with one bomb at no risk to any American personnel. Unfortunately, this option would also destroy the shrine these people elected to hide in. Or, in order to prevent having to destroy the shrine, the sons of all those listening to the conversation could kick down the door and engage those hiding inside in a firefight. This option would prevent the destruction of the shrine, but it would place the American kids doing it at great risk. In all probability, one or more of them would be killed and several would be injured. The senior commander would end the conversation with a question to the elected officials while their constituents listen: "Now, how do you want me to handle this?" You can draw your own conclusion as to how this question would be answered. No building in the world is more precious to those parents than the lives of their children, and if the Imam Ali Shrine is that damn important to the Muslims, then they had better stop hiding in it. Fight the war like we really mean it. Fewer people will actually be killed on both sides if we do.

Additionally, any competent young parent knows that one does not threaten a child for displaying bad behavior, then ignore that same behavior. Yet both America and the United Nations had been doing exactly that with Saddam since the end of the first Gulf War. Perhaps the British woman speaking in London in response to a reporters question regarding the Abu Ghraib prison fiasco said it best when she commented, "What more can you expect from trailer trash Americans." In America it seems as though our politicians only back up threats with force when the economy, a donors deep pockets, or their constituency is endangered. Everything and everyone else is expendable. If that is so, then maybe an elitist government is what Americans deserve! Politicians, be they UN or US, should never issue a threat that they themselves are not prepared to die enforcing. The "School of Hard Knocks" has taught me a valuable lesson: If you do not mean it or cannot do it, then do not say it! Should this not also be a lesson taught in Ivy League schools as well?

Like Vietnam, the fact that America may have gone to war unnecessarily has caused a rift between the pro-war and anti-war groups. It is interesting to note that there are still those who believe that even self-defense may not be a legitimate reason for going to war, and distressing to note that there are still those who believe that criticizing elected officials during a time of war is unpatriotic. To those rejecting war for any and all reasons, I can only suggest that you are living in a dream world and that the realities of life make it too dangerous to live there with you. I will agree that America should not go into the jungle in pursuit of a tiger without cause. But when a tiger comes out of that jungle, as happened on 9-11, *someone* had better have the nerve to shoot it. People like Osama bin Laden, Khalid Sheik Mohammed, and Abu Musab al-Zarqawi possess the same detached, unemotional view of human life that any other hungry predator does. They will never respect your right to life, liberty and the pursuit of happiness. If you are one of those who believes that making a house pet of such animals is the way to deal with them, then you are crazier than they are!

For those who continue to insist that criticizing the current administration is unpatriotic I will remind them that America has been at war with Islamic fundamentalists since the Carter administration. Those people currently deflecting criticism behind a shield of patriotism did not spare previous administrations from criticism, nor should they now. The vacuous logic that one cannot be against the war but still support the troops defies explanation. Using a sports analogy, it is possible for one to be critical of a coach who sent in the wrong play and still support the team.

The belief that the creation of a democracy in Iraq will serve as an inspiration to bordering countries is another skeptical idea. If such a concept actually worked Mexico would not have its people risking death in order to get into America. Anyone who believes that Jeffersonian democracy will spread from Iraq to the government of a neighboring country needs to honestly admit to his or herself that the economic and political freedoms found in San Diego do not exist across the border in Tijuana. And the only thing separating these two cities is a permeable chain-link fence, not several centuries of political retardation. No matter how much blood or how much money we expend, the countries surrounding Iraq will not fare any better than Mexico has.

As part of the critical analysis to understanding 9-11, America seems to have gone through a series of machinations in an attempt to discover which government officials dropped the ball, and what balls dropped allowed the terrorist attack on September 11, 2001 to be so successful. Televised senate hearings were conducted vaguely reminiscent of the Salem witch trials of a bygone era in American history and eerily reminiscent of the more recent Joe McCarthy hearings as neatly coifed politicians waved the finger of blame around the room. Both Clinton and Bush appointees, as well as the Presidents themselves, albeit in a more civil manner, were made to answer questions surrounding who knew what, and when did they know it, in a belated effort to prevent the reoccurrence of another, similar attack. At least this is what the professed purpose of the hearings were announced to be. In my opinion they were little more than pabulum for the masses, conducted more for political party gain than for problem resolution; yet they were entertaining enough that we all watched attentively in the vicarious hope that something good for the nation would come from them. Regrettably, I fear that it will be a false hope. There are too many large egos and too much political power at stake to let something like the truth upset the power balance of the ruling political and special interest elite. I also cynically predict that the only "fix" that was offered at the conclusion of these hearings came with an exorbitant price tag attached that you and I are being asked to pay. A price tag that will do little more than enrich and empower the circle of elitists who promoted it.

However, even if we dismiss the hearings as being all bluster and posture, there is another recent event that received scant media attention more illustrative of the sinister effects of elitism than anything that the Senate hearings might reveal. Unlike the Senate hearings this incident doesn't delve into the operational aspects of either the terrorists or the government that exists to protect us, but it does delve into the ideological reasons of why people hate Americans enough to want to kill us. It goes beyond politics; it goes to the very core of American society.

On March 24, 2004, during the annual Radio and Television Correspondents Association dinner, in a ten minute, mostly puckish, self-deprecating speech, President George W. Bush presented a slide show he called an "election-year White House photo album." In several comical photos he appeared to be searching the Oval Office for weapons of mass destruction, saying as much in his prepared speech, eliciting great guffaws, laughter and applause from the elite audience of journalists, politicians, bureaucrats and other titled guests. That the audience could be so out of touch with reality that they would find humor in the President having been wrong for his announced reason for invading Iraq, resulting in the deaths of several hundred American soldiers and several thousand Iraqis, went virtually unnoticed. Also unnoticed was the observation that not only did the President see nothing wrong with his elitist brand of humor, neither did the speechwriters who wrote it, the many people who heard it during rehearsal, and the large numbers who heard it at the dinner. That many hundreds of Americans could be so callous as to believe that neither soldiers nor Iraqis are worthy of respect is a stunning example of American elitism at its worst. It is why a great and growing portion of the world despises the American ruling elite, the only kind of American many of them have ever observed.

The above is not to single out George W. Bush for criticism; he is as much a victim of elitism as a poster boy for it. Nor is elitism a partisan issue affecting only republicans, democrats suffer from it as well. In fact, elitism is probably the only real bipartisan character trait that exists in Washington, crossing lines of race, gender, career, and party affiliation.

George W. Bush, 43rd President of the United States, did not create the elitist mind-set; it has been around far longer than he has. Nor did he inherit it from his father, George H. W. Bush, the 41st President of the United States. As a former World War II fighter pilot shot down in the pacific, George H. W. Bush tasted the fear of his own death often enough that he would never have cavalierly sent others to their death on a guess. George W. Bush learned to be an elitist the same way all other elitist's learned it: by believing that the world and all the people in it belong to them. A small and privileged group belief that the rights of others are valid only if they do not interfere with the elitist's own personal ambitions.

The 43rd President of the United States also learned the elitist concept that he is above the fray, immune from the hardships and sacrifices required from others. He certainly meets the stereotypical qualifications for being an elitist. Born with a silver spoon in his mouth, educated in an Ivy League school, a member of the exclusive Skull and Bones at Yale, he, like all other elitists, apparently believes that the sacrifices made by others for his personal gain is the natural course of events. As a born again Christian it would be but a small extension for him to also believe that since God gave man dominion over lesser beasts, so too has He given elitists dominion over non-elitists. It is the natural order of things.

Still, whether George W. Bush is a true elitist remains a matter of speculation and opinion. However, that this elitist mind-set dominates much of what passes for politics inside the D.C. beltway is difficult to argue against. Can anyone seriously doubt that if it had been Jenny and Barbara Bush captured in Iraq instead of Jessica Lynch and Shoshanna Johnson, or killed as Lori Piestewa was, that neither the President nor any of the other elitists in attendance would have found humor in erroneously sending young men and women to an early death? Had it been your child or grandchild killed in Iraq would you have found it to be funny? But since it wasn't one of his own daughters, nor were they a daughter of one of his elitist friends in attendance, they were expendable, the butt of a sick joke. Harsh sounding words but words that match the actions of the ruling elite. Not many of their children or grandchildren are braving the dangers of Iraq at the expense of delaying an Ivy League education; yet they have no qualms about sending someone else's son or daughter to war. Ironically, a fact that never seemed to bother me when I was one of those being sent, but now that it will be my grandchildren who are sent, it bothers me a great deal.

This concept of shared sacrifice is one that must be considered by all Americans because it is simply not right that the few should be carrying the burden for the many. And, over time, I have no doubt that it will be as the demand on our military begins to exceed its ability to meet that demand. Terrorism is not a threat that is going to dissipate in the very near future. A return to conscription may well be in the party platform of all aspiring politicians. But what should be of immediate concern to all Americans is our dismal record of previous foreign policy failures. The Bush administration was required to solicit support from other nations following the attack on 9-11 by traveling hat in hand, groveling like a door to door salesman, largely because of previous administration's failures to follow through on past promises, real or implied. Fortunately, with the possible exception of people like Osama, reneging on those past promises resulted in angering only those nations incapable of doing much about it. After 9-11, this is no longer the case. Now, America has made promises — real, implied, or imagined promises — to Russia, China, India, Pakistan, Britain, France, and Israel. All of these countries *already* possess weapons of mass destruction. The stakes have been raised enormously and the consequences of reneging on political promises this time could lead to the direst of consequences as the stage has been set for World War III. What voting America needs to know now from our elected leaders is what was promised to these other countries for their support and when is the bill coming due? This is the real information that should have come out of the 9-11 commission hearings yet scant attention has been paid to it other than by those who have received those promises.

The one constant ray of hope in all this is our military. The many fine young men and women who do the difficult and dangerous work ensuring that you and I do not have to fear a hand grenade being thrown through our bedroom window while we sleep. A common occurrence in many parts of the world and one that we all had a small taste of on 9-11. But, whether we like it or not, America is at war. A fact that our opponent has long known but only recently brought to the attention of our collective psyche, an awareness that even now, in less than three years time, is already slipping to the back of our minds, largely because it involves far too few of us. Except for the immediate families and friends of those killed on 9-11 and the brave young men and women fighting today in Afghanistan and Iraq, the vast majority of Americans are still not being asked to make a sacrifice in order to win this war. During World War II rationing affected all Americans, not just those that were fighting the war. During Korea and Vietnam the draft kept everyone of age aware of how the war was going. Today, an eighteen to thirty-two-year old male can stand on the street corner with his thumb up his butt forever and no one will ever ask him to make a sacrifice for the benefit of someone other than himself. Men like Pat Tillman are the diamonds all too infrequently found in the coal pit of rich American youth.

The real benefit of a draft is incidental, it does not benefit the military directly but, more appropriately, benefits our country. The real benefit of a draft is that young men are placed in uniform who do not want to wear one; a concept seemingly at odds with the ideals of service leaders wanting to retain a professional, all-volunteer military. Yet the odds that draftees will support a "bright and shining lie" in Iraq is no greater today than it was during Vietnam when draftees banded together to expose the fallacies of those wanting to continue prosecuting the war. Something professionals may be reluctant to do. Not many flag rank officers resigned their commissions during the Vietnam War, despite their growing awareness that it had very quickly turned into killing merely for killing's sake. If Iraq is indeed another Vietnam — and the jury is still out on that question — then these same draftees will once again expose the lie.

I mention our military because there seems to be a great deal of hand wringing taking place with America's invasion of Iraq as the next step in the war on terrorism. Like some, I too question the wisdom of this but, unlike some others, I realize that it is already too late to second-guess our efforts. We have grabbed the bull by the horns and under no circumstances should we let go. Not until he is too depleted and too exhausted to continue the struggle. A gun cannot simply be unfired just because one wishes that it could. If we cannot get the United Nations to assume responsibility for Iraq — something that should have been agreed upon before the first shot was ever fired — we have but two options in Iraq: either prosecute the war with total conviction, or get out of the country. Neither are very good options as both are fraught with unintended consequences.

If we prosecute the war with total conviction, more Americans and Iraqis will be killed. That each American soldier who falls has family members to grieve his or her loss is not lost on the politicians or the general public. The heat is already being ratcheted up on elected officials as we surpass our one-thousandth casualty. That each Iraqi who falls has a family to grieve his or her loss is also a fact not to be easily dismissed because it will only result in more terrorists as fathers, brothers, uncles, and friends seek to avenge their death. The methodology required to conduct total war will require that we destroy block after block of Iraqi real estate. Which will save American lives in the short term, but it will culminate in a never-ending cycle of retaliatory violence making Baghdad look like Gaza and the West Bank for decades to come.

Conversely, if America withdraws from Iraq before she completes the mission of

We must accept the lesser of two evils and stay the course.

The military knows all too well what the mission is and what it will take to accomplish it, but it cannot do it without public support. When a pilot is shot down flying in support of some international mission, the countries that signed on to support that mission must be mentally prepared to "fix bayonets" in order to get him or her back. Otherwise, the mission is doomed to fail because it will be shown to have been a bluff. When a country will not back up its words with deeds it needs to keep the troops in the barracks, not send them out to be targets of opportunity for the opposition. I do not sense a "fix bayonets" mentality in some I have spoken with, although they profess not to be isolationists. One cannot have it both ways!

Likewise, futurists must never lose sight of the fact that Precision Guided Munitions do not rescue prisoners or maintain stability during post-combat operations. Only boots on the ground can accomplish either and that means putting soldiers at risk. For the squeamish, keep in mind that whenever a Brigade of the 82nd Airborne division is called to war, when the jump light inside that lead aircraft turns green the young men inside are going to jump out the door. When they get on the ground they are going to kill people just as rapidly and as violently as they can, and the opposition is going to do the same to them. It is what happens in war and soldiers know it, even if they don't like it. If you are one of those who can't stand the thought of this don't ever, EVER, put those young soldiers inside that aircraft. *Pretending* to go to war is not something any soldier was ever trained to do. In a soldier's world it has always been all or nothing. This time let the politicians adjust to a soldier's reality and not the other way around. This time, let's have both a military and a political victory that the entire world can live with. It may well be our last chance.